D1368216

# FUNDAMENTAL CHANGE

This volume is part of a set of four. These volumes together form the *International Handbook of Educational Change,* which was originally published in 1998 as volume 5 in the Springer International Handbooks of Education series (formerly known as Kluwer International Handbooks of Education series), and edited by Andy Hargreaves, Ann Lieberman, Michael Fullan and David Hopkins.

The Table of Contents of the entire *International Handbook of Educational Change* has been printed at the end of this volume.

# Fundamental Change

## International Handbook of Educational Change

Edited by:

Michael Fullan

*Ontario Institute for Studies in Education, University of Toronto, Canada*

 Springer

A C.I.P. Catalogue record for this book is available from the Library of Congress.

The Roots of Educational Change: ISBN-10  1-4020-3289-7
Extending Educational Change: ISBN-10  1-4020-3291-9
Fundamental Change: ISBN-10  1-4020-3292-7
The Practice and Theory of School Improvement: ISBN-10  1-4020-3290-0
Set: ISBN-10 1-4020-3423-7
The Roots of Educational Change: ISBN-13  978-1-4020-3289-9
Extending Educational Change: ISBN-13  978-1-4020-3291-2
Fundamental Change: ISBN-13  978-1-4020-3292-9
The Practice and Theory of School Improvement: ISBN-13  978-1-4020-3290-5
Set: ISBN-13  978-1-4020-3423-7
Springer Dordrecht, Berlin, Heidelberg, New York

The volumes can be purchased separately and as a set.

Published by Springer,
P.O. Box 17, 3300 AA Dordrecht, The Netherlands.

*Printed on acid-free paper*

springeronline.com

Printed in the Netherlands.

# Table of Contents

*III. Professional Development for Reform*

# International Handbook of Educational Change - Introduction

ANDY HARGREAVES
*Department of Teacher Education, Curriculum and Instruction Lynch School of Education, Boston College, MA, U.S.A.*

ANN LIEBERMAN
*Carnegie Foundation for the Advancement of Teaching, Stanford, CA, U.S.A.*

MICHAEL FULLAN
*Ontario Institute for Studies in Education, University of Toronto, Canada*

DAVID HOPKINS
*Department for Education and Skills, London, U.K.*

This set of four volumes on *Educational Change* brings together evidence and insights on educational change issues from leading writers and researchers in the field from across the world. Many of these writers, whose chapters have been specially written for these books, have been investigating, helping initiate and implementing educational change, for most or all of their lengthy careers. Others are working on the cutting edge of theory and practice in educational change, taking the field in new or even more challenging directions. And some are more skeptical about the literature of educational change and the assumptions on which it rests. They help us to approach projects of understanding or initiating educational change more deeply, reflectively and realistically.

Educational change and reform have rarely had so much prominence within public policy, in so many different places. Educational change is ubiquitous. It figures large in Presidential and Prime Ministerial speeches. It is at or near the top of many National policy agendas. Everywhere, educational change is not only a policy priority but also major public news. Yet action to bring about educational change usually exceeds people's understanding of how to do so effectively.

The sheer number and range of changes which schools are now confronting is staggering.

Educators have always had to engage with educational changes of one sort or another. But other than in the last three decades or so, these changes were infrequent and episodic and they never really affected or even addressed the core of how teachers taught (Cuban, 1984). The changes were in things like how subjects were organized, how grade levels were clustered together into different school types, or how groups of students were divided between different schools or integrated within them according to ability, gender or race. Thus when educational

*M. Fullan (ed.), Fundamental Change,* vii–xi.
© 2005 *Springer. Printed in the Netherlands.*

historians chastise contemporary change advocates for ignoring the existence of educational change in the past and for exaggerating current crises and change demands "as a marketing device to promote the new possibilities of education in a new century, designed to appeal to consumers of different kinds who are grown weary of the old familiar product" (McCulloch, 1997), they are only partially right. While educational change has always been with us in some sense or other (as also, of course, has educational continuity), many of the changes are very different now, in both their substance and their form.

Since the 1960s, educational change has became a familiar part of teachers' work, and has more directly addressed issues of what teachers teach and how they should teach it. Following the launch of Sputnik and the emergence of post-war egalitarian ideals, public education has been treated as a crucible of technological and economic advancement and as a creator of greater social justice. In the 1960s and 70s, teachers in many countries had to deal with the rhetoric and sometimes the reality of curriculum innovation in mathematics, science and the humanities. They saw students stay in school longer, the ability ranges of their classes grow wider and the walls of their classrooms come down and then go up again just a few years later. Successive waves of different approaches to reading or mathematical learning swept through their classrooms, each one washing away the marks left by its predecessors.

It was in these times of educational expansion and optimism that educational change really began in earnest - as also did the study of it. From the late 1960s and early 1970s, researchers like Matt Miles, Per Dalin, Lou Smith, Neil Gross, Lawrence Stenhouse and Seymour Sarason studied the growing phenomenon of educational innovation - whether in the shape of large-scale curriculum projects and packages, or in the form of newly-created innovative schools. They showed how and why large-scale curriculum innovations rarely progressed beyond the phase of having their packages purchased or "adopted" to the point where they were implemented fully and faithfully, and could bring about real changes in classroom practice. At the same time, they also revealed how the promise of exceptional innovative schools usually faded over time as their staffs grew older, their charismatic leaders left, and the system withdrew permission for them to break the rules.

As the limitations of large-scale curriculum innovations became apparent, educators began to treat the individual school as the centre or focal point of educational change efforts. School-based curriculum development, and school-based staff development initiatives proliferated in many places, instead of development being imposed or initiated from faraway.

Research on what made teachers effective in their classrooms also expanded to address what made schools effective or ineffective as a whole, and as lists of effective schools characteristics were discovered (such as creating a safe and orderly environment for learning, or setting and checking homework regularly), these were sometimes then used as administrative blueprints to try and make particular schools become more effective over time. Many districts or other administrative authorities initiated "effective schools" projects on this basis. Some schools and districts supplemented and sometimes supplanted this science of school effectiveness with a more loosely defined and humanistically interpreted art of school improvement - the process of how to help schools and their staffs become more effective through setting clear goals, creating staff involvement, measuring progress over time and so forth.

Ironically, this approach to school improvement was then translated back into a rational science by many educational systems. It was treated as a process of planned or managed change that schools could be moved through step-by-step, stage-by-stage, guided by the school's improvement team that its region or district mandated it to have.

When these various school-centred changes and improvements didn't work well enough or fast enough (and sometimes even when they did), impatient educational administrators (and American urban school superintendents with an average job tenure of less than two years can be very impatient indeed), imposed their own reform requirements instead. So too did ideologically driven politicians, whose agendas of educational reform have often been shaped by the desire to create public indignation (which they promise their measures will then answer), or by the private idiosyncrasies of their own educational pasts, (which their reforms are meant to cherish or purge).

This quarter century or more of educational change processes and initiatives that have been meant to alter learning and teaching in our schools, has left us with a mixed legacy. On the one hand, studies of what works and what doesn't across all the different change strategies have created a truly powerful knowledge base about the processes, practices and consequences of educational change. During this period, research studies have shown, for example, how educational change moves through distinctive stages of initiation, implementation and institutionalization; how people who encounter changes go through successive "stages of concern" about how those changes will affect them; and how people respond very differently to educational change initiatives depending on what point they have reached in their own lives and careers.

Some of the research findings on educational change have even been accorded the status of generalizable rules or `lessons' of change. These include the maxims that practice changes before beliefs, that successful change is a product of both pressure and support, that evolutionary planning works better than linear planning and so forth (these `lessons' have been synthesized especially effectively by Michael Fullan, 1991, 1993).

So extensive is the current knowledge base of educational change that it has come to constitute a field of study in its own right - drawing on and transcending the disciplines of sociology, psychology, history and philosophy, as well as the fields of curriculum and educational administration. In a way, educational change has now really come of age - but while this is a significant academic achievement, it is also where the problems of the field - the second part of its legacy - also begin.

Our experience of educational change today is stretching far beyond our experience, knowledge and investigations of it in times gone by. While the existing knowledge-base of educational change is impressive, it is no longer really sufficient to address the unique change problems and challenges that educators confront today.

Contemporary patterns of educational change present educators with changes that are multiple, complex and sometimes contradictory. And the change demands with which educators have to deal, seem to follow one another at an increasingly frenetic speed. A typical primary or elementary school these days may be considering a new reading program, developing cooperative learning strategies, thinking about how to implement new computers, designing a better parent newsletter, and trialling portfolio assessments all at the same time. The portfolio assessments favoured by the region or the district may have to be reconciled with imposed standardized test requirements by the nation or the state. A push to develop a more integrated curriculum and to recognize children's multiple intelligences may be reversed by a newly elected government's commitments to more conventionally defined learning standards within existing academic subjects.

All this can make teachers and administrators feel that the systems in which they are working aren't just complex but downright chaotic. This chaos is partly inherent in societies and organizations where information circulates and decisions are made with increasing speed. It is also the result of educational policy constantly being shaped and altered by different and competing interest groups in an ideological battle for the minds of the young. And sometimes it even results from a kind of *manufactured uncertainty* that more than a few governments wilfully create to arouse panic, to set pretexts for their policy interventions and to keep educators and everyone else off-balance.

Few of the existing theories and strategies of educational change equip educators to cope effectively with these complex, chaotic and contradictory environments

- Rational theories of planned change that move through predictable stages of implementation or `growth' are poorly suited to schools where unexpected twists and turns are the norm rather than the exception in the ways they operate.
- The conventional academic and behavioural outcomes that defined the core of what an effective school should produce in the past are outdated in an age where many people now clamour for schools to develop higher-order thinking skills, problem-solving capacities, and the habits of collaboration and teamwork. Complex as the world of education is, people expect more and more from it, and the effective schools of the past cannot deliver what many expect of schools today.
- Theories and models that helped educators know how (and how not) to implement single curriculum innovations are of little use to schools where innovations are multiple and priorities compete.
  While we have learned a lot about how to improve individual schools or small clusters of schools with additional resources, exceptional leaders, the ability to attract or shed particular kinds of staff members, and discretion to break the

rules; we are only just beginning to understand the challenges of scaling reform up from small samples of improving schools, to entire school systems. The existing knowledge base of school improvement has shown us how to create islands of improvement, but has been less helpful in assisting people to make archipelagoes from islands, and still less in showing them how to build entire continents of change.

It is time, therefore, to reflect at some length about what we already know and have learned about educational change and to explore how the field can and should be pushed further, to help educators understand and deal effectively with the immensely complex change problems that are customary today. Each of the four volumes on *Educational Change* addresses these fundamental issues in its own distinctive way.

## REFERENCES

Cuban, L. (1984). *How teachers taught: Constancy and change in American classrooms, 1890-1980.* New York: Longman.
Fullan, M. (1991). *The new meaning of educational change.* New York: Teachers College Press.
Fullan, M. (1993). *Change forces.* London: Falmer Press.
McCulloch, G. (1997). Marketing the millennium: Education for the twenty-first century. In A. Hargreaves, & R. Evans (Eds.), *Beyond educational reform.* Buckingham: Open University Press.

# Introduction

## Scaling Up the Educational Change Process

MICHAEL FULLAN

*Ontario Institute for Studies in Education, University of Toronto, Canada*

The chapters in this section are divided into three broad categories: (1) those dealing with macro educational change at the societal level (2) those relating to large scale initiatives based on particular reform strategies (3) those pertaining to fundamental transformations of professional development strategies, indeed to fundamental reform in the profession of teaching itself.

There has been a growing dissatisfaction over the past two decades about the slow pace of educational reform. Whatever successes that have been obtained have been confined to individual schools which succeeded here and there. Missing was any sense that educational change could be accomplished on a large scale sustained basis.

The chapters that follow attempt to push forward on the agenda of fundamental change. In the first section the revolution in human development and the learning society is analyzed resulting in the recognition that macro strategies must focus on transformations in how learning occurs. Revolutions in cognitive science have enabled us to understand how learners construct their own deep understanding of knowledge. Suddenly, new technologies have made possible networks of information and people that directly compare the learning of students and teachers alike. These developments are occurring in all countries reflected in the chapters in section one: Canada, Japan, the United Kingdom, and the United States.

In addition to comprehensive reforms relating to education policy, there are a number of large scale change initiatives underway which are based on particular models. These chapters focus on Levin's Accelerated Schools, Comer's School Development Program in the United States, and the National Schools Project in Australia. At the same time, we raise new questions about the roles of communities and community service agencies in school reform. Fundamental change eventually will require radical rethinking of the relationship between schools and communities.

In the third section, professional development is examined in new and more fundamental ways. Professional development, in-service location, staff development and the like have always been identified as important components of any change strategy. Yet the impact of professional development has been limited. The chapters in section three essentially claim that this limited impact is related to

*M. Fullan (ed.), Fundamental Change*, 1-2.
© 2005 *Springer. Printed in the Netherlands.*

superficial or partial conceptions of development. The new conceptions include the development of teaching standards as foundations for reform, the role of teachers throughout their careers as "change agents" concerned with equity, social justice and academic excellence for all, new unionism as teachers' organizations help lead educational reform and restructuring schools for improving teaching in dramatic ways. All of these involve the reconceptualization of professional development for teachers and administrators recognizing their key roles in bringing about large scale educational reform.

Educational reform has proceeded through at least four broad phases over the last third of the 20th century. The 1960s involved large scale aspirations for reform in most Western countries. At the time, there was little appreciation of the complexities of implementation and most of these ambitious efforts failed to bear fruit. Second, the 1970s was a period of downturn and recession with limited attention to fundamental reform. At the same time there was growing dissatisfaction with the role and performance of public schools. This led in the 1980s to stronger central intervention and more demands and mechanisms for accountability. We are at the early stage of a fourth phase in which there is a growing realization that accountability per se is not the answer, and that the "capacity" of the school system and its communities is the key to reform. Fundamental change, then means basic transformation of educational institutions.

As we move to the 21st century, the interest of Western countries, and those around the world, whether they be Eastern Europe, Asia, Africa or Latin America are beginning to coincide. All now appear to agree that transformation of societies – individually and interdependently – is essential, and that educational reform is the critical strategic intervention that will achieve these goals.

Accomplishing educational and societal reform in today's world is a challenge of enormous complexity. The good news is that we know much more, after forty years of research and development, about the educational change process and the strategies required for success. In many ways, the next period of reform could be the defining decade for focusing on fundamental educational reforms. The chapters in this section help set the stage for the next phase of ambitious work on the educational reform agenda.

I: Macro Change

# Beyond Bloom's *Taxonomy*: Rethinking Knowledge for the Knowledge Age

CARL BEREITER

*Ontario Institute for Studies in Education of the University of Toronto*

MARLENE SCARDAMALIA

*Ontario Institute for Studies in Education of the University of Toronto*

*This chapter focuses on how schools could function as places where students become proficient in all aspects of knowledge, including its creation. Traditional forms of knowledge are inadequate because they are based on "mental filing cabinets". New conceptions are based on enabling learners to construct knowledge drawing on a range of information enabling them to obtain greater depths of understanding which they can apply in new situations.*

From two quite different sources comes a similar message: Knowledge is far more important than has previously been realized. One source is the study of wealth creation and economic competition. From this source come such as-yet little understood ideas as knowledge-based economy, knowledge workers, and knowledge as an economic product and as a dominant 'means of production,' taking precedence over labor and capital (Drucker, 1993). The other source is cognitive research, now spanning three decades, on the nature of expertise. This research has demonstrated with great consistency and in many different domains that experts are distinguished from non-experts mainly by the extent and depth of their knowledge, not by their mental abilities, thinking skills, or general cognitive strategies (Chi, Glaser, & Farr, 1988).

These ideas have begun to have an impact on the thinking of educational reformers. In particular, many curriculum reforms are afoot that emphasize depth of understanding. Yet an examination of both the products and the rhetoric of many programs for educational change will reveal that they are based on the conception of knowledge that was current forty years ago, and whose roots go back not only to before the 'cognitive revolution' and before the advent of the 'knowledge society' but to before the printing press and the microscope. It is a conception that trivializes knowledge and subordinates it to a panoply of intellectual abilities and skills of doubtful teachability. It is a conception that fixes knowledge within individual minds and therefore can make little sense of the social and economic role of knowledge.

Our objective in this chapter is to advance new ways of looking at knowledge that are more consistent with current understanding and with the ascendant social

*M. Fullan (ed.), Fundamental Change, 5-22.*

importance of knowledge. The old way of conceiving of knowledge is well represented in an important and still influential work of four decades ago, the *Taxonomy of Educational Objectives, Handbook I: Cognitive Domain* (Bloom, 1956), more familiarly known as Bloom's *Taxonomy*. This taxonomy played an important role in expanding the scope of curriculum objectives and achievement testing beyond those of itemizable subject-matter content, but at the same time it served to entrench the idea that knowledge is only such items of content. In the taxonomy, knowledge occupies the lowest of six levels of cognitive objectives. In explaining this level, the authors suggested that the reader

> . . .think of knowledge as something filed or stored in the mind. The task for the individual in each knowledge test situation is to find the appropriate signals and cues in the problem which will most effectively bring out whatever knowledge is filed or stored (Bloom, 1956, p. 29).

The higher levels of the taxonomy – Comprehension, Application, Analysis, Synthesis, and Evaluation – were conceived of as "intellectual abilities and skills." They constituted the person's capacity to operate on the contents of the mental filing cabinet. Contents of the filing cabinet might go out of date and need to be changed, but the intellectual abilities and skills would continue to serve the person throughout life. Accordingly, they were the objectives of most long-range significance for education (pp. 38–43).

These ideas should sound familiar. They are part of the rhetoric of contemporary educational reform. They do, of course, have some validity. Some knowledge does go out of date (although the great bulk of what we know does not). What one can do with knowledge *is* crucial. But the limitations of these ideas, which we will explore more fully in later sections, can be glimpsed at by considering how they could serve to answer two questions: (1) What does it mean to have a deep understanding of something? (2) In what way is a knowledge worker different from any other kind of white-collar worker? A conception of knowledge that is of no help, that may even get in the way of answering questions such as these, is surely in need of updating itself.

## EMERGENCE OF THE KNOWLEDGE SOCIETY

Taken at face value, terms such as 'knowledge-based economy' and 'knowledge society' do not carry much meaning. When was there ever an economy that was not based on knowledge applied to producing or acquiring tradeable goods? What society does not embody the accumulated knowledge of its past? To impart meaning to these terms, we need to look at historical changes in the status of knowledge.

Throughout most of the human past, knowledge was embedded in traditional practices, tools, and myths. Practices, tools, and myths evolved over time, and in this sense knowledge grew. But, said Whitehead (1925, 1948, p. 91), "[t]he process of change was slow, unconscious, and unexpected." Major advances occurred in response to new conditions, which continues to be the case in traditional societies.

But there was little capacity to envisage and create new conditions. That would have required a detachment of knowledge from its embedding practices and myths, so that ideas could be manipulated and recombined in a speculative way.

Such a detachment or, as we shall say, *objectification* of knowledge began to take place in all the major civilizations a few thousand years ago. Many social factors conspired to bring this about, but the invention of writing systems undoubtedly provided a powerful tool (Olson, 1994). Philosophers, historians, mathematicians, and theologians began to appear. These, along with attendant librarians and scribes, became the first knowledge workers. Knowledge work differed from that of the present day in three important respects, however: (1) There was no general conception of a *state of knowledge*, which advanced through the cumulative contributions of knowledge workers; (2) Knowledge work was not applied to practical arts. Such knowledge continued to be embedded in the various trades and crafts, evolving slowly and with little crossover from one trade to another; (3) Knowledge work of any kind was the province of a tiny minority of the working population.

With the Industrial Revolution came the deliberate application of knowledge in the advancement of practical arts. Yet, according to Whitehead (1925, 1948, p. 92), it was not until the nineteenth century that we got "the full self-conscious realization of the power of professionalism in knowledge in all its departments, and of the way to produce professionals, and of the methods by which abstract knowledge can be connected with technology, and of the boundless possibilities of technological advance." This led to what he called "disciplined progress," progress achieved through the deliberate and orderly pursuit of solutions to theoretical and technical problems.

The next and current stage in the evolution of knowledge work is not very well defined. Peter Drucker, who coined the term 'knowledge society,' dates its emergence as the end of World War II. The change, he said, is that knowledge began to be applied to knowledge, whereas previously it had been applied to materials and to work. This rather barren definition may gain more meaning through use of an analogy. What comes to the silversmith's workbench is silver and what leaves it is still silver, but it is worth more than it was before. The silversmith's work has *added value* to the silver. Similarly, what comes to the knowledge worker's desk is knowledge and what leaves it is also knowledge, but the knowledge worker has done something to add value to it. What arrives might be market research; what leaves might be the draft of a marketing plan. What arrives might be functional specifications for a new software application; what leaves might be technical specifications. What arrives might be excerpts from airline schedules; what leaves might be an itinerary. What arrives might be student journals; what leaves might be entries by the teacher that stimulate further thought. What arrives might be customer complaints; what leaves might be ideas contributed to a design database, or what leaves might be only an organization of the complaints into useful categories. Knowledge work may go on at different levels. It need not always be creative, but it must in some fashion render the knowledge more meaningful, accessible, reliable, relevant, or applicable to particular purposes. Clearly, it takes knowledge in order to do this. In order to organize the customer complaints into a useful set of categories, you need more than 'classification skills,' whatever that might mean. You need to understand the product or service customers are complaining about and you need to understand the contexts within which those complaints are arising and what capacities the organization has for responding. This, as we take it, is the sense in which knowledge work means applying knowledge to knowledge.

We are not intellectual historians. The preceding sketch is highly derivative and no doubt flawed but its main theme is, as far as we are aware, uncontroversial. That theme is the gradual shift from knowledge being completely embedded in practice, myth, and artifact to its becoming objectified as abstract objects that are recognizable human creations and that can be described, compared, criticized, disseminated, improved, discarded, rediscovered, and so on. An important question, accordingly, is whether education has kept up with this transformation. "Professionalism in knowledge," which Whitehead dated from the nineteenth century, can certainly be found in many classrooms, but the literature on teacher professionalization would indicate that it is still to be fully realized. As for students functioning as knowledge workers, engaged in adding value to knowledge, however, this is virtually unheard of except at postgraduate levels. Bringing such a conception into elementary and secondary schooling is a new challenge, which later sections of this chapter will address.


EXPERT KNOWLEDGE

Research on the nature of expertise has been one of the most active areas of cognitive research. The earliest research on expertise, which set the paradigm for much of what followed, dealt with experts at chess. This was a fortunate choice because there was already a firmly established conventional belief that the essence of skill at chess is reasoning ability. To this day, chess is fostered in some school programs as a means of teaching children to think (Marjoram, 1987). However, it was found that chess grand masters did not differ from lesser players in reasoning out the consequences of possible moves. The difference was that grand masters only reasoned about good moves. This seemed to deepen the mystery, but another finding offered a clue. Grand masters had a phenomenal ability to memorize whole chessboard configurations at a glance. Yet it was not that they had generally superior memory abilities. The ability was confined to chessboard configurations and – most interesting of all – only to *meaningful* configurations, which is to say, arrangements of pieces that might actually occur in a well-played game. Give them a randomly arranged chessboard configuration and their ability to memorize it was not much better than that of a novice.

Through a series of ingenious experiments and analyses, Chase and Simon (1973) deduced that the secret of the chess experts' performance was that they knew from memory tens of thousands of patterns in which chess pieces might be arranged. A particular chessboard configuration would consist of a combination of several of these patterns. For them to memorize a chessboard layout in a few seconds was no more difficult than it would be for you to memorize a sequence of 30 letters of the alphabet when they form a readable sentence of four or five words – as compared to what it would be like to memorize the same letters randomly arranged. Thus the secret is knowledge, but not a kind of knowledge that had been appreciated before. It is far vaster in quantity that the knowledge we commonly recognize. It is not readily verbalizable; those who have it are typically not even aware of it. And yet it is integral to what we generally regard as highly intellectual activity.

Similar experiments have been done in many other fields – various sports, medicine, computer programming, weaving, music. In all of them the same kind of evidence shows up indicating vast knowledge of patterns relevant to the activity. But not just any patterns will do. Given textbook physics problems involving pulleys, inclined planes, and the like, novices as well as experts can sort the problems into meaningful categories; but the categories of the novices are based on surface features – pulley problems in one category, inclined plane problems in another, and so on – whereas the categories of the experts are based on the laws of physics that are applicable.

Principled pattern knowledge evidently lies behind a great deal of what we commonly attribute to mental abilities and intuition. The novice physician looks at a patient and sees a dumpy person with thin, oily hair; the skilled internist looks at the same person and sees a familiar pattern of thyroid deficiency. The novice editor sees a 40-word sentence and breaks it into two disjointed sentences. The expert editor sees a 25-word noun clause and changes it to a free modifier, thus rendering the 40-word sentence easy to read. The star quarterback or infielder decides in a split second on a play so brilliant that it takes the sportscaster a minute and a half to explain its rationale. Could the player actually have thought all that out? Of course not. It was a matter of recognizing a principled pattern – principled in the sense that it encapsulated the principles elaborated by the sportscaster.

The lesson in this, however, is not that we should be teaching students tens of thousands of patterns. If there is a place for pattern training at all (which there may well be) it will be at advanced stages of mastering very specific jobs or problem domains. Experts do not generally learn patterns directly but as a byproduct of striving to achieve goals in their domains. Their pattern knowledge is principled by virtue of their pursuing principled goals, trying to get to the bottom of things, reflecting on their mistakes, making use of principles to understand what they are doing and the phenomena they encounter (Bereiter & Scardamalia, 1993).

A better way of approaching the educational implications of pattern knowledge may be the following: With experience, everybody acquires pattern knowledge. That is just how our brains work. They are pattern-learning devices (Margolis, 1987). The only question, therefore, is what kind of patterns will be learned? Will they be patterns that support resourceful, principled action and that keep being elaborated and enriched as experience grows or will they be patterns bound to surface appearances, limited in their potential for growth, and supporting mindless, stereotyped behavior? Schooling should be able to do something about this, even though most pattern learning will take place outside school.

Related to the principled aspect of pattern knowledge is another finding well supported in many areas of expertise. It is the importance of *depth* of knowledge. Among the correlates of chess expertise, accuracy of memory for chess positions is one that distinguishes among levels of skill across the whole wide range covered by chess point ratings. An equally strong correlate, however, is the kind of knowledge obtainable from textbooks: knowledge of chess strategies, important games, and the like (Charness, 1991). Perhaps the most striking evidence of the importance of depth of knowledge comes from a study by Lesgold and LaJoie (1991). This is one of the few studies that has compared experts with experienced non-experts rather than with relatively inexperienced people. The people were employed in troubleshooting defects in airplane test instruments. Lesgold and his colleagues used a wide range of psychological and performance assessments to find out what distinguished the more expert from the less expert troubleshooters. They did not differ in general mental abilities or in troubleshooting strategies. Thus, although troubleshooting is clearly a thinking task, experts did not appear to differ from non-experts in thinking skills. They all knew how to troubleshoot. They did not differ in their basic knowledge of electronics, either, however. Where they differed was in their knowledge of the actual devices they worked with and on. The experts had, according to Lesgold, a very deep understanding of these devices, whereas the others had a more superficial understanding.

Depth seems to be the unifying theme in the bulk of studies on expertise: getting beneath the surface, making contact with the underlying patterns and principles that give meaning and support intelligent action. Understanding in the ordinary sense, marked by the ability to explain, may be a part of it, but deep knowledge goes beyond that to encompass patterns that inform action yet are not available to consciousness. Bloom's *Taxonomy* circles around the idea of depth but never really seizes it. Many of the sample test items at higher levels in the taxonomy seem to require knowledge of some depth. One item at the Analysis level presents the following information:

> Galileo investigated the problem of the acceleration of falling bodies by rolling balls down very smooth planes inclined at increasing angles, since he had no means of determining very short intervals of time. From the data obtained he extrapolated for the case of free fall. (Bloom, 1956, p. 151)

Examinees are then asked to identify the assumption implicit in the extrapolation. To do so would require grasping the logic of Galileo's ingenious procedure, which in turn requires understanding extrapolation at quite an abstract level as well as having a ready command of concepts of acceleration due to gravity and rolling friction. But this is not how the item is advertized. Instead, it is put forth as an item testing the ability to recognize unstated assumptions, as if there were such an ability that would generalize across subject areas. Of course, one must know what unstated assumptions are, but that is also knowledge – knowledge of what Ohlsson (1993) calls "abstract schemas." If research on expertise teaches us anything relevant to this example, it is that having students spend time solving hidden assumption problems while neglecting deeper understanding of physics would be just the wrong way to go.


## ALTERNATIVES TO THE FILING CABINET MODEL

The psychology that informed Bloom's taxonomy was a blend of behaviorism, which was the dominant scientific psychology of the day, and a common sense view, which has come to be called 'folk psychology' (Bruner, 1990; Stich, 1983). From behaviorism came the choice to define educational objectives in behavioral terms and to base the hierarchy of levels "on the idea that a particular simple behavior may become integrated with other equally simple behaviors to form a more complex behavior" (Bloom, 1956, p. 18). From folk psychology came the mind-as-container metaphor (Lakoff & Johnson, 1980), which led to treating knowledge as the contents of a mental filing cabinet.

Behaviorism has since waned as a theoretical program, but the container metaphor persists. Cognitive psychology and artificial intelligence research have elaborated and specified the contents of the container. In addition to the consciously accessible stored facts envisaged by Bloom and his colleagues, the mind as envisaged in mainstream cognitive psychology contains a large number of unnoticed items of factual knowledge or belief and additionally contains rules, which are the basis of skills. These items, furthermore, may be organized into larger structures such as scripts, schemata, semantic nets, production systems, or mental models. Anderson (1993) presents strong evidence for believing that complex skills such as computer programming and geometry proof are built-up one rule at a time.

Thus the container metaphor is far from dead. For the first time in centuries, however, it has begun to come under serious attack. The most direct challenges come from research on memory, which indicates that remembering is not a matter of retrieving an intact object but of reconstructing something anew each time remembering occurs (Schacter, 1989). Another kind of attack is based on the ability of connectionist or neural net AI programs to demonstrate how systems can act as if guided by rules and concepts without actually containing any such objects (Bechtel & Abrahamsen, 1991; Bereiter, 1991). Other attacks are based on the biological implausibility of the container metaphor (Churchland, 1986). These have been strengthened by mounting evidence that people are born with a great deal of what functions as knowledge but that can hardly be mental content fitting the filing cabinet metaphor (Hirschfield & Gelman, 1994). A very different line of criticism comes from research on situated cognition and on the social and discursive bases of knowledge. Here the general argument is that much of what folk psychology assumes to be internal is actually external, sustained by the cultural practices and ongoing discourses that people are engaged in. "[T]he whole point of the discursive turn in cognitive psychology," say Harré and Gillett (1994, pp. 39–40), "is to get away from mythical mental entities."

Unfortunately, it is quite beyond the scope of this chapter to discuss how it is possible to have a knowledgeable mind without stored mental content. A crude analogy will have to suffice. Your comfortable old shoe does not contain a representation of the shape of your foot. When the shoe is not on your foot it looks like any other shoe, but the molecules in the leather have gotten arranged so that when you put the shoe on it moulds itself to your foot (and not to just any foot of equivalent size). Imagine the brain as a supershoe that can mould itself to many different feet that it has encountered in the past. It is a shoe that remembers but that does not contain memories.

From an educational standpoint it is quite legitimate to ask, however, what is wrong with "mythical mental entities" if they produce a theory that works in practice. Folk psychology surely does work well in everyday practice. It works well in education so long as we are dealing with knowledge that can be adequately described by a smallish set of sentences or rules. In those cases, teaching people the sentences or rules is one way (and often a fairly good way) to impart the knowledge to them or at least to get them started in mastering a skill. It is the time-honored way of teaching arithmetic algorithms, for instance. And when a student is getting something wrong in a non-random way, it often helps to think of a rule that fits what the student is doing and then try to get the student to see the inadequacy of the rule. This is a prevalent strategy in the 'conceptual change' approach to teaching in science and mathematics (Scott, Asoko, & Driver, 1992).

Many important kinds of knowledge cannot be adequately described by sentences or rules, however, at least not by a small enough number to be of practical use in education. The use of English prepositions is one example. Rules fail, and a list of actual usages fills a book. Number sense, as distinct from executing arithmetic algorithms, is another (Bereiter & Scardamalia, 1996). On a larger scale, literary skills and the learning that occurs in reading good literature are important kinds of knowledge that can hardly be described in terms of mental content at all. In general, the deeper the knowledge the more difficult it is to describe it in propositions and rules and the less useful it is to deal with it in that way.

The higher-level test items in Bloom's *Taxonomy*, like the previously cited one concerning Galileo and falling bodies, seem from a more modern perspective to call for knowledge beyond what can be readily stated. As Bloom and his colleagues well recognized, students could understand gravity, acceleration, and friction at the level these are typically presented in textbooks and yet be unable to explain the logic of Galileo's experiment or to identify its unstated assumptions. Something more is required, and the authors of the *Taxonomy* sought to capture it by defining a hierarchy of general intellectual skills – what are now called 'domain independent' skills, meaning that they are not tied to any particular knowledge domain but apply across the board. But even if we acknowledge that there could be such a domain-independent skill as 'recognizing unstated assumptions,' students could be well endowed with it and still fail the test item because their understanding of physics and/or extrapolation lacked the necessary depth and coherence.

It is this deeper, more coherent understanding that contemporary research tells us we should be pursuing in education. In order to do so in a purposeful manner, however, we need ways to think about knowledge that allow us to be reasonably clear and definite about what we are trying to achieve yet do not require reducing knowledge to itemizable objects in the mind. Bloom's *Taxonomy* fails, but what is a practical alternative?

In combination, two of the ideas presented so far provide a basis for a more adequate treatment of knowledge objectives. These ideas are, on one hand, the connectionist view of mind as being knowledgeable without containing knowledge items, and, on the other hand, the objectification of knowledge as abstract objects that people create, modify, and use. The two ideas come together in the following proposition:

*The educated mind has various abilities and dispositions. Paramount among these are the ability and the disposition to create and work with abstract knowledge objects.*

## MAPPING LEVELS OF UNDERSTANDING

[S]ome teachers believe their students should "really understand," others desire their students to "internalize knowledge," still others want their students to "grasp the core or essence" or "comprehend." Do they all mean the same thing? Specifically, what does a student do who "really understands" which he does not do when he does not understand? Through reference to the taxonomy as a set of standard classifications, teachers should be able to define such nebulous terms as those given above. (Bloom, 1956, p. 1)

These words from the foreword to Bloom's *Taxonomy* indicate that its authors aimed to elucidate the nature of understanding, at least in behavioral terms. However, as we have seen, the *Taxonomy* does no such thing. With Knowledge occupying the bottom level of the hierarchy, Comprehension occupies the second. The four levels beyond that are not levels of understanding but are levels defined by kinds of performance that depend on but do not clearly reveal understanding. The *Taxonomy* captures the strong intuition that there are levels involved in knowledge. We all recognize a low level characterized by a smattering of facts and deeper levels characterized by coherently connected principles. But the levels of the *Taxonomy* do not constitute levels of knowledge in this sense.

It is also common to recognize levels of capability with respect to knowledge, ranging from some lowly ability to parrot statements to abilities to do intelligent things with knowledge. The *Taxonomy* offers us levels of this kind, but it is not clear that they are very useful levels. They are testable, to be sure, but do they correspond to reasonable educational objectives? The authors of the *Taxonomy* evidently thought so: "Teachers building a curriculum should find here a range of possible goals in the cognitive area" (Bloom, 1956, pp. 1–2). Many educators have used it in curriculum planning. The *Taxonomy* is cited among the sources of the Common Curriculum, for instance, now being introduced in Ontario schools (Ontario, Ministry of Education and Training, 1993). Few would dispute that a good educational program will engage students in plenty of comprehending, applying, analyzing, synthesizing, and evaluating. But these do not constitute a curricular sequence. No sane educator would propose starting with knowledge in grade 1, moving to comprehension in grade 2, application in grade 3, and so on. Rather, the levels of the *Taxonomy* refer to processes that need to go on in concert at all levels, supposedly leading to the attainment of worthy objectives. By not indicating what those objectives might be, however, the *Taxonomy* has, we suggest, encouraged schools to continue an emphasis on low level factual knowledge as the only kind of knowledge that has been clearly identified, supplementing factual instruction with various activities believed to foster domain-independent higher level skills.

These criticisms leave the impression that Bloom's *Taxonomy* represents a failed attempt to map levels of understanding, and that now, after four decades of cognitive science, we should be able to do it right. This would be to misread the lessons of cognitive research, however. A sounder conclusion would be that it is futile to try to define levels of understanding that are applicable across domains, or even across objects within the same domain. Possibly the authors of Bloom's *Taxonomy* tried it and found it couldn't be done. Suppose we have worked out six levels of understanding *Huckleberry Finn* and six levels of understanding the principle of natural selection. What correspondence could we expect to find between the two hierarchies? Would level 4 on one have any meaningful relationship to level 4 on the other? In order to define levels that applied to both the literary work and the scientific principle, we would need to move to a high level of abstraction. The result might be a set of indicators – essentially a set of test item types – much like those of Bloom's *Taxonomy* , or it might be levels of cognitive functioning, perhaps based on the Piagetian stages. In any case, we should have lost any sense of what a deep understanding of *Huckleberry Finn* or of natural selection would consist of.

We have been criticizing Bloom's *Taxonomy* for its failure to address depth of understanding, but we too have skirted the question of what depth of understanding is. The definition we shall offer is so simple that it will appear circular: *Having a deep understanding of something means understanding deep things about it.* Although you might argue that there is more to deep understanding than this, you can hardly argue that there is less. And if you accept that deep understanding must include understanding deep things about the matter in question, then you must abandon hope of a general taxonomy of levels of understanding.

The deep things to be understood about *Huckleberry Finn* have no necessary resemblance to the deep things to be understood about natural selection, even at a very abstract level. Experts may disagree about what the deep things are. This is invariably the case with literary works. Furthermore, we should expect only a weak ordering, even among people who agree on the deep principles. That is, it may be clear that understandings B and C are both 'deeper' than understanding A, but there may be nothing to say about the depth of B relative to C. But in all cases we are talking about the depth of *what* is understood, not about the cognitive processes or skills associated with that understanding. In assessing someone's understanding, we might well make use of the kinds of questions and tasks presented in Bloom's *Taxonomy*, but these would only be tools for getting at the substance of the student's understanding and they would be useless without a conception of what the understandings are that we are looking for. Those understandings would invariably be domain-specific.

The performance standards being developed as part of the New Standards project (National Center on Education and the Economy, 1995) place a heavy emphasis on understanding. Of the eight major standards in science, four of them begin, "The student understands. . . ." The middle-school standard for life sciences concepts reads:

The student understands:

- structure and function of cells, tissues, and organs;
- reproduction and heredity, including genes, traits, and learning;
- regulation and behavior, especially the roles of senses and hormones;
- population and ecosystems, including food webs, resources, and energy;
- evolution, in particular, species, diversity and adaptation, variation, extinction.

For any of these concepts there are things to be understood far beyond the grasp of middle school students, but there are also simple understandings – about the senses and about biological diversity, for instance – that even young children can be expected to have picked up without study (Keil, 1989). Obviously something in between is expected, but what would an intermediate level of understanding consist of? Along with the standards are model evaluative activities with samples of student performance intended to indicate an appropriate level of understanding. Thus, there is an implicit scaling of levels of understanding, but the hard work of determining what actually constitutes adequate understanding of the various concepts is left to be worked out locally, and will need to be done separately for each concept or network of concepts.

The hard lesson to be learned is that there is no shortcut to setting objectives of understanding. The curriculum designer or teacher has to get deeply into the material to be learned, to see what is there that warrants understanding, where understanding can go awry (as research on misconceptions shows that it frequently does), and what the deeper understandings are and whether these are within reach of the students. A model of this kind of analysis may be found in the work of Hunt and Minstrell (1994). In high school physics they identified a large number of what they call 'facets.'

A facet is a convenient unit of thought, an understanding or reasoning, a piece of content knowledge or a strategy seemingly used by the student in making sense of a particular situation. For the most part, our facet descriptions paraphrase the language used by students as they justify their answers, predictions, or explanations. . . . An example from free-fall and projectile motion is "Horizontal motion keeps things from falling as rapidly as they would if they were moving straight downwards." (Hunt & Minstrell, 1994, p. 52)

Over 200 facets were identified just within the areas of mechanics and electricity. Most of these would count as partial or faulty understandings, while a few comprise the principles intended to be taught. The facets were incorporated into a software application called DIAGNOSER, which not only identifies the facets of individual students' understanding but checks for consistency. One could imagine a set of facets developed to capture various novice and expert understandings of *Huckleberry Finn*. These would be specific to that novel and would have very little overlap with facets developed for *The Brothers Karamazov*, for instance. There could also be facets for literary theory, which would consist of understandings about literature in general, although these in turn would be very different from understandings of domains such as history, and facets pertaining to history in general would be very different from understandings of a particular event or epoch. Itemizing the facets of understanding relevant to standard school subject matter could occupy a substantial industry. Unfortunately, such an industry is unlikely to develop; and the task is too formidable for practitioners to carry out independently. And so, instead, we have scope-and-sequence charts and curriculum guidelines which merely name concepts without addressing what constitutes understanding, and general schemes like Bloom's *Taxonomy*, which have no direct relevance to issues of understanding.


LEVELS OF APPROACH TO KNOWLEDGE

If there is no way to characterize levels of understanding in general, and if identifying levels of understanding in particular domains is impractical, this raises doubts about the value of any general scheme of educational objectives. Yet there is an obvious need for educators to take a large view.

One kind of large view is provided by the various societies and education ministries that have produced curriculum frameworks. A number of these are cited in *Performance Standards* (National Center on Education and the Economy, 1995). These can be important in forming the major topical boundaries within which educational activities are to go on and in bringing about changes in those boundaries in response to new knowledge or new societal concerns. It is not reasonable to expect them to do much more than that, however.

Another kind of large view is provided by developmental schemes. There is the well-known Piagetian scheme of development from sensory-motor to concrete to formal logical operations. There are neoPiagetian schemes which do not propose uniform development across all domains but nevertheless propose the same general form of cognitive development in different areas of competence (Case, 1985; Fischer, 1980; Karmiloff-Smith, 1992). These developmental schemes have the virtue, lacking in Bloom's *Taxonomy*, of indicating, for a student at any particular level of attainment, what a reasonable next step should be. Case's model, in particular, has shown itself to be valuable in designing instructional interventions based on developmental levels (Case, 1992).

Something important is still missing, however. Curriculum guidelines specify areas in which knowledge is to be pursued. Developmental models lay out a continuum of increasingly sophisticated performance, applicable to various curriculum areas but we have not taken account of the student's role in the pursuit of understanding and competence. Constructivist thinking convinces us that students need to be more than willing workers. They must be agents, not merely recipients. But what are they to be agents of? Surely, the answer for a three-year-old cannot be quite the same as the answer for a thirteen-year-old, but what is supposed to change? Taking a cue from the briefly sketched history of knowledge, we can speculate that there should be developmental changes in how students approach knowledge itself.

What follows is a provisional scheme of levels of working with knowledge.[1] The levels may be thought of as levels of objectification, which start with viewing knowledge as a mental state and extend to viewing it as consisting of abstract objects. Of the seven levels, the first three are fairly well documented in the developmental and writing research literature. The seventh level corresponds to a mature scientific approach to knowledge. In between, however, are three levels that mark important and little recognized transitions that could form educational objectives in the school years:

1. *Knowledge as individuated mental states.* Research on children's theories of mind (Astington, 1993) suggests that a concept of knowledge begins to emerge with the realization that one person may know something that another does not. Prior to that, knowledge is not distinguished from 'the way things are.' In one common type of demonstration, the child is shown a puppet playlet in which the puppet puts candy in a drawer and then goes away. The candy is then removed from the drawer and put in a cupboard. When the puppet returns, the child is asked, "Where will Bozo look for the candy?" The typical three-year-old will predict that the puppet will look in the cupboard because "that's where it is." The typical six-year-old will predict that the puppet will look in the drawer because it "doesn't know" that the candy was moved. Thus, implicitly, there is some entity – a fact – which a person may or may not know.

2. *Knowledge as itemizable mental content.* According to Donald Graves (1983), a favorite writing topic of six- and seven-year-olds is "What I Know About. . ." something of interest to them. This implies a view of knowledge as items of mental content that can be accessed and reported. At this level, however, knowledge tends to be reported in the order in which it comes to mind. This is true not only of young children but of unsophisticated writers of all ages (Flower, 1979). A consequence of this 'knowledge-telling' strategy (Bereiter & Scardamalia, 1987) is that knowledge tends not to be reflected upon in the course of reporting it, so that writing or telling contributes relatively little to knowledge development.

3. *Knowledge as representation.* Trying to communicate what one knows to a reader, taking into account what the reader already knows and is in a position to understand, represents an important advance not only in language skills but also in how knowledge is conceived. It is no longer just something in the head to be expressed but is something to be represented, shared, interpreted by others. This

stage is indicated by expressions of audience awareness and by the use of explana-
tory devices such as analogies and examples.

4. *Knowledge as viewable from different perspectives.* An important step toward
objectification occurs when students see that the same knowledge can appear in
different contexts and can be viewed from different perspectives. To illustrate, we
take a classroom experiment by Ward and Thiessen (1995), which made use of
CSILE, a student-generated hypermedia database (Scardamalia & Bereiter, 1994).
Third-graders, studying endangered species, each produced a CSILE note describing a different endangered species in their region, its habitat, source of endangerment, and so on – a fairly common activity up to this point. However, using
CSILE's note-linking capabilities, the students all linked their notes to appropriate points on a map of a region, thus allowing students to see what species were
near each other or shared the same habitat. They also linked their notes to a phy-
logenetic tree, allowing them to see biological relationships among their species.
Finally, the students themselves worked out a set of reasons for endangerment,
and linked their notes to appropriate boxes in a diagram of these reasons, thus
affording a third perspective on the same body of knowledge.

5. *Knowledge as personal artifacts.* Although constructivism is widely endorsed
by teachers, it is not so common for students to view themselves as constructors of
knowledge. Viewing oneself as constructing knowledge is quite a step beyond viewing oneself as constructing knowledge representations (Level 3). One kind of
knowledge construction students can grasp readily is the construction of theories.
CSILE provides labels for several different kinds of contributions to collaborative
knowledge building, one of which is "My theory." Notes thus labeled become
discussable knowledge objects. Students will comment on one another's theories:
"I agree with your theory," "My theory is like Jamie's theory," etc. After discussion, a group of students may begin referring to "our theory" or "our solution."

6. *Knowledge as improvable personal artifacts.* When children first begin producing "My theory" notes, they are inclined to treat these as personal opinions, and
thus entitled to the protected status accorded to personal opinions in modern
classrooms, or else as guesses at the truth, to be checked by consulting authorita-
tive sources, which provide the correct theory. This, of course, is not how theories
are viewed among scientists. They are viewed as provisional solutions to theoretical problems, always subject to improvement. Viewing a theory in terms of what
it can and cannot do it, what its virtues are and where it is in need of improvement
thus represents a major advance in conceptualization of knowledge. Such a more
advanced conception is conveyed by a fifth-grade student who, asked how she
would know when she had learned, replied:

> I think that I can tell if I've learned something when I'm able to form
> substantial theories that seem to fit in with the information that I've already
> got; so it's not necessarily that I have everything, that I have all the informa-
> tion, but that I'm able to piece things in that make sense and then to form
> theories on the questions that would all fit together.

7. *Knowledge as semi-autonomous artifacts.* In the preceding quotation, knowledge is still being described as something personal. This corresponds to what Kieran Egan defines as the 'philosophical' stage of educational development, in which there is a focus on "the *general laws* whereby the world works" but "this is not a process of expansion outwards along lines of content associations, it is a closer charting of the context within which the student exists. It is not a further expansion *from* the self, but rather a closer approach *toward* the self" (Egan, 1979, pp. 51–52). Movement to the seventh level involves recognizing that knowledge objects, like other constructed objects, take on a life of their own and can be considered independently of their personal relevance. This does not mean that you become dispassionate and 'objective' in a sense that implies extreme rationality and detachment. You may feel strongly attracted or repelled by an idea, but you recognize that the idea remains unaffected by your feelings, that other people may feel differently about it, and that the idea may turn out to have virtues or flaws that you are presently unaware of and that may change your attitude toward it. Thus, at this level, knowledge objects become things that one can relate to, use, manipulate, and judge in various ways, just like other things in the real world. At this stage, then, 'knowledge work' becomes readily comprehensible. Like any other kind of productive work, it involves adding value; but in this case the things one adds value to are knowledge objects.

Let us be clear that these are levels of *approach* to knowledge. Functioning at a high level does not imply either a high level of understanding of subject matter or a high level of skill in working with knowledge. It implies, rather, that students are in a position to take a sophisticated, constructive role in the pursuit of understanding and to engage in the kinds of purposeful activities that develop knowledge-processing skills. The work of actually achieving deep understanding in a domain and competence in working with knowledge in that domain remains to be done; the hierarchy sketched here pertains to the level at which students can participate in that work.

What is immediately striking about these seven levels of approach to knowledge is how much they are neglected in school practice and how alien they are to discussions of curriculum and standards. Normally, the first level could be safely ignored, because children can be expected to acquire an awareness of knowledge as a mental state through ordinary social experience. But when a child does not acquire it, this could be a sign of something seriously amiss (Astington, 1993, Ch. 9); yet it is not a part of any screening program we know of. The second level does receive attention in whole-language approaches but seldom in traditional approaches to writing. It should be noted that itemizing mental content is not the same as responding to factual questions. Even toddlers can do the latter, but searching memory for anything one knows about a topic implies a more mature cognitive stance. The third level, which involves representing knowledge in communicable form, is the only one regularly addressed in statements of educational objectives and standards. It is usually formulated in the context of writing abilities. The previously cited Performance Standards, for instance, call at each school level for the ability to produce a report that organizes appropriate facts and details, excludes extraneous and inappropriate information, and uses a range of strategies for effective communication.

That leaves four levels, however, that receive virtually no attention in education. These are the levels at which students begin to deal directly with knowledge as such. Prior to that, knowledge is a sort of after-effect of their interactions with texts, people, and the material world. And that, we suspect, is how it remains for most people. They never become 'knowledge workers' insofar as their own knowledge is concerned; much less do they see the world's knowledge as something they can work with, add to, and modify. Yet we are expecting them to assume roles in a knowledge society that require just that kind of engagement with objectified knowledge.

How could schools foster development through the upper levels of the hierarchy? This is a large question, and only the beginnings of answers are available. But it is a researchable question – researchable both through psychological experiments and through classroom action research. The first step is to recognize that the challenge exists, and that has been the purpose of this chapter. Our own research over the past decade has explored the potential of the CSILE learning environment to promote higher levels of approach to knowledge (Scardamalia, Bereiter, & Lamon, 1994; Scardamalia & Bereiter, 1996; Scardamalia, Bereiter, Hewitt, & Webb, in press). Among upper elementary and middle school students we have seen clear evidence of levels 4 through 6. Level 7, which is characteristic of mature scholars and scientists, may not be attainable until late adolescence; but a school population functioning at level 6 would amaze the world.

CONCLUSION

Schools could function as places where students become proficient in all aspects of knowledge work, including its creation. To do so, however, fundamental changes in underlying epistemology and psychology are required. In this chapter we targeted the 40-year-old *Taxonomy of Educational Objectives* as embodying the kind of epistemology and psychology that needs changing. Knowledge, according to Bloom's *Taxonomy*, is analogous to the contents of a mental filing cabinet. The higher level objectives of education are what Bloom and colleagues called "intellectual abilities and skills," which enable people to adapt knowledge to new situations and use it for various purposes. Such a concept fails when it is stretched to cover such contemporary concerns as the creation and allocation of knowledge, knowledge work, knowledge executives, and a knowledge-based economy in which knowledge is conceived as a means of production. Thirty years of research on the nature of expertise has shown, moreover, that what distinguishes experts in all fields is their deep knowledge, not their general "intellectual abilities and skills."

Drawing on insights from recent work on the nature of mind, situated cognition, expertise, and processes of knowledge creation in the sciences, we have tried to outline a different way of thinking about knowledge. Gone is the filing cabinet metaphor and its attendant trivializing of knowledge. Instead, we have a conception of minds as being knowledgeable without containing itemizable knowledge. The challenge, accordingly, is to develop forms of objectives and standards compatible with this view. Two watchwords of a new approach are *depth of understanding* and *objectification*. Because depth of understanding implies understanding deep things about something, no global hierarchy such as that of Bloom's *Taxonomy* can suffice. The 'deep things' need to be identified separately for each object of understanding. Objectification, however, can be characterized in a more general way. Objectification means the prying loose of knowledge from individual mental states and collective practices, making it an object of constructive activity in its own right. Historically, objectification emerged over the course of many centuries. For individuals, we have sketched a series of seven levels or stages that represent increasing ability to deal with knowledge as such – to construct it, view it from different perspectives, criticize it, improve it. Thus, progression through these levels represents an educational objective of particular significance to a knowledge society.

## ENDNOTES

1    The provisional nature of the scheme must be emphasized. We are involved in the early stages of a project titled "Knowledge-Building Indicators," which will develop and test a variety of ways to assess knowledge building in telelearning environments. The scheme presented here is a first pass, based largely on existing research, and will undoubtedly undergo substantial changes as new research is carried out.

## REFERENCES

Anderson, J. R. (1993). *Rules of the mind.* Cambridge, MA: MIT Press.
Astington, J. W. (1993). *The child's discovery of the mind.* Cambridge, MA: Harvard University Press.
Bechtel, W., & Abrahamsen, A. A. (1991). Beyond the exclusively propositional era. In J. H. Fetzer (Ed.), *Epistemology and cognition* (pp. 121–151). Dordrecht: Kluwer Academic Publishers.
Bereiter, C. (1991). Implications of connectionism for thinking about rules. *Educational Researcher*, 20, 10–16.
Bereiter, C., & Scardamalia, M. (1987). *The psychology of written composition.* Hillsdale, NJ: Lawrence Erlbaum Associates.
Bereiter, C., & Scardamalia, M. (1993). *Surpassing ourselves: An inquiry into the nature and implications of expertise.* La Salle, IL: Open Court.
Bereiter, C., & Scardamalia, M. (1996). Rethinking learning. In D. R. Olson &. N. Torrance (Eds.), *Handbook of education and human development: New models of learning, teaching and schooling* Cambridge, MA: Basil Blackwell.
Bloom, B. S. (Ed.). (1956). *Taxonomy of educational objectives: Handbook 1. Cognitive domain.* New York: David McKay Company, Inc.
Bruner, J. S. (1990). *Acts of meaning.* Cambridge, MA: Harvard University Press.
Case, R. (1985). *Intellectual development: Birth to adulthood.* Orlando, FL: Academic Press.
Case, R. (1992). *The mind's staircase: Exploring the conceptual underpinnings of children's thought and knowledge.* Hillsdale, NJ: Erlbaum.
Charness, N. (1991). Expertise in chess: The balance between knowledge and search. In K. A. Ericsson & J. Smith (Eds.), *Toward a general theory of expertise: Prospects and limits* (pp. 39–63). Cambridge: Cambridge University Press.
Chase, W. G., & Simon, H. A. (1973). Perception in chess. *Cognitive Psychology*, 4, 55–81.

Chi, M. T. H., Glaser, R., & Farr, M. (Ed.). (1988). *The nature of expertise*. Hillsdale, NJ: Erlbaum.
Churchland, P. S. (1986). *Neurophilosophy: Toward a unified science of the mind-brain*. Cambridge, MA: MIT Press.
Drucker, P. F. (1993). *Post-capitalist society*. New York: HarperCollins.
Egan, K. (1979). *Educational development*. New York: Oxford University Press.
Fischer, K. W. (1980). A theory of cognitive development: Control and construction of hierarchies of skills. *Psychological Review*, **87**, 477–531.
Flower, L. S. (1979). Writer-based prose: A cognitive basis for problems in writing. *College English*, **41**, 19–37.
Graves, D. R. (1983). *Writing: Teachers and children at work*. Exeter, NH: Heinemann Educational Books.
Harré., R., & Gillett, G. (1994). *The discursive mind*. Thousand Oaks, CA: Sage Publications.
Hirschfeld, L. A., & Gelman, S. A. (Eds.). (1994). *Mapping the mind: Domain specificity in cognition and culture*. New York: Cambridge University Press.
Hunt, E., & Minstrell, J. (1994). A cognitive approach to the teaching of physics. In K. McGilley (Ed.), *Classroom lessons: Integrating cognitive theory and classroom practice*. (pp. 51–74). Cambridge, MA: MIT Press.
Karmiloff-Smith, A. (1992). *Beyond modularity: A developmental perspective on cognitive science*. Cambridge, MA: MIT Press.
Keil, F. C. (1989). *Concepts, kinds, and cognitive development*. Cambridge, MA: Bradford/MIT Press.
Lakoff, G., & Johnson, M. (1980). *Metaphors we live by*. Chicago, IL: University of Chicago Press.
Lesgold, A. M., & Lajoie, S. (1991). Complex problem solving in electronics. In R. J. Sternberg & P. A. Frensch (Eds.), *Complex problem solving: Principles and mechanisms* (pp. 287–316). Hillsdale, NJ: Erlbaum.
Margolis, H. (1987). *Patterns, thinking, and cognition*. Chicago: University of Chicago Press.
Marjoram, D. T. E. (1987). Chess and gifted children. *Gifted Education International*, **5**, 48–51.
New Standards. (1995). *Performance standards: English language arts, mathematics, science, applied learning*. Rochester, NY: National Center on Education and the Economy.
Ohlsson, S. (1993). Abstract schemas. *Educational Psychologist*, **28**(1), 51–66.
Olson, D. R. (1994). *The world on paper: The conceptual and cognitive implications of writing and reading*. New York: Cambridge University Press.
Ontario, Ministry of Education and Training. (1993). *The common curriculum, grades 1–9, working document*. Toronto: Publications Ontario.
Scardamalia, M., & Bereiter, C. (1994). Computer support for knowledge-building communities. *The Journal of the Learning Sciences*, **3**(3), 265–283.
Scardamalia, M., & Bereiter, C. (1996). Adaptation and understanding: A case for new cultures in schooling. In S. Vosniadou, E. de Corte, R. Glaser & H. Mandl (Eds) *International perspectives on the psychological foundations of technology-based learning environments.*(pp.149–163).Mohwah, N.J: Laurence Erlbaum Associates.
Scardamalia, M., Bereiter, C., & Lamon M. (1994). CSILE: Trying to bring students into world 3. In K. McGilley (Ed.), *Classroom lessons: Integrating cognitive theory and classroom practice* (pp. 201–228). Cambridge, MA: MIT Press.
Scardamalia, M., Bereiter, C., Hewitt, J., & Webb, J. (in press). Constructive learning from texts in biology. In K. M. Fischer & M. Kirby (Eds.), *Relations and biology learning: The acquisition and use of knowledge structures in biology*. Berlin: Springer-Verlag.
Schacter, D. L. (1989). Memory. In M. I. Posner (Ed.), *Foundations of cognitive science* (pp. 683–725). Cambridge, MA: MIT Press.
Scott, P., Asoko, H., & Driver, R. (1992). Teaching for conceptual change: A review of strategies. In R. Duit, F. Goldberg, & H. Neidderer (Eds.), *Research in physics learning: Theoretical issues and empirical studies* Keil, Germany: Schmidt and Klannig.
Stich, S. P. (1983). *From folk psychology to cognitive science: The case against belief*. Cambridge, MA: MIT Press.
Ward, D. R, & Thiessen, E. L. (1994, August). *Endangered species* (Technical Report of Instructional Unit): CSILE project. Toronto: OISE.
Whitehead, A. N. (1925, 1948). *Science and the modern world* (Mentor ed.). New York: New American Library.

# Human Development in the Learning Society

DANIEL P. KEATING

*Ontario Institute for Studies in Education of the University of Toronto*

*New models of learning are radically changing our conception of education. Education for human development in the learning society requires collaborative learning and involves focusing on knowledge-building. These changes arise from shifts in educational goals, from increasing diversity of populations, and from new conceptions in learning and knowledge. Life long learning, schools as learning organizations, and the integration of schools into a broader community that promotes learning will be required for human development in the information age.*

The core question of this *Handbook* is how best to achieve desirable educational change. As soon as we ask that question, a host of prerequisite questions assert themselves. What is the goal of the educational change, or, more bluntly, what educational change is desired? What is our understanding of the fundamental processes of change, which might enable valued educational change to occur? What is the broader context of societal change within which the educational change will take place? Vast complexity is introduced when we admit these and other similar foundational questions into the discussion, yet, if we do not take them on, we are forced to operate in a piecemeal fashion.

A coherent conceptual framework with a sufficiently broad perspective may enable us to make sense of the complexity and to address these questions in an integrated fashion. In the Human Development Program of the Canadian Institute for Advanced Research, my colleagues and I have sought to explore and articulate such a conceptual framework (Keating, 1995b, 1996b; Keating & Mustard, 1993; Task Force on Human Development, 1992). The first goal of this framework is to understand human development in its broadest sense, linking together perspectives on individual development across the lifespan; on the health, competence, and coping capacity of human populations; and on the social organization of human activity. The second goal is to explore the possible future directions for human development in the contemporary era, and to identify key elements that may contribute to more desirable directions.

We have used the term a "learning society" to capture this idea. Although this term is fraught with the potential for misinterpretation, it does connect a number of key themes essential for constructive change. Among these are that change is a continuous process, that it can be brought to conscious awareness in which goals are made explicit, that it involves the broader society and not just communities of experts, and that collaborative learning is crucial to effective societal adaptation.

*M. Fullan (ed.), Fundamental Change, 23-39.*
*© 2005 Springer. Printed in the Netherlands.*

It is important to clarify potentially major misconceptions which may arise from the use of each of the constituent terms. Learning is not to be restricted to the individual acquisition of knowledge or skill already attained by others (as in, say, "learning to read"), but also to include activities better described as collaborative knowledge building and innovation (Bereiter & Scardamalia, 1996). Traditional psychological notions which viewed learning as a purely internal set of processes describing the adaptation of the individual to a relatively fixed external environment (the "to be learned" material) represent one type of obstacle to this broader understanding.

Society is to be seen as not only a collection of institutions and practices, but also as a culturally integrated organization of institutions and practices, whose organization is in itself capable of adapting and learning from experience. It has become commonplace to speak of learning organizations capable of effective institutional memory, collaborative goal seeking, and continuous improvement, all of which occur in a real sense at the group rather than the individual level. A learning society can be usefully regarded as a generalization of the learning organization (Keating, 1995a).

This introduces one further potential misconception which is that collaborative efforts depend on uniformity of goals among the individual members of a group. From this misconception it is easy to dismiss the notion of an effective learning organization (or learning society) merely by taking note of the ubiquity of conflict and competition in human activity. The heart of this misconception is the view that competition and cooperation are exclusive states. It can be observed in many well functioning complex systems that cooperation and competition are linked in a dynamic tension which is essential to the system's functioning. Neural competition at the level of cells and cooperation at the level of systems is but one well documented example.

The goal of this chapter is to outline the conceptual framework on human development and the learning society which we have been constructing, with a particular focus on the critically important issue of educational change. It is perhaps obvious, but should be made explicit, that the success of a learning society is crucially dependent upon the available human resources (or human capital, to use the economists' term), as well as upon the patterns of social organization to employ those resources. Notions of "social capital" (e.g., Putnam, 1992) capture some important elements of this perspective. The important point here is that education is central to the formation of both human capital and social capital. To create a learning society, we must address the central role of education.

## CONTEMPORARY SOCIAL CHANGE IN HISTORICAL CONTEXT

We are experiencing rapid social and economic change as we approach the 21st century. The perceived rapidity of these changes not only generates a sense of disorientation among many individuals, but also presents major challenges to societal adaptability. Societies must cope simultaneously with global economic competition, the demand for new competencies in the population, the provision of opportunities for health and well-being throughout the population, and the maintenance of the social fabric for nurturing, socializing, and educating the next generation. Successfully meeting these challenges sets the foundations for future population health and competence, economic prosperity, and social cohesion. But many of the traditional societal forms and practices may experience difficulty in adapting to change, and new forms which may be able to meet these challenges have yet to emerge clearly.

The pace, magnitude, and complexity of social change are often perceived as overwhelming and uncontrollable. This perceived lack of control can then distort our perceptions of the challenges and opportunities, further diminishing our ability to respond and adapt to change. This core dynamic – accelerating change and decreasing sense of control – makes thoughtful planning and reform difficult to achieve, whether in education or other social institutions.

We may start to break this cycle by appealing to a combined evolutionary and historical perspective that takes note of the fundamentally social nature of humans, and of the many different patterns of organizing social life with which we have experimented. I have previously summarized some key elements of this perspective (Keating, 1996b).

Like almost all of our close relatives – non-human primates – *Homo sapiens* is a social species. We play, work, interact, learn, and reproduce in social groups throughout our lives. We develop in social relationships from the earliest period of life, as do most other primates, but we remain dependent on the caretaking of others for a longer time than any other primate. At the core, then, we need social groups to survive.

Moreover, our early experiences – most of which occur through social interactions – play a critical role throughout life in how we cope, how we learn, and how competent we become. The nature of the social environment in which we develop is thus a key determinant of our quality of life. Diverse life outcomes – positive and negative – are closely associated with identifiable differences in early social experiences. In turn, the quality of the human social environment is partly a function of the competence that is available within the society. The nurture, education, and socialization of new members of the group depend on the skills and commitment of more mature members, and on social arrangements that facilitate high quality interactions among generations.

Many of these demands are neither historically new nor species specific. But we face additional challenges unknown to our human and pre-hominid ancestors. Although we share much in common with our primate cousins, humans appear to be unique in having developed the capabilities of conscious self-reflection, cultural transmission of skills and knowledge through language and other symbolic means, cumulative technological development, and civilization. In evolutionary terms, these are quite recent changes in our lives (Keating, 1995a; Keating & Mustard, 1993).

We can get a better sense of how recent they are by using a calendar year analogy. Take 100,000 years as an estimate of the time elapsed since the emergence of fully modern humans, and place it on the scale of a single year. Using this baseline, we can note that our species first moved into small urban centres, supported by agriculture, about the end of November, and started an industrial revolution on the afternoon of New Year's Eve. Only a few minutes ago, we launched experiments in instantaneous global communication, information technology, and multicultural metropolism. This recency is further exaggerated if we use the earlier starting point of the emergence of consistent tool-making and tool-use by hominids, which may go back as much as 2.5 million years.

The origins and mechanisms of this evolutionary process remain controversial (Dennett, 1995), but several important features have gained fairly broad consensus. Consider first the social sophistication of non-human primates. From this perspective, we can see that complex social arrangements and behaviours among humans are not merely a function of cultural experiences; other primates are also skilled social strategists (Tomasello, Kruger, & Ratner, 1993). Much of our "intuitive" understanding of how to function in groups thus has a lengthy evolutionary history, which has embedded in us many elegant "designs" for social interaction, although some of them may present obstacles to further adaptation – wariness of "others" may be one such design feature.

At some critical juncture, we added language capabilities to this already rich social mix, yielding apparently infinite potential for complex communication. Language enables much more complex social communication, and may even have arisen initially out of a need to maintain cohesion in larger groups (Donald, 1991; Dunbar, 1992), although there is much controversy at the moment regarding the evolutionary history of human language (Dennett, 1995). The larger group size may have contributed economic benefits of organization and specialization of work, permitting more effective exploitation of harsh habitats as well as a primitive form of shared risk.

The teaching and learning of special skills were also enhanced by language, and an accelerating cycle of technological innovation and development ensued. Apparently unique to *Homo sapiens*, this unification of language and tool use was put forward by Vygotsky (1978) as the starting point of fully human intelligence, both phylogenetically and ontogenetically.

At a later critical juncture, the evidence suggests that we drew on our increasing symbolic and instrumental sophistication (that is, better language and tool use) to establish connections *between* troops and tribes. This is a signal accomplishment, which we might justifiably designate as the initiation of human "experiments with civilization" (Keating & Mustard, 1993). We can date the origins of this new design pattern in human activity to about 40,000 – 50,000 years ago (Stringer & Gamble, 1993), when the remarkable onset and spread both of symbolic forms (particularly cave painting and sculpture) and of more complex stone technologies, which had been previously unchanged for perhaps two million years, coincided. The rapidity and coincidence of these emerging forms suggests the innovation of language-based cultural diffusion, which implies in turn the capacity to work with others outside one's own group and to innovate on a collaborative basis.

It is important, however, not to romanticize this prehistoric past. Ample evidence supports the pervasive nature of human conflict, among individuals and between groups, then and now. Cooperation did not displace conflict (recall the earlier discussion about misconceptions of their relationship), but new designs for inter-group collaboration and diffusion are likely to have afforded substantial material advantages to groups who took it up, even against the backdrop of persistent inter-group conflict. A contemporary manifestation of the misconception is the belief that cooperation is a natural and desirable state of humanity, for which only the educational opportunities to exercise it are needed in order to induce it. The evidence suggests rather the contrary. Both competition and cooperation represent potential human activities, but persistent and effective cooperation has to be highly supported by well-designed educational structures and practices which acknowledge and account for the equally human propensities toward competition and conflict.

Although formal education as an innovative human design was still millennia away, we can confidently speculate that the onset of "experiments in civilization" occurred together with – and was crucially and mutually dependent upon – the onset of what we can reasonably describe as "education" in the broad sense.

The accelerating pace of technological and social change appears to be based, then, on our species-specific penchant for collaborative learning across (formerly rigid) group boundaries. Enhancing this new design for learning through progressively more efficient cultural means – oral histories, formal instruction, writing, and now information technologies – contributes directly to this acceleration.

Changes in the means of communication also have non-trivial consequences for cognitive activity – how we think, what we know, and how we learn. A well understood example is the connection between the practice of literacy and the development of logic, argument, reflection, and metacognitive understanding (Cole & Scribner, 1974; Olson, 1994). As literacy spreads, so do literate habits of the mind.

This analysis suggests that the combination of a new technology for communication with new capabilities in the population creates a potent new medium for discourse among previously isolated groups and individuals – and thus new opportunities for innovation. In concert with changes in social communication (such as language, literacy, and now information technology and knowledge media), we have continued to discover new means for extracting material subsistence from the earth.

The agricultural revolution first enabled the congregation and settlement of large groups of humans in specific places over a durable period of time – in other words, cities. The organization of production in agricultural societies demanded that a relatively large proportion of the population was needed to provide direct physical energy – plowing, sowing, reaping, and so on. Thus, only a small portion of the population was directly involved in the acquisition and expansion of knowledge which was potentiated by the agricultural revolution. Literacy and numeracy, for example, remained rare skills over long historical periods – and into the present in less affluent societies. Yet the potential for rapid and systematic accumulation of knowledge owing to the opportunities for collaborative learning was historically realized, as was the onset of new social designs, including formal education and cumulative science.

The next major revolution in social forms occurred very recently. The industrial revolution removed human labor from the direct energy loop required for material production (Rosenberg & Birdzell, 1986), but created a demand for ever more complex arrangements for the organization of labor. Note again that these technological innovations were mutually dependent upon concomitant changes in social structures and practices.

These examples illustrate an on-going, mutually causal interplay between technological and social innovation. This may be difficult to visualize initially, as we are more accustomed to linear or main effect models, in which an isolated cause yields a specific outcome. But as we trace these four major transformations in our species' history, we can see that changes in technology generated demands and opportunities for changes in societal functioning, and changes in society generated demands and opportunities for technological innovation:

- language and complex communication within the group (100 to 50K before present [BP] (Donald, 1991);
- intertribal communication and cultural diffusion (about 40K years BP);
- the agricultural revolution and settled urban civilizations (about 10K years BP);
- the industrial revolutions (about 0.5 to 0.1K years BP), from steam to electrical;
- the information and knowledge revolutions (now).

Another such transformational moment thus seems to be upon us, in the form of existing information technologies and knowledge media-instantaneous and thoroughly diffused global communication; unlimited knowledge storage and retrieval; sophisticated techniques for data analysis, simulation, and visual representation; and artificially intelligent design with robotic manufacture.

Unique among species, then, we have created what systems theorists call an iterative feedback loop between our ways of using material resources and the ways in which we organize our social lives. This new pattern of cultural and social change continually reshapes the ecological habitats in which we live and work – and in which subsequent generations will develop (Keating & Mustard, 1993). The essence of this "innovation dynamic" is shown in Figure 1.

Modes of teaching and learning also evolve in response to these broad social and technological shifts. But since evolutionary changes are by definition trial and error, we can not be assured that any given historical trend in education is beneficial rather than harmful. Dewey's (1963) cogent criticism of formal education as overly abstract and insufficiently practical, as the ascendance of "book learning" over hands-on apprenticeship, spoke to this concern, a concern echoed in many contemporary educational critiques (Bruner, 1990; Lave, 1988; Rogoff, 1990). As

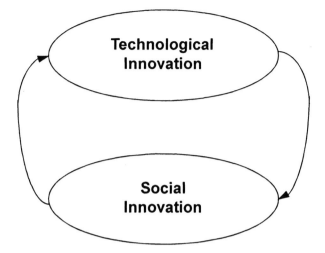

**1. Precision Stone Tools**
   **Intergroup Learning**

**2. Agricultural Resource**
   **Urban Congregation**

**3. Industrial Manufacture**
   **Taylorism / Urban Linkages /**
   **Market Mechanisms**

Figure 1: The innovation dynamic.

the pace of change accelerates, there may be insufficient time for societal adaptation by trial and error. In these circumstances, understanding the core dynamics in order to guide progressive change becomes more critical.

Designing an educational system capable of responding to these demands requires that we attend simultaneously to the broad historical forces which have shaped human development, to the fundamental processes of individual and collective human development, and to the nature of contemporary educational practices.

From this perspective, then, several lessons for educational change leap to mind. First, it is important when designing educational change to keep in mind where the broader dynamic of change is headed, at least as much as where it has been. We may well be able now to design a highly effective educational system to serve an industrial age, but it will not likely serve our goals very well.

Second, the nature of the design process for change needs to be better understood. Given the accelerating pace of change, it is essential to try to create now an educational system capable of self-renewing change, of conscious adaptation. It seems likely that top-down design processes may be both too unwieldy and too insensitive to local conditions to succeed, at least for long. Bottom-up design processes may hold more promise, but risk incoherence and pure reactivity unless they are guided by a coherent conceptual framework which can shape the discourse about changes in design.

Third, we should beware of hubris as we attempt to meet these challenges. We have been shaped by thousands of millennia of hominid evolution, which gives us much potential but also many constraints, only some of which we understand very well at this time. We have even less experience of knowing how to adapt to the experiments in civilization which the innovation dynamic keeps churning up. The hubris is that, despite these inherited constraints and limited experience, we should be able to solve these complex problems forthwith. As they remain unresolved, we sometimes lapse into looking for someone or some group to bear the blame, rather than recognize the inherent difficulty and complexity of the problems. Solution-focused discourse would appear, under these circumstances, to be a better use of human resources than identifying the blameworthy. Although resistance to productive change may arise from self-centered goals, such as retaining power, or from personal apprehensions, such as fear of change, we should recognize that some of the most formidable obstacles to change lie in the inertia of complex systems themselves.

## EDUCATIONAL CHANGE AT THE DAWN OF THE INFORMATION AGE

We can link these perspectives on the broader social forces with the specific issue of educational change. A productive comparison can be drawn between educational practices and beliefs that evolved in the industrial age and those that may serve us better in an information age.

These domains of educational change can be thought of as falling into three main groups:

Table 1: Characteristics of Education in the Industrial and Information Ages

|  | Industrial Age | Information Age |
| --- | --- | --- |
| Educational goals | Conceptual grasp for the few; basic skills & algorithms for the many | Conceptual grasp & intentional knowledge building for all |
| Anticipated workplaces | Factory models, vertical bureaucracies | Collaborative learning organizations |
| Nature of diversity | Inherent, categorical | Transactional, historical |
| Dealing with diversity | Selection of elites, basics for broad population | Developmental model of life-long learning for broad population |
| Pedagogy | Knowledge transmission | Knowledge building |
| Prime mode of learning | Individual | Collaborative |

- the changes arising from shifts in educational goals, which are in turn tied to broader societal changes and to the nature of work in evolving economies;
- the changes arising from increasing diversity of populations which schools are expected to serve, which are related in turn to emerging political perspectives on inclusiveness and to major demographic shifts from urbanization to expanding global immigration patterns (Keating, 1995b);
- the changes arising from our new conceptions in learning and knowledge building, based on our improving grasp of fundamental processes in human development (Keating, 1996b; Olson & Torrance, 1996).

CHANGING EDUCATIONAL GOALS

In an industrial era, only a few people were required to plan and innovate (the "heads"), whereas the masses were expected merely to execute repetitive tasks (the "hands"). An educational system in such circumstances would ideally function as an honest selection mechanism, to assure the best and brightest become heads. This never worked well in practice, as schools being a part of society tended to reproduce social class distinctions based on non-relevant factors, especially social class.

In any case, this selection mechanism is far less relevant in an information age, where positions in bureaucracies are far less stable, credentials are less of a guarantee of status, and the nature of work is changing at a furious pace. The decimation of middle management in both the private and public sectors is but one example of this. Enterprises and organizations that are capable of adapting to rapidly shifting conditions will become more dominant, and to support this we need to expand competence more broadly and deeply through the population than we have been able to do previously.

Related to this is the reality that information technology, especially networking capabilities like the Internet and the World Wide Web, reduces the absolute value of acquired knowledge and stored information by making it readily available (Keating, 1995a). In these circumstances, the advantage accrues to those whose goal is knowledge building (Bereiter & Scardamalia, 1996). This highlights an example of educational change that is innovative but counter-productive: the student who produces an Internet-based "research paper" that is dense with up-to-the-minute information, none of which has been processed at a deep or conceptual level. Neither novelty nor change is inherently good – or bad. In order to design effective educational change, we need to be guided by a coherent conceptual framework.

The innovation dynamic (see Figure 1) may afford a better grasp of the challenges facing education in the current context of massive societal change. Many observers have suggested that we appear to be at the cusp of change, but also that there may be radically different possible paths for the future.

One path (Path B in Figure 2) has captured the attention of science fiction writers and social science prognosticators alike. This path is put forward by many as the most likely outcome – the path of least resistance, if you will. Simple inertia

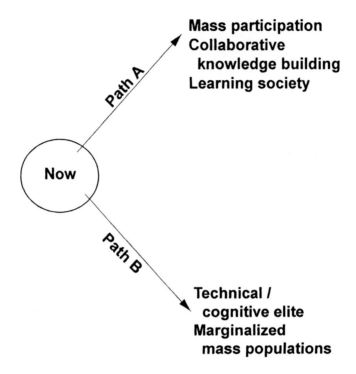

**Figure 2: Schematic view of possible future pathways.**

from our current directions seems to lead toward the separation of a technology or cognitive elite from increasingly marginalized mass populations. And of course that division is not just within societies in the technologically advanced world, but also between the developed and the developing world. Given current directions in terms of deskilling and unemployment, Path B does seem to have a high probability.

Conceptually at least, there are alternate pathways. One alternative suggests that we need to conceive a way of introducing technology that would encourage mass or universal participation in collaborative knowledge building, not only about our material and economic existence, but also about our social functioning and societal structure. The generic concept then that holds these ideas together is the notion of a learning society, represented as Path A.

As already noted, many would predict that Path B is almost inevitable from where we now stand. But when complex systems are at major change points, as we know from looking at many different dynamic systems in many different domains, their variance increases dramatically, as does the potential for fundamental realignment. It is also true in these moments that small pushes to that system can move it down different paths – the well-known "butterfly effect." Is it possible to push these systems toward a more virtuous cycle, onto a path that has the positive features of Path A and therefore enables us to avoid some of the very worrisome features of Path B? Probability estimates are wildly unstable in the midst of fundamental change, and are not of much practical value for such a broad question. But if it is possible, it is clear that education will need to play a key role in such a system transformation. It will need to focus on two key tasks: optimizing human development throughout the population to enable mass participation in important economic and social tasks; and constructing the core social patterns of collaborative learning and innovation which will be a key for an effective learning society.

Many of the central aspects which differentiate these two possible pathways invoke important features of human development. A knowledge economy relies heavily on the human resources of its population, including health, coping, and competence. Making effective use of these human resources requires attention to the social organization of those resources, whether in support of the economy (that is, workplace organization for production) or the society (that is, community coherence). These dimensions can be viewed as the human development components of the innovation dynamic – the optimal development of human resources and the effective organization of those resources.

## EDUCATION'S ROLE IN OPTIMIZING HUMAN DEVELOPMENT

One clear implication from these revised educational goals is that we need to expand competence more broadly and deeply through the population than we have been able to do previously. The tensions between excellence and equity, between proponents and opponents of traditional standards, and between regular and special education, take on a new character in this light. We need to base *all* education on a more explicit and conceptually sophisticated developmental model. In particular, it is distinguished from the selection or categorical model of education which emerged under quite different historical circumstances. The legacy of that earlier model creates some substantial barriers to effective educational change.

Previously, I identified several key characteristics that distinguish the developmental from the categorical model of education (Keating, 1990). These include the recognition that there are multiple pathways to the development of expertise, not just one; a shift in focus away from underlying cognitive abilities and toward understanding the fundamental cognitive activities that we engage in as we acquire expertise; an appreciation of the importance of domain specific expertise as well as more general habits of learning and thinking; and a shift in assessment from a primary goal of categorical placement, toward a guided attempt to inform instruction so that it is maximally relevant to the child's development at that point in time. Elsewhere, I described an example of how this might be applied to a particular sector of students who have been poorly served by both regular education and the special education model: gifted students – or in our new terminology, developmentally advanced students (Keating, 1991).

In that previous discussion, I summarized the core conceptual distinction in this way:

Those individuals who give evidence of being best *adapted* to current social and educational practices, revealed in test scores and school performance, are defined in the categorical model as most generally *adaptable* (that is, intelligent) due to a more optimal underlying design. A consequence of this conflation of two quite different meanings is the assumption that educational difficulty is legitimately explained as a failure of adaptibility of the student.

From a developmental perspective, we recognize that success in a particular ecological . . . niche is not necessarily a sign of adaptability to a wide range of niches. Moreover, we are more likely to look for ways in which the instructional environment has failed to adapt to the developmental diversity that differential histories inevitably generate. By shifting the onus from a lack of adaptiveness in the child to a lack of adaptiveness in the setting, we can begin a close examination of the ways to design better learning environments, rather than simply demarcating presumed design flaws in the child (Keating, 1990, p. 264).

The key point is that we need to attend more closely to the developmental needs of each child, regardless of an identifiable diagnosis or categorical label. This understanding offers a realistic way to achieve educational integration of all students. When supplemented by the exciting work on the linkage between collaborative learning and networked learning environments, the prospects for escaping the unhelpful dichotomies between regular and special education, and between excellence and equity, begin to seem more realistic.

## EDUCATION'S ROLE IN BUILDING THE LEARNING SOCIETY

It grows increasingly clear that knowledge of all types is always a social and cultural product. As advanced information technologies spread, this social nature of knowledge will become ever more apparent. The emerging picture of science as a collaborative and cumulative discourse captures the essence of one key self-organizing social system. Differences among societies in how well they are able to make use of the social nature of knowledge may determine, in part, how effective they will be in building successful, innovation-based economies.

In other words, socially distributed intelligence may become increasingly central to societal success. It depends in turn on the diversity of talent available in the population *and* on the ways in which human groups interact to become units of learning.

One difficulty is that this runs against the historical trend of viewing knowledge, skill, and expertise as a strictly individual possession, and to view one role of education as the validation and certification of that individual knowledge. Much of the resistance to collaborative learning models is precisely the concern about the submersion of this educational activity.

This is, of course, the now familiar competition-cooperation dynamic in yet another guise. When rewards are distributed (partially) on the basis of individual accomplishment, then the risks of cooperation are magnified. But knowledge building – as opposed to knowledge transmission – occurs far more effectively in collaborative networks than in individual study. It also likely enhances individual skill acquisition (Bereiter & Scardamalia, 1996).

In light of the educational goals discussed above, it makes sense to recognize this as a real tension, and to examine possible solutions from a coherent framework. Maintaining individual accountability and effective developmental progress for each individual are entirely possible within a collaborative knowledge building model. We need to reconcile this necessity for change with the reality of a pervasive selection-based model.

This is just one example of the type of barriers to educational change that will be encountered. Many educational practices and beliefs are interlocking, which makes it difficult to engage in meaningful change which persists. In dynamic system terminology, the current practices and beliefs form a "stable attractor state," from which it is difficult to move, because each specific change implicates a host of others. It is this system inertia which is often pointed to by critics from outside the educational community.

It has often happened that schools are the focus of serious social criticism for a range of perceived shortcomings. Professionals of many types who have devoted their careers and their intellectual and emotional energy in the field of education see this criticism as a double-edged sword. On the one hand, they are understandably defensive in response to such critiques, especially when they are launched by those who have not invested themselves in this pursuit, and who claim instant expertise on extremely difficult, if not intractable problems. Particularly when criticisms do not ring true to teachers' and students' everyday lives, the value of these instant solutions is justifiably doubted. On the other hand, there is a temptation to join in even the most damning chorus of criticisms because they perceive more clearly than others the depth of the problems and the difficulty of achieving real and lasting change.

From a learning society perspective, neither the response of defensiveness nor despair is warranted or useful. Rather, the particular nature of current concerns about schooling in our society offers a unique opportunity to make substantive changes. The current alignment of social pressures and growth in our conceptual understanding represent a transformational moment in the role of education in society, and how we approach this opportunity is likely to play a significant role in the outcome of that transformation.

We can identify some conditions that may enable major transformation. These include a deepening awareness among educational practitioners that the institution is not functioning well, and that more than small changes are called for. Added to this is a growing recognition in the larger society that successful schools, and thus successful students and graduates, are fundamental to the future well-being of society.

The reality is that we need schools to work well for society to prosper. They represent an enormous collective investment in the social infrastructure for developing human resources. Dismissing this investment and starting from scratch is not only not feasible, but also wantonly wasteful of the abundance of talent and commitment that already exists among professionals involved in and committed to education. It becomes increasingly apparent that major transformations are necessary, amounting in effect to reinvention of the institutions of education. Some recent simulations of how large and complex systems do change suggest that a widespread perception of the necessity for change is itself a substantial contributing factor to the likelihood that change will occur.

If our educational goals are focused on building a learning society, we can identify a number of key themes that will likely be important as we move forward (adapted from Keating, 1995b).

- *Lifelong learning is essential to a learning society, and we need to learn how to facilitate this.*

As students enter school from increasingly diverse backgrounds, their habits of learning and academic readiness attained prior to the onset of schooling vary substantially. At the beginning and throughout the school years, we must find ways to encourage a positive attitude toward learning. A central ingredient is that students must perceive clearly the potential benefits for their effort, in particular a range of realistic pathways linking education with meaningful opportunities for participation in economic and social life.

- *Schools can not do it alone.*

The early experiences of some children may make it difficult for them to learn under most typical educational circumstances. We need to build stronger links among families, schools, and communities to reduce the number of children who enter school as dysfunctional or marginally functional learners. Where the erosion of the social fabric has reached an advanced stage, in what Garbarino (1994) has called socially toxic environments, the prospects that schools can fully redress the negative outcomes for all children are dim. As a society, we need to consider how best to prevent such problems from occurring (Keating, 1996a).

- *Competence develops along multiple pathways within and between individuals.*

We need to accommodate the fact that different children will require different educational experiences to help them develop, and we must be prepared to adapt instructional and learning settings accordingly (Keating, 1990). We need to enhance the capabilities of schools to support developmental progress along the full diversity of pathways that they encounter. Virtually all children retain sufficient plasticity to develop meaningful competence, if we can discover appropriate educational experiences for them.

- *Diversity arises from differing developmental histories – cultural, gender, class, and individual. Diversity offers both challenges and opportunities. Understanding such diversity and forging common goals must proceed simultaneously.*

Too often commentators highlight the difficulties we have encountered in our initial attempts to include all members of the population in formal education. Although the challenges are great, we need to reflect on the potential benefits to organizations and societies arising from diversity. For example, possessing a larger storehouse of potential cultural solutions to social problems creates opportunities less readily available in more monocultural societies. It is not an automatic benefit, however, as we must be prepared to do more than tolerate diversity. We must discover how to learn from each other in pursuing common goals. We *do* share many aspirations in common, especially regarding children and youth, and learning how to provide high quality social environments for them – in and out of school – is a key building block for social consensus (Keating, 1990).

● *Schools need to become learning organizations, both to ensure continuous improvement in educational practice and to teach students how to function well in such organizations.*

Recent work on human groups shows that organizations which grow and adapt best tend to learn collaboratively (Brown & Duguid, 1991). Key ingredients include shared and clearly understood goals; open, lateral networks for the flow of information and expertise; and reasonable distribution of gains from group efforts. A legitimate social expectation of schools is that they should prepare students for work. In doing so, we need to focus on the ways in which work is organized in currently successful enterprises, not just on past workplace arrangements. A step in the right direction would be to devise ways in which schools and school boards can themselves become learning organizations, harnessing the diversity of professional expertise in a collaborative effort to enhance the learning of all students. Historical forms of educational leadership that preserve a hierarchical distribution of power are likely to impede this effort.

● *A developmental model for education and learning should replace the prevailing normative, categorical model.*

We need to invent a new educational model for the information age in order to build a learning society. Many of the established structures of education were forged to meet a set of social and economic demands that arose during the industrial revolution. We now need to re-examine those structures in a fundamental way. For example, the structure of special education emerged as an interplay between the progressive policy of mainstreaming and life normalization, on the one hand, and, on the other, the perceived need for medical justification of the required additional resources. An ironic consequence is that parents whose children are not learning well are compelled to lobby for their child to receive a diagnosis of (presumed) organic deficiency in order to receive extra help. Resources that might be used better for instruction become diverted to supporting a quasi-judicial system to verify and defend a diagnosis. In addition, it leads us to focus more on a presumed lack of adaptibility in the child rather than on attempts to discover how to adapt our instruction to better meet the child's developmental needs.

● *We need to integrate schools into a broader community and societal effort to provide high quality social environments that promote and support learning.*

Compared with the private sector, the diffusion in education of best practices, as we build our knowledge of them, proceeds slowly and painfully, and often not at all. This is one consequence of a vertically-arrayed bureaucracy, in which centralized decision-making generates obstacles by its very existence. Thus far, limited success has been achieved from efforts at centrally guided, rather than community based, cross-sectoral integration involving schools, social and child care services, parental and family resources, and volunteer services. Cutting across these solitudes to create horizontal arrays of information flow and mutual support is an important task for a learning society. The design and building of learning networks, supported by emerging information technologies, affords opportunities for linking community resources and for diffusing best practices more rapidly across communities.

- *Finally, in order to sustain the adaptibility of educational systems, it is necessary to engage the broader society in an on-going discourse about continuous improvement, which is based upon a shared conceptual understanding of the goals, importance, and limitations of education.*

One of essential features of a learning society is the continuous monitoring of the health and development of its members. Such population monitoring would place educational outcomes high on the list of important aspects to monitor. It is distressing to realize how much more attention is paid to the monitoring of economic performance, and environmental impacts, than to human development (Keating & Mustard, 1996). In order to make effective use of such information, however, we need to provide both the technological and conceptual infrastructure for informed community discourse on how best to adapt education to the changing needs of contemporary societies. It is only through such on-going societal investment in education that there is any real hope of lasting (that is, self-renewing) educational change. In other words, achieving the goal of a learning society requires acting as if it were so, and learning how to do it as we proceed.

## REFERENCES

Bereiter, C., & Scardamalia, M. (1996). Rethinking learning. In D. R. Olson & N. Torrance (Eds.), *Handbook of education and human development: New models of learning, teaching and schooling* (pp. 485–513). Oxford: Blackwell.

Brown, J. S., & Duguid, P. (1991). Organizational learning and communities of practice: Toward a unified view of working, learning, and innovation. *Organizational Science, 2*, 40–57.

Bruner, J. (1990). *Acts of meaning.* Cambridge: Harvard University Press.

Cole, M., & Scribner, S. (1974). *Culture and thought: A psychological introduction.* New York: Wiley.

Dennett, D. C. (1995). *Darwin's dangerous idea: Evolution and the meanings of life.* New York: Touchstone/Simon and Schuster.

Dewey, J. (1963). *Experience and education.* New York: Collier Books.

Donald, M. (1991). *Origins of the modern mind: Three stages in the evolution of culture and cognition.* Cambridge, MA: Harvard University Press.

Dunbar, R. (1992). Why gossip is good for you. *New Scientist, 136*, 28–31.

Garbarino, J. (1994, October). *Child development in socially toxic environments.* Paper presented at the Ninth Rochester Symposium on Developmental Psychopathology, Rochester, New York.

Keating, D. P. (1990). Charting pathways to the development of expertise. *Educational Psychologist,* **25**, 243–267.

Keating, D. P. (1991). Curriculum options for the developmentally advanced: A developmental alternative for gifted education. *Exceptionality Education Canada,* **1**, 53–83.

Keating, D. P. (1995a). The learning society in the information age. In S. A. Rosell (Ed.), *Changing maps: Governing in a world of rapid change* (pp. 205–229). Ottawa: Carleton University Press.

Keating, D. P. (1995b). The transformation of schooling: Dealing with developmental diversity. In J. Lupart, A. McKeough, & C. Yewchuck (Eds.), *Schools in transition: Rethinking regular and special education* (pp. 119–139). Toronto: Nelson.

Keating, D. P. (1996a). Families, schools, and communities: Social resources for a learning society. In D. Ross (Ed.), *Family security in insecure times: Vol. 2. Perspectives/Vol. 3. Building a partnership of responsibility* (pp. 153–176). Ottawa, ON: Canadian Council on Social Development.

Keating, D. P. (1996b). Habits of mind for a learning society: Educating for human development. In D. R. Olson & N. Torrance (Eds.), *Handbook of education and human development: New models of learning, teaching and schooling* (pp. 461–481). Oxford: Blackwell.

Keating, D. P., & Mustard, J. F. (1993). Social economic factors and human development. In D. Ross (Ed.), *Family security in insecure times* (Vol. 1, pp. 87–105). Ottawa, ON: National Forum on Family Security.

Keating, D. P., & Mustard, J. F. (1996). The National Longitudinal Survey of Children and Youth: An essential element for building a learning society in Canada. In *Growing up in Canada: National longitudinal survey of children and youth* (pp. 7–13). Ottawa: Human Resources Development Canada and Statistics Canada.

Lave, J. (1988). *Cognition in practice: Mind, mathematics, and culture in everyday life.* Cambridge: Cambridge University Press.

Olson, D. R. (1994). *The world on paper: The conceptual and cognitive implications of writing and reading.* Cambridge: Cambridge University Press.

Olson, D., & Torrance, N. (1996). *Handbook of education and human development: New models of learning, teaching and schooling.* Oxford: Blackwell.

Putnam, R. D. (1992). *Making democracy work: Civic traditions in modern Italy.* Princeton, NJ: Princeton University Press.

Rogoff, B. (1990). *Apprenticeship in thinking: Cognitive development in social context.* New York: Oxford University Press.

Rosenberg, N., & Birdzell, L. E. Jr. (1986). *How the West grew rich.* New York: Basic Books.

Stringer, C., & Gamble, C. (1993). *In search of the Neanderthals: Solving the puzzle of human origins.* London: Thames and Hudson.

Task Force on Human Development. (1992). *The learning society.* Canadian Institute for Advanced Research, Research Publication #6. Toronto: CIAR.

Tomasello, M., Kruger, A. C., & Ratner, H. H. (1993). Cultural learning. *Behavioral and brain sciences,* **16**, 495–552.

Vygotsky, L. (1978). Mind in society: The development of higher psychological processes. In M. Cole, V. John-Steiner, S. Scribner, & E. Souberman (Eds.), *Mind in society: The development of higher psychological processes.* Cambridge, MA: Harvard University Press.

# Educational Reform Networks: Changes in the Forms of Reform

ANN LIEBERMAN

*Teachers College, Columbia University*


MAUREEN GROLNICK

*Teachers College, Columbia University*

*New professional learning "networks" are expanding which link people together for common purposes of learning. These networks typically involve a sense of shared purpose, psychological support, voluntary participation and a facilitator. A number of specific networks are described. Analysis shows that networks have great power, but they are also fragile, necessitating continuous negotiation of tensions.*

## THE REFORM MOVEMENT AND NETWORKING

Even as public schools struggle to serve the needs of all children in an increasingly diverse population, the changing nature of our technology and economy has raised the stakes for education. Without a rewarding or stable market for unskilled or semi-skilled workers, economic mobility has become increasingly dependent on skills and competencies taught in a school setting, and on certifications of high school and college degrees. At the same time, as communities diversify and fragment, schools remain one of the few unifying centers to which most members of our society belong at some time in their lives.

In attempting to reshape classroom practices created for the social and economic realities of the last century, many teachers, administrators and researchers have become members of networks committed to building educational programs that better reflect the needs of contemporary students, schools and communities. While some of these networks have ideological foundations such as a commitment to democratic decision-making, many are joined together by interests in subject area, technology, pedagogy and school change.[1]

Since educational approaches that depend on teacher interdependence and collaboration in the construction of curriculum differ fundamentally from the norms of a profession that has traditionally isolated its members with their classrooms, ideological and technological changes inherent in reform efforts have elicited an unprecedented interest in networks, coalitions and school/university partnerships.

40

*M. Fullan (ed.), Fundamental Change, 40-59.*
© 2005 *Springer. Printed in the Netherlands.*

Teachers, administrators and researchers, many for the first time in their professional lives, are making common cause with one another as colleagues. These collaborations are helping to redefine professional learning by going beyond the often didactic forms of traditional professional development to engage and involve participants actively in their own learning.

The necessity for building a professional community has become a recurring theme in reform literature (Lieberman, 1988; Little, 1993; McLaughlin & Talbert, 1993). Contemporary research is documenting the need for genuine colleagueship, support for teacher learning, faculty innovation and continued professional commitment – all characteristics of professional community (McLaughlin & Talbert, p. 9).

## THEORIZING ABOUT NETWORKS

Encouraged in part by change theory coming out of the locally based community organization reform work of the 60's, and by earlier interest in studying networks as sources of influence (Kadushin, 1976) – educators, sociologists and political scientists developed an interest in this form of social organization as a vehicle for educational reform. They studied such networks, theorized about their potential and actively tried to implement them. Their work – often linked to research on existing educational networks – developed definitions, described various types of networks and offered analyses of how they function.

The term network is understood to refer to a social web of people connected by links over which such things as objects, labor, affection, evaluation, knowledge prescription, influence and power flow, (Miles, 1978, p. 2) and in which most participants are connected with each other through no more than two links (Kadushin, 1976). Networks link different kinds of people for different purposes, using a variety of forms.

Networks can be distinguished from each other based on the degree to which they are "instituted," the nature of their links and the extent to which they are visible. American political parties, for example, are highly instituted, are interstitial in their links and very visible while "corporate overlap" (the practice of overlapping membership among corporate boards) is instituted, interstitial, but generally invisible. (The Mafia, job-finding nets and invisible colleges – the connections researchers use to share scientific information – are also in this category (Kadushin, 1976). They can also be distinguished on the basis of their function or purpose such as community groups that operate in a community development, social planning or social action (or "movement") model (Rosenbaum, 1977). Community development style groups assume that the problem facing their community is a lack of communication and common purpose and they try to bring all elements of the community together in commonly supported projects. Groups that adopt a social planning model are normally found in more prosperous communities and assume that their function revolves around long term local planning and analysis.

In contrast to these more collaborative approaches, the social action model operates on the assumption that the main problem they face is a larger community characterized by an unjust hierarchy of power and privilege. Such groups see their task as that of confronting an unyielding establishment (Rosenbaum, 1977).

Community action groups sustain themselves by imbuing their membership with a strong "we against thee" ethos and necessarily engage in conflict (Rosenbaum, 1977). Such groups depend heavily on leaders who normally also have other daily life commitments and require effective staff support if they are to be successful. Community planning groups are also very leadership dependent, relying heavily on professional research and development staff. The function of these groups also requires that they work closely with (many would argue come under the domination of) the business and government organizations and agencies from which it normally must seek the funds necessary to sustain its cadre of professional staff (not to mention the access necessary to enable its plans and programs to have some chance of being adopted) (Rosenbaum, 1977). In contrast to these two, the community development style organization requires leadership that is focused on and skilled at facilitation as they try to bring more and more people into the organization (Rosenbaum, 1977). While educational networks might superficially appear to conform to this last model, there are certainly elements of confrontation in many reform initiatives – especially those intended primarily to meet the needs of poor and minority children. In other efforts strategic collaboration with business and government organizations that have power and influence may also be problematic.

In addition to incorporating elements of the community action and community development models, most educational reform networks also function as practitioner networks. Common to many professions long before they developed in education, these networks connect practitioners across organizations. They can provide a vehicle for sharing information and serve as a route to professional mobility. Practitioner networks create a sense of professional belonging and offer a source of status and prestige to participants (Schön, 1977).

Whatever model they adopt, educational networks share a number of characteristics. These include:

- a sense of being an alternative to established systems
- a feeling of shared purpose
- some mix or sharing and psychological support
- an effective facilitator
- an emphasis on voluntary participation and equal treatment

(Parker, 1977)

If success is measured in terms of simple survival, not all networks make it. If, in addition, the success of educational reform networks is to be judged in terms of the persistence of their innovations, few of the 1970's educational reform networks accomplished their mission. Networks such as the Boston West Biology Teachers' Network, the National Diffusion Network, the Ford Foundation Comprehensive School Improvement Program, the Northern Westchester Resource Network, and the Tri-University Network have left us with an important fund of knowledge and experience, but little in the way of lasting educational reform. The goal of educational networkers has been to bring together combinations of teachers, school administrators, university personnel, parents and community members – within or across role groups – to enact reforms that will enable local schools to better meet the needs of students. However, the intractable quality of our century-old school "grammar," and the fragile and often ephemeral nature of social networks, suggest that there is much to be understood if this approach is to be successful.

We know from work done in the 1970's that networking leads to the need for cognitive flexibility and the ability to play complex roles, but that within organizations those most likely to participate are managers – those with a more cosmopolitan rather than local identification (Granovetter, 1973, 1983). We also know that successful networks are based on voluntary participation and egalitarian treatment (Parker, 1977). Even as their popularity spreads and their numbers grow, networks should not be too tightly structured or formally organized. They thrive on the unpredictability, serendipity and informality that supports the initiative, energy, peer support, shared meaning and trust characteristic of many networks (Miles, 1978). These analyses are helpful, but they also suggest dilemmas. Teachers are part of a profession that has long isolated them in the classroom. Far from being cosmopolitan, many would not include the district, or even the whole of their building, as part of their territory. Many networks directed towards systemic change are based on a coalition of districts rather than individuals. While the superintendent and her cabinet may volunteer, the teachers are drafted. The public school system, like most organizations, is based on a system of hierarchy. Treating the superintendent as equal to a classroom teacher re-orders the relationship in a way that is very different from the culture of the school. In order to effect a significant transformation in American education, networks must have an impact that goes beyond a small group of teachers or a few schools. As the network grows, this becomes more and more difficult to accomplish without organization and structure.

## STUDYING CONTEMPORARY NETWORKS

At the National Center for Restructuring Education, Schools and Teaching (NCREST) at Teachers College we have been learning more about educational reform networks, while helping to support and, in some cases, organize them. Extended discussions with the leaders of three of the networks organized by NCREST led us to study a larger number of networks – 16 in all. We sought answers to such questions as: How do these networks evolve and take shape, and how do they build commitment to common purposes What activities bind people together in these networks and how are they organized? Who leads these networks and how do they do it? What institutional supports do these networks depend on and from where does the money come? What tensions and dilemmas do they face in the process of developing and sustaining themselves?

We chose networks that had been in existence long enough to have a history and that linked people together who were of different status and who played many roles. We also looked for networks that reflected a variety of organizational forms. In addition to interviewing the leaders, we collected their newsletters and other print materials to expand our understanding and gain further insight into these seemingly improvisational arrangements that were so hard to characterize theoretically or conceptually, but so effective in practice.

## HOW DO THESE NETWORKS EVOLVE?

"You've got to have a compelling idea . . . a dust particle around which to coalesce . . . but it has to be compelling to the *coalescees.*" (Network Leader)

We found that the individual story of each network's inception and evolution was very much a function of the context from which they emerged. They developed in many different ways. Some began with informal conversations which led to broader and deeper purposes, while others started with a lofty vision and then developed practical ways of engaging people in the day-to-day work that supported that vision. Still other networks were begun by charismatic leaders who represented, or even embodied, educational values that were cherished by participants. Viewed close up, any one of these processes could seem almost untidy – even happenstance – as common purposes and concerns brought participants together around a "compelling dust particle."

We began in one rural school where the principal wanted to change. Another school heard about our discussions . . . then seven to eight other schools eventually came to a meeting and said, "Let's form a league looking at schools as democratic institutions. (Network Leader)

## PATTERNS OF DEVELOPMENT

Tracked from a distance, the networks we studied followed at least four discernible patterns. For some, (like Foxfire, and The League of Professional SCHOOLS described above), it was a slow, evolving process in which one activity gave rise to another and eventually led to the need for a more systematic way of connecting. Others, (the National Network for Educational Renewal and DEWEY), were more intentional from the outset. They originated with an explicit plan, such as linking the restructuring of schools with the simultaneous renewal of teacher education, or connecting districts with similar populations and a commitment to equity in education. In a third pattern we observed, participants were drawn together by a strong leader who embodied their educational values and vision, (North Dakota Study Group, Harvard Principals' Center). In a fourth pattern, networks were formed to support educators as they tried to develop and support their reform ideas in an indifferent or even hostile environment, (Center for Collaborative Education in New York City).

True to the form of an organization that is based on the needs of its participants, and adapts to its own circumstances, a number of the networks we studied combined elements of more than one pattern. (Foxfire evolved from small scale teacher workshops and the need to connect workshop graduates who taught writing in isolated settings. It also derived much of its initial momentum from work of a very charismatic leader.)

## HOW DO NETWORKS BUILD COMMITMENT?

Networks build commitment in direct proportion to the extent to which members feel they have a voice in creating and sustaining a group in which their professional identity and interests are valued. The ways in which people are brought together affects the interplay between participants' developing relationships with each other and with the ideas that will form the basis of their work. Collaborative relationships build trust, essential to the development of ideas, and ideas build network interest and participation as they themselves are transformed by the participants and fed back into the network (Schön, 1977). In this process, by which the relationships participants have with each other and the ideas they share is extended to a commitment to a larger organization, the fabric of the network is woven. Through an expanding series of connections, members become committed to each other and to larger ideas and ideals that expand their world and their work.

Regardless of how these networks evolved, critical first relationships were built on meetings, conversations and activities that created opportunities for people to gain information while receiving psychological support (Parker, 1979). Whether original purposes were broad or narrow, focused or only loosely defined, seems of less importance than that those being brought together feel not only that what they are doing is worthwhile and productive, but that they themselves play a defining role in the work.

## WHAT ACTIVITIES SUPPORT NETWORKING?

The activities sponsored by a network serve many interrelated purposes. Speakers provide information and inspiration – conferring a sense of validation by an outside authority. They can also focus on particular problems, giving people alternative ways of thinking and acting. This process builds identification with a larger group of colleagues and commitment to purposes beyond one's own classroom, school or district. Such activities support the sort of reciprocity which motivates members to contribute to the larger project, believing that it will be helpful to their individual work as well (Kadushin, 1976, p. 36). However, most problems in education are not solved by the mechanical application of simplistic schemes or panaceas. Peer presentations have the advantage of offering insights into the complexities of the process from colleagues who share comparable goals and constraints.

The effects of collaboration extend in many directions. Working actively with others strengthens the investment participants have in the network; the work becomes, quite literally, their own and they develop relationships that bind them more closely to the group. Connecting with other members across schools, institutions, roles and geography enables participants to develop more complex views of the issues they are concerned about, and encourages them to take different perspectives and different ways of knowing into account (Granovetter, 1973).

Engaging educators in activities in which they learn to work interdependently, reflect on their practice, value their own expertise, play leadership roles and respond flexibly to unanticipated problems and opportunities is as central to the purposes of networks as it is to the processes of school reform. Sometimes the gap between the norms of the network and the professional expectations of the schools can be the source of some tension. Educators, accustomed to meetings and staff development activities for which someone else provides the agenda and leads the session, may initially perceive the more open ended style of network gatherings as too loose or unstructured. Activities which draw on participants rather than experts for professional knowledge may be experienced as "sharing ignorance." Networks try to transcend these perceptions and provide meaningful professional experiences that are based on collaboration. But who facilitates the changes in norms and expectations? How do the activities get organized? Who makes it all happen?

## WHAT DOES EFFECTIVE NETWORK LEADERSHIP LOOK LIKE?

Leadership may be one of the least studied aspects of networks, coalitions and partnerships. Although Parker (1977) speaks about a "facilitator" of a network, he gives few details as to what this means and what facilitators actually do. Leadership is, however, important to the network constituency because it must represent the vision of the network, and encourage and inspire others without inhibiting them from taking on similar responsibilities.

For most this is accomplished through the quality of their individual interactions with members of the network and the extent to which their own work is collaborative. As heads of organizations that supported strong professional identities on the part of their members, the leaders we studied found that their role was based more on brokering and facilitating than directing. Despite these commonalties, the particulars of network leadership varied with the purposes, membership and setting of each organization. Network leaders themselves also brought a personal and distinctive style into the mix that ultimately became their role. Several examples help illustrate how leaders of different networks defined network leadership.

*In The Southern Maine Partnership* – leadership evolved from an exclusively university function to one that depended heavily on membership responsibility. The centerpiece of this partnership became the conversations between school and university-based educators and there was no effort to prescribe what the schools should do with the ideas that were discussed; the leadership limited itself to creating a format for discussion. Participation was built on an underlying assumption of parity between school and university personnel which came to symbolize the partnership. In addition to scheduling meetings, inducing colleagues to participate, visiting districts and keeping the communication flowing, it was the leaders' job to protect this parity in the face of any tendencies to return to the old hierarchies.

*In the League of Professional Schools* – leadership has been heavily influenced by the League's early commitment to democratic schooling. Member schools are represented by teams made up of a principal, teachers, staff and parents. In developing plans these teams must receive 80% approval of their faculty. The teams report to the League Congress, made up of representatives from all the different regions where there are League schools.

While leadership of this network has consistently involved brokering, it has also involved reminding participants of their commitment to democratic education; the central question being, "How do we authentically engage people in their own learning – learning that connects them to others and to the common good?" Although these underlying values were introduced initially by Carl Glickman, he saw his role as seeing that the emphasis on shared leadership, democratic ideals and commitment to community became embedded in the structure of the network.

*In the Foxfire Teacher Outreach Network* – the form leadership and learning took was marked by the founder's experience as a classroom teacher. Eliot Wigginton developed a way of teaching secondary school English that connected students' own experiences to their literacy development. As teachers began to come to Rabun Gap, Georgia to take courses, he recognized the need for a support system to help them practice what they learned. Foxfire explicitly committed itself to developing the teacher-leaders who would head regional networks to meet that need.

MAINTAINING COLLABORATIVE MODELS

These profiles illustrate some of the different entry points for network beginnings and the roles that leadership can play in building a network community. At times, facilitating networks appears to be about making phone calls, raising money, establishing connections, forming groups, finding places to meet, and brokering resources and people. However, it is also about creating "public spaces" in which educators can work together in ways that are different in quality and kind from their institutions, as well as from much that is considered standard professional development. It may be building structures that encourage a respectful dialog between and among school and university personnel, or modeling more collaborative stances toward learning and support, enunciating important ideals (as in the National Network for Educational Renewal, Foxfire and the League of Professional Schools), or leaving room for emergent goals, (as in the Southern Maine Partnership, the Breadloaf Rural Teacher Network and the Consortium for Educational Change). As five of our network leaders put it, it is about: "providing a challenge, not a delivery of services"; "figuring out how to push people along and give them what they want at the same time"; "understanding the tension between the values of the network and the problems of the field"; "facilitating teachers' work outside, so that they can make changes inside"; and "keeping the focus on the partnership way of doing work". It is also about figuring out how to sustain these networks and help them develop and deepen their work while the education dollar continues to shrink.

## WHERE WILL THE MONEY COME FROM, AND AT WHAT COST?

Of the sixteen networks studied, fourteen received significant or complete support from private or corporate foundations. The two that did not were started by constituents in the public school system (the Mission Valley Consortium and the Consortium for Educational Change; the former initiated as a collaboration among three school districts and the latter by a regional branch of the Illinois National Education Association). Those networks with sources of support in addition to foundations received money from universities (6), United States Department of Education (2), National Education Association (1) and participating school systems (2).

Three-fourths of the network representatives who contributed to the study affirmed that the struggle to find funding was an important part of their story. In some instances the pursuit of funding actually helped to create the network because it encouraged prospective constituents to share available moneys more broadly by forming a network. (The Elementary Teachers Network in New York City is an example of this.) Alternatively, funders actually built networking into the conditions of the grant, (as with the funding of the DEWEY network).

Foundation funding can, however, also produce great tensions for networks. Matthew Miles' admonition of twenty years ago still stands, that finding primary funding outside the collaboration can be "fatal"(Miles, 1978, p. 33)[2]. The Network of Progressive Educators struggled over the very name of their network, with many members arguing that the word "progressive" would be unappealing to prospective funders. (It might indeed have contributed to the difficulty of getting funds.) In another instance, a funder felt entitled to exert ongoing influence on the emphasis a network placed on each of its multiple goals. Often, the needs of many foundations for an assessment that documents outcomes can be at odds with the process oriented work of many networks. One interviewee said: "No one wants to pay the bill for a network. The problem is wired in. It's not clear to anyone who the beneficiaries of a network are and what the outcomes should be. All the data are soft."

There were other tensions that occurred consistently within all of these networks. From our perspective, the dynamics inherent in these tensions appeared to be central to the process of how networks organize, build new structures, learn to collaborate, and develop a sense of community. The changing needs, constant negotiations, and flexible resolutions keep networks flourishing. While the resolutions to these tensions were heavily influenced by the context and character of each network – sometimes obscuring their similarities – the tensions themselves were common to all of them.

## THE POWER AND FRAGILITY OF NETWORKS: HOW DO NETWORKS NEGOTIATE THEIR INEVITABLE TENSIONS?

The avowed intention of network participants is to build their organizations around the real work of educators; the tensions included: negotiating between the purpose of the network and the dailiness of the activities that constitute network "work"; dealing with the balance between "inside knowledge" and "outside knowledge"; creating a structure to resolve contradictions between centralization and decentralization; moving from informality and flexibility to more formal and rigid forms as the network grew; and making decisions about how inclusive or exclusive membership policy should be.

*1. Can networks integrate ideals with the everyday work of educators?*

Initially, many networks simply attract participants who agree with their stated purposes, which in some cases may represent lofty ideals and/or longstanding aspirations. Alternatively, compelling purposes can be driven by ideas that promise to transform classroom practice in specific ways. Educators with shared philosophies often form networks and other networks, made up of several different groups with different roles or perspectives may decide to work together in the interests of improving schools, before they have developed an all embracing philosophy. Some networks have a single focus and there are networks that have a more systemic mission.

No matter what the purpose of the network, activities have to be compelling enough to keep people coming back for more. This can be a challenging tension. In the Consortium for Educational Change, where they are trying to forge a reform partnership between the teachers' union and the district, activities were first directed at bringing people together who played very different roles in disparate organizations. Because the purposes had to be broad enough to be inclusive, it was difficult to devise activities that advanced these purposes without being too broad to be of interest to any of the participants.

In some cases the tension is a creative one, and purposes actually emerge from the activities that are created by the network. In the Southern Maine Partnership, conversations within many different groups of school and university educators built the partnership. The initial purpose was to provide a collegial environment in which participants could talk about educational ideas to bridge the gaps between their two cultures, but as these discussions proceeded, the larger purposes of school reform developed.

**Table 1: Purposes and Participants, and the Contexts of the Sample of Educational Reform Networks**

| Network | Participants | Purposes | Contexts |
|---|---|---|---|
| **Breadloaf Rural Teacher Network** | secondary school English teachers and their students | ease the isolation of teachers in rural schools across the country | national – electronic |
| **Center for Collaborative Education** | New York City public schools; teachers and directors | to promote education reform and school restructuring based on the successful practices of its member schools | (NYC affiliate Coalition of Essential Schools) |
| **Consortium for Educational Change** | districts that, in conjunction with their N.E.A. union leadership, commit to involvement – superintendents, school boards, union leaders and, increasingly, community members | build trust and collaboration between the teachers' union and district/school administrators | regional |
| **Diversity and Excellence Working for the Education of Youth (DEWEY)** | 8 school districts selected because of their increasingly diverse student populations; administrators, teachers and university based educators | share and support practices that promote diversity and excellence | regional (Westchester and Rockland Counties in New York) |
| **Four Seasons** | teachers | collaboration among three networks to build knowledge about how teachers learn, use and shape authentic assessment | national -electronic |
| **Foxfire Teacher Outreach Network** | secondary school English teachers | support individual teachers who have adopted the Foxfire approach to the teaching of writing and learning and to integrate that approach into the life of the school | national |
| **Harvard Principals' Center** | public school principals in the greater Boston area | provide a professional support network for principals committed to school improvement | regional |
| **(Harvard) Teachers' Center** | teachers from the greater Boston area | to provide teachers committed to their own professional growth and to school improvement opportunities to learn and share with like minded colleagues | regional |

**Table 1: Continued**

| Network | Participants | Purposes | Contexts |
|---|---|---|---|
| **Breadloaf Rural Teacher Network Institute for Literacy Studies – Elementary Teachers' Network** | primarily elementary teachers | promote effective literacy instruction using the primary language record as the focus | regional (NYC) |
| **International Network of Principals' Centers** | principals' centers, both nationally and internationally | connect the professional support networks that serve school principals | international |
| **Mission Valley Consortium** | all members of the Mission Valley school community | review and revise curriculum in participating districts and build a sense of shared ownership and commitment to curriculum reform | regional |
| **National Network for Educational Renewal** | school-university partnerships | to promote the simultaneous renewal of schools and the education of educators | national |
| **Network of Progressive Educators** | teachers, teacher educators, parents, public and private schools, child advocacy organizations, | provide a professional network for people who share the same values and beliefs about progressive education | national |
| **North Dakota Study Group** | educators committed to the principles of progressive education who have been invited to join | bring together educators from across the country who are committed to progressive education, support democratic schools and are interested in assessment | national |
| **Program for School Improvement –League of Professional Schools** | schools committed to shared governance, instructional initiatives and action research | to help create schools that are driven by internal decisions based on the school's own criteria for success – "democratic schools" | regional/national |
| **Professional Development Schools** | professional development school partnerships, university and school-based educators | to share support and build knowledge about professional development schools (school-university partnership) | national |
| **Southern Maine Partnership** | school districts | to help schools reflect on their own practice/move toward restructuring and help the university reflect on and restructure its preparation of educators (evolved over time). | regional |

NEGOTIATING THE TENSION

It is imperative that reform networks find ways to build connections between larger or emergent meanings of their work, and the logic of the specific activities that maintain them. Such clear connections help teachers, such as those in the DEWEY network, remember that when they are working on the detailed design of a block schedule, its ultimate success depends on the extent to which it supports equality of access for students. It is also important to note that many participants are first drawn to a network by the organization's activities – its focus on issues of immediate professional concern to them, or on opportunities for teachers to work together – rather than by its broader purposes. Participation in an activity, even if it does not seem of major importance, may lead new members to ultimately identify with the network's goals and contribute something from their own perspective. It is this dialectic, between the larger meaning of the network's goals and the concrete vitality of its daily activities, that grounds its purpose and ennobles its practice.

*2. Teachers and/or the "experts": Whose knowledge counts?*

Whatever the purpose, networks must take a stance on *what* and *whose* knowledge should inform the work of the network. This is particularly true for educational reform networks, as they are often trying to forge connections between communities and/or different role groups that encompass a variety of perspectives and have different ways of knowing, developing and using knowledge (Lytle & Cochran-Smith, 1992). Teacher and principal knowledge developed in the context of their work is of a different order from the knowledge of university researchers or that of outside experts. Simply reading and studying "outside" knowledge may fail to help participants make connections to the world of practice as they experience and live it in their particular contexts. But while networks have to find ways to accommodate these different ways of knowing, a network that deals only with experiential or context-specific knowledge may cut itself off from knowledge that inspires new ideas, expands personal and professional vision, or helps teachers and administrators invent new techniques and processes for improving their practices. In the worst of situations, participants might "just be sharing ignorance."

Most networks embrace both "inside" and "outside" knowledge, although no two networks appear to do it in quite the same way. The synthesis is affected by what the purposes are, how participants are involved with practical and conceptual ideas, and where the knowledge and ideas come from. Teachers in a Level 1 Foxfire course are exposed to a philosophy as well as a method born out of teaching practice. The primary work of the network, which joins teachers together who have taken the course, flows from the questions raised by teachers who are attempting to implement the project method with their students. But, as the network has matured, teachers have increasingly sought additional pedagogical knowledge and broader understandings of educational and school improvement.

In the League of Professional Schools participants receive a research packet after they have designed what they want to work on and outside knowledge informs their plan. The Southern Maine Partnership started with participants reading articles for group discussion, but incorporated the problems and agendas of the participants into their discussions as the network developed.

One of the fundamental differences between conventional professional development and networking activities is that, in networking, both outside knowledge *and* the content knowledge of school based educators are acknowledged as important sources of agenda building. How and when these resources are used has to do with the purposes, the context and the organizational arrangements of the network's central governing group and its participants.

NEGOTIATING THE TENSION

Within the profession itself teachers have not yet developed a tradition of sharing their own expertise among themselves. Networks play a major role in providing opportunities for teachers to validate both teacher knowledge and teacher inquiry. By organizing activities around shared work, networks give recognition to the validity of the classroom educator's experience, while broadening the base of that experience through collaboration. As teachers become more secure about what they know, they are more willing and able to pick and choose among resources beyond their classroom doors for what they need to know and to articulate problems in more complex ways.

*3. Centralization or Decentralization: What Does it Look Like When Networks Organize?*

While some networks are loose federations of people who come together to support, discuss and learn together (e.g., The Network of Progressive Educators or The International Network of Principals' Centers), others create tighter structures and build norms of membership by working to internalize explicit goals (League of Professional Schools, National Network of Educational Renewal). Some form for specific – even local – purposes, subsequently broadening their agendas as the networks' roots take hold (e.g., Breadloaf, Foxfire, Harvard Principals' Center).

Each organizational tendency suggests a complimentary style of organization: centralized, decentralized or what we might call "evolving." The forms are not always rigidly adhered to however, since their effectiveness might be reduced. For example, a typical "district office" approach might be very efficient, but fail to involve the membership in helping to shape the work. A totally "grass roots" approach, on the other hand, might promote a committed membership but fail to link with other partners who have different perspectives, different knowledge bases or different ways of working. An effective network organization creates ways to engage participants directly in the governance and leadership of the organization, while maintaining the flexibility to organize complex, and potentially far reaching operations. Some examples show the variety:

*Southern Maine Partnership* – This network avoids being "staff driven" by diffusing responsibility among the participants. The superintendents of member districts meet once a year to decide on policy. They discuss the kinds of activities that have transpired during the year and decide which ones they should continue to support and which should be dropped, based on the interests of the membership. Each project has a school team working with a university team, keeping the work rooted in the schools.

*The League of Professional Schools* – a national network, has a more elaborate organization based on a system of faculty selected site committees at every school. Where Southern Maine might be described as loose and flexible, the League could be considered a tight network. Schools are organized into regional chapters and are represented in a congress that is made up of chapters from all the regions. The leadership of the regional chapters are very active in making decisions. The role of the university is to provide consultation to the site committees to help them define their work. In this way the university provides "outside knowledge" to be used to deepen the schools' understanding of the work they want to do.


NEGOTIATING THE TENSION

Mechanisms, roles and structures that forge collaboration must be consciously designed to achieve greater decentralization. In addition to their awareness of their own desires to retain control, network founders and facilitators encourage participation when they recognize that many teacher participants have not had the opportunity to play professional leadership roles in the past. Administrators, who are accustomed to models of individual accountability rather than shared leadership, may find that the transition to a collaborative organizational style can, at times, produce confusion and frustration, discouraging the participants. Ultimately, however, learning to collaborate and work with people who have different orientations to building knowledge is what many members find to be one of the most powerful experiences of participating in a network.


*4. Can Networks Scale Up Without Losing the Intimacy and Informality that Attracted Original Participants?*

Because networks are not tied to district specifications and particular inservice days, they are freer to create informal mechanisms to bring people together – serving food at meetings perhaps, or meeting over dinner; they can set aside whole days for conferences or convene retreats in more isolated settings. Networks develop their own ways of working, depending on context and/or character, often designing unique and informal ways of communicating and meeting that become particularly associated with their network "work". For many years the core activity of The Network of Progressive Educators has been an annual meeting with "inside" and "outside" speakers who legitimate and support progressive education practices while intellectually challenging the membership. The NNER creates task forces, special regional conferences and, where appropriate, makes use of the expertise of consultants. The League of Professional Schools began by organizing a congress to represent its member schools while, the Southern Maine Partnership started with an activity they called "dine and discuss." The tension arises as the network matures: trying to sustain the flexible forms of work that are a source of its strength, the network central office or leadership often tries to institutionalize them so that they will last. To give conferences, money must be raised, people must be hired and rooms must be rented. To develop collaboration across schools, districts, or role groups, activities must be organized and facilitated, and work must be coordinated. The energy, initiative, peer support and trust developed informally within each network is often threatened as the organization seeks ways to stabilize and expand (Miles, 1978, p.43). The more success networks experience, the more they reach out to other areas and the more pressure they feel to expand their bureaucracy. Protecting what makes a network special becomes more difficult as it grows, requiring time, effort, and most of all, creative solutions to the problems of success.

## NEGOTIATING THE TENSION

As a network expands, it moves beyond the core of "true believers" who helped shape its alternative culture, its "way". New recruits may find it more difficult to make the transition to professional development activities that are not run in the tidy, answer oriented way to which they have become accustomed. In addition, sheer numbers challenge the intimacy and the informality of the original network. The transition from an informal and flexible organizational culture that is invitational toward its members, to one that is more formal, more rigid and less inviting, is common to growing organizations. It is a critical issue for reform networks, however, because their institutional culture is central to who they are and what they do.

*5. The Already-Converted and Everyone Else: How is Membership Related to a Network's Purposes?*

At different times in a network's life, criteria are established for membership that are – explicitly or implicitly – shaped by the purposes of the network. Is the central purpose of a network to bring together like-minded people who will develop and expand each other's knowledge? Such a group might restrict membership to educators who already share a particular perspective. Is it to provide a way of talking across districts to share resources and improve schools? In such a network efforts would be made to enlist the broadest possible base of participation. Should anyone who wants to join be allowed to become a member? All networks have to determine *who* should be included in their membership and *how* expansive the network feels about recruiting new members.

In the Southern Maine Partnership, the personnel of any school district in the region may attend the variety of activities available by simply paying a nominal fee for the year. Any pressure to participate comes from other members. By contrast, the DEWEY network restricts participation to eight school districts and, in pursuit of systemic change, actively recruits as many eligible members as possible. In yet a third variation, the League of Professional Schools admits only schools that commit at the outset to develop their own plans for democratic schools. They must agree not only to do the work themselves, but to subsequently share their work with others. Similarly, the National Network for Education Renewal has a membership based on school-university partnerships that commit to the network's postulates for renewal.

Each network must decide how, when and/or if, they will bring in new members. These decisions lead to dealing with the problem of how to socialize new members into the network. Some provide specific activities for new members (League of Professional Schools, Breadloaf) that help to define membership, while others provide activities that are always open to new members (Southern Maine Partnership, Consortium of Educational Change). Regional networks often reach a point where size becomes a problem; sometimes instead of growing larger, they encourage the formation of new networks who share their vision and purpose, thereby gaining new organizational partners.[3]

## NEGOTIATING THE TENSION

Networks face a Hobson's choice when they decide whether or not to restrict membership in their network. Members who have already committed to the purposes of the organization, or take a course on its fundamental precepts, can usually be counted upon to support the work of the network enthusiastically. In most cases, however, the reform tends to remain with those invested members who qualified to join the network in the first place.

For networks with a more open approach to membership, the issues are quite different. While there is the potential to include and convert a much broader membership, open enrollment networks must struggle to create the investment in purpose of its participants that more exclusive networks can often take for granted. When open networks try to establish themselves across a whole district, they tackle even more complex issues. They have to find ways to interest and attract members who perform different roles and functions, members who are struggling to make sense of the purposes of the network, at the same time that they are trying to form new kinds of working relationships with colleagues who are on different rungs of the school system hierarchy.

WHAT WE HAVE LEARNED: UNDERSTANDINGS FOR THE PRESENT

We found networks have a confounding duality to their nature. On the one hand, some networks would be all but impossible to replace as a part of our lives. How would we find the best place to get our car repaired, locate a responsible babysitter, or get a fix on a local politician, if it weren't for our information networks? Recently, when a school board made a surprise appointment for superintendent at a late night meeting, the news had spread throughout the town among parents, and up and down the county among educators, long before any morning papers hit the streets. This sort of networking is a spontaneous and irrepressible part of our lives as members of a community. On the other hand, networks that are consciously organized and facilitated often seem quite fragile. In our study we found that leaders who were too directive discouraged participation while those that did not communicate a clear vision left participants adrift. Organizations that were too tight stifled creative energies, while those that were too loose lost touch with the needs of an expanding membership. While connections among participants might be strong at planned gatherings, sustaining on-going communication required close attention to systems. In one of the most active networks, everyone was given an e-mail account and used it. In another, the idea never caught on.

This delicacy derives in part from the difficulty we always have when art, or artifice, tries to imitate life. The "natural" networks thrive because they operate outside any formal system, and can evolve in immediate response to the needs of their participants. When they cease to be useful, they fade and are replaced by other networks that better fit the problem at hand. A constructed or facilitated network runs the risk of an inevitable emphasis on maintaining the network as an institution, rather than keeping its innovative or problem solving stance (Parker, 1979). Beyond the problem of nurturing the flexibility and responsiveness of robust "natural" systems in a planful way, educational reform networks are trying to take root in a field that has cloistered its professionals for years. The "egg crate" school, with a single teacher to a single room, has isolated colleagues from each other since before the turn of the century. Schedules that place most teachers on-duty for all but a forty minute block in an eight hour day, have further blocked communication and collaboration. Without discretionary time, any stimulus from outside their building, or responsibilities that require collaboration, teachers have connected with each other in the way piece workers might at a factory – around the coffee machine and at lunch time, *outside* of their work.

As the reform movement supports the transformation of teacher roles into much broader areas of practice – developing curriculum and assessment, setting standards and evaluation practice, for example – these roles will carry powerful and authentic opportunities for teachers to work together and learn from each other (Darling-Hammond & McLaughlin, 1995). It is these transformations that have fueled the growth of educational networks, even as the networks themselves work to support, shape and sustain the transformations. But this is a period of transition. In any given setting, school change initiatives may be ahead of network support systems, or reform networks may be well in advance of movement towards reform on the part of the schools. Teachers are now finding themselves being asked to bridge two entirely different professional cultures. The culture they entered twenty years ago assumed that as long as they conformed to the curriculum and solved most of their own problems, they would have autonomy within their classroom. They were largely judged on the basis of their self-reliance and accountability was individual. As the culture of teaching changes, teachers are now expected to collaborate and to share responsibility for the work they do together; their work has become visible outside their classroom. Even as they are given more responsibility, many teachers experience this as a loss of control. They are being confronted with a new set of conditions and few, if any, referents or experiences to draw upon.

In this changing context educational reform networks are playing a significant role. They enable network participants to gain the experience of addressing educational challenges as full members of a professional community that respects *their* knowledge and *their* definitions of *their* problems – regardless of position, role or status. Identifying and solving problems collaboratively, educators learn to tolerate the frustration and ambiguity that is built into a meaningful examination of existing practice, gaining confidence, both personally and professionally, in their knowledge and abilities. They become increasingly vocal and effective members of the schools and other institutions where they work, helping to influence – directly and by example – the direction and practice of not only the people they work with, but of the organizations themselves.

In a society that is undergoing unprecedented demographic and technological change, the problems of education are too complex to be solved by educators acting as a collection of independent practitioners, alone and on their own. Since formally constituted educational institutions change slowly and reluctantly, reform networks are coming to serve as vehicles for the collaborative development of innovative and far reaching solutions to educational problems that are permeating large systems. These networks are indeed new forms for advancing the professional, organizational and pedagogical reforms that contemporary education so urgently requires.

## ENDNOTES

[1]   Portions of this chapter have been adapted from "Networks and Reform in American Education" by A. Lieberman and M. Grolnick first published in the *Teachers College Record,* 98, 1, Fall, 1996.
[2]   Miles is referring to the need to protect the norms that bind people to the network from external demands of a funder who might distort the meaning of the network to its members.
[3]   This happened in Maine where a group of districts created a new network in northern Maine, learning from their southern partners.

# REFERENCES

Darling-Hammond, L., & McLaughlin, M. (1995). Policies that support professional development in an era of reform. In *Practices and policies to support teacher development in an era of reform.* (NCREST Reprint Series, pp. 2139). New York: NCREST.

Granovetter, M. S. (1973). The strength of weak ties. *American Journal of Sociology,* **78**(6), 1360–1380.

Granovetter, M. S. (1983). The strength of weak ties: A network theory revisited. *Sociological Theory,* **2**, 201–233.

Kadushin, C. (1976). *Introduction to the theory of macronetwork analysis.* Unpublished manuscript. New York: Columbia University

Lieberman, A. (Ed.). (1988). *Building a professional culture in schools.* New York: Teachers College Press.

Little, J. W. (1993). *Teachers' professional development in a climate of educational reform* (NCREST reprint series). New York: NCREST.

Lytle, S., & Cochran-Smith, M. (Eds.). (1992). *Inside-outside: teacher research and knowledge.* New York: Teachers College Press

McLaughlin, M. W., & Talbert, J. (1993). *Contexts that matter for teaching and learning.* Stanford: Center for Research on the Context of Secondary School Teaching.

Miles, M. (1978). *On networking.* (Unpublished manuscript). Center for Policy Research. Washington, DC: National Institute of Education.

Parker, A. (1977). *Networks for innovation and problem solving and their use for improving education: A comparative overview.* (Unpublished manuscript). School Capacity for Problem Solving. Washington: National Institute of Education

Parker, A. (Oct. 3, 1979). *Some challenges for disseminators building networks* (Speech delivered at the National Seminar). Networking: An Essential Dissemination Process. Washington D.C.: National Institute of Education.

Rosenbaum, A. (1977). *Social networks as a political resource: Some insights drawn from the community organizational and community action experiences.* (Unpublished manuscript). Network Development Staff, School Capacity for Problem Solving Group. Washington, DC: National Institute of Education.

Schön, D.A. (1977). *Network related intervention.* (Unpublished manuscript). Center for Policy Research, Washington, D.C.: National Institute of Education.

# Educational Change in Japan: School Reforms

N. KEN SHIMAHARA

*Rutgers University*

*This chapter explores Japan's education reforms in the 1980s and 1990s. The present school system was built to promote Japan's industrialization, and has now become obsolete. The thrust of education reform over the past decade has been how to diversify schools away from uniformity and rigidity. Strategies include: introducing new curricula, implementing innovative high schools, and increasing the autonomy of universities to improve curriculum, teaching and research.*

## INTRODUCTION

This chapter explores Japan's education reforms in the 1980s and 1990s. Many of the reform initiatives in the last decade laid the groundwork for continued campaigns to overhaul schools in the 1990s. The main purpose of the chapter is to highlight major changes in Japanese education that have been occurring for the past decade.

Formal education is a function of society, and, although it is a conservative cultural agent, it gradually changes in response to societal demand. Japan underwent two sweeping school reforms since the Meiji Restoration, which repudiated Tokugawa feudalism in 1868, and ushered in the modern era. The first comprehensive reforms occurred in 1872, when Japan laid out a national school system in which elementary education became compulsory. It was a bold and progressive system, largely copied from the one current in France. The modern Japanese school system was perfected by 1890 through a series of overhauls and expansions. The second comprehensive reforms were launched immediately after World War II, and they altered Japan's pre-war school system fundamentally.

Whereas the first education reforms were initiated by Meiji leaders in response to the nation's urgent need to create the human resources required for modernization, the post-war education reforms were imposed and implemented under the close supervision of the Occupation authorities. In early 1946, the United States Mission on Education was invited to Japan to recommend education reforms. Members of the mission used the current U.S. education system as a model for formulating their recommendations. The Education Reform Committee, appointed by the Japanese government as a counterpart to the U.S. mission, played a critical role in reviewing the Americans' recommendations and drafting final recommendations for reforms to be legislated. The recommendations led to the establishment

60

*M. Fullan (ed.), Fundamental Change, 60-72.*
© 2005 *Springer. Printed in the Netherlands.*

of a uniform system of co-education that offered six years of elementary, three years of lower secondary, three years of upper secondary, and four years of university education (Rohlen, 1983; Shimahara, 1979; Shinoda, 1979). This post-war education system has remained relatively unchanged until the present time.

Prior to the 1980s, the only major campaign to overhaul the Japanese post-war school system occurred in the early 1970s. In 1967 the minister of education charged his advisory council, the Central Council of Education, to deliberate on school reforms to meet changing social and economic demands. The Council completed its report in 1971, delineating a new vision of Japanese education (Central Council of Education, 1971). The 1960s witnessed industrial and economic expansion unparalleled in Japanese history. In response to the auda-cious personal "income-doubling plan" launched by the government in 1961, the Ministry of Education assumed centrality in embarking on many new initiatives: implementing a revised curriculum; enhancing science and technical education; implementing national achievement tests; expanding secondary and higher educa-tion; and further revising math, science, and technical education (Kinoshita, 1983; Shimahara, 1992; Yamaguchi, 1980). Personal incomes tripled within a decade, as did international trade. Industry was desperate for ever greater numbers of better trained people, and it demanded that education be upgraded. Reflecting the tenor of those times, enrollments in high schools and four-year colleges increased from 57.7 and 9.2 percent, respectively, of all youths in 1960 to 82.1 and 24 percent in 1970, a phenomenal change within a single decade. In short, the reform report was issued at a time when Japan's unparalleled socio-economic transformation was taking place.

Notwithstanding the Central Council of Education's audacious vision, it failed to receive undivided support from within the Ministry of Education and national legislators to implement its entire recommendations. The Ministry of Education was divided into the "internationalists," who aggressively attempted to advance reforms, and the conservative bureaucrats, who rejected radical changes (Schoppa, 1991). Top bureaucrats within the Ministry, who guided the development of Japan's postwar school system, stubbornly defended the status quo. The recommenda-tions were partially implemented in the 1970s, however, and, perhaps more significantly, laid out parameters of reform issues during both the 1970s and 1980s.

EDUCATION REFORM MOVEMENT IN THE 1980s

*Reform Issues*

Whereas the 1971 reform concentrated on expanding the nation's adaptability to further industrial development and concomitant social change, reformers' principal concerns in the early 1980s were how to deal with negative social consequences of Japan's school system and the advanced industrial and economic structure. The 1980s reform campaign was launched to deal with these problems on a much broader scale than the 1971 reform initiative, and it was directed by the Prime Minister, who showed a political commitment to education reforms.

One salient issue, among others, that prompted the education reform campaign in the 1980s was the widespread phenomenon of deviant adolescent behavior, including school violence, bullying, refusal to attend school, and other forms of juvenile delinquency (Shimahara, 1986). It peaked at the middle school level across the nation, challenging long-standing norms of society. The Japanese, especially adolescents, were affected by the rise of the information society, changes in family and industrial structures, internationalization, and concomitant centrifugal social forces, all of which contributed to the diversification of adolescent needs and values. Japan became obsessed with adolescents' school violence. The rise of adolescent deviant behavior reflected a lack of fit between a static school system and dynamic social and industrial structures (Amano, 1986).

Another factor that encouraged the reform movement in the 1980s was Japan's concern with its future development (Shimahara, 1986). Japan's long-standing fixation with the West as the source of all things modern has been reversed. The West had served as the model for industrialization since the Meiji Restoration, and during the ensuing century catching up with the West became Japan's coveted national goal. But in the 1970s and 1980s Japanese development gradually shifted from industrialization guided by the "catch-up" ideology to unprecedented technological advancement for which there was no ready-made model. That was an unparalleled historical development for which Japanese government and industry had not adequately prepared (Economic Council, 1983). The education reform movement of the 1980s was in part stimulated by Japan's political concern with technological and scientific development in the next several decades.

Other prominent issues during the education reform movement in the 1980s included: effects of Japan's uniform, egalitarian education on students; negative consequences of overheated competition in university examinations; the need to create strategic plans for life-long learning; and effects on education of the rise of an age of information-intensive society and internationalization (National Council on Educational Reform, 1988; Ministry of Education, 1989).

Above all, the chief problem challenging reformers was to overhaul the uniform education that was becoming dysfunctional in a fast changing society. Uniform education in Japan is a legacy of the Meiji and post-war school systems, which had been highly effective in preparing literate human resources for industrialization during the "catch-up" era. But it was losing its effectiveness in a society, which was demanding diversity, rather than uniformity, in schooling. Reformers saw this to be a primary issue (National Council on Educational Reform, 1988).

Since he became prime minister in 1982, Yasuhiro Nakasone was interested in launching a campaign for education reform. By the spring of 1984 he had become thoroughly acquainted with the critical issues of Japanese education and was ready to move ahead. Preparation of the Bill to establish the National Council on Educational Reforms (NCER) was already under way under his leadership, and the bill passed in the national legislature in the summer of 1984. NCER was a national task force under direct control of the Prime Minister and completely independent of the Ministry of Education. It had four divisions responsible for education for the 21st century; activating educational functions of society; reforming elementary and secondary education; and reforming higher education. NCER took three years to deliberate on recommendations for school reforms and issued four reports.

*Implementation*

The Ministry of Education plays a key role in overseeing local authorities' compliance with national standards and policy, while each of the 47 independent prefectural boards of education is charged with educational administration. Under this structure of Japanese educational administration, the Ministry of Education assumed responsibility for creating new policies in response to NCER's recommendations.

Here I will highlight major reform initiatives that the Ministry of Education began implementing in the late 1980s. The first cluster of reforms was focused on improving primary and secondary education. It included: a revision of the primary and secondary curricula to enhance students' adaptability to changing society, the mastery of basic knowledge and skills, and moral education; measures to improve student guidance; initiatives to diversify high school education; and beginning teacher internships and upgrading teacher certification standards.

Among these initiatives, beginning teacher internships were the most coveted program of the Ministry of Education, and substantial national subsidies are provided. Every year this one-year program involves all the beginning public school teachers at the elementary and secondary schools. Its purpose is to improve the quality of teaching and broaden neophyte teachers' perspectives under the supervision of a full-time mentor. Interns are expected to work closely with the mentor to improve a broad range of competence, including teaching, classroom management, and student guidance. They are also required to participate in an out-of-school, inservice program involving workshops, lectures, and observations 30 times a year, which is organized by the inservice education center of the prefectural board of education. Further, a retreat for five days is organized to provide intensive inservice education (Ministry of Education, 1994; Shimahara & Sakai, 1992).

High school restructuring became a pivotal campaign in the 1990s. It will be discussed in some depth in the next section.

The second cluster of initiatives aimed to overhaul higher education (Ministry of Education, 1994). A University Council was created in the Ministry of Education, and its primary charge is to review strategic plans in higher education and make policy recommendations. Following the NCER reports, the University Council formulated specific recommendations to reform all levels of higher education. Implementation of these recommendations is currently under way. These reforms will be explored in the last section.

The third campaign was to enhance an effective life-long learning system. For this purpose, the Ministry of Education created a Bureau of Life-long Learning to coordinate locally organized adult education, cultural, and sports programs. Further, a law for promoting life-long learning was enacted by the national legislature to provide funding and other support for prefectural-level organizations. The Council on Life-long Learning established by this law in 1992 issued a reform report emphasizing the augmentation of recurrent education, the promotion of volunteer activities, the expansion of students' activities outside schools, and the extension of learning opportunity for adults.

The fourth campaign was to expand international education to stimulate Japan's internationalization: expanding exchange of students with foreign countries; improving Japanese language instruction for foreigners; improving the instruction of foreign languages for Japanese students; and enhancing school programs for Japanese students living overseas.

Thus far I have sketched education reform initiatives in the 1980s. In the next section I will focus on Japan's reform efforts in the 1990s, which ensued from the earlier campaign to overhaul schools.

## REFORMS IN THE 1990s

By virtue of the fact that educational change is additive and more often than not spiral, it is slow unless it is imposed as a consequence of war or revolution. As mentioned, Japan's post-war school reform was drastic, because the pre-war system was virtually replaced with an American system. But since then it followed a cumulative and spiral process. School reforms in the 1990s, however, are additive building on the 1980s highly publicized nationwide reform movement. When the National Council on Educational Reform completed the four reform reports, its recommendations appeared to be too ambitious and broad. Moreover, they were even diffuse and general. Concrete reform agendas, however, gradually emerged from the late 1980s and early 1990s. This section will focus on the restructuring of upper secondary and higher education.

### High School Structuring

In Japan, compulsory attendance is required only through middle school, and currently 96 percent of middle school graduates are enrolled in high schools. Of these high schools 76 percent are public and only 24 percent are private.

High school education is the most critical stage of schooling in terms of transition to college and employment. High school education has a strikingly lasting impact on adolescents because the most pivotal element of that education is preparation for intense university entrance examinations. These examinations have a dominant influence on high school students' cognitive and motivational orientation toward schooling. More than 30 years ago Vogel (1963), author of *Japan's Middle Class*, noted:

No single event, with the possible exception of marriage, determines the course of a young man's life as much as an entrance examination, and nothing, including marriage, requires as many years of planning and hard work. . . . These arduous preparations constitute a kind of *rite de passage* whereby a young man proves that he has the qualities of ability and endurance for becoming a salaried man. (p. 40)

Vogel's comment is based on his observation at a time when only 10 percent of high school graduates went to college. Now the intensity of preparation for entrance exams is even greater, as 43 percent of youths advance to college. The preparation is escalated and largely institutionalized, requiring much more prolonged drilling at preparatory schools, which exist outside the school system.

Educational credentials and skills are key to employment, social status, and promotion. Since the Meiji period (1868–1911) education has eminently contributed to the shaping of Japan's meritocratic society (Rohlen, 1986). This accounts for the importance that Japanese attach to education, as well as to the demanding entrance examinations for high school and university. Entrance examinations, however, have had a significant polarizing effect on youths, resulting in considerable disaffection in a large proportion of students. As Japan became a mature, affluent society, social mobility, observed for two decades in the 1960s and 1970s, declined, and youths' aspirations for success were remarkably cooled down (Amano, 1986). As pointed out earlier, it became increasingly evident that Japan's school system had become ineffective and even dysfunctional in satisfying diversified youth values and needs.

Currently 75 percent of high school entrants attend academic high schools, and the remaining 25 percent, vocational high schools. The former high schools are ranked by a single criterion in each prefecture or region: the number of students admitted to top universities. High schools draw applicants from a number of middle schools within a prefecture, which is usually divided into several large districts. Middle school students compete for admission, through entrance examinations, to academic high schools with good reputations. However, a large percentage of students end up attending vocational schools only because their chances for admission to academic schools are remote.

Suffice it to suggest that university entrance examinations by and large mold the dominant orientation of high school education in Japan. This is a chief issue as reformers see it (Central Council of Education, 1990). It goes without saying that diversity in high school education is severely limited. Japan's high school education failed to reflect the diversity of industry and economy and although students have been diversified with respect to their ability, needs and goals, high schools failed to offer programs that reflected student diversity.

Following NCER's reform reports, in 1989 the Ministry of Education charged the Central Council of Education with making further recommendations to reform educational structures (Central Council of Education, 1991). One important aspect of the charge was to consider how to diversify high school education. The Council urged greater latitude in the curriculum and students' freedom to choose courses.

Subsequently the Ministry of Education set up a task force, the Committee for Enhancement of High School Reforms in 1991. It issued four reports in two years to recommend plans to restructure high school education (Ministry of Education, 1993). Its central theme was to revamp high school education to empower students to link their personal interests and future aspirations to formal learning in the school.

The Committee's main recommendation was to implement a comprehensive program in each academic high school whose central was to promote students' career aspirations based on a broad study of both academic and specialized vocational subject. This comprehensive program would attract students by offering an alternative to the exclusively college-bound program. The comprehensive program would consist of four parts. The first would include the common requirements for all high school students. The second part would feature three common areas for students in the comprehensive program, identified as industrial society and human life, basic studies of information technology, and independent study on selected problem. The third part would encompass rich clusters of elective courses, including: information, industrial management, international cooperation, regional development, biotechnology, welfare management, environmental science, and art and culture. And additional optional studies would make up the fourth part.

The Ministry of Education's (1993) survey indicates that at least 14 high schools in various prefectures opened a comprehensive program as a pilot undertaking by 1995. Thirty other prefectures were considering adding the program in public schools. All in all, given the fact that the comprehensive program requires rich resources and is in its trial stage, it seems to be off to a fairly good start.

I will turn to another promising restructuring in high school education. In the past decade and a half what is often identified as a new type of high school has emerged offering students diverse programs and flexible course selection. Among new types of schools are "comprehensive high schools" that offer attractive, rich programs. The expansion of innovative high schools was enhanced by reform initiatives in the 1980s and 1990s. Although the development of these schools is still in a formative stage, they are expanding throughout the country, extending alternative high school education to youths. According to the latest survey conducted by the Ministry of Education (1993), 42 innovative schools were in operation in 23 prefectures, and 14 such schools were scheduled to be opened within a few years.

By way of illustration, I will cite a few schools identified as new types of schools. To date, the best known comprehensive school in Japan is Ina Gakuen High School outside Tokyo, established in 1984 (Nishimoto, 1993). It enrolls 3,300 students and offers 164 courses; its seven programs include the humanities, natural science/mathematics, languages, health/physical education, arts, home economics, and business. At this school, students are permitted to choose half the courses that make up their entire program, providing them with latitude to select courses that promote their interests. An ambitious comprehensive high school will be opened in Makuhari, Chiba Prefecture in 1996. It will enroll 2,100 students and offer five programs, including the humanities, natural science/mathematics, international studies, information science, and arts. Students will take all the required courses in their sophomore year, enabling them to choose the remaining courses with few restrictions in the junior and senior years.

Other new types of schools include schools that specialize in international studies, economics, information technology, technology, electronics, information industry, and the like. Two schools will be mentioned here as examples of these schools. Narita, which had been a prefectural academic high school, was changed to an international school in 1991, incorporating both English and international programs. Tokyo Metropolitan International School was opened in 1989. Both schools emphasize strong language and international studies programs, in addition to a regular academic program. Students in these schools receive rich language training and an exposure to cross-cultural studies.

Policy initiatives that have led to the development of new types of high schools will be briefly discussed in the following. During the American occupation comprehensive high schools were initially introduced but failed in the 1950s owing to several reasons. The first critical reason is that Japanese policymakers, who were unaccustomed to the concept of comprehensive high schools, considered them ineffective, and the second was funding shortfalls (Kaneko, 1986). Consequently, high schools were differentiated into academic and vocational schools. This reorganization of high school education was part of an extensive national campaign to restructure occupation-led reforms in the 1950s (Komori, 1986).

Several factors contributed to the renewed interest in comprehensive high schools and other innovative schools. As early as 1971, in its reform report the Central Council of Education (1971) pointed out the need for diversity in high school education in response to increasing variance in students' ability, aptitude, and aspirations. Subsequently the Association of Prefectural Superintendents of Schools (1978/1994) addressed the diversity theme by setting up a task force, which eventually proposed structural changes in high school education. The task force published a noteworthy reform report (1978/1994) in 1978 proposing several innovative measures, including: credit-based high schools; effective use of resources by clustering two or three high schools on the same site to permit students to select courses offered by any cluster school; and six-year high schools designed to provide continuity throughout secondary education. This report stimulated further explorations of alternative high school education, which eventually led to the development of new types of schools.

The report was timely for several reasons. A demographic projection that the population of high school age would surge throughout the 1980s, especially in suburbs of large cities, demanded a substantial increase of new high schools. Moreover, the nation's mood for education reforms was growing around 1980, and the Ministry of Education had just revised the elementary and secondary curricula to "humanize" schooling and provide latitude and freedom in the construction of school programs. These demographic changes and support for school reforms enhanced the attractiveness and the subsequent public acceptance of new types of school. As the National Council of Educational Reform gave the needed political legitimation to the birth of innovative schools, they started to develop in the 1980s. They are further expanding in the 1990s, stimulated by continued public support and further reform initiatives.

The restructuring campaign also involved vocational high schools which, as mentioned earlier, suffer the image of second-class status. To make them attractive and relevant to changing economic and technological needs, local school authorities are creating innovative vocational programs. As of 1993 there were 224 innovative vocational schools across the country, with such unique programs as biotechnology, information technology, electronic mechanics, international economics, and the like (Ministry of Education, 1993). Such programs were planned in 74 schools in 31 prefectures.

Currently a small fraction of the country's 4,181 high schools is participating in these innovative initiatives, and the success of the comprehensive program is uncertain. Nevertheless, the high school reform campaign has the potential of paving the way toward further diversifying Japan's uniform high school education to respond to students' varying aspirations, aptitudes, and needs. Bolstering that potential, it is reported that as of 1995, 10 and 40 percent of public and private academic schools, respectively, have developed some sort of innovative programs (Ogawa, 1995).

*Restructuring in Higher Education*

Japanese higher education is now in a transition from the post-war system to an emerging system capable of meeting challenges in an age of global economy, information, advanced technology, expanded life expectancy, and life-long learning. The post-war system met Japan's needs for economic growth and industrialization during the time when Japan was catching up with the West. Higher education was uniform, adhering to the national standards established by the Ministry of Education and proliferated rapidly in response to the nation's economic growth. Four-year colleges numbered only 180 in 1949, when post-war higher education started, increased to 534 in 1994, while the number of two-year colleges swelled from 246 in 1955 to 595 in 1994. The augmentation of colleges, however, was represented largely by an increase of private institutions, which currently constitute 73 percent of four-year colleges and 84 percent of two-year colleges. Enrollment of high school graduates in colleges dramatically expanded from 10 percent in 1955 to 24 percent in 1970 and 43 percent in 1995. Suffice it to say that Japan's higher learning has literally become mass education.

The higher education system consists of a three-tier structure: four-year colleges, two-year colleges, and higher technical colleges, which offer five-year programs that accept middle-school graduates as entrants. In addition, there are nearly 3,500 technical schools, in which 860,000 students are enrolled offering post-high school education in a variety of technical fields.

As Kazuyuki Kitamura (in press) points out, the phenomenal growth of higher education in Japan largely occurred without guided policy, unlike elementary and secondary education, which has been a policy priority in the Ministry of Education. He argues that Japan had no comprehensive policy on higher education until the beginning of the 1970s. The government had a "laissez-faire" policy, if any, especially for the private sector, suggesting no control with respect to direction of expansion and little support, despite its predominance in higher education enrolling nearly 80 percent of the college population. It may be noted, however, that as mentioned earlier, the government had national regulations for establishing institutions of higher education.

Policy initiatives to direct the development of higher education started to develop only after the widespread campus unrest in the late 1960s, which eventually led to the proliferation of proposals to reform higher education presented by universities, government agencies, business and political circles, and other groups (Kitamura, in press). The Central Council of Education's 1971 reform report, which was referred to in the earlier section, also presented an ambitious proposal for the national planning of higher education and public subsidies to private colleges. Subsequently, although national legislation on subsidies to private institutions was enacted in 1965, the nation's fever for the reform campaign subsided with little substantial changes in higher education.

Consequential impetus to overhaul higher education was eventually injected late in the 1980s when the National Council on Educational Reform (1988) completed its reform deliberations. Although NCER's recommendations to restructure tertiary education were broad and relatively brief, they outlined the essential parameters of restructuring in the 1990s. There was broad public support for the recommendations because of the mounting domestic and international demands for reforms inherent in the emergence of a new age of global economy, scientific and technological development, and life-long learning. Salient among the recommendations were the establishment of a University Council whose responsibility is to make policy recommendations, as mentioned earlier, and liberalization of national regulations for the establishment of curriculum, programs, and institutions (NCER, 1988). The University Council, an advisory body in the Ministry of Education established in 1987, at last began formulating national plans for higher education.

In 1991, the University Council (1991A) made a broad range of specific recommendations to overhaul higher education which constituted a framework of reforms. These recommendations are influential in stimulating current reforms at all levels, including two- and four-year colleges and graduate schools (Amano, 1994). Several initiatives will be mentioned here to illuminate the direction of the reform movement at the higher education level (for further analysis see Amano, 1994). Following the University Council's recommendations, the Ministry of Education liberalized its regulations to encourage the development of diverse and unique programs and institutions. In the past these regulations were a major source of constraints, replicating uniformity in programs of higher education throughout the nation. In the history of Japanese higher education, deregulation identified as Taikoka is an epoch-making move encouraging colleges and universities to offer unique curricula and programs.

Deregulation also led to the development of non-traditional faculties and coherent integration of general education and specialized programs at the undergraduate level. Until the 1990s the Ministry's rigid regulations contributed to the perpetuation of a flat, unprepossessing curriculum required of all freshman and sophomore students, although when introduced in the late 1940s, it was designed to provide students with rich liberal education. Faculty who took charge of general education were also treated as low-status teaching staff.

Another significant initiative in the Japanese reform context is enhancement of access to higher education for part-time students and adults. Until recently higher education was restricted largely to traditional full-time students, leaving Japan far behind other advanced countries in promoting a life-long learning system (see Ministry of Education, 1994). A campaign to create evening and part-time programs at the undergraduate and graduate programs is now under way to meet the needs of the diversifying population.

The third important campaign is to expand graduate education to offer advanced training and research opportunity for a larger population to meet enhanced demand. As the University Council (1991B) points out, graduate education is far less developed in Japan than in other advanced countries, relative to access, facility, funding, enrollments, and attainability of PhDs. For example, as of 1989 the ratio of graduate students per 1,000 persons is only 0.7 in Japan as compared with: 7.1 in the United States; 33.5 in the United Kingdom; and 2.9 in France. To promote graduate studies, the Ministry of Education liberalized program regulations and encourages universities to create diverse graduate schools/programs by offering enhanced funding (University Council, 1991B).

The fourth campaign under way is the enhancement of accountability through the evaluation of university programs involving self-studies and external reviews (Kitamura, in press). In view of the fact that Japanese higher education has no tradition of self-evaluation, this campaign is significant and challenging. Further, to improve the quality of faculty and mobilize them within the system of higher education, the University Council proposed in 1995 to replace the current tenure practice with an appointment system according to which faculty in all ranks would receive appointments for a specific term (Asahi Shimbun, 1995). Reappointments would require a review of faculty accomplishments, including teaching effectiveness. It is a controversial issue that is being debated now.

Other reform campaigns address the internationalization of higher education and the diversification of two-year colleges and technical higher schools to meet differentiating needs of students who are drawn from local communities (University Council, 1991A). It is relevant to mention that the expansion of higher education has recently been slowed because of demographic shifts. The population of 18-year-olds peaked in 1992 and totaled 2,050,000, and it is expected that it will progressively decrease to 1,290,000 in 2007. Unless the enrollment of nontraditional students dramatically increases, intense competition for survival among institutions of higher education is likely to ensue in the near future. Put differently, this demographic trend offers colleges and universities an opportunity to develop programs at all levels aimed at non-traditional students and carry out the reform initiatives mentioned above to attract students. Now emphasis is not on expansion but improvement of the quality of teaching and learning and diversification of learning opportunities.

## CONCLUSION

The present school system was built to promote Japan's industrialization and modernization, but now that Japan has surpassed that phase of development, and a post-industrial society is on the horizon, the system is becoming obsolete. Japanese workplaces, social discourse, and various dimensions of everyday life are now profoundly influenced by the global economy, information, internationalization, and diversified values and needs. The lack of fit between schools and the changing society of which I spoke is inherent in the conservative nature of educational policy and practice. The National Council on Educational Reform was quite blunt in enunciating the issue: "The most important [initiative] in the educational reform to come is to do away with the uniformity, rigidity, closedness and lack of internationalism. . ." (NCER, p. 26). Diversification is a key word that educational, business, and political reformers choose today to characterize Japan's social transformation.

The thrust of education reforms for the past decade have been how to diversify schools from the elementary to the graduate school levels. This reform campaign has entailed a broad scope of strategies, including: introducing new curricula at the elementary and secondary levels, implementing innovative high schools and programs providing diversity and choice, Taikoka or deregulating higher education, increased autonomy of universities to improve the curriculum and quality of teaching and research, and diversification of higher education.

The Ministry of Education began other initiatives to provide students with increased freedom and relaxation. Beginning in 1992 it introduced a new school attendance policy, requiring students to attend schools five days a week, instead of six days as in the past. The Ministry aims to increase the enrollment of foreign students in institutions of higher education from the current level of 52,000 to 100,000 in the near future. These new drives are consistent with the reform efforts to achieve diversity in Japanese education.

But obstacles to achieving reform goals, however, cannot be underestimated. Schools and universities are slow to recognize that structural changes in society require corresponding reforms in their practice. The challenge Japan faces is how far reformers' initiatives can be brought to fruition.

## REFERENCES

Amano, I. (1986). The dilemma of Japanese education today. *The Japan Foundation Newsletter*, **8**(5).
Amano, I. (1994). *The university: An age of change*. Tokyo: University of Tokyo Press.
Asahi Shimbun. (1995). A daily newspaper, September 19, p. 1. Association of Prefectural Superintendents of Schools (1978/1994). Study report on the development of high schools. In K. K.

72    *Shimahara*

Henshubu (Ed.), *Primary documents on high school education: Reform reports* (pp. 183–196). Tokyo: Gakuji. Shuppan. (Original work published 1978).
Central Council of Education. (1971). *Basic policies for the comprehensive expansion of school education.* Tokyo: Mombusho.
Central Council of Education. (1990). Subcommittee progress report concerning the school system. Published in *Journal of Educational Administration* (Kyoshoku Kenshu), January, 1991, 150–205.
Central Council of Education. (1991). *Education reforms for a new age.* Tokyo: Gyosei.
Economic Council. (1983). *Japan in the year 2000.* Tokyo: JapanTimes.
Kaneko, T. (1986). Postwar education reforms and the establishment of the high school system. In K. Komori (Ed.), *A comprehensive study of reforms of the high school system.* Tokyo: Taga Shuppan.
Kinoshita, S. (1983). The postwar curriculum. In M. Okazu (Ed.), *The encyclopedia of curriculum* (pp. 25–36). Tokyo: Shogakkan.
Kitamura, K. (in press). Policy issues in Japanese higher education. *Higher Education Policy.*
Komori, K. (Ed.). (1986). *A comprehensive study of reforms of the school system.* Tokyo: Taga Shuppan.
Ministry of Education. (1989). *Outline of education in Japan 1989.* Tokyo: Ministry of Education.
Ministry of Education. (1993). *Progress report on reforms of high school education.* Tokyo: Ministry of Education.
Ministry of Education. (1994). *Our nation's education policies.* Tokyo: Mombusho.
National Council on Educational Reform. (1985). *First report on educational reform.* Tokyo: National Council on Educational Reform (English).
National Council on Educational Reform. (1988). *Recommendations on educational reforms.* Tokyo: Okurasho Insatsukyoku.
Nishimoto, K. (1993). How to create a comprehensive program. *Monthly Journal of High School Education,* **26**, 23–29.
Ogawa, H. (1995). High school reform in the third year. *Nihon Keizai Shimbun* (daily economic newspaper), p. 17, November 4.
Rohlen, T. P. (1983). *Japan's high schools.* Stanford: Stanford University Press.
Rohlen, T. P. (1986). Japanese education: If they can do it, should we? *American Scholar,* **55**, 29–43.
Schoppa, L. (1991). *Education reform in Japan: A case of immobilist politics.* London: Routledge.
Shimahara, N. (1979). *Adaptation and education in Japan.* New York: Praeger.
Shimahara, N. (1986). Japanese education reforms in the 1980s. *Issues in Education,* **6**, 85–100.
Shimahara, N. (1992). Overview of Japanese education: Policy, structure, and current issues. In R. Leestma & H. Walberg (Eds.), *Japanese educational productivity* (pp. 7–33). Ann Arbor: Center for Japanese Studies, the University of Michigan.
Shimahara, N., & Sakai, A. (1992). Teacher internship and the culture of teaching in Japan. *British Journal of Sociology of Education,* **13**, 147–161.
Shinoda, Hi. (1979). Training of elementary school teachers. In H. Shinoda & T. Tezuka (Eds.), *History of schools,* pp. 13–98. Tokyo: Daiichi Hoki.
University Council. (1991A). *Aiming to develop diverse universities: A collection of reform recommendations.* Tokyo: Gyosei.
University Council. (1991B). *Aiming to develop diverse universities: Plans for higher education after 1993 and reforms of graduate schools.* Tokyo: Gyosei.
Vogel, E. (1963). *Japan's middle class.* Berkeley: University of California Press.
Yamaguchi, H. (1980). Modern problems of the curriculum. In S. Sato & H. Inada (Eds.), *School and curriculum.* Tokyo: Daiichi Hoki.

# National Strategies for Educational Reform: Lessons from the British Experience Since 1988

MICHAEL BARBER

*Institute of Education, University of London*

*This chapter takes the British case as an example of how national and local policies affect educational reform. Factors affecting school performance and reviewed strategies for improvement are considered in terms of a policy framework that combines elements of pressure and support. The roles of both individual and local governments are outlined with a view to establishing combined strategies for educational reform.*

## INTRODUCTION

There have been moments in the last decade when it has seemed as if central government has dictated the entire agenda in the United Kingdom. A series of Acts of Parliament between 1986 and 1993 altered for good the education landscape in England and Wales, or so it seemed. In Scotland, with its own separate education system, legislation of similar extent if not intensity followed. Yet in classrooms, in the millions of micro-learning events which taken together make up young people's experience of education, how much has really changed?

This question reveals the limits to the power of apparently all-powerful governments such as that in the United Kingdom. Other national governments, such as those in the United States, Canada and Australia which unlike that in the UK, have to operate in the context of either a separation of powers or a federal constitution or both, are in an even weaker position to change education at the classroom level.

Given this context, this chapter examines the potential of central and local government to change radically what happens in schools and classrooms and, simultaneously considers the limits on that potential. It draws predominantly on the British experience but refers from time to time to international experience. Its generalisable principles ought to be universally relevant, even if they will not always be practical politically.

## STANDARDS

The first and perhaps most important point concerns the government's treatment of 'standards'. The revised National Targets for Education and Training will

73

*M. Fullan (ed.), Fundamental Change,* 73-97.

include one suggesting that 85 per cent of young people in England and Wales should achieve five grades A-C at GCSE (or the equivalent) by the year 2000. In Scotland there is a different target appropriate to its different examination system. The young people who will take GCSE, an examination normally taken at 16+, in that year started secondary school in September 1995. The challenge of meeting this target is therefore immediate. To many in the education service the target seems ludicrously unrealistic, yet it is pitched at the kind of level needed if the UK is to keep up with the international competition. In Japan, for example, roughly 80 per cent of an age cohort achieve the equivalent of two British "A levels" compared to a figure of about 40 per cent in the UK. In both Germany and Japan the apparently ambitious targets set for the UK have already been surpassed (Dearing, 1996, p. 3).

Raising standards, however, is not just a matter of international competition. It is also necessary to take account of the rapidly changing job market.

> By the year 2000, 70 per cent of all jobs in Europe will require cerebral rather than manual skills. Some experts suggest that as many as 50 per cent of these jobs will require the equivalent of higher education or a professional qualification.
>
> (Evans, 1994, p. 15)

Nor is the case for higher standards purely a matter of economics. It is also an issue fundamentally related to the success of a democratic society in the 21st century. The social consequences of extensive under achievement will become increasingly dire. Already we have evidence of a clear, if indirect, link between educational failure and crime. We also know that a high degree of education and self-confidence are requirements for full participation in a democratic society. The fruits of a successful education system are therefore much more than purely economic.

Even this is not the full extent of the case for higher standards. The fact is that the range of threats to the future existence of the planet, from global warming to the pressure of population growth, will increasingly focus minds. We will require more ingenuity, knowledge, and understanding than ever before to solve these immense challenges early in the next century.

It is this wide range of demands for higher standards that explains why governments across the Western world are giving such attention to improved educational performance. Passages from the speeches of Bill Clinton, John Major, Tony Blair and Paul Keating are often interchangeable. All of them gaze in awe at the economic and educational achievements of Pacific Rim countries and await with some anxiety the arrival of the Asian century.

Although standards, measured in these terms, are clearly too low in the UK, it is important to recognise that for many young people they are rising and have been rising for a number of years. Indeed if the available indicators are to be believed there has never been a time when standards have risen as much as they have in the last decade. In 1994 over 53 per cent of those entered achieved five grades A – C at GCSE compared to fewer than 30 per cent in 1987. The average improvement at GCSE is, therefore, around 3 per cent per annum since 1988. There has been a similarly steady improvement at A level over the same period. Meanwhile staying on rates at both 16 plus and 18 plus have soared. By 1994 over 70 per cent of the age group remain in education after the age of 16 compared to only 35 per cent 15 years earlier, while participation in higher education has more than doubled since the mid-1980s. Over 30 per cent of young people now enter higher education. Thus for a significant proportion of young people, indeed perhaps for the majority, standards appear to have risen.

However there is simultaneous and disturbing evidence that for other young people standards are at best static, and perhaps falling. The evidence from both OFSTED, the inspection agency, and elsewhere suggests that reading standards in primary schools may have fallen in the early 1990s. As many as 30 per cent of lessons in junior schools were considered inadequate in the 1995 report of Her Majesty's Chief Inspector (OFSTED 1995). It is not uncommon, these days, for secondary heads, normally in private, to explain that they are admitting ever more pupils at age 11 with reading ages of 9 or less. Indeed a significant number of secondary schools are now employing reading tests at the beginning of the year 7 in order to set a base line for examining their own value added impact. In one of the more successful inner London boroughs, the average reading age of pupils in the first year of secondary schools is nine years and nine months. This kind of disadvantage at the start of secondary school is all too likely to prevent pupils from making the most of the crucial years between 11 and 16. Evidence published by the Secondary Heads Association in 1995 and OFSTED again in 1996 confirmed these fears (OFSTED, 1996). At the other end of the schooling system the evidence is disturbing too. The Basic Skills Agency has discovered that as many as 15 per cent of 21 year olds have limited literacy competence and 20 per cent have limited competence in Mathematics.

It is interesting to set this evidence on standards against the Keele University database of Pupil Attitudes to Secondary School, a database which includes the views of over 30,000 young people. This shows that somewhere between 20 and 30 per cent of secondary school pupils are bored or lacking in motivation. They are "the Disappointed". Another 10–15 percent are more actively hostile to school and likely to disrupt the education of others. They are "the Disaffected". As many as another 5 – 10 percent truant regularly and in some urban areas have unofficially left school altogether and become the "the Disappeared". In short it would seem that the attitudinal data confirms the data on standards. While half or slightly over half are doing reasonably well, concern over the rest remains justifiable (Barber, 1994, 1996).

If this is the overall national picture then it should be borne in mind that the gloomy parts of it are likely to be accentuated in Britain's urban areas. The groups which are under-achieving include a disproportionately high number of boys, working class students and students in deprived urban areas. The fact that a disproportionate number of those who under-achieve are in urban areas does not, in any sense, justify having lower expectations or setting lower standards for pupils there. It does mean acknowledging, given the social circumstances in many of

Britain's urban areas, that it takes more time, energy, commitment, skill and resources to enable pupils to reach those high standards. Government policies at either local or national level which fail to recognise these facts are unlikely to succeed.

Perhaps not surprisingly in these circumstances not all schools manage. Some become ground down by the weight of social pressures and the demands of a never-ending series of educational policy changes. The central issue for policymakers is to create a framework which increases the chances of success and reduces, and perhaps ultimately even eliminates, the chances of failure for all schools and especially urban schools. The starting point for such a policy must surely be the extensive knowledge we now have of what characterises effective schools and what can be done to help schools that are not yet effective to improve. This is the theme of the next section of this chapter.

## IMPROVING PERFORMANCE

There is now an overwhelming consensus about the characteristics of effective schools. The last year or two has seen the publication of a series of reviews of the literature in this field. The conclusions of all them are similar. Following the most comprehensive review of the recent literature in this field Sammons, Thomas and Mortimore (1995) arrived at the following list of eleven characteristics.

Other recent research is demonstrating that even within an effective school there are significant variations in the effectiveness of different departments or aspects of the school and indeed that within a particular school the extent of effectiveness for different ability groups varies too (Sammons, Thomas, & Mortimore, 1995). These findings can help school managers to analyse and understand what is required to help their own schools improve.

Helpful though it is to be able to describe an effective school, doing so does not solve some important problems. Firstly, the evidence from major studies in school effectiveness in this country has limitations. There has, for example, been insufficient work on the study of historically ineffective schools and the evidence suggests that one cannot easily translate the characteristics of effectiveness determined through studies of effective schools and apply them, unthinking, to schools that are less than effective. In Britain work by a number of researchers is beginning to rectify this (Barber 1995, Myers 1995; Stoll, 1995; Reynolds, 1995). Secondly, the studies of school effectiveness have tended to focus on school and departmental level factors rather than on aspects of classroom practice. Surely one of the next frontiers for research is to examine what it is that characterises effective teaching and, adding to the complexity, to explore the relationships between the teachers' performance and the management context. Thirdly, there has until recently been insufficient overlap between the study of school effectiveness and the study and application of the processes of school improvement. Increasingly in this third area there is progress both in terms of research and practice. For example, the Institute

## ELEVEN FACTORS FOR EFFECTIVE SCHOOLS

| | | |
|---|---|---|
| 1 | Professional leadership | Firm and purposeful |
| | | A participative approach |
| | | The leading professional |
| 2 | Shared vision and goals | Unity of purpose |
| | | Consistency of practice |
| | | Collegiality and collaboration |
| 3 | A learning environment | An orderly atmosphere |
| | | an attractive working environment |
| 4 | Concentration on teaching and learning | Maximisation of learning time |
| | | Academic emphasis |
| | | Focus on achievement |
| 5 | Purposeful teaching | Efficient organisation |
| | | Clarity of purpose |
| | | Structured lessons |
| | | Adaptive practice |
| 6 | High expectations | High expectations all round |
| | | Communicating expectations |
| | | Providing intellectual challenge |
| 7 | Positive reinforcement | Clear and fair discipline |
| | | Feedback |
| 8 | Monitoring progress | Monitoring pupil performance |
| | | Evaluating school performance |
| 9 | Pupil rights and responsibilities | Raising pupil self-esteem |
| | | Positions of responsibility |
| | | Control of work |
| 10 | Home-school partnership | Parenting involvement in their children's learning |
| 11 | A learning organisation | School-based staff development |

of Education School Improvement Network at London University and the Keele University Centre for Successful Schools are both consciously designed to bridge the school effectiveness – school improvement divide.

The most significant problem, unaddressed in the school effectiveness research findings, is that being able to describe an effective school does not necessarily indicate what is needed to help an unsuccessful school to become successful. The steps required to help a school turn itself round are, from a policy point of view, more important to know yet significantly less researched. However there is a growing body of evidence about what works and it is important to summarise this as a prelude to determining a policy framework (see, for example, Brighouse, 1991; Hopkins 1994; Myers, 1996; Barber & Dann, 1996; Hillman & Maden, 1996). There are many processes which appear to contribute to improving schools. Six appear to come through loudly, clearly and consistently in the recent British literature, so much so that they are now consistently highlighted in government publications and have informed policy on, for example, leadership development and school self-evaluation. While there is no theoretical justification for separating these processes from others, such as parental involvement, these are the ones that have been given emphasis in the British context.

The first of these six features is that improving schools tend to have a clear sense of direction. This is harder to establish in urban schools because of the many pressures upon them but it is also more crucial since the status quo is rarely acceptable to either the staff or the pupils or the local community. There is thus a premium in such schools on effective leadership and on a management approach that can generate both a vision of the future and a shared culture and commitment to the schools' direction. One way to achieve this is for the school to have a development plan prepared after widespread consultation. It can become the central text for individual teachers, departments (in secondary schools) and others involved in planning aspects of a school's provision. In short everyone must believe in it, if it is to have an impact.

Once this is established, it is also important that urban schools, to use Michael Fullan's evocative phrase, 'practise fearlessness' (1991). Once the school has established its own destiny and its plans for how to move towards it, school leaders need to recognise that they cannot do all the things that external organisations – central government, national agencies and local authorities – will ask them to do. There is simply not enough time for them to be able to do so and implement their own plan. Thus the choice is stark: either things fail to happen by default, or, surely more sensibly, schools decide that they will not do some of the things that they have been asked to do. A good example of schools practising fearlessness in the UK at present is the refusal of 80 percent of secondary schools to carry out the daily act of collective worship required by statute. Practising fearlessness also implies being prepared to take risks in pursuit of improvement in a changing world. In the most rapidly improving schools, senior management encourages innovation throughout the school and encourages staff to take the risks that are inevitably involved.

Thirdly, increasingly schools that know what they intend to do (and what they are not going to do), set clear targets for themselves. These ought to identify timescales, success criteria, necessary resources and the staff responsible. It then becomes a vital part of management to monitor the implementation of agreed targets and to build on them. Where targets are not met the school is then in a position to ask itself the question why and engage in a process of review and development. Where targets are met they can contribute to building confidence among the staff. The government is so enamoured of targets that it is currently legislating to require schools to set targets for performance in the core curriculum subjects. Several good examples of target-setting are reported in a recent DFEE publication (1996) on the theme. The following examples are taken from it.

## GROVE PRIMARY SCHOOL, BIRMINGHAM

*Action*

Each child in the school is expected to progress 'half a National Curriculum level per year', at the very least, and pupils falling below this are quickly identified in order to accelerate their progress. Pupils achieving above their expected rate of progress are encouraged to move forward as far as they can.

The school commissioned an IT package to provide an assessment database which could be used in a variety of ways. Assessment data is used, for example, *to identify and provide for differentiated groups of pupils.* Teachers log assessment data from the core subjects into the database every term. They use the information to select teaching groups for different purposes: 'fast track' English and mathematics groups, and to identify pupils with special educational needs. For example, pupils in Years 5 and 6 operating at National Curriculum levels 4 and 6 in English are grouped together; while pupils not reaching level 1 or 2 are grouped as a special needs group for intensive support. These pupils are assessed six times per year against English and mathematics criteria from within National Curriculum level 1 and 2. Teachers can then detect progress and redeploy resources in the most sensible way. For example, pupils' progress is formally recorded at six weekly intervals on letter sound, for instance, and on their ability to write to dictation and form letters. Meanwhile, teacher assessment of these skills and activities is ongoing. The formal recording of progress at regular intervals allows the class teacher and the Special Needs Co-ordinator to see how best to arrange the support of individuals and groups of pupils as well as giving a more finely tuned indication of progress than the National Curriculum levels alone.

*Effect*

The quality of teaching is very good in mathematics, and is well informed by effective assessment, which is used to constantly raise pupils' attainment in mathematics. 'Fast track' pupils in mathematics in Years 4 to 6 work confidently together; they enjoy and talk about their mathematics with each other, and are aware of the National Curriculum level at which they are working. *Last year four pupils achieved a higher grade GCSE pass in mathematics.*

Spelling was identified as a weakness and the teaching programme was changed to address the concern. Regular spelling homework, an award scheme and daily assessment were introduced. This action has led to measurable improvements in spelling. The school has now identified punctuation as an area for attention across parts of the school.

Teachers make effective use of the database to evaluate the quality of provision and to redeploy resources. The school produces graphs to show the progress of a year group in a core subject, to make comparisons between different intakes at the same point, to compare predicted and actual performance and to compare teacher assessment against National Curriculum test results. The database show up imbalances between year groups which have implications for the organisation and the curriculum, for example if a class or group is performing significantly lower than expected.

## PRINCE ALBERT PRIMARY SCHOOL, BIRMINGHAM

*Action*

Internal assessment in the school identified weaknesses in mathematics. Teachers have introduced a range of strategies to improve the resources for mathematics and to target some pupils for intensive support. These strategies have been underpinned by a curriculum-wide change in classroom management so that teachers give more sustained support to individual pupils. Standardised tests in mathematics, and of key stage National Curriculum tests and teacher assessment are used to identify small groups of pupils for intensive teaching sessions during a six week period.

*Effect*

The percentage of Year 3 and Year 6 pupils achieving above the national average in standardised test scores has doubled in the last four years. The upward trend began following the general school-wide changes in teaching mathematics. The introduction of intensive teaching for sustained periods of time resulted in a dramatic improvement in the test results. The school is well aware of the dangers of teaching to a test and has ensured that a range of assessment approaches and teaching methods is in place.

## BOYS AND ENGLISH IN WAKEMAN SCHOOL, SHROPSHIRE

Target-setting in the English department is one part of a wider concern to raise standards of achievement in this school. The school's inspection in 1994 had drawn attention to the relatively weak examination results of the boys compared to those of the girls. This confirmed the English department's already established concern with the matter following the publication of HMI's report *Boys and English*.

*Action*

The department's response took several forms. They used a questionnaire, followed up by more detailed individual interviews with some of the pupils to examine the differences in attitudes to, and views of, English of boys and girls. Using the information gained, the department made changes in teaching and curriculum to take the teaching as supportive of boys as it had been of girls. The teachers also revised their assessment procedures so as to focus more closely on specific aspects of attainment in English. They grouped the pupils into broader ability sets to improve the gender balance, girls having previously predominated in top sets.

Target-setting involves giving the pupils clear information about the progress they have made to date and the steps they need to take to improve their work. Initiatives are directed at both boys and girls although they arose out of a particular concern about underachievement by boys. During the work the department has been supported by the LEA.

The first initiative was introduced on a trial basis last year and is to be extended to all pupils this year. As Year 11 pupils approach their GCSE examinations and after the pupils have been told the grades they are predicted to get, they are mentored. The pupils have detailed and specific discussions with the teachers about their progress and about what they must do to improve on their predicted grades.

*Effect*

In the trial last year, the pupils who had taken part in the mentoring system gained GCSE grades at C or above which were 25 per cent better than the results which had been predicted before the mentoring took place.

Fourthly, there seems to be growing evidence to suggest that openness about performance data within a school is a vital ingredient of improvement. Schools are greatly helped in this process if school authorities provide them with high quality data, a factor which has been taken seriously in the quality assurance strategies of, for example, Scotland, New South Wales and Singapore as well as English counties like West Sussex and Shropshire (e.g. Cuttance, p. 1995). This is part of the process of developing a common language about performance. It is also critical to ensuring that no part of a school or individual teacher is able to hide relatively poor performance. Where there is under performance, on the whole successful schools bring it into the open and debate it. However, openness does not apply solely to performance data. It also applies to discussions about teaching approaches and philosophies and about the budget. Roland Barth (1990), for example, in 'Improving Schools from Within', suggests that encouraging discussion in staff rooms about approaches to teaching is an important feature of a successful school and of a learning staff. The same applies in general to the whole process of evaluating a school's performance. Essentially the staff should both formally and informally be constantly engaged in researching and reflecting upon their own practice across all aspects of the school. This is more a matter of culture among the staff than of time or resources. In short, improving schools appear to engage in what might be described as restless self-evaluation and use the available evidence to underpin the process.

Fifthly, and following directly from the previous point, a successful urban school requires a learning staff (Stoll & Fink, 1996). This is partly a matter of having a carefully planned professional development strategy which is related both to the school development plan and to the schools' teacher appraisal scheme. It is partly too a matter of ensuring that staff have opportunities to take part in courses and conferences away from the school, and in some cases, in higher degree courses. However, it is also very much a matter of encouraging staff to learn from every day events and from policy initiatives. For example, one of the great benefits of the national scheme of teacher appraisal, introduced in 1989, has been to encourage much more widespread classroom observation. Again and again in a recent evaluation of teacher appraisal (Barber, Evans, & Johnson, 1995) teachers refer to the value they gained from being appraisers which provided them with the opportunity to watch other colleagues teach. Often the learning experience of being the appraiser has been as valuable as being appraised, if not more so.

Finally, it is demonstrably good practice for a school to consider all its staff, not just its teachers, as members of the learning community. For many years teaching support staff were neglected in professional development terms as indeed in many other ways. There is now a growing body of evidence of good practice in the involvement of teaching support staff in all aspects of the management of a school including planning processes, professional development and decision making. The best example identified in a study of urban education initiatives, undertaken at Keele University, was in Nottingham where the nine primary schools were making highly effective use of teaching support staff, not only in administrative and support functions but also in the teaching and learning process (Barber & Dann, 1996). The teachers in these schools did not feel threatened by support staff in a classroom. On the contrary they recognised that having additional support in the classroom enabled them to play their role as teacher and professional leader much more effectively. This is not a minor issue. The number of teaching support staff in schools in the UK is growing rapidly. According to the 1995 School Teachers' Review Body Report 'there was an increase of nearly 40,000 in the number of non-teaching staff employed in schools' between 1991 and 1994 (STRB, 1995).

In some cases, external assistance or significant changes in personnel are necessary to enable these improvement processes to begin. The following interventions or strategies developed after external evaluation are currently high on the British agenda. The introduction of national inspection in 1992 and new powers for government to take over schools found by inspectors to be failing in 1993 has led to a focus on strategies for improving ineffective schools. A range of strategies have been developed for doing so, including the following:

*i)  Changing the Head*

Where the leadership has been poor this can make all the difference. Teachers who have been performing poorly or moderately can, given the right management context, become effective teachers. The new headteacher or principal in these circumstances needs to establish clear goals, focus on a few central priorities to bring about some visible progress within a short time and recognise that significant change may take some time. There is a leadership skill, barely recognised in the management literature, which might be described as keeping faith. This is needed most starkly in the months and sometimes year or so after improvement processes have been established but before they bear fruit.

*ii)   Changes in the Staff*

These are sometimes necessary but can prove very difficult to achieve through standard procedures which normally result from lengthy negotiations between management and unions and in the name of fairness or protection of the rights of staff often include several steps or stages each of which can take many weeks or even months. Some heads who have successfully turned round schools talk of the 'unofficial' means they used to drive out inadequate teachers, a process which is inevitable if official procedures are too cumbersome. There has been a fierce and high profile debate in England and Wales in 1995 and 1996 about whether school inspectors should have the power to trigger competence procedures, where they observe poor teaching.

*iii)   Providing External Consultancy*

A school that is failing may well be incapable of designing its own improvement strategy. An external consultant, from an LEA or elsewhere, can make an important contribution. The 'critical friend', beloved in education jargon, can be effective in already successful schools too. The focus, however, needs to be on creating the capacity for sustainable improvement rather than on creating dependency. In other words consultants do not improve schools; they help to create the conditions in which schools can improve themselves.

*iv)   Changing the Culture*

Removal of staff is only an issue affecting small numbers and in some cases no staff at all in a given school. In any case, a school leader who believes change is simply a matter of removing staff whose competence or compliance is question-able is deluding him or herself. It is as important to change the culture and create:

- a sense of purpose and direction
- high expectations of staff and pupils
- a climate of self evaluation
- a focus on teaching and learning
- a belief in the possibility of success

This is easier to say than do, but undoubtedly involves attention to small but symbolic details as well as larger structural issues. Much of the literature on educational change including Fullan (1991) and Stoll and Fink (1996) gives care-ful attention to this aspect of change.

*v)    Learning Networks*

Some schools have found that their improvement is enhanced if they link up with other schools either via a local authority or school district or via a university. Being part of a network encourages risk taking and enables schools to share ideas and expertise. It also encourages the development of a shared language of school improvement, referred to earlier. There are many examples of such networks. The school of education at the University of Toronto is at the heart of a "Learning Consortium" including some local school districts and many local schools. In the UK, the Two Towns project in Staffordshire involving Keele University and the IQEA project based at the Cambridge Institute of Education are examples.

*vi)    Investment in Teacher Development*

A school's policy for professional development needs to make effective use of limited resources, and to be seen to be fair. Similarly, local and national systems need to invest in teacher development. The idea of a learning profession and, at school level, a learning staff among whom professional development and reflection are a constant feature of practice is a powerful but as yet underdeveloped notion. In an era of change unless all staff are learning there is considerable risk that an organisation will stagnate or slide. The problem for publicly funded schools in the Western world is that this growth on the demand for teachers to learn has occurred at a time of public expenditure constraint. The temptation for school authorities is to spend what money there is on "visibles" such as equipment and reduce expenditure on "invisibles" such as staff development. This is one reason why so many educational reforms have not resulted in real classroom change.

There is a growing body of literature on ineffectiveness in this country as a result of these policy developments (Barber, 1995; Stoll, & Myers, 1997). However, improving just under 300 failing schools (as of January, 1997) does not solve the broader challenge of raising standards across urban areas. While the broad thrust of government policy is to make schools responsibile for their own improvement, there is some acknowledgement from national policymakers that schools in disadvantaged areas may find the challenge overwhelming unless they receive consistent and steady support at local level. For this reason, in 1994 Keele University was commissioned by OFSTED, the inspection agency in England, to study the characteristics of successful urban education initiatives involving more than one school. The results of that study, have a direct bearing on the argument here. The analysis suggested that in inner city areas, schools involved in collaborative projects or learning networks have a greater opportunity to improve. It also revealed that in over sixty of England's urban areas there were significant projects designed to assist in the improvement of urban schooling. Some of them involved substantial commitments of time, money and energy. The vast majority of them were initiated by local education authorities, many involved not only the school authorities but also universities and local employers and had sought additional funding, perhaps from charitable sources to act as a catalyst for change. We arrived at what we described as sixteen propositions which indicated what kind of practice was likely to be successful in these circumstances. These are summarised below.

*Proposition 1*: There is a great deal of concern at the local level about urban education and this has generated a wide variety of initiatives designed to address urban education problems.

*Proposition 2*: Loose collaboration rather than formal structures provided the pattern for the organisation of urban-education initiatives, but LEAs will remain the most important players in the game.

*Proposition 3*: Management of structures need to reflect the loose nature of collaboration and to place initiative firmly with the schools involved.

*Proposition 4*: The scope and range of projects does not coincide with the extent of urban educational need: rather it reflects initiative in the LEAs, HEIs and/or TECs in a given area

*Proposition 5*: There is a lack of clarity in some projects about success criteria.

*Proposition 6*: Clear measurable targets for the progress of urban-education initiatives are essential.

*Proposition 7*: Significant amounts of money are, in some cases, being spent relatively ineffectively.

*Proposition 8*: Small amounts of additional funding, spent well, can make a huge difference.

*Proposition 9*: External attention and recognition can help inspire a school.

*Proposition 10*: Participation in an initiative is not an alternative to getting the in-school factors right.

*Proposition 11*: For the monitoring and evaluation of an initiative to be effective it needs to take into account schools not involved.

*Proposition 12*: Co-operating agencies as well as schools can benefit from urban school-improvement initiatives.

*Proposition 13*: The emphasis of urban-educational improvement is on secondary schools in spite of the fact that there is more potential gain to be made in primary education.

*Proposition 14*:   Planning the end of an initiative needs to come at the beginning.

*Proposition 15*:   Some university departments of education are in a position to make a major contribution to improving education in urban areas.

*Proposition 16*:   Educational consultants are making a contribution to urban educational improvement, which is under-estimated by this survey.

(Barber & Dann 1996)


## THE POLICY FRAMEWORK

In England and Wales Education Acts have followed each other with such bewilderingly rapidity over the years since 1988 that it is sometimes difficult to pick out the underlying principles from the mass of detail. Many other education systems suffer from the same sense of not knowing which way to turn. School reform has, at times, been characterised, not just in the UK, by a sense of crisis and a series of politicians who are more concerned to be seen to be doing something than they are about precisely what they do. Certainly in the UK many of the features of what Kerchner and Mitchell (1988) call intergenerational conflict have been apparent in the early 1990s. In spite of this whirlwind of activity and the fact that there are many ways in which the present policy framework is in need of amendment, the reforms in England and Wales have pointed the way to some important principles. The following paragraphs are an attempt first to identify these emerging principles and then to show how they might be refined in order to have their full potential impact. I am conscious, at this point in the argument, of moving from summarising what is essentially a set of research findings to examining a set of principles for which the evidence is as yet insufficient and which are the subject or significant controversy. Though I intend to write about these principles in robust and confident style (partly in order to provoke controversy), I recognise that they are open to question and indeed will admit to sensing more doubt myself than might be apparent from the written style.

The first principle that emerges, as the mists clear, is that *school improvement is a task for the schools*. This apparently simple statement – though on one level what Tom Peters would call "a blinding flash of the obvious" – is far from being universally accepted. Nor has it been the basic premise of education policy in the United Kingdom for most of the 20th century. Following the delegation of both resources and accountability to school level in the reforms of the late 1980s and early 1990s, it has become the central premise of the policy of both government and Opposition. The same shift has occurred to a greater or lesser extent in other parts of the world with New Zealand leading the way (Whitty, 1996).

Perhaps not surprising, the teaching profession has been more anxious about schools becoming the point of accountability than about taking responsibility for their budgets. In England and Wales the published tables of schools' performance have been the subject of continuing controversy and regular independent inspection has hardly been welcomed. Nevertheless, above all in a democracy, it seems difficult to construct an argument against those with responsibility for a public service being held to account for their use of public money and their contribution to the public good. It seems improbable that any imaginable government in the rest of this decade, and probably beyond, would undo this shift towards both greater autonomy and accountability at school level. Furthermore, over time, the evidence suggests that schools are increasingly taking a balanced view of these changes. There is recognition among head teachers that the pressure of these accountability measures does spur them to improvement. For example, while there has been great anxiety generated by the public focus on a small number of seriously failing schools, recent research suggests that in most schools preparation for inspection has led to improvement and that following inspection there is a concerted effort to address any problems the inspectors have identified.

Thus in a fundamental way, the British government has been right about this issue. The problem is that crucial details of its approach to both autonomy and accountability were flawed. Thus, for example, its political obsession with the notion of grant-maintained schools – which have opted out of the local authority – has led it to distribute funds inequitably. The result has been, at times, to discredit an otherwise unimpeachable principle.

The second principle, that follows from the first, is that *the task of those outside of schools is to create a framework which increases the chances of success in schools and reduces the chances of failure.* Michael Fullan (1991) has argued that successful implementation of any given policy requires those implementing it to be simultaneously provided with support and put under pressure. This pressure-support paradox, which has been increasingly recognised as a crucial consideration in the UK, is a profound insight into successful public policy. Among other things, it can provide politicians and officials with an effective and relatively simple means of evaluating the likely impact of a package of measures. Since the war the United Kingdom has rarely achieved the right balance of pressure and support in its education policy. One might generalise ruthlessly and argue that successive governments provided thirty years of support without pressure and then (since the mid 1980s) ten years of pressure without support. The job for government in the late 1990s and beyond is surely to provide both (Barber, 1995).

There are various ways in which effective pressure might be applied. One is the establishment of targets. In addition to the National Targets for Education and Training which have been established in this country along lines similar to those in the United States, it is essential that all schools benefit from targets for improvement against their previous performance. These can be established at the level of both the school and the locality. Certainly target-setting has been a vital feature of Tim Brighouse's strategy for raising standards in Birmingham (Brighouse, 1996) and, according to the recent report from the DFEE quoted earlier, of schools in many other parts of the country. Politicians of all the major parties are in 1996 working hard to promote a target-setting culture in education.

The second means of applying pressure is to establish the case for the publication of performance data. The debate has so far been an unsatisfactory one with the government arguing in favour of publishing solely raw results and the teaching profession, generally-speaking, arguing against publication of anything at all. It ought to be possible to move towards a model which does more to recognise prior attainment so that the indicators show not just absolute performance but also value-added. It would also be much more satisfactory to move towards the notion of three or four indicators, which taken together, summarise the performance of the school. One recent report in the UK suggested that in addition to raw results, a value added indicator and a school improvement index should be published (SCAA 1994). These three statistics taken together would probably give a broadly accurate picture of whether or not a school was performing successfully. That combination of indicators would also ensure that any school, even one with an advantaged intake, which is failing, or relatively speaking under-performing, would be unable to hide behind the misleading statistics that are currently published.

The third element of pressure on schools ought to be independent inspections. It is entirely reasonable in a democracy for public services to be subjected to periodic inspection. The inspection system in England and Wales could be enhanced if it gave greater emphasis to school self-evaluation and provide a greater support for improvement in the post-inspection period. In particular, the inspection system ought to be more subtle in its distribution of time and resources and to concentrate any post-inspection improvement resources on the schools which have been found, either through the published performance indicators or through inspection, to be relatively under-performing. Plans published in 1996 for the future of inspection in England and Wales show awareness of this kind of thinking (OFSTED 1996). Finally, in terms of pressure, there needs to be a much clearer national policy for ensuring effective intervention in schools which are found to be failing. This aspect of pressure is examined in greater depth later in the chapter.

Support, the essential corollary of pressure, should come from a range of factors too. Firstly, there should be a commitment to resourcing education consistently over several years. Authorities ought to consider, at the very least, the introduction of three year funding horizons. At present in the UK the inadequate system of staggering from one year to the next, without any clarity about medium term funding support, is disruptive of school improvement efforts. This was a point made vigorously by the national inspection agency, OFSTED, in its report on 'Access and Achievement in Urban Education' where it argued that 'Resources need to be allocated on a more consistent and long term basis and bear a closer relationship to educational need' (OFSTED 1993).

Secondly, there needs to be much greater investment in teachers' professional development, particularly in urban areas. This is partly because the pace of technological and social change and the increased expectations of education mean that ever more is demanded from teachers. Teachers too often become ground down by the multiple pressures of their work. For this reason investment in their continuing development and maintaining their freshness ought to be a priority.

Mechanisms for funding for professional development will vary from one country to another. Whatever the mechanism, investment is needed at three levels: in the development of the teaching profession as a whole, in institutional change and in individual teacher development.

Thirdly, there ought to be much greater investment in local and school level innovation through provision of funds ear-marked for this purpose. In the UK almost all innovation-funding is targeted on the implementation of national priorities. The Lucretia Crocker Fellowships, for which individuals or team teachers could apply, adopted in the 1980s in Massachusetts were a small but significant means of supporting and disseminating teacher-led innovation.

Fourthly, it is becoming increasingly clear, in the UK at any rate, that teachers' workload – reckoned to be an average over 50 hours per week for primary teachers and much higher for headteachers – is in part made up of work which could be done more cheaply and efficiently by either administrators or assistants. If their numbers were expanded it might reduce "burn out" among teachers and enable them to give higher priority to their own learning needs and to pedagogy.

It is also essential for government to invest in the provision of a range of extra curricular activities, homework clubs, and other after school options which would provide for young people attractive and motivating alternatives to the dubious attractions of the street. These activities both support schools and reduce to some extent the impact of undesirable social trends among young people. Where schools have provided an array of after school activities, as in parts of Stoke-on-Trent and in Hammersmith and Fulham for example, they have been successful both in attracting significant numbers of pupils and in raising standards of achievement (Barber & Dann 1996; Myers 1996). Indeed the evidence suggests that by encouraging significant numbers of young people to volunteer to achieve more, such activities have a positive effect on the formal curriculum through contributing to improved peer group attitudes.

Tim Brighouse has begun to explore, in Birmingham, how a wide range of activities after school and in school holidays might be given priority, coherence and structure through coming under what he has described as University of the First Age, aimed at pupils in early teenage (Birmingham LEA, 1996). This would be a means of both enabling enthusiastic teachers to provide activities in their chosen areas of expertise – from chess to soccer, from design to Latin – for pupils interested in pursuing them, and a system of accrediting those activities so that they could be recognised by employers and higher education institutions.

If this balance of pressure and support were established, it is possible to imagine that many more schools than at present would succeed. In general the aim should surely be to encourage schools to achieve conditions for sustainable improvement. From this one can deduce a third policy principle, namely that *external intervention should be in inverse proportion to success*. This of course requires that there is generally accepted definition of success and that means of evaluating school performance have been established. Once this is the case intervention would come when there was clear evidence of school failure or at those moments when the risk of failure is known to be higher, such as at the moment when the headship passes from one head to another or when, for whatever reason, there is excessively high staff turnover.

In the case of the government of England and Wales, there has been a shift between 1994 and 1996 towards the adoption, consciously or otherwise, of this policy principle. In the years immediately following the implementation of the market reforms of the late 1980s, the government's view appeared to be that the market would take care of success or failure. It appeared to believe that if a school was failing it would lose customers and eventually go out of business. In other words the assumption was that the education market would operate like the business market. For a number of reasons this analysis was flawed. Unlike business there is not always an alternative product – another nearby school – which can replace the inadequate one. In any case, the evidence repeatedly shows that most parents support and believe in the school their child attends even when objectively it is shown to be under-performing (Barber, 1994). And, of course, children caught up in a school which has spiralled into decline are, in effect, denied their entitlement.

In 1993 the government legislated to give itself the power to intervene directly and take over the management of a failing school if the local authority in which it is situated has not either improved it or decided to close it. Following the 1993 legislation a new section of the Department for Education, the School Effectiveness Division, was established to oversee policy in relation to all schools which inspectors have found to be under-performing. Since then its main goal has been to ensure that the local authority responsible for any failing school takes appropriate action. In some cases it has found it necessary to exert pressure on local authorities. In one case, the case of Hackney Downs School, government took the view that the school was so poor and its relations with the local authority so poisoned, that there was no alternative but to use central government's powers of intervention. The minister appointed a team which, after several weeks of investigation, recommended closure and found places for the pupils at other more effective schools nearby (NELEA, 1995).

Direct intervention is a high risk strategy for central government and is likely to be used only sparingly. The threat of such intervention is, however, a powerful lever over local authorities. An OECD seminar on "Combatting Failure at School" held in November 1995 in London found that the British government's position was unusual (Stoll & Myers 1996, forthcoming). Only New Zealand and some parts of the United States have remotely similar arrangements. Nevertheless, the principle of intervention in inverse proportion to success which is beginning to emerge in the UK may provide a starting point for policy-thinking elsewhere.

THE IMPLICATIONS FOR POLICY

If these are the policy principles, what do they mean for national government and local government? The final section of this chapter looks at each of these levels of the education service in turn. Much of the argument that follows is based on the way in which power is distributed in the British system. However, it should be clear how the various proposals could be used at different but appropriate levels within, for example, a federal system such as that in Australia or Canada.

## The Role of Government

The role of national government is relatively straightforward to establish, though much harder to execute, given the discussion above. First, of course, it has responsibility for establishing the policy framework. This does not mean only the laws and regulations governing education but also the climate in which policy development takes place. This includes the establishment of effective working relationships with the teaching profession, local education authorities and other "producers" of education as well as, of course, consumers. In some countries, this is a matter for state level rather than Federal level decision. However, government at all levels in all countries significantly influences cultural attitudes to education. Secondly, national government clearly has the prime responsibility for setting out the resource framework. In England and Wales, this is not simply a matter for Department for Education and Employment; it also requires the Department of the Environment which shapes local government expenditure and, ultimately, the Treasury which establishes the overall framework for government expenditure, to consider carefully the impact of their decisions on education as the school governors' and parents' revolt over education spending in 1995 demonstrates.

National government in England and Wales also has responsibility for the National Curriculum and the national framework for assessment and examinations. Now that the government – finally – has established a workable National Curriculum, the main task for it and its successors over the next five years is to keep it under review and prepare for a thorough overhaul of it in the year 2000. There is no doubt that as and when various crises arise in the next few years, there will be repeated demands for the revision of one or other part of the National Curriculum. National government must resist the temptation to tamper with the curriculum until the five years of promised stability are over, otherwise the National Curriculum as a whole will be brought into disrepute. There were times between 1990 and 1993 when it seemed that ministers would alter the curriculum on a whim. As a result, teachers ceased to take is seriously, expecting that it would be likely to change at any moment. Fortunately, since 1994, politicians have resisted this temptation.

National governments normally also have control or influence over national assessment and the qualifications framework. This is of central importance, since through national assessment schools across the country can gain a common language of standards and achievement and compare their performance to that of others. It is also important because it provides what might be called the currency of exchange between the education system, employers and the public. The growing concern across society for higher standards of performance has led to a growing emphasis on outcomes. It is through the qualifications framework that this information is conveyed publicly. At the same time, qualifications must motivate learners and enable teachers and schools to do their job.

With the National Curriculum, and potentially national assessment, in place, it becomes another crucial function of government to establish a national set of performance indicators. So far the government in England and Wales – but not Scotland – has insisted on the publication of raw examination data school by school but it has encouraged, too, the development of value-added and improvement indicators. Since the Labour Party has also advocated the publication of raw results, improvement indices and value added data, it is likely that incremental development in this area will continue through the 1990s. At present, the system of performance indicators is still establishing its credibility, and their promotion and explanation will require more work. Performance indicators can only play a significant role in the national policy framework if they have widespread credibility.

Performance indicators make up only one of a number of strands of the quality assurance system in the UK. The national inspection system, under which every school is due to be inspected once every four years is of perhaps even greater importance. The government is currently considering how to refine the system once every school has been inspected for the first time. Applying the policy principle outlined above (that external intervention should be in inverse proportion to success) it seems likely that in future OFSTED inspection will vary in its intensity according to what the performance indicators and other evidence suggested about a school's success. Where there were significant concerns a more thorough inspection would be required with the possibility of clear follow-up action. More successful schools, on the other hand, would undertake a self-review which could validated by an external consultant. This would combine the best principles of the English and Welsh inspection systems which emphasise accountability and the Scottish or New South Wales models which emphasise self-evaluation.

Creating the structure is not enough. Central government also needs to provide consistent leadership. That requires leading politicians, especially the Prime Minister, to urge consistently higher standards and to draw the public's attention both to the pressure the government is applying and the support it is providing. It is interesting to note that it is not uncommon for political leaders in the western world (including George Bush, John Major and Bill Clinton) to begin their terms of office by emphasising the importance of education and then to lose interest in it rapidly when they discovered how difficult it can be to bring about change in the sector. That kind of fleeting leadership will be inadequate in the decade ahead. The creation of a learning society requires, in short, a learning government.

As part of its leadership role a government might consider setting demanding targets for the education service. Both the British and American governments have invested substantial political capital in education and training targets or "goals." However, unless these are translated by local government or schools into targets for improvement, they are unlikely to change attitudes and motivate those who spend their daily lives working in education. Where it does happen, as in Birmingham or Lewisham in the UK, it can help to bring real change.

A government also has an obligation (which over recent years it has failed to carry out in England and Wales, although it had done better in Scotland) to promote research and development in education. The Department for Education and Employment has a limited budget for research and little sense of strategy. It compares very unfavourably with the Department of Health and is blatantly inadequate in the context of the many challenges facing the education service. In particular, for example, there has been far too little national investment in research into the relationship between communications technology, pedagogy and educational achievement. This area is rich with possibilities but remains, sadly for the moment, largely undiscovered territory, though a review of this area of the DFEE's work appears to be in progress during 1996.

Finally, national government needs to build a creative functioning partnership with local government. In a federal system, federal, state and local government need to co-operate. One of the powerful lessons of the Asian education success stories is the sense of unity and purpose in relation to education. There is some evidence that in 1994 and 1995 the British government began to recognise the need to rebuild its relations with local government after a decade of conflict during which the relationship reached a low ebb at a great cost to young people and teachers across the country. Now that central government has become increasingly pragmatic, local government has been slow to respond, not least because the bruises of the previous decade are still very much in evidence. It seems improbable that the huge leap in standards required in the UK can be brought about while different tiers of government are at war or working under the terms of an armed and uneasy truce. This is a major concern and depends on both national and local government focusing not on short term self-interest but on long-term educational standards. This is, incidentally, a separate issue from party political control. It has been possible in the past for effective collaboration to transcend party politics in relation to education. Given the growing cross-party consensus about the need to raise standards and the means of doing so – features which are in evidence in north America, Europe and Australasia – there is a firm foundation for effective co-operation in the future.


THE ROLE OF LOCAL GOVERNMENT

Education reform in the late 1980s and 1990s was so much driven from the centre, there were times when it seemed that local government would become irrelevant. Partly this was a result of central government's hostility, partly it was a result of legislative change and partly it was a result of some local education authorities becoming so demoralised that they began to write themselves out of the script. However during 1994 – when central government had clearly both over-reached itself and lost its way – there was a positive revival of morale and activity at local education authority level. Local authorities such as Birmingham, Nottinghamshire, Lewisham and Essex began to create a new role for themselves in spite of the deprivations of the early part of the decade. What is more this role is turning out in many ways to be more creative and constructive than the old management and administration functions that LEAs have been forced to surrender. In systems where a constitution guarantees the existence of local government in a way which it does not in Britain, this role is just as important.

Crucial to the role of a successful local education authority in the late 1990s will be offering community leadership and providing a sense of direction for a three to five year period. School districts in the United States could do the equivalent task. It is interesting that recently a spate of LEAs have taken to writing strategic plans which cover the five years into the start of the century. This suggests a growth in confidence and a renewed determination to provide the local leadership that is so essential to transforming attitudes and promoting successful education, particularly in urban areas. The evidence suggests that in establishing collaborative school improvement initiatives in urban areas, the LEA has played the leading role in bringing together the other partners such as business, community organisations, local higher education institutions, FE colleges and other organisations in support of school improvement (Barber & Dann, 1996). Though it is possible to imagine urban education initiatives without LEAs, it seems from the evidence that there would be far fewer of them and that they would be significantly less likely to succeed. Even the successful higher education urban education networks such as the one at the Institute of Education in London are often stronger as a result of working with and through LEAs. It is worth pointing out that this function of LEAs is of immense significance although it is not written down in law. There are similar collaborative ventures in many countries such as that at Halton in Canada which has made a significant contribution to improving education performance. The impact of an arm of government is often less a function of its legal powers that of its sense of direction, vision and skill in building partnerships.

The same applies to the next important function. LEAs are well placed to provide schools with extensive performance data relating, for example, to examination results, test results and financial and management information, though they are not required to do so. Comparative data which enable schools to examine their own success and approaches in comparison with those of other schools in the same geographical areas or to those with similar intakes cannot, by definition, be provided by a school alone. It is almost unthinkable that any school on its own could find the time to gather sufficient data from other schools in order to provide itself with comparative data even if it had the expertise. For an LEA on the other hand this is a relatively straightforward matter. Many LEAs are already performing this role excellently. Nottinghamshire, Surrey and Shropshire for example provide excellent data to all their schools. In urban areas LEAs such as Islington are doing a similarly effective job.

Information is only one aspect of the support that LEAs can provide. Many LEAs now offer schools a range of training, consultancy and advice which schools are able to buy into as and when they believe they need it. This too can be helpful and the delegation of the funding of it to schools has, as many people in LEAs will admit, often improved the quality and responsiveness of the services that LEAs provide. By contrast, where local government is unresponsive and heavily bureaucratic, it is less able to promote successful school level change as many American school districts have found. Cincinnati School District, for example, made more progress with reform after it had stripped out half the posts in the central bureaucracy – under pressure from the local teacher union – than it had done before (Kerchner & Koppich, 1993).

In addition some LEAs have been able, even in times of financial stringency, to find small but significant sums of money at the margin of the projects in order to fund local level innovation. Lewisham, for example, has funded a highly successful school improvement initiative for its secondary schools as has Hammersmith and Fulham (Myers, 1996). Essex has provided £300,000 to assist the deprived urban area of Tilbury in recovering from devastating and historic underachievement and low expectations (Barber & Dann, 1996). Since any successful organisation depends, as the management textbooks constantly remind us, on innovation coming from all levels, it is essential that innovation is promoted at school and local as well as national level. It is obviously beneficial if schools take the initiative in the promotion of innovation, it is a substantial risk for any single school to invest a substantial amount in any given innovation. For one thing such innovation can draw away precious resources from core activity and for another innovation is often treated with caution and suspicion by parents. Keele's data on parents' attitudes to schools suggests that while about 60 percent of parents would like, in general, to see some changes in the school that their child attends, it is virtually impossible to put together a majority of parents in favour of any particular strategy. Few proposals for change win the approval of more than a third of the parents and most have significantly less. LEAs, on the other hand, can find the money and help a group of schools build the confidence to take the risks which are a necessary part of successful change.

Another critical role for local education authorities, particularly relevant in urban areas, is to intervene in cases where there is a risk of school failure. This role parallels the role ascribed by Charles Handy to central office of business organisations, a role he calls "the right to invasion" (Handy, 1994). Central government in this country has, with some justification, often pointed out that LEAs are hardly in a position to claim the role of intervening in failing schools since there are too many cases of failing schools which have been consistently neglected over a long period. However, in a climate of partnership in which day to day management is delegated to schools, it seems sensible that the responsibility for intervention is placed, at least in the first instance, with LEAs. Ideally, a local government intervention should come before a school slides into serious failure. This requires it to have sensitive processes for identifying changes in school performance. If it leaves intervention later, it is likely to be much more difficult and much more expensive. While this should be a primary responsibility for LEAs, central government in England and Wales retains the right to intervene ultimately if an LEA has not succeeded in tackling a failing school. The justification for this in principle is that where a school failure is being tolerated, the rights of pupils are being infringed. There is no doubt that the government's intervention in closing Hackney Downs School not only benefitted the pupils who had been betrayed there, but also encouraged LEAs across the country to examine whether they were taking sufficiently seriously their own under-performing schools.

There are many other functions of local government in relation, for example, to special education. This section has concentrated on those activities which can do most to help schools improve themselves. If local government takes on the role described in this section, it could become the driving force at local level of a nationwide crusade to raise standards.

## REFERENCES

Barber, M. (1994). *Parents and their attitudes to school,* Keele University, Keele.
Barber, M. (1995). *The dark side of the moon: Imagining and end to failure in urban education,* TES/ Greenwich lecture.
Barber, M., & Dann, R. (1996). *Raising educational standards in the inner cities: practical initiatives in action,* London: Cassell.
Barber, M., Evans, A., & Johnson, M. (1995). *An evaluation of the national scheme of teacher appraisal,.* London: DFEE.
Barth, R. (1990). *Improving schools from within.* San Francisco and Oxford: Jossey-Bass,.
Birmingham LEA. (1996). *The university of the first age,* Birmingham: Birmingham LEA.
Brighouse, T. (1991). *What makes a good school?* Stafford: Network Education Press.
Brighouse, T. (1996). Urban deserts or fine cities? In M. Barber & R. Dann (Eds.), *What makes a good school?* Stafford: Network Education Press.
Cuttance, P. (1995). Building high performance school systems in *School Effectiveness and Improvement*
Dearing, R. (1996). *Review of qualifications for 16–19 year olds: Summary report.* London: HMSO.
DFEE. (1996). *Setting targets to raise standards: A survey of good practice.* London: DFEE.
Evans, A. (1994). *Industrial change in Europe.* Eurotecnet Synthesis Report. London: HMSO.
Fullan, M. (1991). *The new meaning of educational change.* London: Cassell.
Handy, C. (1994). *The empty raincoat: Making sense of the future.* London: Arrow Books.
Hopkins, D. (1994). *Towards a theory for school improvement.* Sheffield: ESRC Seminar.
Kerchner, C., & Mitchell, D. (1988). *The changing idea of a teacher's union.* Lewes: Falmer Press.
Kerchner, C., & Koppich, J. (1993). *A union of professionals: Labour relations and educational reform.* New York: Teachers College Press.
Myers, K. (1995). *Intensive care for the chronically sick.* Paper for the European Conference on Educational Research, Bath.
Myers, K. (1996). *School improvement in practice: The schools make a difference project.* London: Falmer.
North East London Education Association. (1995). *The future of hackney downs school.* London: DFEE.
OFSTED. (1993). *Access and achievement in urban education.* London: HMSO.
OFSTED. (1995). *Annual report of her majesty's chief inspector.* London: HMSO.
OFSTED. (1996). *Consultation on arrangements for the inspection of maintained schools from September 1997.* London: HMSO.
OFSTED. (1996). *The teaching of reading in 45 inner London primary schools.* London: HMSO.
Sammons, P., Thomas, S., & Mortimore, P. (1995). *Accounting for variations in academic effectiveness between schools and department: Results from the differential school effectiveness project.* Paper for European Conference on Educational Research, Bath, England.

School Curriculum and Assessment Authority. (1994). *Value-added performance indicators for schools.* London: SCAA.

School Teachers' Review Body. (1995). *Fourth report.* London: HMSO.

Stoll, L. (1995). *The complexity and challenge of ineffective schools.* Paper for the European Conference on Educational Research, Bath, England.

Stoll, L., & Fink, D. (1996). *Changing our schools.* Buckingham and Philadelphia: Open University Press,.

Stoll, L., & Myers, K. (1997). *No quick fixes.* Buckingham: Open University Press.

Whitty, G. (1996). *Creating quasi-markets in education: A review of recent research on parental choice and school autonomy in three countries.* unpublished paper.

# Quality in Schools: Developing a Model for School Improvement

MEL WEST

*Institute of Education, University of Cambridge*

*This chapter examines the Improving the Quality of Education for All (IQEA) model used in England to help schools develop the internal capacity to engage in continuous development. It identifies the key dimensions of external support required for school development. The outcomes arising from IQEA are considered in relation to the model and its underlying strategies.*

## INTRODUCTION

It is now seven years since the Improving the Quality of Education for All (IQEA) Project was initiated at the University of Cambridge Institute of Education, in collaboration with schools and local educational authorities in London and East Anglia. Since then it has spread into the North of England, and more recently to Iceland and to Puerto Rico, where local projects have been established. This chapter will not attempt to catalogue the Project's development. It does not represent the 'case-history' – which can be found elsewhere (See Hopkins, Ainscow & West, 1994) – nor does it observe the chronology of the development of the various aspects. Rather it seeks to explain the ideas which underpin the Project, and to outline the main components of the improvement model.

The chapter presents these ideas in five main sections. First, the chapter deals with the construct of a successful school, since the way we define 'success' has a profound influence on both the scope and the style of school improvement efforts. Second, it explores the notion of "capacity" for improvement, because our experience tells us that unless a school is working to make changes to its current arrangements at both school and classroom levels progress is difficult to achieve and harder to sustain. Third, it considers the IQEA improvement model as a strategic approach to internal development which acknowledges the reality of external demands. Fourth, it (briefly) describes the ways we have encouraged project schools to 'organise' themselves for sustained improvement effort and what we have seen as the key dimensions of external support. Finally, it offers some reflections on the various outcomes we see emerging from the project.

However, it may be helpful if some clues to the thinking which lay behind the Project are given at the outset, as inevitably my colleagues and I came to this journey feeling that we had learned something from our previous travels. Thus,

*M. Fullan (ed.), Fundamental Change, 98-119.*
© 2005 *Springer. Printed in the Netherlands.*

for example, we brought to the Project the shared belief that school improvement is for all schools and all students. We do not believe that any school can feel entirely satisfied with its current provision – even the most successful of our schools could, indeed must, continually seek out ways to improve the quality of outcomes and of experience for its students. Consequently, we share a parallel belief that within the school we must be aware of these outcomes and experiences in each individual case – what happens to or for the 'average' student may conceal as much as it reveals about the quality of schooling.

We also believe that the impetus, the effort, the creativity needed to improve schools must come largely from within. In this, we find ourselves in agreement with Roland Barth, who has argued that school improvement is most likely to succeed when it is based on the skills, aspirations and energies of those closest to the school. Contrasting the potency of internally generated improvement activity with the sterility of many of the externally driven reforms, he suggests that:

> Schools have the capacity to improve themselves, if the conditions are right. A major responsibility of those outside the school is to help provide the conditions for those inside.(Barth, 1990)

This acknowledgment of the general competence and potential to be found in schools chimes with our own various experiences; but it is necessary to develop both management and classroom arrangements to create 'capacity'.

This approach also sits well with the de-centralization of school systems which has spread through many countries and is well established in the United Kingdom. In such de-centralized systems the response to national policies is determined at the school level, but most often the number of policies requiring a response is greatly increased. Therefore, the issue is not so much whether a school is able to assimilate a particular change or develop a particular programme or approach – but whether the school can develop itself continually over time to meet the various challenges and opportunities which arise. This means for us that any model for improvement needs to have within it the seeds of regeneration. We felt strongly at the outset of this Project that it should lead to a way of thinking, a set of approaches within project schools which could be used repeatedly, which would enable the schools to become self-renewing communities. This does not mean that we expected them to close their doors to outside influences and support, but that we anticipated a clarity about purposes and organizational arrangements that would help them to exert their own control over development activities in the future.

## A SUCCESSFUL SCHOOL: DEVELOPING THE CONSTRUCT

From the outset we hoped that IQEA Project schools would be encouraged to develop what Peters and Waterman (1982) have referred to as 'a bias for action'. That is, we wanted them to identify development priorities, make development plans and implement these vigorously. We were aware that many school improvement programmes had become little more than 'recipes' for specific, externally controlled developments. Further, too often, what was called school improvement seemed in reality to be an organizational or staff development programme with tenuous connections to classroom practice or student experience. We were also mindful that the recent reforms in the United Kingdom had led to a new emphasis on accountability and on school effectiveness. The 'measurement' of school performance, the ranking of schools according to performance, the debate about what might happen to 'failing' schools, all placed great emphasis on those pupil outcomes that were easily measured.

Like many of our colleagues in the schools, we were uncomfortable with the assumptions underpinning this narrow approach to effectiveness, but we were also aware of the failure of school improvement programmes to penetrate to the point of impact. We felt, therefore, that we needed as a basis for our work with the Project schools to re-conceptualize what was meant by a 'successful' school, to develop a construct or a series of constructs which we could share with teachers from Project schools, which would offer new opportunities for discussions about ends and means, outcomes and processes. Inevitably these are discussions which take us back to the fundamental purposes of education. Without rejecting the emphasis on 'basic' and 'work' skills which have become widespread (and particularly popular with politicians), we felt that a more holistic view of schooling would provide a sounder basis for improvement effort at the school level.

Of course, as we have argued elsewhere (West & Hopkins, 1996) any fruitful reconceptualization is likely to involve a return to the basic goals of those who, in their different ways, have attempted to improve the quality of schooling, and therefore to a reminder of the core purposes of schools themselves. This means critical scrutiny of the 'effectiveness' and 'improvement' traditions. It will not be sufficient to simply 'merge' the two approaches by seeking out those areas on which the two groupings can agree – both because what can be agreed and what is right are not always the same thing, and because there is a need to transcend the vocabularies and question the 'truths' of both paradigms.

In particular, as a pre-requisite for meaningful dialogue, it is necessary to detach the term 'effective school' from the narrow and particular connotations it currently processes. It is time to acknowledge that effective schools are the legitimate goal of all those currently involved in research and development work within the two traditions. But neither an "academically successful school" (a much more accurate description for those schools which top the league tables) – or a "processes approved" school (which seems to be what much of school improvement has been about) is necessarily effective, since to be truly effective a school must satisfy a series of different but equally valid criteria.

Carl Glickman has recently posed similar doubts about the current direction for public schools in the United States:

> What difference does it make if we graduate 100 per cent of students, or if SAT scores rise twenty points, or if our students beat other countries in achievement in science when they have not learned how to identify, analyze and solve the problems that face their immediate and larger communities?

Our country would be better served by schools that produce caring, intelligent and wise citizens who willing engage in the work of a democracy than by schools that produce graduates who do well on isolated subgoals.(Glickman, 1993)

Other North Americans have stressed similar values in their call for a "restructuring" of schools. Elmore (1990), for example, calls for a clearer focus on the way teaching and learning is conceived in schools, on the organization and internal conditions, on the distribution of power within the school system. Lieberman and Miller's (1990) 'five building blocks of restructuring' show the same emphasis, and are explicit in identifying all students as the target of improvement efforts. Fullan (1993) describes how the 'Learning Consortium' in Ontario has sought to establish radical structural/cultural arrangements that support the integration of classroom and school improvement, encourage networking and partnership in learning.

It was a similar sense of frustration with traditional approaches to school effectiveness and a common desire to identify and capture the essence of a 'living' school which led us to propose that IQEA project schools should take a broader and more adventurous view of success. Accordingly, we encouraged the schools to give as much weight to the quality of experience they offer their students, and the access to this experience, as they do to measurable student outcomes. Equally, we placed importance on the notion of partnerships that could support the school and promote learning – particularly partnerships with students, with teachers, with parents, with the school's various communities. Finally, we sought to promote the relationship between developing teachers and developing schools.

Identifying these different dimensions to the construct of a successful school has inevitably been a major influence on the design of the IQEA Project. This influence can be seen clearly in both our desire to establish 'capacity' or 'conditions' for improvement within the school, and in the particular conditions (both management and classroom arrangements) we have focused upon. It can be seen in the strategy we promoted in the project schools, which places emphasis on their own assessment of needs, opportunities and priorities for action. We hope it has also been reflected in our own support activities, where we have tried to act as partners to the schools as they pursue their own priorities, rather than external "experts" who can tell them what these priorities should be.

## GENERATING THE CAPACITY FOR IMPROVEMENT

As pointed out above the notion of 'capacity' for improvement has been important in our work. Specifically, we have identified a number of distinct strands to this capacity. For example, there is the capacity to recognize when external demands for change offer opportunities for internal development. There is the capacity to manage change to and beyond the point of implementation. There is the capacity to develop the culture of the school to support new methods of working, rather than simply reorganizing. There is capacity to scrutinize and develop classroom practice. Each of these strands contribute, and we have tried to address all of them in our work with project schools. However, we have found that the capacity to organize the school effectively (management arrangements) and the capacity to organize the classroom effectively (classroom arrangements) are strands which both require and are amenable to systematic programmes of enquiry and development within each school.

Inevitably, any attempt to define these two sets of arrangements must be to an extent arbitrary, reflecting as it does our own conceptualizations, our own vocabulary. However the very fact that describing the arrangements reveals our own conceptualizations and establishes, with our partner schools in the project, a common vocabulary is important, since it facilitates systematic training (by providing organizing categories) and promotes and enables debate. We do not claim therefore, that the "arrangements" we encourage the project schools to develop constitute a definitive description of either management or classroom practice within improving schools. We do feel, however, that they provide a coherent framework for school and teacher development activities that can foster and then remain anchored to real improvements.

## MANAGEMENT ARRANGEMENTS

The management arrangements are concerned with the way the school is organized to identify needs and to develop, implement and evaluate responses to these needs. They are important individual components of responsive management, but together they build the capacity for improvement by creating a framework for planning and supporting change. These arrangements (see Hopkins & West, 1994) relate to how the school:

- Makes use of school-based data
- Plans for development
- Co-ordinates activities and groups
- Conceptualizes leadership
- Links staff and school development
- Involves key stakeholder groups and communities

A brief description of what we mean by each of these arrangements follows.

### 1. Using Enquiry and Reflection

As I noted earlier, national reforms in the education system of England and Wales have produced unprecedented pressures for change at the level of the school. Changes in curriculum content, processes and assessment have been enshrined in legislation – requiring adoption at a pace which many schools feel is beyond their capacity. In addition to creating a potentially de-skilling context in which individual teachers must work, the logistics of implementing these changes have proved a severe test for even the most confident of management teams. So much so, it may seem strange to be arguing that schools should actively adopt a focus upon school improvement activities at a time when many teachers are finding that all their time and energies are consumed in trying to assimilate into their schools the range of 'unavoidable' changes currently required.

However, we have observed that those schools which recognize that enquiry and reflection are important processes in school improvement find it easier to sustain improvement effort around established priorities, and are better placed to monitor the extent to which policies actually deliver the intended outcomes for pupils, even in these times of enormous change. Ironically, however, we have found that information gathered by outsiders, be they inspectors or consultants, is often seen as having more significance than information which is routinely available to those within the school community. Further, we have observed that where schools understand the potential of internally generated information about progress or difficulties, they are better placed to exploit opportunities and to overcome problems. A major area of focus, therefore, in our work with IQEA Project schools has been to review the current use made of and to consider the opportunities for improved future use of school-based data.

## 2. Collaborative Planning

The quality of school level planning has been identified as a major factor in many studies of school effectiveness. Such studies have also identified the nature and quality of school goals as important, and collaborative planning and clear goals as key process dimensions. Our own experiences also lead us to see links between the way planning is carried forward in the school and the school's capacity to engage in development work. However, we have also noted that there is rather more to successful planning than simply producing a development plan – indeed often the quality of the 'plan' as a written document is a very misleading guide to its influence on the course of events – it is the link between planning and action which in the end justifies the effort we put into planning activities. This practical focus on the impact of planning rather than the technical merits of different planning systems or approaches has led us to stress a number of points when working with IQEA Project Schools on this condition.

The school's improvement plans need to be clearly linked to the school's vision for the future. Indeed, the notion of priorities for planning arise from the vision, and where there is a lack of congruence between the school's long term goals and a particular initiative it is hard to build commitment amongst staff. One way of tying together school and individual goals is through widespread involvement in the planning process. In some ways, involvement in planning activity is more important than producing plans – it is through collective planning that goals emerge, differences can be resolved and a basis for action created. The 'plan' is really a by-product of this activity, and almost always needs to be revised, often several times. The benefits of involvement in planning are, however, more durable.

### 3. Co-ordination Strategy

Schools are sometimes referred to as 'loosely-coupled systems'. This 'loose' coupling occurs because schools consist of units, processes, actions and individuals that tend to operate in isolation from one another. Loose-coupling is also encouraged by the goal ambiguity that characterizes schooling (West & Ainscow, 1991). Despite the rhetoric of curriculum aims and objectives, schools consist of groups of people who may have very different values and, indeed, beliefs about the purposes of schooling. We have therefore identified the school's capacity to co-ordinate the actions of teachers behind agreed policies or goals as an important factor in promoting change.

In our work with the IQEA Project Schools we have pursued a number of strategies which, we have found, improve the quality of co-ordination. At the core of such strategies are communication systems and procedures, and the ways in which groups can be created and sustained to co-ordinate improvement effort across a range or levels of departments. Of particular importance are specific strategies for ensuring that all staff are kept informed about development priorities and activities, as this is information vital to informed self-direction. We have also found that awareness amongst staff of one anothers' responsibilities cannot always be assumed. A further factor is the 'informal' organisation – all schools are made up of a number of informal or self-selected groupings which rarely coincide with formal work units. The attitudes and behavior adopted by these groups often have a profound effect on the individual's willingness to undertake formal tasks. As a consequence, it is important not to overlook the impact of informal organisation on formal structures, and a co-ordination strategy needs to take account of informal contacts which influence (and can often contribute directly to) the quality of effort.

What is needed, therefore, is a well co-ordinated, co-operative style of working that gives individual teachers the confidence to "improvise" in a search for the most appropriate responses to the situations they meet. In other words, we are seeking to create a system coupled by ideas, and shared understandings of purpose, not one conforming to pre-determined behaviors.

### 4. Leadership Practices

There is considerable evidence in the studies of school effectiveness that leadership is a key element in determining school success. Perhaps such studies have over-emphasized 'leadership' at the expense of 'management' – our own experience suggests that these are both important characteristics of the effective school

– but they do underline the cultural significance of this term for teachers. Most recently, studies of leadership in schools have tended to move away from the identification of this function exclusively with the headteacher, and have begun to address how leadership can be made available throughout the management structure and at all levels in the school community. This shift in emphasis has been accompanied by a parallel shift in thinking about leadership itself, with an increasing call for 'transformational' approaches which distribute and empower, rather than 'transactional' approaches which sustain traditional (and broadly bureaucratic) concepts of hierarchy and control (see Hopkins, Ainscow, & West, 1994).

Within the IQEA Project we have deliberately set out to promote discussion about leadership style within participating schools, and to help staff from different levels in the school to share perceptions of how leadership operates. Such discussions have identified a number of key aspects of the leadership role. The first underlines the responsibility of school leaders in establishing a clear 'vision' or set of purposes for the school.

The second relates to the way individual knowledge, skills and experience are harnessed, and the extent to which the school is able to transcend traditional notions of hierarchy or role in bringing together the "best team for the job". A third aspect is the way leadership is used in group or team meetings. Leader behavior is obviously an important determinant of group effectiveness, but a strong commitment to the quality of relationships within the group can sometimes lead to over-cohesiveness, with a corresponding decline in the quality of critical thinking which individuals bring to the group. Fourthly, we have been keen to explore with participating schools the opportunities for 'spreading' the leadership function throughout the staff group. This means accepting that leadership is a function to which many staff contribute, rather than a set of responsibilities vested in a small number of individuals or jobs.

## 5. Staff Development Policies

Staff development is inextricably linked to school development. In the quest for school improvement powerful strategies are required which integrate these two areas in a way that is mutually supportive. In turn, powerful strategies that link staff development to school improvement need to fulfil two essential criteria. First of all they need to relate to and enhance ongoing practice in the school and, secondly, they should link to and strengthen other internal features of the school's organization. Unless the staff development programme leads towards overall school improvement then it tends to become a series of marginal activities.

Further, it seems reasonable to assume that improving the conditions for supporting the learning of teachers in school will have an impact on the conditions they provide for their pupils. To this end it is important that a school has a well thought out policy for teacher development. This must go beyond the traditional patterns through which teachers attend external courses, or, more recently, the use of one-shot school-based events. It is vital that strategies for staff development should be linked to school improvement. As such these should be concerned with the development of the staff as a team, as well as with the evolution of its thinking and the practice of individuals.

### 6. Involvement

In the research literature on effective schools there is strong evidence that success is associated with a sense of identity and involvement that extends beyond the teaching staff. This involves the pupils, parents and, indeed, other members of the school's community. It seems that some schools are able to create positive relationships with their wider community that help to create a supportive climate for learning. Though it may be difficult for a particular school to establish whole community links overnight, it does seem reasonable to expect that strategies for the active involvement of two key groups, pupils and parents, should be more straightforward. Within the IQEA schools, we have tended therefore to focus on ways in which these two groups can be brought more directly into the school's planning and decision making processes.

The start-point for such involvement is the adoption of clear policies which encourage participation into the school – the onus should not be left on the groups themselves. Rather, methods for gaining access to the school need to be published and supported by appropriate attitudes towards potential partners.

### CLASSROOM ARRANGEMENTS

Though the description of management arrangements cannot be considered definitive or comprehensive, it represents the clearest lessons which appear to emerge from our recent work. In a similar vein, we have tried to identify the classroom arrangements which are most often associated with successful learning.

These arrangements are concerned with the quality of the learning environment, and the teacher's practice is clearly the most important determinant. We have therefore been analyzing teacher behaviour in those classrooms that appear most successful, and out of this analysis we have identified a series of practices which are most often present. These relate (see West, Hopkins, & Beresford, 1995) to the extent to which teachers:

- Establish authentic relationships with students
- Maintain appropriate boundaries and expectations
- Draw on a repertoire of teaching approaches
- Engage in classroom level curriculum development
- Evaluate their own teaching
- Talk with each other about pedagogy

These arrangements are amplified below.

## 1. Authentic Classroom Relationships

Many studies of effective schooling have indicated that the teacher-student relationship is at the heart of the learning process. This is not simply a philosophic proposition emerging from a belief in equity, but a practical contributor to effective schools. Consequently, it is a theme which continually appears in writings on effective classrooms. Brandes and Ginnis (1990) quote the evidence gathered by the Committee of Enquiry into Discipline in Schools (Children's Legal Center, 1988), which indicated that behavior and commitment improve when teachers treat students fairly and with respect, work to build up co-operative and supportive relationships, demonstrate concern for students' needs and welfare, and give students meaningful responsibilities within the learning partnership. The essence of this high quality relationship which teachers create within their classrooms is described as 'unconditional positive regard'.

However, descriptions of what a high quality relationship involves are harder to find than exhortations that such relationships be developed. In our own work, it seems that the student responds best when the relationship with the teacher is authentic – that is both teacher and student see themselves as partners in the learning process, and there is mutual respect and acceptance and reciprocal expectation. Though the detail varies, we have noted that such relationships can be created at any stage of schooling.

## 2. Establishing Boundaries and Expectations

It is apparent from our observations of practice that where teachers act in concert, demonstrating similar ranges of approaches and behaviors, these patterns are learned quickly by students, who then recognize them as cues. Nowhere is this more evident than in the expectations of students behavior and commitment. Consistent adherence to an announced code is an important determinant of student response. Where rules are clearly set out and faithfully followed, most students seem to learn very quickly to function within the boundaries established.

There are obvious side-benefits to clearly articulated and consistently enforced rules, for example, the level of support these offer of the teacher who is comparatively weak. But the main impact seems to be on the classroom climate, and therefore on the possibility of developing the other classroom conditions listed above. Because of this, the clarification of classroom 'rules' and expectations benefits individual teachers by contributing to the quality of the learning environment. Collective agreement and consistent behavior across teachers is a very potent influence indeed on student response.

## 3. The Teacher's Repertoire

That the range of teaching approaches influences the quality of learning outcomes has been clearly established (see especially Joyce & Weil, 1972; Joyce & Showers, 1988). However, it is also clear that particular teaching styles have come to be associated with particular subjects. This is most evident in the secondary sector, where single subject teaching is the norm, but there are also many primary schools where a change in learning opportunity is most often associated with a change in subject content.

Within the IQEA Project schools we have been able to look at the preferred learning styles of some groups of pupils. These studies reveal both that within any teaching group preferred learning styles vary between students and that, for any one student, preferred learning styles vary according to the subject content. Genuine entitlement therefore requires that there is a range of teaching approaches in use in each subject of the curriculum, and not merely a change in method between, for example, mathematical and physical education. Preliminary findings suggest that where the teacher employs a range of teaching approaches more students demonstrate high levels of involvement in and commitment to the goals of the lesson.

## 4. Curriculum Development

Despite the very high levels of external prescription, we have observed that some teachers still find time and space for classroom-level curriculum development. Perhaps to be expected, such development or modification of curriculum materials seems to be most evident where teaching is conducted in mixed ability groupings. Essentially, curriculum development offers a strategy for differentiating common curriculum requirements, and, at its most effective, it can be seen as a method of enfranchising the student. Within the IQEA Project, we are currently mapping the ways in which individual teachers make such adaptions at the classroom level, and the effect on student involvement and response which this engenders.

One issue emerging is that even the most detailed and prescriptive curriculum model is some way short of a "blue-print" for classroom activities, so that there is often more scope for individual adaption than teachers have realized. A second finding is that where teachers develop schemes of work which address method and means of assessment alongside content, the opportunities for teacher-level development are more clearly seen.

## 5. Self-Evaluation

The management arrangements outline how a general commitment to enquire into and reflect about what is happening in the school enhance the school's capacity for improvement. There is a natural counterpart to this activity in the classroom setting – a commitment to evaluate methods and impacts at classroom level, and to develop or change teaching behaviors in light of this. As the focus within the IQEA Project schools has shifted away from how the school is managed to a more explicit focus on classroom practice, we have seen that many teachers have taken what has become "the habit of enquiry" with them. Consequently, there appears to be a much more self-conscious and open commitment to enquire into and reflect on classroom processes and outcomes.

Teachers who are self-critical of their practice as a matter of routine appear, in the IQEA Project schools at least, to be those teachers who have the most extensively developed 'repertoires', and also seem to be those teachers who are most aware of the many things that are happening in the classroom at any one time. There is also a close overlap between those teachers in the Project schools who engage in regular self-evaluation and those who engage in classroom level curriculum development.

## 5. Focus on Pedagogy

Working as we do, in constant contact with teachers and frequently spending time within schools, we have been surprised by the relatively small amount of 'teacher talk' that relates directly to matters of pedagogy. We have found that teachers talk freely about such things as school structures and management, policies, micro-politics. Many discuss curriculum content, or pupils, or resources on a daily basis. But the majority seem able to get through most working days without referring specifically to the way they teach or how students learn.

Yet, it can be argued that there is nothing more important for teachers to talk about than their own teaching and their students' learning. Indeed, if teachers are 'professionals' in the technical sense then, surely, their professionalism centers on their pedagogical expertise. Certainly, we have no reason to believe that teachers know better than any other group within society what students should learn (though often they have very clear ideas on this subject), but we can expect them to know in detail how students learn.

Within the IQEA Project schools there has been a deliberate attempt to focus on issues of pedagogy, to form pedagogical partnerships in which teachers can observe and reflect on one anothers' teaching, and, as often as possible, to celebrate the quality of teaching which is achieved.

## THE IMPROVEMENT STRATEGY

Identifying arrangements which increase the school's capacity to improve is an important stage in the process, but it does not in itself lead to improvement. This is evident from the many attempts which have been made over the years to "backward map" (Reynolds, 1992) the characteristics of "effective" schools onto schools which generate poorer outcomes. At best, training teachers in these areas may increase the quality of staff development programmes, but the link between the development of teachers and the development of their schools remains elusive. We have been concerned, therefore, to ensure that the development of capacity or potential for improvement at the school level is linked to some clearly focused improvement project within each school – a concern we find reflected in, for example, the Accelerated Schools Project (see Hopfenberg et al., 1993; Finnan et al., 1996). The key question is how capacity can be exploited, how the arrangements within the school can be tied in with specific improvement efforts.

Our approach here can be outlined through reference to the improvement 'model' which underpins our thinking. The model starts not with abstractions about the kinds of 'vision' or goals that may 'inspire' the school community, as we have ample evidence from our previous work with schools that quality of vision is independent of quality of schooling – many schools with entirely laudable vision statements seem unable to reflect these in practice; many of the best practices we have seen have never been formalised into school goals. Rather, we have encouraged our Project schools to begin by auditing the quality of experience they currently offer their students – the quality they deliver in the classroom, not the quality they aspire to in plans. Essentially, we are asking our Project schools to start from where they are, rather than to imagine where they would prefer to be. We have found that when schools look closely at what they currently provide, and then, in the context of their own constraints and opportunities, consider what can (or indeed must) be done, the generation of goals and priorities for action remains 'grounded' in the realities of the school.

The conceptual model of how quality improvement takes place can thus be simply illustrated (see Figure 1). Our assumption here is that the starting point for improvement effort is student outcomes – indeed, we might define improving the quality of schooling in these terms, as a deliberate programme aimed at reducing the discrepancy between the outcomes we desire for our students and the outcomes they actually achieve.

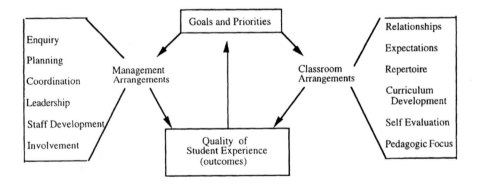

**Figure 1: A quality improvement model.**

The desired improvements in these outcomes form the basis for specific goals – the priorities which will guide and focus teacher energies. But we cannot expect "priorities" to galvanize efforts if there are too many. Often, this means that decisions about priorities must be made, moving from the separate, perhaps even conflicting, priorities of individuals or groups to a systematically compiled set of priorities which represent the overall needs of a whole school community. Hargreaves and Hopkins (1991) have suggested that two principles should guide this process of choice among priorities:

1.  Manageability: How much can we realistically hope to achieve?
2.  Coherence: Is there a sequence which will ease implementation?

To those principles we have added a third,

3.  Consonance: The extent to which internally identified priorities coincide or overlap with external pressures for reform.

In practical terms, this means that within the 'family' of IQEA project schools each school is pursuing its own particular improvement priority. The IQEA project offers a way of thinking about and working on school improvement, but the decision about what to improve must in each case be determined by the individual school in relation to its individual circumstances and opportunities. We have previously written (Hopkins, Ainscow, & West 1994) about the range of priorities project schools have selected, attempting to give some sense of the sorts of activity going on. Such accounts explain why the notion that each school should focus on priorities relevant to its own particular circumstances is central to our conceptualization of the improvement process, and also illustrate how "capacity" can be created and tapped into to support the school's work, since it will be the quality of the management arrangements and the classroom arrangements that determine whether the priorities identified lead to improvements in outcomes or not.

Essentially then, the arrangements are mediating variables, through which ideas about improvement are given substance. Often, one or more of the arrangements will need to be developed if this transformation is to be successful. But there is a difference between (for example) developing co-ordination because it is necessary to improve co-ordination to meet an identified goal or priority, or developing the repertoire of a group of teachers because this is necessary to meet an identified classroom priority, and simply addressing these areas for their own sake.

The strategy followed in the project is, then, relatively straightforward, at least conceptually. Identify areas for improvement from an analysis of what is currently happening, select a limited (we discourage schools from trying to pursue more than two or three priorities at one time) number for action, then develop the school's management and classroom arrangements as necessary to enable the priority to be pursued in appropriate and supportive conditions. We believe that Project schools have demonstrated the wisdom of linking activity related to priorities with activity to develop the school's management and classroom arrangements. We have also noted that this process becomes "easier" with time, as the schools develop capacity and learn to use it, building on successive improvements in successive years. We have suggested that by addressing specific improvements alongside a more general commitment to ensure that the best possible 'arrangements' are in place the school is, in effect, developing the culture, rather than simply organising or reorganising around current priorities. Indeed, we feel that an effective school improvement strategy offers the most reliable means of enhancing school culture.

## ORGANISING FOR IMPROVEMENT

Any project carried out in partnership with a number of schools requires a number of practical arrangements to be made. Such arrangements need to embody the expectations which the various partners can hold with regard to one another, as well as the methods of organizing the project. The arrangements which have governed and supported the partnership between IQEA schools and the Project team can be briefly summarized as:

- The IQEA contract
- The School Cadre Groups
- Development and Support
- Evaluation

## THE IQEA CONTRACT

It was seen as important from the outset that collaborating schools and project team members all demonstrate real commitment to the project. Consequently, a set of ground rules for commitments from participants was drawn up. Though, not a legal arrangement, we felt it appropriate to refer to the ground rules as a 'contract' – since they related to the in-school management of the project and set out what we considered to be the minimum conditions necessary for a fruitful partnership. There were as follows:

- The decision to participate in the project is made as a result of consultation among all staff in the school.
- Each school will designate a minimum of two members of staff as project co-ordinators (one of whom is the head teacher or deputy head) who attend days of training and support meetings (the group of co-ordinators is known as the 'project cadre').
- The whole school will allocate substantial staff development time to activities related to the project.
- At least 40 percent of teachers (representing a cross-section of staff) will take part in specified staff development activities in their own classrooms. Each participating teacher will be regularly released from teaching in order to participate in these classroom based aspects of the project.
- Each school will participate in the evaluation of the project and share findings with other participants in the project.

Having established these expectations as far as possible, the next step was to help each school to design a strategy for achieving its developmental priorities and establishing the appropriate conditions for improvement. As we have already pointed out, the details of this strategy had to be particular to particular schools, taking account of the nature of the priorities that had been agreed, the existing conditions and the resources that were available.

## THE CADRE GROUP

Since development must be concerned with the school as a whole, it must be designed in such a way as to impact upon all levels in the organization. Specifically, our focus was on three levels (see Figure 2) and the ways in which these interrelate. The whole school level is to do with overall management and the establishment of policies, particularly with respect to how resources and strategies for staff development can be mobilized to support school improvement efforts. Within the school there is a level where activity is carried forward by working groups. Here, the concern is with developing collaboratively the details of and support for improvement activities. Finally, at the individual teacher level the focus is on developing classroom practice.

We take the view that in very effective schools these three levels of activity are mutually supportive. Consequently a specific aim of the IQEA Project has been to devise and establish positive conditions at each level and to co-ordinate support across these levels. It is in this connection that we have established a team of co-ordinators in each school whose task included the integration of activities across the various levels. We refer to these co-ordinators, as the cadre group. They are responsible for the day-to-day running of the improvement project in their own schools and also for creating links between IQEA ideas and approaches, school level improvement priorities and practical action.

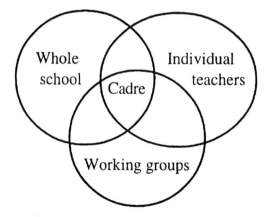

**Figure 2: The role of the Cadre Group.**

## DEVELOPMENT AND SUPPORT

The cadre members take responsibility for co-ordinating the development of the project within the school, but there are a number of forms of support available. One is the training provided to cadre groups, which takes place away from the school. The training is focused around the management and classroom arrangements outlined above, but also creates time for school cadre groups to discuss and to plan for development in their own schools. In this way it is intended to help them to review their own management and classroom arrangements, on the one hand in light of 'theory' and 'practice' elsewhere, that we are able bring to them, and on the other in light of their own development goals and priorities. Essentially, we are inviting them to consider whether there are conditions they can develop at the school level which will facilitate the progress of their own improvement programmes. These training days also offer the advantage of building a network between cadre members from different schools, though this needs to be supplemented by support which reaches into the school.

LEA advisers linked with the project have been one way of providing such support. Many of the project schools have an identified LEA adviser/officer who has taken on this role. Project team members have also taken on this role: each school has a link with a particular team member and, through this link, access to the whole team. Support provided from these sources ranges from simply joining in the school's own deliberations and discussions, via help in planning or guidance towards possible sources of help or ideas, to involvement in staff development activities within the school alongside cadre members, which can be offered to the whole staff or to sub-groups.

A further source of support is the project manual, a collection of information, activities and readings grouped around the conditions (Ainscow et al., 1994). The resources in the handbook include many short, focused staff development activities which cadre members are encouraged try themselves, and (where appropriate) to organize for colleagues in the school.

## EVALUATION

The IQEA Project places considerable importance on the need for inquiry, reflection and evaluation within schools. The collecting of school-based data of various kinds for the purpose of informing planning and development is seen as a powerful element within each school's strategy. Consequently, the schools are expected to collect data about progress towards the achievement of developmental priorities; about progress in establishing conditions for improvement; and, of course, about student and teacher outcomes. Agreement that these data are to be shared is one of the specifications of the project contract.

Within the project, journals kept by the cadre members provide a common approach to recording relevant information. In general terms the journals provide a detailed account of events, decisions and processes that occur, as well as summaries of significant outcomes that have been noted. Cadre members are also requested to write reflective comments, indicating their personal reactions to what occurs, and mapping their involvement in the project over time. In this way individuals can monitor the progress of the school's project and, at the same time, record developments in their own thinking and practice.

Toward the end of each school year cadre members are encouraged to prepare an evaluation report which provides a summary of developments in their school. It is intended that the reports and the process leading up to their preparation will be of value within the school. Indeed, it is assumed that they will be distributed to all members of staff. The reports are also used by the project team to gain an overall picture of the developments in each school's project. Issues raised in the reports are discussed during follow-up visits and cadre meetings.

Throughout the period of the project the Project Team make regular visits to each school to support cadre members in their work and, at the same time, to collect additional data. All these data are systematically processed on a continuous basis, in order to build up a clearer picture of the activities going on in each school. These findings are also being fed back to the school in order to inform development processes. In this respect the project can correctly be characterized as a process of collaborative inquiry within which all partners are contributing to its evolution.

SOME REFLECTIONS

I stated at the beginning of this chapter that it was not my intention to provide an account of the IQEA Project itself, but rather to outline some of the ideas and approaches which have influenced its development. However, I will offer two examples of the sorts of development in which IQEA project schools have become involved. Both illustrate how systematic enquiry and classroom based staff development (management arrangements) can combine with (e.g.) a review of teaching repertoires, or curriculum development (classroom arrangements) to improve the quality of learning opportunities provided.

One of the project schools has, over the past year, been investigating the quality of learning opportunities and outcomes. This exercise was planned in three phases. In the *first phase*, teachers in the participating subject departments (eight in all) formed "Research Groups." These research groups then planned classroom level enquiries focusing on the quality of learning. Though each department selected its own points of focus, in each case there was a commitment to pursue this focus within a range of classrooms, and to pool the outcomes at a departmental level. This sharing of experiences and reflections on the quality of learning itself raised a number of issues about teaching approach and classroom organization, and there was a commitment to identify and to replicate the best practices across the department. In the *second phase*, departmental research groups exchanged experiences and findings, with a view to identifying issues of whole-school interest and areas for whole-school development. In the *final phase* these were followed up and a deliberate strategy to disseminate best practices (supported where necessary by appropriate training) implemented.

Already much has emerged from this collaborative exercise in classroom level enquiry. The technology department, for example, has looked at how colleagues use homework within the context of their teaching, and also at the response of students to the way homework is used. This revealed significant differences in practice between teachers. It also indicated that for many students some of the homework set, rather than being a tool for learning, actually reduced interest in and commitment to the subject. The department is revising its policy in light of the findings, and it is clear that this investigation will have implications for other departments.

Other departments looked at student response to different teaching approaches, at students' own learning behaviours and teacher planning and delivery. Each departmental research group felt that it had produced something of value for their colleagues which could benefit the students in that department. Many have thrown up issues which will need further enquiry or have wider implications. But there is a clear sense of empowerment amongst those who have been involved. It seems that if the confidence to take a critical and self-critical look at classroom practice can be established, then classroom level enquiry and reflection can do much to increase the quality of learning

In another project school, the focus for development was the use of differentiation in catering for different learning styles and differing abilities of students. The original intention was to adapt existing schemes of work within the department so that each would incorporate tasks suited to a range of learning styles. (The typology used was based on Kolb, 1984.)

Teachers were paired for the purposes of observation, and a schedule of questions for the teacher and of the observation foci for the lesson was drawn up. Teachers were asked about the scheme of work being used in the lesson, their confidence in it, the objectives of the lesson and any bases on which student grouping was made. The observation schedule recorded instances of differentiation by task and by outcome, the setting of targets and the nature of teacher interventions. The impact of any variation in teaching approach on the lesson format was also noted.

Following this enquiry, a document was produced that defined differentiation, and presented a series of strategies which could be used in the classroom to achieve it. (The document stressed the importance of such things as accurate assessment of where students are in terms of their learning and the need for personalised as well as group targets.) This format for planning was not only adopted within the school, it has also been widely networked across schools in the IQEA project.

These are merely fragments of what has been taking place in the project schools, and, as Henry Levin has pointed out, premature judgements are easy to make but outcomes need to be viewed over time and with caution. Nevertheless, typically project schools can point to similar instances, where systematic attention to the facilitating arrangements has enhanced the school's capacity to improve classroom experience.

But, individual examples notwithstanding, we have also been reflecting on our wider involvement with the schools, and can offer some observations on the Project as an improvement initiative. First, the IQEA approach seems to be a sensible way to promote improvement at a time when de-centralisation of systems is transferring more and more decision making powers into the school. The United Kingdom, Iceland, Puerto Rico have (to varying degrees) all embarked on de-centralisation programmes. These programmes have emphasized the school as the centre for planning and development – bringing new problems of policymaking, of management, of control into the schools. Whether it is to pursue improvement or not, these schools need new levels of clarity about purposes, about priorities, about progress. The Project schools tell us that working within the IQEA framework has helped to focus attention on and develop ways of responding to these new challenges.

Second, there is the issue of empowerment of teachers. Of course, 'empowerment' has become a rather over used term in recent years – and often seems little more than a mechanism for extending internal accountability and control. But, within the Project, we have seen genuine empowerment of groups of teachers, as they have come to be centrally involved in identifying, planning for and implementing their own improvement programmes. Typically, this process has started with the cadre group, but in many instances it has spread out from there to embrace other groupings. The linking of individuals and groups to activities which they then take responsibility for managing, appears not only to increase the levels of commitment and job satisfaction of the teachers involved, it also helps to re-shape organisation structure. Thus we have begun to see structures developed in light of purposes and priorities – a notion which is less common than might be expected in schools. The development of such structures and the extension of empowerment are particularly important issues in the Icelandic and Puerto Rican contexts, where there is little history of internal structures for managing the school, and we believe that teachers from IQEA schools in these countries are finding their way towards mutuality as they work on the project.

A third observation concerns the quality of dialogue within the schools. Where all teachers can be drawn into discussion about the school's current strengths and weaknesses, and its opportunities for development, then the quality of debate within the school increases perceptibly. Such discussions are both strengthened by and contribute to the spread of empowerment, the growth of mutuality. They also help to focus teachers' thinking and creativity upon the same issues at the same time, lending considerable momentum to change efforts.

Fourth, is the beginning of dialogues across schools. Schools are strangely insular organizations. Many seem to have become inoculated against practices and ideas from elsewhere, and getting them to share their thinking and their expertise with one another has never been easy. A feature of the IQEA working method is that the 'training' sessions bring together on a regular basis groups of colleagues from different schools. In these sessions openness and exchange are encouraged, and we have noted that, over time, the teachers from the different schools begin to discover their common interests and to develop levels of cooperation and trust. Looking closely at one another's practice, visiting one another's schools are important sources of ideas, and the networking between the schools in the Project is a powerful force for development.

Finally, there is the issue of our own role – what is it that external consultants should be doing to assist and support those teachers who are leading improvement efforts in their own schools? Are there key tasks which determine whether or not an improvement intervention is successful? These are questions which we continue to debate, both amongst ourselves and with the Project schools. There are some things we have learned – for example, it is important to perceive the role as working with the schools, and not on them, and each school is different so while it may be possible to have the ingredients in hand, there will be no single recipe. But there is much more that remains to be unravelled.

Nevertheless, we believe that within the IQEA Project lies an approach to school improvement which offers a firm basis for the development of the individual school, while retaining sufficient flexibility to be adaptable to the circumstances of many schools. We know, however, that it is the teachers from our Project schools who have made the model work, for their schools, for their students, for themselves. If there is an over-riding lesson from the IQEA Project, it is that teachers improve their schools, and that the first priority for any school improvement initiative must therefore be to engage and to engage with teachers.

## REFERENCES

Ainscow M., Hopkins D., Southworth G., & West, M. (1994). *Creating the conditions for school improvement. A handbook of staff development activities.* London: David Fulton.

Barth R. (1990). *Improving schools from within.* San Francisco California: Jossey Bass.

Brandes D., & Ginnis P. (1990). *The student centred school.* Oxford: Blackwell Education.

Elmore, R. (1990). *Restructuring schools.* San Francisco, California: Jossey Bass.

Finnan C. & Associates. (Eds.). (1996). *Accelerated schools in action: Lessons from the field.* Thousand Oaks, California: Corwin Press.

Fullan M., Bennett, B., & Rolheiser-Bennett, C. (1990). Linking classroom and school improvement. *Educational Leadership,* **47**(8), 13–19.

Fullan M. (1993). *Change forces: Probing the depths of educational reform.* Lewes: Falmer Press.

Glickman, C. D. (1993). *Renewing America's schools. A guide for school based action.* San Francisco, California: Jossey Bass.

Hargreaves D. H., & Hopkins, D. (1991). *The empowered school.* London: Cassell.

Hopfenberg, W. S., Levin H., & Associates. (1993). *The accelerated schools resource guide.* San Francisco, California: Jossey-Bass.

Hopkins D., Ainscow M., & West, M. (1994). *School improvement in an era of change.* London: Cassell.

Hopkins D., & West, M. (1994). Teacher development and school improvement. In D. Walling, (Ed.), *Teachers as leaders.* Bloomington Indiana: Phi Delta Kappan.

Joyce, B. & Showers, B. (1988). *Student achievement through staff development.* Harlow: Longman.

Joyce, B., & Weil, M. (1972). *Models of teaching.* Needham Heights Massachusetts: Allyn and Bacon.

Kolb, D. (1984). *Experimental learning.* Englewood Cliffs: Prentice-Hall.

Lieberman, A., & Miller, L. (1990). *Staff Development for Education in the 90s: New demands, new realities, new perspectives.* New York: Teachers College Press.

Peters, T. J., & Waterman, R. H. (1982). In search of excellence: Lessons from America's best run companies. London: Harper and Row.

Reynolds, D. (1992). School effectiveness and school improvement. In D. Reynolds & P. Cuttance (Eds.), *School effectiveness*. London: Cassell.

West, M., & Ainscow, M. (1991). *Managing school development*. London: David Fulton.

West, M., & Hopkins, D. *Reconceptualising school effectiveness and school improvement*. Paper presented at American Education Research Association Annual Conference, New York, April 1996.

West, M., Hopkins, D., & Beresford, J. *Conditions for school and classroom development*. Paper presented at European Conference on Education Research, Bath, September 1995.

# School Administration In Russia: Centralization Versus Decentralization

DALE MANN

*Teachers College, Columbia University*

VLADIMIR BRILLER

*Education Development Center, Inc.*

*This chapter focuses on the development of school administration in Russia. The process of decentralization is experienced in terms of the difficulties and tensions involved in moving from a previously hierarchical system to one involving more school-based autonomy. Regional and local differences are identified as the process of decentralization evolves in Russia.*

## BACKGROUND: SOCIAL/ECONOMIC TRANSFORMATION AND SCHOOL REFORM

Russia needs to re-invent many of its social and political institutions and it needs to re-engineer its economy. School reform is not a necessary condition for economic transformation as America in the 1990s and Japan in the 1960s have demonstrated. For the economy, schools may be a long-term brake; they are not a short-run accelerant. Civic and social transformation turns on the culture, the media, the structure of opportunity more than it does on whether or not middle school students make field trips to their country's capital. In Russian terms, the three TV stations broadcasting MTV from Moscow are likely to have a more profound effect on young people than a new edition of "Modern Civics for a Modern Russia."

Still, whether or not public school administrators in Russia can decentralize the operations of their schools is a significant question. Regional variations and changing labor force demands both require more flexibility than centralized governments can manage. The financial collapse of central institutions puts a premium on local initiatives. And, capturing the energy, creativity and loyalty of local populations for local institutions is a central dynamic of democracy.

Is it possible for the administrators of Russia's 65,000 local schools to operate them in ways that depart from their country's historic habits and current reality? Russia's thousand year tradition of authoritarian government was simply continued by communism's central control disguised as central planning. There were many indicators in the communist-operated school system of Russia's tendency to autarky – single textbooks for every grade and every subject, mandated and

*M. Fullan (ed.), Fundamental Change, 120-136.*
© 2005 *Springer. Printed in the Netherlands.*

produced by the state; school finance determined to the last ruble by Moscow; the administration of school buildings hyper-regulated and micro-managed by 2,000 memos a year from "The Ministry"; a lack of professional associations independent of the government, and a saturation of ideology.

The centrifugal disintegration of the Soviet Union had three effects on Russian school administrators. First, the central government was nearly bankrupted and is thus less able to wield power through budget control. Second, the moral bankruptcy of communism stripped the central institutions of their ideological, normative authority. Third, there was an unevenly shared conclusion that schools should participate in transforming Russia so that it could compete and participate differently in the world.

The first two changes created the possibility of more local autonomy. The third change – a need to make the economy more competitive and the society more open – created an argument in support of local autonomy.

Russia has 1,500,000 teachers and 140,000 school administrators. The teachers do not have the time or the organizational resources to transform their schools. If it is to happen, it must at least begin with administrators. This chapter presents the only empirical analysis of school administrators in the country's history[1]. It documents their readiness to create and/or to accept local responsibility for their own schools.

STUDY QUESTIONS

In the Winter of 1994, we asked 1,399 school administrators from six diverse regions of Russia 54 questions about issues of school governance and decision making. The group was representative of all Russian administrators and included principals, chairpersons of "subject methodology units" (similar to central office curriculum specialists), and local and regional superintendents. (See Endnote 1 for the research design).

In Western education, proponents of decentralization argue that autonomous school decision making can affect teaching and learning and may thus lead to improved student outcomes. Others argue that the current state of research is insufficient to establish a causal or even an empirical link between decentralization and student outcomes (Davies & Hentshcke, 1994).

But, if you are a Russian school "leader" earning less than your teachers but with no job security, and if you are still responsible for meeting classes while administering a 3,000 student institution in which the teachers have not been paid for four months, then the Western curiosity about the relation between forms of governance and student outcomes will seem academic at best. The administrators we studied had practical, immediate concerns – who could force them to do what? What were the likely consequences of what actions? And especially, who would pay for what and how could they be assured of that?

## WHO CAN FORCE WHOM TO DO WHAT? THE SOURCES OF INFLUENCE

The sources of influence can be divided into four groups.

1. *The Russian Federation Ministry of Education.* This is the Moscow headquarters (*Chistoprudny Boulevard*) which still issues rules and regulations for the whole country. Just as other countries find it desirable to maintain national institutions that attend to national level education, so do the Russians. The issue of course is the amount of power held at that level compared to other levels.

2. *The regional and district authorities.* In the 1992, *Act of the Russian Federation on Education*, regions and districts were allowed some fiscal control. Regions and municipalities can raise (different amounts) of money locally and they can determine how that money is disbursed. At the same time, the Federation Ministry retains an amount of fiscal control and has recently begun to experiment with lump sum budgeting for selected schools.

3. *The parents, teachers and students.* These are the clients of educators and, to the extent that educators regard themselves as servants of the public, parents especially are the constituents of educators. In most systems, the intimate and diurnal interaction among administrators, teachers and parents produces significant influence on the administrators from the other groups. Several cultural factors made that less the case for school administrators under the Soviet system. The Communist Party and the central Ministry preempted anyone else's putatively legitimate authority. The Russian respect for learning elevated and insulated school people. And central financing kept local hands off the power of the purse.

4. *The respondent herself/himself.* This is especially important in instances where a superordinate *dictat* conflicts with personal/professional judgement. In the West, race and social class combine with scarce resources to produce dilemmas of this sort. The same sorts of personal conundrum grow out of Russia's current conflicting tendencies. Whose views should be honored, the genuinely respected war veteran who literally saved the country and now passionately wants to retain a chauvinist civics curriculum? Or the newly rich entrepreneur who would have the schools teach economic and social Darwinism?

How school administrators orient themselves is at the heart of the prospects for decentralization. Two of the sources – the Russian Ministry and the regional and local authorities – are hierarchically above school administrators and, arguably, are therefore comfortable, traditional sources of guidance. The teachers and the students are down the organization chart. In many Western countries, parents are recognized as a legitimate source of direction for public schools and some school organization charts elevate them to that station. In the absence of functioning democracy at the local level, the location of parents in the current Russian configuration of authority is less clear. The role of one's own self as a source of authority is similarly unclear, at least in current theory. What do the data say? Table 1 reports the respondents' estimates of the strongest source of influence.

In light of the ferocious competition for very scarce public resources, self-reliance is a good choice. The next to last place ranking of the national Ministry

**Table 1: Sources of Influence on School Administrators**
**(Most to Least)**

| Place | Source | Number Choosing |
|---|---|---|
| 1. | Self | 635 |
| 2. | Municipal Government | 599 |
| 3. | Teachers | 486 |
| 4. | Students | 261 |
| 5. | Regional Government | 216 |
| 6. | Ministry of Education | 165 |
| 7. | Parents | 131 |

is a measure of how quickly things have changed. And, if the goal is to locate power close to those affected (a corner stone of democratic government), the primacy of the municipal government is as heartening as the dead last place of the parents is disheartening. The 1992 legislation assigns district officials the authority to approve budgets, inspect schools and evaluate administrators and teachers. The influence of parents varies between urban and rural places: in urban places, 63 percent of administrators credit parents with some influence but only 49 percent of the directors of rural schools agree.

One of Russia's leading scholars of school administration, Konstantin Usha-kov, has been attacking the still continuing isolation and dependence of some school administrators by intervening in the school's climate and culture (1994b). And, by introducing innovations such as job descriptions and role playing simu-lations, Ushakov is working to create new models for the "ideal administrator" and the "ideal teacher" (1993, 1994a).

Today, most schools in the U.S. operate as a dual system. The core technical activity of schools, what goes on in classrooms, is loosely supervised (Weick, 1976). Teachers have the *de facto* autonomy within broad guidelines to close the door and run their classrooms as they see fit. On the other hand, non-instructional activi-ties such as testing and pupil placement are tightly supervised.

Russian schools also operate as a dual system, but this duality is connected first to the external environment, which is treated by the building administration and school faculty as hostile. In return for protection, the faculty "pays off" the administration with loyalty and obedience (Ushakov, 1994b).

Eighty-six percent of administrators (1,198 people) rank teachers as the most influential force despite the fact that Russian teachers do not have as much legal power as do their Western colleagues. (Soviet trade unions were in reality "state organs." Far from being sometimes antagonists with independent financing, they resembled "company unions" in the distant past of Western trade unionism.) Rus-sian administrators often consider themselves to be teachers who temporarily became administrators and *include* themselves in their estimate of the power of teachers.

Sixty-eight percent of administrators believe they are influenced by students. We are skeptical about that claim: Soviet ideology celebrated "child-centered" schooling. In fact, schools offered only education focused tightly on communist ideology. The State curriculum and the unitary goal of "new Communist man" made individualizing instruction a sin. Discovery learning was permitted only in math and science. Schools were presented with production quotas for graduates geared to the supposed needs of the economy including the preparation of manual laborers. Rural students were often assigned to harvest labor. Approximately 400,000 children with disabilities (the Russian phrase translates as "defectology") were isolated, under educated and therefore consigned to lives of deprivation[2].

## WHO HAS A BIGGER EFFECT ON ADMINISTRATORS – SUPERIORS OR SUBORDINATES?

Given Russia's unbroken history of top down and authoritarian government, one would expect that superordinates would be a far more potent source of influence than subordinates. Reciprocal power between the governed and the governors is a fairly sophisticated, subtle concept, even in established democracies. Almost half (48 percent, 668) of the respondents mention they are more influenced by superiors than by subordinates; about the same proportion (44 percent, 614) believe they are more influenced by subordinates. Eight percent declined to answer. It has been said that 'the Renaissance never got to Russia', but in light of the even distribution of administrators willing to recognize that they both govern and are governed by their subordinates, this too may be changing.

## INFLUENCE ON FUNCTIONAL DOMAINS BY SOURCE

Among other things, the 1992 Law on Education denounced centralized examinations and tests. While there remains a national curriculum, most testing is done at the local level. The issue of a national curriculum is sensitive and complicated. In other countries of the former Soviet Union, the first task of school reform was to strip "the Red topics" out of the textbooks (after which, often, not much remained). But Russia remains a federation which incorporates more than 100 different languages and those language groups reflect ethnic identities and nationalist loyalties even where the "nation" ceased to exist 500, 600 years ago. The Russian problem is like the American problem – *"E Pluribus Unum"* ("Out of many, one") and thus there is a continuing debate about safeguarding "Russian educational space." The national (minimum) curriculum is one way to attempt its preservation.

The respondents believe that the Ministry of Education is in control of the curriculum, especially regarding the issues of what gets taught and which books are used. They assign the least influence to parents and students.

*Personnel issues.* The administrator herself/himself and the district authorities are identified as the most important figures in deciding on personnel except for the issue of professional training (see Table 2).

Table 2: How School Administrators Feel They Are Influenced On Curriculum Issues by Source

| Curriculum issue | Source of influence %/(N) | | | | | | | |
|---|---|---|---|---|---|---|---|---|
| | Min | Tch | Reg | Dis | Self | Stu | Par | N/A |
| Which books are used | 30 (1242) | 19 (780) | 22 (916) | 15 (616) | 8 (354) | 2 (102) | 3 (134) | 1 (53) |
| What gets taught to students | 27 (1132) | 17 (696) | 21 (874) | 14 (590) | 11 (480) | 5 (218) | 4 (187) | 0[a] (20) |
| How studentsare tested | 8 (325) | 24 (1017) | 8 (335) | 15 (611) | 22 (925) | 4 (153) | 4 (147) | 16[a] (684) |
| Mean | 21 (900) | 20 (831) | 17 (708) | 14 (606) | 14 (586) | 4 (158) | 4 (156) | 6 (252) |

*Note.* Min = Ministry of Education; Tch = teachers; Reg = regional authorities; Dis = municipal authorities; Self = the respondent her/himself; Par = parents; Stu = students; N/A = no answer.
[a]Errors due to rounding.

Teacher training can be divided into two parts: undergraduate preparation, the prerogative of the pedagogical universities which continue to be governed by the Ministry of Education; and in-service training that is provided by regional and district educational authorities in cooperation with the Institute for Upgrading Teachers' Qualifications. These institutes are supervised by regional or city educational authorities. The decision of who is to be trained, and when, is usually made by the district and school administration (Saprykin, 1990).

For observers who expect that the Soviet celebration of worker participation would have created a major role for teachers in school governance, the low estimate of teachers, even in curriculum matters bears some explanation. First, whatever the rhetoric, teachers were never allowed to participate in school governance (nor were local administrators). Second, there are still no teacher organizations, independent of the government, which can mobilize teachers to influence local personnel decisions. Both facts increase the relative power of the school director.

Dismissing teachers is a special case. In the former, State-dominated system, the Russian phrase for losing your job was, "crossed out of life". Hanging on to a job, any job, is a survival issue given the lack of alternate employment in the fragile Russian economy. The combined influence of subordinates – teachers, parents, and students (28 percent) – is bigger than that of the regional and district authorities (23 percent) and 14 times bigger than that of the Ministry of Education (2 percent). This, despite the fact that the Ministry issues regulations on dismissal. Although it is commonly believed in Russia that constant disapproval from parents and students can force a dismissal, such cases are in fact extremely rare.

*Budgets.* The issue of budget control is reflected in the responses to the questions of who exercises the most influence over the total budget and over each department's budget. Local school administrators have been emancipated from the central Ministry; the school district is reported to be far more powerful than any other source of influence (see Table 3). At the same time, joint teacher/parent influence is practically negligible. School administrators do not believe parents and teachers are capable of contributing to the budgetary process (they have their own, chronic family economic crises?) and even if they wanted to, administrators *do not know how* to involve parents and teachers.

## IMPORTANCE OF SCHOOL ADMINISTRATORS FOLLOWING ORDERS AND BEING LOYAL TO AUTHORITIES

Schools are bureaucracies the world over. The plus side is a certain regularity and even equity of service; the minus side is often a mindless pathology. The previous regimes recognized that independent schools would be social dynamite. They selected school administrators for dependability, predictability, malleability and loyalty and that was often measured by Party service. We measured the current reality: how important did administrators think it was to follow orders?

When all the answers to the question about loyalty and willingness to follow orders are combined, 51 percent of respondents think that it is important for a school administrator to be loyal to the three different levels of government and to follow orders. But while 62 percent believe in loyalty to municipal or local government, only 32 percent think it is necessary to be loyal to the central government (see Figure 1) and that is an intriguing measure of decentralization in process.

## "DECENTRALIZATION": ALTERNATE REALITIES IN RUSSIA

The word "decentralization" can mean many things to a Russian school administrator: first, economic independence ("My school is now paid for locally."); second,

**Table 3: Russian School Administrators' Estimate on the Sources of Influence Over the School Budget**

| School budget | Source of influence %/(N) | | | | | | |
|---|---|---|---|---|---|---|---|
| | Dis | Self | Reg | Min | Tch | Par | Stu |
| Each department's budget | 38 (1090) | 29 (830) | 17 (500) | 5 (154) | 7 (196) | 3 (72) | 2 (44) |
| Total budget | 35 (989) | 16 (460) | 27 (763) | 16 (457) | 2 (56) | 3 (92) | 1 (33) |
| Mean | 36 (2079) | 22 (1290) | 22 (1263) | 11 (611) | 4 (252) | 3 (164) | 1 (77) |

*Note.* Errors due to rounding. Dis = municipal authorities; Self = the respondent her/himself; Reg = regional authorities; Min = Ministry of Education; Tch = teachers; Par = parents; Stu = students.

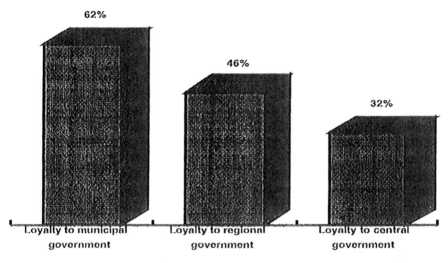

62%

46%

32%

Loyalty to municipal government | Loyalty to regional government | Loyalty to central government

Figure 1: Administrators' Attitudes Regarding Issues of Loyalty.

functional independence ("Why be bothered by Moscow? We make our own decisions here."); or third, geographic independence ("Do you really imagine that a Moscow bureaucrat will endure 10 hours on two different Aeroflot planes to inspect this school?"). At the same time, those who believe they are independent economically may believe themselves still to be dependent functionally and so on.

We used factor analysis of item responses among respondents to map this part of their political/administrative conscious. The responses clustered around three dimensions – political, economic and psychological decentralization.

Political decentralization (.65710) describes decision making independence. Economic decentralization (.68780) relates to the "golden rule" – whoever has the gold, rules. Psychological decentralization (.79745) measures the willingness of school administrators to separate from their past and create a new future.

The political decentralization scores support the earlier analysis of the continuing salience of hierarchy for a substantial fraction, about half, of Russia's administrators.

Economic decentralization is impacted by the still evolving reality of finance for local schools. The central government, regional government, municipal government, a sponsoring institution (e.g., a local pharmaceutical plant or a fishing fleet), or other local sources can all participate in paying for schools. The group for whom the economic factor was most salient made all their decisions according to who was providing the most money – what got taught to students; which books were used; how students were tested; how teachers were hired, trained, evaluated, and dismissed. They also made decisions about school morale and climate, about school budget, and about their future goals – all according to the source of money. If most of the money came from the Ministry, then they took their signals from that level. Similarly, they were also sensitive to municipal sources or local sources.

Throughout, centrally-oriented administrators were more grateful for guidance than resentful. They have no training in site level decision making, their own authority is unclear, and Russian history teaches a certain prudence.

In 1997, the average school administrator's income was $75 a month, mostly from a single source. The salary has increased since, but the cost of living has increased even more. To stay on the job with such a salary requires devotion to education. It also means frustration and anger because in spite of government promises to equalize educators' salaries with those of industrial workers, school people are paid 50 percent less. (To fill the gap, school administrators continue to meet classes and thus qualify for some amount of pay as teachers.) Wage exploitation is one explanation for the 54 percent of the respondents who think that the main obstacle to education reform is the "low prestige" of schooling. Communist ideology had always celebrated manual labor, e.g., trolley operators made more than engineers. Paradoxically, the press to be admitted to private schools and universities continues unabated as does the general cultural respect for learning.

What school people perceive as "low prestige" is more likely triage decision making on the part of governments who have to allocate chronically scarce resources among economic sectors all of which are collapsing if at different rates. This is "if it is not broken, don't fix it" logic. Russian schools continue to open every morning, the universality of literacy is a world leading accomplishment and the scientific establishment continues to function.

We recommend moving school finance as close to local schools as possible. Second, we recommend lump sum budgets to schools. The recommendations assume that administrators are ready for change. Some are, some are not. From our evidence, particularly with respect to personnel and curriculum matters, most are not yet prepared or willing to make independent decisions and that may relate to the third factor, psychological decentralization.

Seventy-five percent of the respondents believe that they can influence their own schools. Curiously, the same school administrators who feel dependent about political and economic factors claim psychological independence. In a country with as many contradictions as birch trees, explanations are chancy. The 1992 law announced a new local freedom but there is no money to support local judgements. The Ministry has theoretically and sometimes practically been supplanted by regional and local authorities, but it continues to issue regulations and orders. Most local administrators recognize that they are now expected to do what none of them has ever done before, run their own schools. Authority without resources, responsibility without independence, expectations without support. Rational models are not always the most powerful explanations (Richards & Height, 1988).

## SOCIO-DEMOGRAPHIC AND BIO-SOCIAL VARIATIONS

Do these attitudes and practices vary across the multitude of Russian circumstances? If they do not, then the monolith prevails and Russian school administrators have not begun to differentiate themselves and their institutions.

But if there are variations, then those differences may illuminate what seems to be working in the reformation of Russian public school leadership. We examined possible differences by gender and age, by hierarchical position (superintendent, school director, etc.), and by region (wealth varies greatly across Russian regions). We assembled responses to the items that had the most discriminatory power about centralization and decentralization. We then created a four-point "centralization" scale where a respondent's belief in a Moscow-centered universe was a "1" and a school or district centered belief was a "4".

## THE SUMMARY DISTRIBUTION OF ATTITUDES TOWARD CENTRALIZATION

The mid-point of our four-point centralization-to-decentralization scale is 2.5. The mean value for all 1399 respondents was 2.59, just slightly over the line toward a decentralized, district centered attitude. Although there are no prior data for comparison purposes, that slight tilt in this group is very probably progress. The fact of significant variation across the group (the first decile is 2.292 and the last decile is 2.955) is certainly progress in differentiating school practice and in moving toward the flexibility and responsiveness available through decentralization.

*Men and women administrators.* The sample had 864 female and 535 male respondents. The mean of the female respondents on issues of centralization was 2.49 (s.d., .38). The mean of the male respondents was 2.57 (s.d., .36). The difference is statistically and programmatically significant in that men are more locally oriented than are women. Why? One hint is in recent history, the other in tradition. By tradition, men were accorded more autonomy than women. Additionally, in the last five, post-Soviet years, 70 per cent of the newly appointed administrators have been men, a group presumably less burdened by the past. (Across the whole sample, age is not related to attitudes toward centralization. That is a bit of a surprise since older administrators will have had far more experience with the previous system. But what is the consequence of that exposure? Familiarity breeding contempt and rejection? Or familiarity conditioning incumbents to the traditions of the *ancien regime*? Because both are probably operating in our sample, the likely result is a lack of significant difference.)

*Location in the hierarchy.* The chain of command for Russian schools now more closely resembles a Western model with local superintendents and individual school directors. The exception remains the "chairpersons of the district methodology units." Historically, these people were the enforcers of political correctness. That happened through school inspections, pupil testing and especially teacher training. (Inspection scores still affect salary.) The position has been continued and although the singular dogma no longer applies, so many of the incumbents are holdovers from the Soviet days that they are widely regarded as obstacles to reform.

Table shows the distribution of attitudes by position with school directors being significantly more independent than the "methodology chairs".

Earlier we saw that municipal authorities are regarded as the most powerful sources of direction for school directors. But those same municipal authorities are fiscally dependent on both regional and federal governments. For school directors, superintendents are "shock absorbers" who take part of the federal and regional pressure.

The data document that there is a statistically significant difference between superintendents and chairpersons of the district methodology units. There is also a highly significant statistical difference between school directors and superintendents, and between school directors and chairpersons of the district methodology units. To summarize, school directors feel more decentralized from the central authorities than district superintendents and much more decentralized than the often retrograde chairpersons of the district methodology units. Superintendents also feel more decentralized than chairpersons of the district methodology units.

REGIONAL DIFFERENCES

Russia is mammoth – eleven time zones; some of the coldest places on earth to regions that grow tea; a European country west of the Urals and an Asian country east of those mountains; St. Petersburg and Moscow are world class conurbations profoundly different from rural and village Russia. Because one test of government is the ability to capitalize on divergent strength, we chose six of Russia's 88 administrative units (republics, *kraj, and oblasts*) to study.

Attitudes to decentralization, innovation, and Western management practices were tested across the six regions.

- Krasnoyarskiy kraj is one of the biggest – about a million square miles. Krasnoyarsk is in the north with some of the world's lowest temperatures. It used to be host to the *gulag*. People who work in Krasnoyarskiy kraj get hardship bonuses.
- Chuvashskaya republic is one of the smallest – less than 7,000 square miles.
- Nizhegorodskaya oblast is in the center of Russia, on the Volga and at the intersection of historic West-East trading routes. It was the first to start Western oriented market reforms.
- Nizhegorodskaya oblast was a center of the defense industry, heavily populated, with lots of science institutions.
- Samarskaya oblast is located on the Volga river.
- Stavropolskiy kraj is known as the bread basket of Russia with a comparatively wealthy rural population.
- Sverdlovskaya oblast is the biggest in the Urals region, famous for its heavy and defense industry.

The data suggest that school administrators from four regions: Stavropolskiy kraj, Krasnoyarskiy kraj, Samarskaya oblast, and Sverdlovskaya oblast believe themselves to be more decentralized than school administrators from Chuvashskaya republic and Nizhegorodskaya oblast (see Table 5).

Table 5: The Difference in the Level of Decentralization Between Means Based on Regions

| Mean | Region | Difference | | | | | |
|---|---|---|---|---|---|---|---|
| | | Gr1 | Gr2 | Gr3 | Gr4 | Gr5 | Gr6 |
| 2.5696 | Stavropolskiy kraj | | | | | * | * |
| 2.5628 | Krasnoyarskiy kraj | | | | | * | * |
| 2.5599 | Samarskaya oblast | | | | | * | * |
| 2.5434 | Sverdlovskaya oblast | | | | | * | * |
| 2.4470 | Nizhegorodskaya oblast | | | | | | |
| 2.4461 | Chuvashskaya republic | | | | | | |

The fact of variation is progress for post-Soviet Russia. In fact, on closer examination, it turns out that the Nizhegorodskaya school administrators are objecting not to Moscow's domination but to the amount of supervision from their regional authorities.

*Urban/rural Differences.*

While the bulk of our sampled administrators practiced in either urban or profoundly rural places, a small group (17) could be classed as suburbs. There were not statistically significant differences in attitudes by kind of place. Although urban administrators are more visible and therefore more vulnerable to federal, regional, and municipal authorities, they were just as likely or as unlikely to feel themselves independent as were their colleagues.

Nonetheless, there are profound differences among schools in the different settings. Rural Russia is starved for resources (a Russian aphorism states, "70 percent for Moscow, 30 percent for Russia"). The Soviet system of internal passports (really, restrictions on travel) was intended, among other things, to stem the flow of talent from villages to the cities. Rural life is so difficult that it is often the case that school administration positions are offered to literally anyone who will take them. There are two main groups of rural school administrators in the sample: (a) young (25–35 years of age) and inexperienced (1–5 years of administrative experience); and (b) comparatively old (50–66) and experienced (more than 10 years in administration).

The first, inexperienced group feels strongly dependent on Moscow-supplied textbooks and curriculum. Such dependence is encouraged by the older faculty members who are often not willing to change anything in their practices (especially not for the miserable salaries they receive). The data document that there is also a very large personnel turnover among young rural school administrators. They prefer to look for better paid jobs and to treat school administration as an intermediate step in their career. With only a weak link to the profession they are unlikely to pursue independent decentralized policies.

The second group consists of the people who have been administrators for many years and who are not likely to find another job. They prefer obedience and would like to preserve everything unchanged.

Rural school administrators need incentives to stay on the job and pursue reform. Those incentives should not come from Moscow since that would only increase dependence. The incentives should come from municipal authorities and can be provided in the form of free training and retraining, bonuses, extra days of paid leave, job security, professional recognition, and so on.

That is why, when selecting educators for administrative positions, age should not be a determining factor.

## SUMMARY

In 1992, the then Minister of Education told one of the authors that school reform in Russia was doomed to a "Potemkin village fate" (the showcase facades constructed on the banks of the Volga to impress the Czarina with totally illusory progress). The chief obstacle, he believed, was school administrators almost all of whom had been selected by the Party for their stolid obedience.

On this evidence he was half right, half wrong. About half of Russia's school administrators are shifting their orientation, changing their practice, asserting their own authority to fill the vacuums created by the collapse of the previous regime. That is remarkable progress, particularly so in light of the lack of rewards, the near total absence of resources, and the ever present prospect of punishment (in Russia, as elsewhere, 'no good deed goes unpunished').

Administrators are one of the pivots of an improvement policy. Centrally powered strategies are no longer available, moreover of the 70-years of Soviet Union historical experience, they are unacceptably counter-productive and ineffective. The conclusion does not invalidate the accomplishments of Russian schooling. They were real and they were worthy. But it does say that the governance system turned out to be inadequate.

But if a school system the size of Russia's cannot be driven from the top, neither can it be led from the bottom. Thus, the importance of administrators and of better administration. The current generation of Russian policymakers are world class in their willingness to try new arrangements. They instituted school boards and when they did not work, they let them die. They have tried parent choice and vouchers, chartered for-profit schools and encouraged public schools into market ventures. Electing school heads did not work, but at least it was tried *and* the mistake was fixed.

While there is still a distance to be traveled to fully decentralized and democratic schooling, the fact of the matter is that Russian educators have begun and have great prospects for success. They deserve respect and help.

## NOTES

1. The data were collected through a 54 question, 340 item paper questionnaire. Given the understandable Russian cultural resistance to "that which is written down" and its previously draconian

consequences, one early task was to familiarize respondents with the procedures (and limited uses) of survey research. A room full of Russians will inexorably turn what is in the West an unremarkable individual task, filling out a survey, into a group-think exercise with small groups instantly formed to determine what "the best" or at least "the acceptable" answer should be to any question.

We searched for joint associations between our attitudinal variables of interest and demographic and socioeconomic characteristics such as age, gender, extent of administrative experience, size of school, geographical region and urbanicity. Western studies often include racial composition and wealth but for Russia in the 90's both were irrelevant. The economic differences were among regions with high (Krasnoyarsk) and low (Stavropol) costs of living. School administrators' ages in the sample varied between 26 and 68. The number of female school administrators in the sample (62%) is about the same as the number of female school administrators in the country (61%).Administrators' experience varied from a few months to 34 years.

The size of the population is 65,234 schools and more than 150,000 school administrators. Our sample size of 1,399 is big enough to keep the standard error less than 2.6 percent, or + 1.3 percent. The survey was distributed among 1,597 school administrators; the researchers got 1,537 responses of which 1,399 were useable. Those 1,399 included school superintendents, chairpersons of subject methodology units, and school directors (principals) from Novosibirsk, Krasnodar, Krasnoyarsk, Nizhniy Novgorod, Samara, and Stavropol regions.

Multiple regression analysis was used for continuous data (age, experience, etc.), and a t-test was used for the discrete data that had two groups (e.g., male and female). Data that had more than two groups were analyzed by an ANOVA test.

2. Decile Distributions of School Administrators According to Attitudes Toward Decentralization

| Percentile | Value |
|---|---|
| 10 | 2.292 |
| 20 | 2.408 |
| 25 | 2.447 |
| 30 | 2.457 |
| 40 | 2.545 |
| 50 | 2.593 |
| 60 | 2.667 |
| 70 | 2.727 |
| 75 | 2.773 |
| 80 | 2.818 |
| 90 | 2.955 |

Variance is .09; skewness -.51; minimum-1.00; maximum-3.67.

# ENDNOTES

[1] 'The authors had the support of the Soros Foundation and the World Bank in the conduct of this analysis. They are grateful to Dr. Jody Spiro, then Executive Director for CIS countries in Soros Foundations and Steven J. Heyneman of the World Bank.When asked about their needs, Russian school people often identify "the humanizing of schools" which turns out to mean, among other things, minimizing the physical and moral abuse of students. Only schools with "special needs" (i.e., schools for students with physical or mental disabilities – 20 in the sample) are totally dependent on the Ministry of Education. They get their budget directly from Moscow. One of the most troubling barriers to cross-cultural communication with Russian school administrators stems from the communist habit of appropriating the terminology of democracy but loading it with very different realities. "worker participation", for example, meant the opportunity to support "State organs." "Democracy" existed within the narrow and peculiar confines of the Party hierarchy. While "planning" is generally understood as the decomposition and scheduling of tasks toward a goal, a

middle-aged Russian will hear the same word and think, "their manipulation of me." In fact, that was the response of a Siberian administrator to our questions. The numbers after each factor report the extent to which the items that compose that factor are related to one another.

[2]   "Training" for school administrators continues largely unchanged from the previous regime's model: find a 'good teacher' and have that person attend a month-long, in-service course about pedagogy and psychology. That model was the school based reflection of communist ideology – workers were always more important than bosses and thus, since teachers were more important than administrators, special support for administrators would have violated the dogma. It also suited Soviet purposes since the nominal "leaders" of the school never had the resources to create that dangerous entity, an independent school.

## REFERENCES

Richards, C. E., & Height, R. (1988). Accountability and performance: Incentives for school principals. *Public Productivity Review*, **21**(1), 15–27.

Saprykin, V. S. (1990). Upgrading the qualifications of organizers of public education. (1990). *Soviet Education*, **32**(5), 21–31.

Simonov, V. P. (1994). *Pedagogicheskoje rukovodstvo v srednej shkole* [Pedagogical management for secondary schools]. Unpublished manuscript.

Ushakov, K. (1994a). *Training school administrators in Russia*. Unpublished paper commissioned by the World Bank).

Ushakov, K. (1994b). *Incentives for school administrators*. Unpublished paper commissioned by the World Bank.

Ushakov, K. (1993). Po puti osoznaniya sovmestnykh tselei. Nekotoryie elementy tekhnologiyi upravleniya [Realizing shared goals: Some elements of management technologies]. *Direktor shkoly* **2**, 31–35.

Weick, K. E. (1976). Educational organizations as loosely coupled systems. *Administrative Science Quarterly*, **21**, 1–19.

II: Large Scale Strategies for School Change

# Accelerated Schools: A Decade of Evolution

HENRY M. LEVIN

*Stanford University*

*The Accelerated Schools Project is designed to create schools that provide enriched and accelerated learning opportunities for all students throughout the curriculum. This chapter assesses the first decade of Accelerated Schools which has grown from two pilot schools in 1986 to almost 1000 schools in 1996. The key factors and changes in the development of the project are considered in light of the lessons learned in making sense of large scale change.*

## BACKGROUND

The Accelerated Schools Project is designed to create schools that provide enriched and accelerated learning opportunities for all students throughout the curriculum. It is especially focused on those schools with high concentrations of students who are at-risk of educational failure, schools that have devoted themselves traditionally to less challenging instruction through assuming that such students need remediation. It is premised on the assumption that through challenging educational experiences that build on student strengths, all students can be brought into a rich educational mainstream and become academically able. The Project completed its first decade in 1996, having grown from just two pilot schools in 1986–87 to almost 1000 elementary and middle schools in 40 states and ten regional centers at the beginning of its eleventh year. ("Accelerated Schools Project: Celebrating a Decade of School Reform", 1996/97). It is presently projected to continue developing for two more decades, a planned life of 30 years. However, it was not spawned with such an ambitious plan.

The purpose of this chapter is to describe and analyze the evolution of the project to this point. I believe that such documentation is important because it's lessons may inform others on how a small research project was scaled up and refined in order to expand. This evolution is witness to the need for continual learning and modification. In this process, plenty of mistakes were made and will continue to be made. The key to our survival, expansion, and accomplishments is found in how we identified problems and responded (sometimes reluctantly) to what we had earlier believed were sound and effective strategies. This perspective is particularly important because it contrasts with the common myth that effective designs for change are formulated in pristine form as "treatments" or interventions. In recent years, it has become widely recognized in the literature on school

*M. Fullan (ed.), Fundamental Change*, 137-160.
© 2005 *Springer. Printed in the Netherlands.*

organizations that schools are not inert entities that can be altered predictably and purposively. To the contrary, schools can modify interventions imposed on them so that the "treatment" is altered far more than the "host" and looks different from site-to-site (e.g., Fullan, 1982; Berman & McLaughlin, 1977). But, there is much less recognition of how these types of lessons are also useful for monitoring, understanding, and modifying continuously the developmental path of an intervention as it goes to scale. The purpose of this chapter is to document this evolution for the Accelerated Schools Project in the hope that it can contribute to the knowledge of others who are contemplating or engaged in educational change.

The organization of this chapter will follow the evolutionary metaphor. I will begin with the origins of the project including my own metamorphosis from an economist to an economist-educator and the genesis of the ideas behind Accelerated Schools. I will follow this foundation with the experience of establishing pilot schools to test the intervention and refine it. From there I will focus on our first attempts to replicate the early results through expansion and scaling up. Unfortunately, the first attempt to scale up the intervention did not yield the pristine successes that we expected, so the next section will report the attempts to redesign the replication and expansion. In the final section I will discuss the building of support structures and the need to continually strategize to overcome the obstacles that inhibit change.


FROM CONCEPTION TO GESTATION

Although I have been on the faculty of the School of Education since 1968, I do not have a traditional background in education. My PhD. is in Economics, and prior to my arrival at Stanford I had worked as an economist at the Brookings Institution in Washington, D.C. Although I had served a stint as a long-term substitute in social studies at a junior high school in Washington, D.C., I had no pretensions about being an expert on curriculum, instruction or teacher training. My specialty was in the economics of education and human resources, and my professional work addressed issues in the financing of education, educational productivity, and workplace productivity. In the latter guise I had taken a special interest in worker participation and democratic work organizations and had published extensively on these subjects (e.g. Levin, 1976, 1983; Jackall & Levin, 1984). I had also worked extensively on issues of educational reform, especially as they relate to changes in the workplace (Carnoy & Levin, 1976, 1985; Rumberger & Levin, 1989) and community control of schools (Levin, 1970a). Although I had done some fieldwork for projects on the workplace, the methodologies that pervaded most of my past work were quantitative including mathematical and econometric models (Levin, 1970b, c; 1974).

I mention all of this in advance because it is clear that I was not especially well-suited to undertake directly an educational reform with deep pedagogical roots. At best I had the knowledge of workplace organizations, and particularly participative and democratic ones to draw upon. The segue into my attempt to change schools had its origins in my response to the publication of *Nation At Risk* which provided a scathing indictment of our educational system (National Commission on Excellence in Education, 1983). Since my professional career had been launched during the War on Poverty of the middle sixties, I had a special interest in what were called disadvantaged populations. I was startled to find that the national debate asserting a crisis in education as exemplified in *Nation at Risk* had nothing to do with the educational plight of the impoverished of the nation, but only those fortunate enough to enter the college preparatory track in anticipation of enrollment in higher education.

Reports such as *Nation at Risk* and the slew of other reports calling for national educational reform addressed primarily the educational status of secondary school students in academic tracks, and particularly the decline in their test scores over the previous two decades and their poor test score performances in comparison with those of students in other countries. Although these reports called for more required academic courses and more demanding courses in high school, they said nothing about students who were dropping out because they found the present regimen too difficult or had opted for a non-academic course of study.

I decided to turn my attentions to the so-called educationally disadvantaged student to find out what had happened. I began by studying issues of definition and demography and proceeded to educational practices and outcomes for these students and their continuation into adult life. In short, I found that: (1) By almost any definition, the numbers of educationally disadvantaged students had risen because of rising poverty rates among children, increasing immigration, and rising numbers of children in families under stress; (2) These students enter school without many of the developmental skills and behaviors that schools value, and they get farther and farther behind academically the longer they are in school and have high drop out rates (Kaufman, McMillen, & Sweet, 1996); (3) Their poor educational foundation leads to low productivity, poor employment prospects, costly involvement in the systems of criminal justice and welfare, and the spawning of another generation of disadvantaged. By 1984, I completed the first of two reports on this subject(Levin, 1985, 1986), but by this time I had also become curious about solutions.

Why hadn't we made more progress over the twenty years of Title I and Chapter I and all of the other categorical programs? What about the exemplary programs disseminated by the National Diffusion Network that had been "shown" to demonstrate success? What did recent research say about school effectiveness for educationally disadvantaged or at-risk students? How did teachers, other school staff, parents, and students view their schools? And, to a naive outsider (myself) what does one observe in these schools that leads to success or failure? During the 1985–86 academic year I was obsessed with the answers to these questions. I read considerable research; pursued sites of projects of the National Diffusion Network; visited and observed numerous schools and classrooms; and interviewed school staff, students, and parents at sites around the country.

There were many surprises. First, many of the usual criticisms of the schools seemed patently absurd. I saw few teachers who were not arriving early and leaving late with handfuls of work to be completed at home. Many school staff met in the evenings and weekends to prepare for major school events. The pace of work was continuous and demanding with many external disruptions and the challenges of responding to the diverse needs of students from many different cultures and backgrounds. Interviews with teachers confirmed to me their obvious insights and great desires to succeed as well as their frustrations with the failures of conventional school practices. Most of the classrooms were stifling in their obsessions with low-level basic skills and repetitious drill and practice. Calls to projects of the National Diffusion Network brought additionally, discouraging insights. Many that had been listed only a few years before no longer existed at their original sites. Even those that were continuing were unable to provide longitudinal evaluations of their effectiveness. Some of the projects seemed promising, but they were piecemeal at best, focusing on a particular subject or instructional technique rather than on school-wide reform.

Worst of all was the notion of remediation. The Webster's New Collegiate Dictionary (1979) describes remediation as the "act or process of remedying" where remedy is defined as "treatment that relieves or cures a disease" or "something that corrects or counteracts an evil" (p. 970). Presumably, children who are put into remedial programs are children who arrive at school with "defects" in their development that require repair of their educational diseases, evils, or faults. But, the school repair shop is peculiar because children are never repaired. Rather, they are likely to remain in the repair shop for their entire education whether it is labeled as Title I, LD (learning disability), or any of the many categorical labels. This, in itself, convinced me that programs that slow down the pacing of the curriculum and reduce its depth, emphasize drill and practice, proscribe meaningful applications and problem-solving, and ignore or derogate the experiences and culture of the child will have a predictable effect in stunting the educational development of the child. Although educational remediation was designed with the best of intentions, one must judge it by its results. Once in the repair shop, children will be treated as permanently damaged goods and view themselves in that way for the rest of their educational careers.

The obvious solution seemed to be to do the opposite. If children arrive at school without the skills that schools expect, slowing-down their development through remediation will get them farther behind. If all the young are ultimately to enter successfully the academic mainstream, we must accelerate their growth and development, not retard it. This notion was further reinforced by the fact that the only educational stimulation and excitement that I saw in schools with high concentrations of at-risk students was in the few classrooms characterized as "gifted and talented" or "enrichment." In these classes, students were identified according to their strengths and provided with educational activities and projects that built on those strengths. Instead of being stigmatized with labels as "slow learners," they were celebrated for their talents. And, learning was palpable in those classrooms as their highly valued and stimulated students were continually motivated and challenged to think, reflect, create, and master.

By the late Spring of 1986 I had written a six page, single-spaced memo calling for accelerated schools for at-risk students which was adapted as a short article in *Educational Leadership* in March 1987 (Levin, 1987a). The idea was to create a school that would accelerate the development of all of its students by building on their strengths rather than searching for and "remediating" their weaknesses. However, the ideas in themselves would not carry the day because they opposed the conventional wisdom and practices that prevailed on the subject of educating at-risk students. To succeed, we would have to transform profoundly the culture of the school, a task that some (e.g. Sarason, 1982) thought was not possible. Accordingly, I asked my colleague Larry Cuban to assist me during the summer of 1986 to find pilot schools in two San Francisco Bay area school districts that might work with us to implement the ideas, schools with high concentrations of children in at-risk situations.

It should be noted that I had given little thought to the transformation process, that is how to get schools to shift from their traditional practices to accelerated ones. Rather, I had attempted to describe why schools should move to acceleration and what those practices might consist of. I was not fully aware in the early eighties that the major challenge to educational reform is not coming up with good ideas, but getting those ideas in practice. I had a hint about this from the work of Cuban (1984) who provided impressive evidence that historical attempts at school reform had been overwhelmed by constancy rather than change. Fullan (1982) too had stressed that change in schools is not straightforward. But, personal experience is a far more powerful teacher than readings and theory, and I was about to learn the challenges on a first-hand basis.

Fortunately, previous experience and a fortuitous event conspired to assist me. The first was that I had spent more than a decade studying worker democracy (Levin, 1982), worker cooperatives (Jackall & Levin 1984) and how workers manage their own work organizations. This gave me a unique view into how democracy can create more productive work organizations, even though I had not yet tied these lessons to schools. The fortuitous event that occurred was the involvement of an unusually capable group of graduate students had heard about what I had in mind and asked to join the project. They consisted of a former director of Title I in a school district, a former elementary school principal, a former teacher, and a number of graduate students drawn from non-educational backgrounds who were inspired by the philosophy and ambitious goals of the project. In addition, my wife, Pilar Soler, a Latina with teaching experience, joined the activity.

## BIRTH OF PILOT SCHOOLS

By the fall of 1986 we had located two schools that had been nominated by their school superintendents to consider becoming accelerated schools. In both schools more than 80 percent of the students qualified for free or subsidized lunches, an indicator of poverty. But, there the schools departed considerably in their characteristics. The smaller school, which I will call Alpha, had only about 350 students comprised of about 30 percent Hispanic, 27 percent African-American, 24 percent Chinese, and about 19 percent others including Filipinos, Pacific Islanders, Native Americans, and less than 10 percent Anglos. About one-third of the students were drawn from the local neighborhood, and two-thirds were bussed to achieve racial balance in compliance with a district-wide court mandate. Many of the students from the local neighborhood lived in a public housing project that had a notorious reputation for drugs and violence.

The other school (I will call Beta) was about twice as large with Hispanics accounting for over 90 percent of its enrollment, mostly children of recent Mexican immigrants from rural villages. Both schools shared high student turnover and very low student achievement whether assessed by standardized test scores or direct evaluation of their written work and discourse both inside and outside of the classroom. Neither school had much evidence of parent participation, and even parent-teacher conferences and major school events showed relatively sparse attendance. Disruptive incidents were frequent in both schools, with a constant stream of students headed to the school office for discipline.

Each school was assigned a team of three to four Stanford participants including myself who spent one or two days a week at the school observing classrooms and school events and interviewing teachers, support staff, parents, and students. Within a few weeks our teams were viewed as part of the schools with many invitations to team members to observe lessons and visit classes. During this period we provided written versions of the ideas behind accelerated schools to all staff and made short presentations at staff meetings. We made it clear that we would not move forward unless the schools voted to make a five year commitment to the project. That commitment came in February 1987 for Alpha and at the end of the school year for Beta where both staffs voted unanimously to adopt the accelerated schools philosophy and practices.

We recognized that we needed to implement a process of change in which the school staff and parents would be the main actors, and we would serve as facilitators. We then initiated a process in the two schools that was a crude precursor of our present approach. We engaged the participants in extensive work on developing a vision based upon detailed discussions on what a dream school might look like and how it would work. We also set out an exploration of what aspects of the school would need to change over the next five years to achieve that dream. We then worked with the staff and parent representatives to assist them to choose those priorities that were most important and that should receive initial attention. These priorities became the basis for establishing cadres and a steering committee which included representatives of the cadres as well as members-at-large from support staff and parents.

By this time we had delineated three principles for creating democratic and accelerated schools in which staff, students, and parents would take responsibility for creating powerful learning environments: unity of purpose, empowerment with responsibility, and building on strengths (Levin, 1987b), and we began to work these into the change process. At each school the process was somewhat different. For example, under the guidance of its Stanford team, Alpha worked heavily on group process and meeting management to avoid some of the disruptive problems of the past. Beta worked at using a Deweyan-inspired process of inquiry to address its challenges. Both schools had cadres addressing parental involvement, student behavior, school organization, and student learning with an emphasis on language at Beta.

We had not developed either the extensive taking stock or the specifics of the powerful learning components of the project, but only that the schools should focus on enrichment rather than remediation. Progress was slow initially. Both schools had a range of teachers, from highly talented ones using constructivist approaches to large numbers who used more traditional teacher-center lessons buttressed by a heavy emphasis on classroom discipline and drill exercises. But, as they began to work together, we saw discussions leading to the creation of thematic units both within and among grades that combined all of the subjects and extended them into field trips and school events. With strong principal support, parents came in increasing numbers to Alpha as parent volunteers and participants in all school events. Beta's parental involvement revolved primarily around major school events rather than parent volunteers with greater diffidence about working in the school among the parents, most of who had come from rural Mexico. Disciplinary problems plummeted as both schools adopted a more consistent approach using praise, role modeling, and a uniform set of values as well as developing a more supportive school climate. Most teachers, but not all, began to look for strengths in all students and to share their successes in the informal conversations at lunchtime, yard duty, and prior to meetings. Student attendance began to improve, and teacher morale rose considerably. The quality of student work began to rise, slowly at first as reflected in student projects and writing. Because of the well-known limitations in the standardized test scores, they were not the prime focus for assessment. Nevertheless, as a by-product of the process, test scores began to rise by the third year. According to district test data, one of the schools went from almost the bottom among 65 elementary schools to the top third.

By this time Beta's principal had been transferred to another position and replaced with a new principal who lacked background in and insights into accelerated schools. Unfortunately, the new principal refused to participate in training workshops. [Since then we have been confronted with other districts that have ignored the specific leadership needs of accelerated schools in assigning principals, often undermining the process and returning the school to its traditional functions. This has resulted in the creation of a district change project to address these and other district support questions. It has also generated an extensive effort on our part in trying to understand the roles and requirements of effective principals for accelerated schools (Christensen, 1994, 1995).]

For every hour spent in the schools by the Stanford teams, there were many hours devoted to trouble-shooting, problem-solving, development of training exercises, and meetings on strategy. The two teams met regularly to share both results and challenges and to solve new problems that had arisen. Although both schools were enthusiastic about the ideas behind accelerated schools, they resisted changes in their daily practices in the initial stages. In many cases, excellent decision processes and wonderful solutions lost out to the comforts of tradition and a preference for cosmetic changes. All of these experiences in the two school settings honed (and sometimes dulled) our own skills, but also inspired us with possibilities as we saw children formerly relegated to remedial classes taking on advanced work and enrichment activities and prospering academically. We learned that real change is not smooth and continuous, but proceeds in fits and starts and must necessarily address tension and conflict rather than avoiding them. Teaming, mutual support, and solidarity can only succeed when past conflicts, divisiveness, and isolation are overcome. As time went by in the two schools, more and more of the learning experiences drew upon the cultures and experiences of the students and engaged them in real-world activities, projects, and research endeavors.

## SCALING UP: FIRST EFFORTS

By 1988 publicity on the project through publications (Levin, 1987a, b, 1988 a, b) and word-of-mouth had generated interest in other states and school districts. With our assistance, the State of Missouri launched five accelerated schools in the autumn of 1988. Team members from Stanford designed and delivered the training, based upon what we had learned from the pilot schools to school teams during the summer of 1988. The State of Illinois received a grant to establish Accelerated Schools in 1989 without our involvement. When we were apprised of the grant, we recommended beginning with just a few pilot schools. However, the state decided to launch 25 schools without either experience or infrastructure. We were requested to work with regional service centers around the state to support these schools, but neither the logistics for such support or the cooperation of the centers materialized. Although we were able to provide a one day informational conference to school representatives, the schools received no specific training with exactly the mixed consequences that one would expect. A few schools were able to make progress, but many were not.

    All of this experience made us aware that we needed to begin to work on formalizing both the process of becoming an accelerated school and incorporating that process into programs of training and support. In the autumn of 1989 we began this second phase with the involvement of two new staff members, Wendy Hopfenberg and Pilar Soler. Hopfenberg became the first full-time staff member with specific responsibility for launching accelerated middle schools, but eventually her responsibilities would expand considerably. Soler, my wife, was a Lecturer in Spanish and Portuguese at Stanford and was working at one of the two pilot schools. She took an interest in further development of the Accelerated Schools Process and training. Eventually she would undertake leadership in Accelerated Schools training development. At the same time we received a two year grant to develop a training program that would be used to prepare school teams to launch their own accelerated schools.

    During the spring of 1990, we worked together to flesh out the overall steps of the accelerated schools process and to prepare initial training materials and activities. At the same time, Brenda LeTendre, one of the original Stanford team members had moved to Missouri, and she began to develop the logistics and the content of the team training that would be offered in the summer of 1991 at regional sites around the country. Hopfenberg, Soler, and I began to work on the various stages of the school transformation process, taking advantage of an opportunity to test the new training in Seattle in the spring and autumn of 1990. Also, in the autumn of 1990 we were able to do our first training of a full school staff with weekly follow-up at our first pilot middle school. Fortunately, we were able to incorporate an ethnographic assessment project at that site which provided documentation of both the process and its impact (Finnan, 1992).

We also recognized the limitation of centralizing all of our activity at a single national site and began to design a strategy based upon regional centers. In 1989 we received support to launch our first four satellite centers in New Orleans, Houston, Los Angeles, and San Francisco. These centers were designed to build regional capacity for accelerated schools, starting with a single pilot school at each site and expanding over time. After three days of intensive training of satellite staff in the spring of 1990 and with the assistance of staff from our National Center, each of the satellites launched an Accelerated School in the fall of 1990. These pilot schools and satellite centers were monitored and mentored by our personnel, so that we were able to observe closely the impact of the training model and provide support and trouble-shooting at each center and school site.

## Formalizing the Transformation Process

This constant work on the transformation model drew from direct and collaborative experiences drawing on a number of different school settings which enabled us to construct a systematic process of change that embodied fully our three principles of unity of purpose, decision making with responsibility, and building on the strengths of all the participants.

## (1)  Unity of Purpose

Unity of purpose refers to the common purpose and practices of the school in behalf of all its children. Accelerated Schools require that the schools forge a unity of purpose around the education of all students and all of the members of the school community, a living vision and culture of working together to fulfill this vision. Accelerated Schools formulate and work towards high expectations for all children through daily practice, not slogans, and children internalize these high expectations for themselves.

## (2)  *Empowerment with Responsibility*

Empowerment with responsibility refers to members of the school community, parents, students, and staff, taking responsibility for making informed decisions and for their consequences. That is, all constituents must participate in school life. The school is no longer a place in which roles, responsibilities, practices, and curriculum content are determined by forces beyond the control of its members. The school takes responsibility for the consequences of its decisions through continuous assessment and accountability, holding as its ultimate purpose its vision of what the school will become. This is accomplished through a parsimonious, but highly effective, system of governance and problem solving that ensures participation of students, staff, and parents in the daily life of the school.

## (3)  *Building on Strengths*

Traditionally, schools have been far more assiduous about identifying the weaknesses of their students than looking for their strengths. In an Accelerated School, all students are treated as gifted and talented students, because the gifts and talents of each child are sought out and recognized. Such strengths are used as a basis for providing enrichment and acceleration as well as addressing areas of special need. Strengths include not only traditional categories of talent and multiple intelligences (Gardner, 1983), but also student interests, experiences, and cultural origins. These are used to create powerful learning strategies that build on these strengths. However, in addition, the Accelerated School process searches out and builds on the strengths of all school staff and parents.

From the beginning we constructed the process of school transformation to embed these three principles in all activities rather than to treat them as a checklist. That early formalization of process continues to be at the heart of Accelerated Schools, although it has been deepened and refined considerably in subsequent years. Obviously, a process that has been developed over many years cannot be easily summarized in a few paragraphs, but details are found in Hopfenberg, Levin et al. (1993) and in other sources (e.g. Levin, 1996).

The process begins with school "buy-in" at which time the school becomes familiar with the Accelerated Schools model and its requirements through school visits, videotapes, readings, and discussion. After considerable exploration and discourse, the school community takes a formal vote on whether it wishes to move ahead, devoting the next years to accelerated school transformation. A 90 percent approval by the full school staff, parent and community representatives, and student representatives in middle schools is required today, although 75–80 percent was the requirement in earlier years.

Schools that complete the buy-in process are engaged by Accelerated Schools' staff in making arrangements with the school district to set aside the time requirements for working together and the selection and training of a coach. After these requirements are satisfied and the coach is trained, the school receives initial training on Accelerated Schools philosophy, principles, and practices, and the transformation process. Participants begin the process by taking stock, getting to know virtually every important facet of their school and school community including both strengths and challenges (Hopfenberg, Levin et al. 1993: 60–74). Participants learn and practice new research skills and effective group decision making during the taking stock phase. This phase typically takes several months and culminates in a reporting out of what they have learned.

Taking stock is followed by a deep process of vision setting by the school including parents, students, and all school staff, a process of continuous information gathering and discourse over the next months (Hopfenberg, Levin et al., 1993, pp. 74–83). The taking stock is viewed as a starting point, and the vision as a future framework for a transformed school. The school begins the journey of getting from "here" to "there" by comparing what it has learned in taking stock with where it wants to be. From this the school sets out its highest three to four priorities (Hopfenberg, Levin et al., 1993, pp. 82–86). The agreement on priorities is followed by the establishment of the first cadres – the small groups that will work on each priority – and assignment of staff, parents, and community members to each cadre, usually through self-selection. The final stage is that of deciding how to construct the steering committee using representatives of the cadres and members-at-large. All of these initial phases of the process provide hands-on experience and practice at problem solving, working together democratically, eliciting and building on the ideas of the participants, and creating a unified community.

Governance of the school is done through the work of the cadres, their coordination by the steering committee, and ratification of decisions by the entire school community or school-as-a-whole (SAW) (Hopfenberg, Levin et al. 1993: 86–93). Cadres and steering committee follow an inquiry (Hopfenberg, Levin et al., 1993, pp. 95–137) or problem solving process which is introduced to the school along with team-building and meeting management (Hopfenberg, Levin et al., 1983, pp. 139–158). The entire school works on creating powerful learning situations for its students for both school-wide programs and individual classrooms (Hopfenberg, Levin et al., 1993, pp. 159–280). Much of the internal staff development is devoted to this constructivist approach to learning, using highly engaging strategies that incorporate integrated changes in curriculum, instruction, and context (school climate and organization) and that lead to accelerated learning of children. The powerful learning approach is used for both school-wide change ("large wheels") and for classroom change ("small wheels") (Brunner & Hopfenberg, 1995; Keller & Soler, 1995).

In short, an Accelerated School works continuously at a process of looking for unity in what the school and its children are and will become. Decisions are made through a governance system in which all must participate in a healthy collaboration with emphasis on systematic problem solving using inquiry methods and assessment. It means a school that creates powerful learning situations for all children, one that integrates curriculum, instructional strategies, and context (climate and organization) rather than providing piecemeal changes limited to periodic changes in textbooks, training, and instructional packages. It means a school whose culture is transformed internally (Finnan, 1994) to encompass the needs of students, staff, and parents through creating stimulating educational experiences that build on their identities and strengths. But, having established and refined the process in pilot schools is not equivalent to replicating it systematically in new schools.

*Bringing the Process Into Schools*

The challenge in 1990 was how to incorporate this process into a system of expansion beyond the pilot schools that we were working with directly. For both philosophical and practical reasons we knew that we would have to build capacity at local sites rather than depending upon long supply lines from Stanford University. We decided that the most promising approach was to train teams of representatives drawn from the major stakeholder groups from those local schools. Beginning in 1990 we began to plan a major training initiative for the summer of 1991. During that summer we trained school teams from 70 sites in five day workshops at 7 regional locations around the U.S. Teams were composed of 8–10 persons comprising teachers, support staff, parents, site administrations, and central office persons, eight to ten persons, providing them with an understanding of the Accelerated schools philosophy, principles, process, and practical skills for transforming their schools.

The five days of intensive training focused on taking stock, vision, setting priorities, school governance and decisions, and powerful learning for acceleration (Hopfenberg, Levin et al., 1993). Specific training was provided in team building, problem solving, meeting management, and creating powerful learning experiences as well as in initiating and supporting the major activities of the transformation process.

It had taken five years to develop the essential components of the Accelerated School and to incorporate those into our training. The team training in the summer of 1991 enabled an expansion to over 100 schools nationwide in the autumn of that year. But the expansion did not come off as we had expected. During the autumn of 1991 we made assiduous efforts to follow-up the new schools that had been launched. Each of these schools had presumably gone through our "buy-in" process the previous year in which they read and discussed materials on accelerated schools, watched a half-hour video tape that we had produced, and, in a few cases, visited Accelerated Schools or had teachers and other staff from existing Accelerated Schools visit their school to make presentations and answer questions. Following this process the full school staff and parent representatives (and student representatives at the middle school) voted on whether they wanted to become an Accelerated School with 80 percent support required for moving forward. At that point the schools had put together their teams that were sent to summer training, the training was accomplished, and the schools were launched in the fall of 1991. At least that was the design.

*Assessment of Team Training*

Our follow-up of the newly launched schools in November 1991 provided some astonishing feedback. Roughly one-third of the schools had gotten a good start and were following the process smoothly. Another third had gotten started, but were having a difficult time. One third had not been able to get started at all. This was not an impressive record, given how carefully we had worked on the training and implementation process. Evaluations of the training also had suggested a high level of understanding, enthusiasm, and satisfaction. To put it mildly, we were very disappointed. And we decided to explore why the training had not yielded a high level of success. Every school was followed up with telephone interviews, and in a few cases we were able to do site visits. This assessment yielded important insights.

We found that some of the schools had not followed the "buy-in" process that we required. The principal had simply certified that they had. Thus, the school staffs were resistant to being told that they would now receive training to become an Accelerated School when they had not been involved in the decision and had little or no knowledge on what this was about. In a few cases members of the school team had learned about the training only during the week prior to the event. Many schools also faced a struggle between the insiders that constituted the school team and outsiders who were to be converted to a new set of practices through staff development at the school site. The school team typically had a high level of internal cohesion and bonding derived from its shared summer experience which extended to social activities and references to "inside" jokes and accelerated school lingo. Staff members who had not been part of this experience felt excluded. As a result they resisted collaboration. Their attitude was that if the team wanted to follow the accelerated school model, they could go ahead on their own. Clearly, that would not work in an accelerated school.

In many instances the intensive content of the training over a five day period had overloaded the teams with information that caused them to confuse or forget significant portions of the process. In a few cases the schools were not provided with the staff development days that the district had promised and the principals did not have the commitment or leadership skills that were required. In two cases, principals were moved to other schools before the year began. For all of these reasons the success rate of the expansion was not high.

At the same time we were able to contrast the results of the team training with our more successful experiences from our original pilot schools and the first year of the new accelerated middle school. In all of these cases our National Center for the Accelerated Schools Project had provided coaches to work with the entire school staff, parent representatives, and student representatives simultaneously. With this approach there were no insiders and outsiders as with the team approach, and there was continuous follow-up of the school with weekly visits and assistance. The middle school had been the subject of an ethnographic study of change over its first year (Finnan, 1992). Finnan found that through continuous coaching and mentoring, the entire school was able to undertake what Finnan (1992) termed an "internal transformation process." The coaches had continuous support from the National Center, so that they did not have to worry about having to remember everything about the Accelerated Schools Model from a single training.

## REDESIGNING THE SCALING UP PROCESS

This led to a major change in our approach to scaling up, and paradoxically, a return to an earlier time. The lessons that we learned from the assessment of team training were the following:

- Schools need a highly-trained local coach who can work with them on a regular basis rather than relying on a one-shot training of a school team.
- Training, subsequent mentorship and eventual certification of coaches needs to be integrated into a systematic training model.
- It is crucial to train and support an entire school community at the same time rather than a team or portion of the school. All members of the school and parent and community representatives need to share in the entire experience of transforming their school.
- Our confirmation of the "buy-in" process must assure that schools are ready to be launched.
- Making training sessions participative and engaging is not enough. Both the training of schools and coaches must be based upon constructivist principles in which the values, ideas, and practices are fully embedded in activities undertaken by trainees rather than in more traditional activities and presentations ("Constructivism and the Accelerated Schools Model", 1994).

### A Formal Coaching Model

Accordingly, we initiated a radical redesign of our accelerated schools training model that drew upon the lessons that we had learned from almost six years of experience. In preparation for launching a new set of satellite centers and a cadre of district and state coaches, the new design would include:

- new procedures for school buy-in and forging of agreements with districts for support of accelerated schools in terms of coaching support for training and weekly follow-up and staff development days;
- interview and selection of coaches by our staff;
- an intensive eight day training-of-trainers workshop for coaches that is completely activity-based and embodies a constructivist learning process that we would like to see emulated in schools;
- regular followup of coaches by the National Center through telephone, email, and correspondence as well as site visits to the coaches and schools to provide mentorship and support;

- an end-of-year retreat for the coaches to share experiences and provide feedback to the Project ;
- continuous support and assessment of coaches in the following years to prepare them for full certification so that they can help train other coaches and work independently with schools; and
- the establishment of a database for keeping track of all schools, satellite centers, and coaches.

This ambitious undertaking required design of new procedures, a training process, training activities and case studies, and a system of regular communications with and monitoring of coaches and their schools and districts. In short, it required a radical restructuring of the National Center's training and follow-up model.

Most of the planning and design activity took place in the winter and spring of 1992. At the same time we were completing *The Accelerated School Resource Guide* (Hopfenberg, Levin et al., 1993) which was made available in preprinted form in time for coaches' training in the summer of 1992. Our first attempt was tested on a small group of coach-trainees in the early summer and modified for the larger training. Thirty-seven trainees participated in teams of at least two persons from each of 16 districts or state departments of education. Trainees had to complete extensive applications showing their familiarity with and desire to initiate accelerated schools. Each had to have links with a school that had gone through the buy-in process prior to the summer. Each was also interviewed by telephone for suitability and provided with materials from *The Accelerated Schools Resource Guide* as well as other materials in order to enable them to prepare for the training.

Fortunately, the trainees embraced the new forms of training, and the mentorship and follow-up enabled us to both monitor the progress of schools and coaches and get active feedback from the coaches on the progress of their schools. They were also able to identify areas of training that could be strengthened and to suggest real world challenges for case studies. This feedback has provided us with a continuing source of information for improvement. One or more site visits to each school also enabled our training team to support schools and coaches directly, to make observations of progress, and to engage in joint trouble-shooting where obstacles needed to be surmounted. At the end of the year we held a two day coaches' retreat which enabled the coaches to provide advice for us on future training as well as to share experiences with each other and engage in collaborative problem-solving.

The process of mentoring and feedback provided considerable assistance in revising the training and follow-up in subsequent years. Some things worked well and were retained. Others had to be improved, and we used our own inquiry approach to address them. Each year has been characterized by changes in the training that derive from the field experiences of the coaches as well as our own research on different aspects of the process. In addition, the coaching model has been introduced to our satellite centers which have expanded to ten regional centers with another five in the developmental stages. The satellite centers initially co-trained their coaches with assistance from National Center staff, but followed up their own coaches. They have also brought their coaches to retreats and have networked them and staffs from local accelerated schools at seasonal conferences for accelerated schools.

Within a year we also initiated a three and one-half day training workshop for principals in the autumn, following the launching of the school. To a large degree we have benefited from research that the Project has done on effective principal leadership in Accelerated Schools (Christensen, 1995). By experiencing the first stages of the process in their schools, the interest and attention of the principal is piqued, resulting in a very participative and attentive involvement among principals in the training workshop. Principals also participate in a principals' retreat in the Spring, enabling them to address their specific needs and to contribute to the knowledge of the Satellite Centers and National Center.

The overall result is that we have been able to build a community of about 300 coaches nationally who have had a range of similar challenges and experiences. Some of the coaches are drawn from universities and state departments of education, but most are employed in the central office of their school districts. This has enabled them to participate in getting district support for Accelerated Schools. Although some schools have sought to use principals and teachers as coaches, we have been reluctant because the coaching role is quite different than the role of teacher or site administrator. It is very difficult for a member of the school staff to work effectively in urging a resistant principal to support accelerated school practices of sharing decision making power. Many principals have difficulty in trusting the governance process and tend to undermine it by discouraging it or ignoring it. A good coach needs to be able to communicate honestly with the principal on these behaviors and how to overcome them. At both regional and national retreats and with the assistance of a Network Newsletter, coaches are able to share ideas and assist each other and help the National Center to make improvements.

## BUILDING SUPPORT STRUCTURES

At this writing the Accelerated Schools Project is beginning the eleventh year of an anticipated thirty year life. Although I have stressed the direct efforts at development and expansion, such growth requires far more than training, coaching, and follow-up. It requires building an institutional and knowledge base and a means of effective communication and dissemination. Most notable in this regard are the further development of our network of regional Satellite Centers; the continuing focus on assessment and evaluation; the provision of publications and communications; the deepening and expansion of capacity on powerful learning strategies, and interventions with districts to provide more supportive environments for sustaining Accelerated Schools. The purpose of this final section is to address briefly these support activities as well as to raise important unresolved issues that need our continuing attention.

*Satellite Centers*

By 1989 we realized that expansion and scaling-up depended upon local capacity and ownership of Accelerated Schools. As we noted above, this perspective led to our launching of regional satellite centers of which the first four were established in 1990. All of the initial satellite centers were university based and were expected to work with and develop schools in their regions. These institutions were viewed as regional institutions that would undertake many of the National Center's functions in their geographical areas. They were designed to work initially with pilot Accelerated Schools in order to get hands-on experience, but to eventually undertake research, training, evaluation, publications, and to transform administrator and teacher preparation at their institutions to accommodate accelerated schooling practices.

Personnel at these centers received training in the Accelerated Schools process in the Spring of 1990 and launched pilot schools in the fall with the assistance of personnel from the National Center at Stanford. These centers were expected to build their capacity over time through engaging additional personnel and expanding to new schools as well as undertaking the other functions. We viewed this as a developmental process and provided technical assistance to centers as well as networking events and annual retreats to collaborate and share ideas. In 1992 we added five new centers with special emphasis on establishing accelerated middle schools. We also moved from a strictly university-based sponsorship of centers to ones sponsored by state departments of education and one sponsored by a local district.

By 1995 we had lost two of the original centers when their original funding ran out. Neither had developed a capacity for self-support or expansion despite considerable technical assistance from our National Center. We found that even with the best of intentions, these initiatives do not always succeed. In some cases the institutional base is inappropriate for such endeavors, and in other cases problems of turnover in personnel or lack of commitment are obstacles to survival. These lessons taught us what arrangements need to be in place and what types of support we needed to provide to have a higher probability of successful Satellite Centers, lessons that have been embodied in our programs for establishing and sustaining such centers. With the continuing growth of our Satellite Center movement, we had 10 centers in 1996 with at least another five in the process of being established. In contrast to the initial formation of Satellite centers, new centers are expected to provide their own funding. Satellite Centers are distributed around the Nation with locations in California, Colorado, Illinois, Louisiana, Massachusetts, Missouri, Nevada, North Carolina, South Carolina, and Texas and with new centers forming in Florida, Milwaukee, New York, Oregon, and the San Diego Area and discussions in Ohio and Kentucky. The established centers are working with 17 to 150 schools, and most are continually expanding.

Centers are expected to meet a set of foundational standards to ensure reasonable consistency and quality control for their regions. These are embodied in a satellite agreement that sets out their roles and responsibilities and those of the

National Center. The most recent development entails the establishment of a National Policy Advisory Board comprised of representatives of the Satellite Centers and the National Center that is responsible for establishing both standards and processes of ensuring compliance for all member centers. This development represents a direct voice from the Satellite Centers in the governance of the Accelerated Schools Project as well as an increasing role on their part in sharing responsibilities of planning and direction. Beyond these foundational standards it should be noted that each center is at a different stage of development. Some are in the early stages, working with pilot schools and "training" their own personnel. Others have developed their own coaching model, co-training coaches with the assistance of National Center staff, and others have gone through this stage and are training and mentoring coaches independently. Several are working on transforming teacher-training programs and doing research. Virtually all are sponsoring conferences and retreats for school staff.

Ultimately, we expect our Satellite Centers to represent the larger building blocks of the Accelerated Schools movement, providing coaches' and schools' training, networking, research, evaluation and transforming teacher and administrator preparation in their regions. To do this effectively, both the number of centers and the extent of their operations will need to grow. This is a major goal of the National Center to build regional and local capacity and ownership through satellite centers with the National Center playing a supportive role with its own programs on research, training development, evaluation, and dissemination. Of course, the staff of the National Center will continue to do some coaches' training and school coaching in order to continue to assure that all of our staff have first-hand knowledge of the challenges and experiences of centers, coaches, and schools, and in order for us to test new ideas.

*Evaluation*

Evaluation and assessment are central to Accelerated Schools at every level including those of pupils, classrooms, school as a whole, coaches, Satellite Centers, and our National Center (Assessing Accelerated Schools 1995–96). Since one of our three principles is empowerment to make decisions and responsibility for the consequences of those decisions, we need to know the consequences. Over the first decade we have grown from simple observational assessments of schools and classrooms to a three part assessment process. Our first concern is whether schools have adopted the process, values, practices, and decision-making that are integral to the Accelerated School. Second, we have developed an approach to see if the decisions generated by that process are actually implemented. Third, we have worked with schools and coaches to ascertain the impacts of these decisions and the overall process on student and school outcomes including such results as the quality and variety of student work; improvements in student achievement, attendance, and participation and in parental participation; and reductions in special education placements and retentions in grade. We have also focused on changes in classroom and school climate and issues of racial and gender equity. Each year we issue a summary of results (e.g., Accelerated Schools Project, 1995).

In addition, we have developed an "Internal Assessment Toolkit" that schools and coaches begin to use in the second year of the process to document progress and to identify bottlenecks (Accelerated Schools Project, 1995). This toolkit includes an extensive data portfolio on the school, a coaches log, and an application of benchmarks for school development. This toolkit is designed for the steering committee and the coach to work together to gather documentation that is useful for assessment. Schools are expected to use the data including those on pupil assessment, program assessment, and schoolwide assessment to address their challenges and validate their successes. In addition, the National Center has developed an overall data base on each school that makes use of the data portfolio provided by schools.

In addition to these types of evaluations, a number of schools have been subjected to formal evaluations that compare their progress with similar comparison schools that are not accelerated (e.g., McCarthy & Still, 1993; Knight & Stallings, 1995). These have shown superior results for Accelerated Schools over comparison schools, even though no additional funding has been provided for the former. The Manpower Development Research Corporation has designed a randomized assignment model which we intend to use in a district where we have accelerated middle schools that can be compared with more conventional middle schools (Cave & Kagehiro, 1995). Finally, we have emphasized ethnographic studies (e.g., Finnan, 1992; Peters, 1996 a, b) to gather rich data on school transformation and student processes.

*Powerful Learning Models*

At the heart of an Accelerated School is a learning process that is connected to the school vision and goals and to student and teacher strengths and that links curriculum, instructional strategies, and school context (climate, resources, organization) to a constructivist learning model. One of the goals of the transformation process is to introduce all teachers to the development and use of powerful learning strategies and to expand the schools' capacities to provide powerful learning throughout. The various dimensions of powerful learning are found in Hopfenberg, Levin et al., 1993, Chaps. 5–8. Powerful learning assumes that the best results are achieved by predicating the educational process on the assumption that all students are gifted and talented so that student strengths become key to teaching and learning as opposed to their weaknesses. We have found the implementation of powerful learning to be a major challenge in that it is inconsistent with most traditional teacher training, with assumptions about the needs of at-risk students, and with traditional school culture. The result is that we have put a special effort into the study of and implemention of powerful learning (e.g., Keller & Soler, 1995).

Two particular projects are worthy of mention. First, we have developed a powerful learning project that is attempting to gather examples of powerful learning that can be used to demonstrate how its principles are applied to create effective teaching and learning strategies. Gradually, we are developing a catalog of such examples to provide illustrations and to use in training. In addition, this project is observing individual classrooms in a small sample of schools to document changes in classroom strategies as the school transforms from a traditional school to an accelerated one. Starting from before the transformation, we have made periodic observations of classrooms to document change in order to understand the change process. The second project is just getting started. It is an attempt to establish a powerful learning laboratory in a local school district that can be used to provide extensive training in powerful learning to teachers, coaches, and teacher trainers from the higher education community. Through a month-long summer laboratory experience, participants will develop their own powerful learning projects that they will implement over the subsequent year and document with portfolios. They will be brought together periodically to discuss progress and lessons learned and to assess each other's results.

*Supportive Districts*

One of the major challenges to Accelerated Schools and to school restructuring more generally is the fact that most school districts are not organized and equipped to support the changes. For example, districts often do not take into account the type of leadership that is required for these schools (Christensen, 1995) and simply assign principals according to who is available or who is "deserving" of this administrative role. Districts regularly rotate principals among schools without concern for matching school needs to principal capabilities and interests, and successful principals at Accelerated Schools have been transferred frequently to other schools, breaking the bond that has been created. Often such principals have been replaced by ones with no interest in the Accelerated School philosophy or practices, and the transformation comes to an end. In other cases, districts have not honored their agreements to provide release time for district coaches or the staff development days that were promised. Changes in personnel and a complex diffusion of responsibilities across different school programs and personnel undermine the stability of district commitments too. Accordingly, we have undertaken a study of district organization and functioning in order to assist districts to provide more supportive and sustainable environments for their restructured schools.

*Publications*

Accelerated Schools must be buttressed not only by their coaches and districts and by networking activities with other schools, but also by research and publications that respond to their needs. In addition to a source book on the project and transformation process (Hopfenberg, Levin et al., 1993) and one that shows the ideas in practice ( Finnan, St. John, McCarthy, & Slovacek, 1995), the Accelerated Schools Project provides a regular newsletter to a mailing list of about 13,000 practitioners, policy makers, and researchers. The *Accelerated Schools Newsletter* focuses on a specific topic for each of its three annual issues, combining research findings with information from schools and practitioners on that topic. One or more schools is featured in each issue to illustrate how they have addressed challenges covered by the topic. Recent issues of the *Newsletter* have focused on district support, assessment, troubleshooting inquiry, coaching, powerful learning, and leadership. In addition, the Project has published separate research papers on a wide range of subjects that are central to the needs of accelerated schools including interactive technologies and powerful learning, special education in accelerated schools, and effective principals in accelerated schools. A *Network Newsletter* is also provided to coaches to support their work and provide the latest information on Accelerated Schools developments. And the Project also has a site on the World Wide Web with considerable information and an index (www-leland.stanford.edu/group/ASP).

*High Schools*

A major future agenda is the extension of the model to high schools. At the present time, we are working with a district that has developed accelerated and elementary middle schools and is now beginning to work with two pilot high schools. We expect to learn considerably from this collaborative venture how to incorporate the accelerated schools process into high schools so that students can move along accelerated pathways for all of their elementary and secondary years. In addition, a small number of high schools have adopted the Accelerated Model, with particular success for creating small alternative schools to prevent dropouts (Soler & Levin, 1996). At the same time we are exploring ways of working with the Carnegie Middle Schools Project and the Coalition of Essential Schools to learn how accelerated elementary and middle schools might feed into high schools with similar philosophies from other movements.

A POSTSCRIPT

A decade of toiling in the vineyards of educational change has taught us many lessons. The first is that most of the theory, advice, and cheerleading on educational change comes from those who have not themselves engaged in sustained efforts to work with schools collaboratively to get deep changes. To them, collaboration means that academics and consultants offer the ideas, and the practitioners carry them out. When the reforms fail, the practitioners are blamed for the failure. In my view this is completely wrong because those who assert their theories and formulas for change have never tested their own ideas. Nor do they take any risk.

8

But, worse than the implicit arrogance is the failure to understand the connection between theory and practice. Designing change requires implementation of ideas and assessment by the designer. As I have emphasized throughout this chapter, the deepest understanding derives from the juxtaposition of ideas with implementation, feedback and reformulation; of theoretical insights with direct participation in and ownership of the change process. In contrast, those who provide "expert" advice typically proffer abstract theories and checklists rather than a track record of success at effecting school change.

In my view even the most sensible and compelling guidelines, when they haven't been tested directly, represent hypotheses on change rather than knowledge about change. They may work; they may not work. They should be tested collaboratively by their progenitors in actual school settings to see if they work prior to urging them on educational practitioners. And educational practitioners should always ask their "experts" such questions as: "Where have *you* done this? What have been the results? Where can I see it happening and explore the process myself before considering adopting it?"

A second insight is that all deep school change represents *internal* transformation of school culture. I agree with Sarason (1982) that changes in school culture cannot be imposed upon the school, a point that is also supported by Fullan (1982). Change occurs because those who will be affected by it are able to decide for themselves the future that they will work towards. At best we can provide a process to stimulate change and enable the participants to work together productively in behalf of students and communities. That is certainly a lesson that we have learned directly from the Accelerated Schools Project.

Finally, I return to my original theme in which over a decade of work with hundreds of schools, districts, and coaches and thousands of teachers and students has shown. Any attempt to get deep educational change will represent a lot of trial and error, even with collaborative planning and considerable experience. Strategies that work in some settings will not work in others. Constant assessment is necessary to identify what is working and what is not and why. This knowledge can be used to improve considerably the change process. Even the most experienced person engaged in educational change must still be a student at heart, always seeking, always learning.

## REFERENCES

Accelerated Schools Project. (1995). *Accomplishments of accelerated schools.* Stanford, CA: National Center for the Accelerated Schools Project, Stanford University.

Assessing Accelerated Schools. (1995, 1996). *Accelerated Schools,* 5(2).

Accelerated Schools Project: Celebrating a decade of school reform. (1996, 1997). *Accelerated Schools,* 6(1).

Berman, P., & McLaughlin, M. W. (1977). *Federal programs supporting educational change: Factors affecting implementation and continuation* (Vol. 7). Santa Monica, CA: Rand.

Brunner, I., & Hopfenberg, W. (1995). Growth and learning in accelerated schools: Big wheels and little wheels interacting. In C. Finnan, J. McCarthy, & E. St John (Eds.), *Accelerated schools in action: Lessons from the field* (pp. 24–46). Monterrey Park, CA: Corwin Press,.

Carnoy, M., & Levin, H. M. (1976). *The limits of educational reform.* New York: Longman.

Carnoy, M., & Levin, H. M. (1985). *Schooling and work in the democratic state.* Stanford, CA: StanfordUniversity Press.

Cave, G., & Kagehiro, S. (1995). *Accelerated middle schools: Assessing the feasibility of a net impact evaluation.* New York: Manpower Development Research Corporation.

Christensen, G. (1994). *The role of the principal in transforming accelerated schools: A study using the critical incident technique to identify behaviors of principals.* Doctoral dissertation, School of Education. Stanford, CA: Stanford University.

Christensen, G. (1995). Toward a new leadership paradigm: Behaviors of accelerated school principals. In C. Finnan, E. P. St. John, J. McCarthy, S. P. Slovacek (Eds.), *Accelerated schools in Action: Lessons from the field.* Thousand Oaks, CA: Corwin, 185–207.

Constructivism and the accelerated schools model. (1994). *Accelerated Schools,* **3**(2), 10–15.

Cuban, L. (1984). *How teachers taught: Constancy and change in American classrooms 1890–1980.* New York: Longman.

English, R. A. (1992). *Accelerated schools report.* Columbia, MO: Department of Educational and Counseling Psychology, University of Missouri.

Finnan, C. (1992). *Becoming an accelerated school: Initiating school culture change.* Stanford, CA: National Center the Accelerated Schools Project, Stanford University.

Finnan, C. (1994). School culture and educational reform: An examination of the accelerated schools project as cultural therapy. In G. Spindler & L. Spindler (Eds.), *Cultural therapy and culturally diverse classrooms* (93–129). Monterrey Park, CA: Corwin Press.

Finnan, C., St. John, E. P., McCarthy. J., & Slovacek, S. P. (1995). *Accelerated schools in action: Learning from the field.* Thousand Oaks, CA: Corwin.

Fullan, M. G. (1982). *The meaning of educational change.* New York: Teachers College Press.

Gardner, H. (1983). *Frames of mind.* New York: Basic Books.

Hopfenberg, W., Levin, H. M., & Associates. (1993). *The accelerated schools resource guide.* San Francisco: Jossey-Bass Publishers.

Jackall, R. & Levin, H. M. (Eds.). (1984). *Worker cooperatives in America.* Berkeley and Los Angeles: University of California Press.

Kaufman, P., McMillen, M. M., & Sweet, D. (1996). *A comparison of high school dropout rates in 1982 and 1992.* Technical Report NCES 96–893, National Center for Education Statistics, U. S. Department of Education. Washington, D.C.: U.S. Government Printing Office.

Keller, B. M., & Soler, P. (1995). The influence of the accelerated schools philosophy and process on classroom practices: A preliminary study. In C. Finnan, J. McCarthy, E. St.John, & S. Slovacek (Eds.), *Accelerated schools in action: Lessons from the field.* Monterey Park, CA: Corwin Press: 273–292.

Knight, S., & Stallings, J. ( 1995). The implementation of the accelerated school model in an urban elementary school. In R. Allington & S. Walmsley (Eds.), *No quick fix: Rethinking literacy programs in american elementary schools* (pp. 236–252). New York: Teachers College Press.

Levin, H. M. (1970a). *Community control of schools.* Washington, D.C.: The Brookings Institution.

Levin, H. M. (1970b). A cost-effectiveness analysis of teacher selection. *Journal of Human Resources,* Winter, 24–33.

Levin, H. M. (1970c). A new model of school effectiveness. In A. Mood (Ed.), *Do teachers make a difference?* (pp. 55–78). U.S. Office of Education. Washington, D.C.: U.S. Government Printing Office,

Levin, H. M. (1974). Measuring efficiency in educational production. *Public Finance Quarterly,* **2**(1), 3–24.

Levin, H. M. (1976). A taxonomy of educational reforms for changes in the nature of work. In M. Carnoy & H. M. Levin (Eds.), *The limits of educational reform* (pp. 83–114). New York: Longman.

Levin, H. M. (1982). Issues in Assessing the comparative productivity of worker managed and participatory firms in capitalist societies. In D. C. Jones & J. Svejnar (Eds.), *Economic performance of participatory and labor-managed firms* (Chap. 3). Lexington, MA: Lexington Books.

Levin, H. M. (1983). Education and organizational democracy. In C. Crouch & F. Heller (Eds.), *International yearbook of organizational democracy,* (Vol. I): *Organizational democracy and political processes* (pp. 227–248). New York: John Wiley,.

Levin, H. M. (1985). *The educationally disadvantaged: A national crisis.* Philadelphia: Public/Private Ventures.

Levin, H. M. (1986). *Educational reform for disadvantaged students: An emerging crisis.* West Haven, CT: National Education Association.

Levin, H. M. (1987a). Accelerated schools for the disadvantaged. *Educational Leadership,* **44**(6), 19–21.

Levin, H. M. (1987b). New schools for the disadvantaged. *Teacher Education Quarterly,* 14(4), 60–83.

Levin, H. M. (1988a). Accelerating elementary education for disadvantaged students. In Council of Chief State School Officers, *School success for students at risk* (pp. 209–226). Orlando, FL: Harcourt Brace Jovanovich, Publishers.

Levin, H. M. (1988b). *Towards accelerated schools.* New Brunswick, NJ: Center for Policy Research in Education, Rutgers University.

Levin, H. M. (1996). Accelerated schools after eight years. In L. Schauble & R. Glaser (Eds.), *Innovations in learning* (pp. 329–352). Mahwah, NJ: Lawrence Erlbaum Associates.

McCarthy, J., & Still, S. (1993). Hollibrook accelerated elementary school. In J. Murphy & P. Hallinger (Eds.), *Restructuring schools: Learning from ongoing efforts* (pp. 63–83). Monterrey Park, CA: Corwin Press.

Merriam-Webster. (1979). *Webster's new collegiate dictionary.* Springfield, MA: G. & C. Merriam Company.

National Commission on Excellence in Education. (1983). *Nation at risk.* Washington, D.C.: U.S. Government Printing Office.

Peters, S. (1996a). *Inclusive education in accelerated schools: The case of Plumfield Elementary School.* East Lansing, MI: School of Education, Michigan State University.

Peters, S. (1996b). *Inclusive education in accelerated schools: The case of Vista Middle School.* East Lansing, MI: School of Education, Michigan State University.

Rumberger, R. & Levin, H. M. (1989). Schooling for the modern workplace. In Commission on Workforce Quality and Labor Market Efficiency, U.S. Department of Labor, *Investing in people* (pp. 85–144), Background Papers, (Vol. I). Washington D.C.: U.S. Government Printing Office.

Sarason, S. B. (1982). *The culture of the school and the problem of change* (2nd ed.). Boston: Allyn and Bacon.

Soler, P., & Levin, H. M. (1996). *Second chance schools and the accelerated school model.* Presented at the International Conference on the Project of the Second Chance School, Institut De La Mediterranee and European Community, Marseille (December 9–10).

# Systemic Reform in a Federal System: The National Schools Project

MAX ANGUS
*Edith Cowan University*

WILLIAM LOUDEN
*Edith Cowan University*

*This chapter represents a case study of the National Schools Project in Australia. The difficulty of sustaining national alliances among government, unions and schools is considered. The lessons for addressing systemic reform are identified in terms of the interplay of regulator frameworks and the requirements of restructuring, instructional improvement and workplace conditions at the school level.*

## THE NATIONAL SCHOOLS PROJECT

*Strange Bedfellows*

The dissonance between the rhetoric and the reality of school reform is so striking that many teachers understandably respond with cynicism to calls to renew their commitment to school improvement. Teachers can reel off innovation after innovation that has come and gone. Their cupboards are full of relics of last year's panacea. Scholars, such as Goodlad (1984), Cuban (1984, 1990), Cohen and Grant (1993) and Tyack and Cuban (1995) have documented the durability of the basic ways of teaching in the United States. The picture in Australia is much the same. It is not that schools and classrooms are impervious to new ideas (the evidence suggests the contrary) or that the ideas are without merit, rather the ideas fail to grip before they are swept away by some scheme that is purported to be newer and better. To outsiders, teachers must appear as inveterate tinkerers, finessing the margins while leaving the core structures unchanged.

Conventional wisdom pinpoints ownership as a key ingredient of successful school reform. Usually, there is not enough of it, or it is not shared around enough: governments want their way without having to convince the teaching profession that the reforms are in the teachers' interest; schools want to do things differently without first demonstrating that their plans are in the public interest; academics come up with bright ideas that are purported to be in everyone's interest but usually are not. In this environment teacher unions in Australia have played a conservative role, trying to block reform proposals emanating from the large, centralised

161

*M. Fullan (ed.), Fundamental Change, 161-184.*
© 2005 *Springer. Printed in the Netherlands.*

state education departments which threatened to change working conditions of their members without compensatory salary increases. Since most fundamental reform proposals involve some modification to the work practices of teachers, proponents of systemic school reform have frequently found themselves in opposition to teacher unions. Yet to proceed in the face of union opposition guarantees a rapid and extensive evaporation of teacher acquiescence. More than 70 percent of Australian teachers in the public sector belong to state unions and nearly 50 percent of private sector teachers belong to independent teacher unions (Schools Council, 1990). In the wars between *Them* and *Us*, the employers – the school system authorities – have invariably been which positioned by teachers as *Them* and the teacher unions as *Us*.

Imagine, then, a scenario in which governments, unions and teachers are jointly committed to bring about some agreed changes to the ways that schools operate. Until 1991, this would have seemed a fanciful prospect in Australia, quite unprecedented. Yet it occurred over three years, albeit tentatively and with a struggle. Commonwealth and state governments (and their state education bureaucracies) managed to work collaboratively with unions in order to support changes initiated by the schools themselves. The vehicle was the National Schools Project. What happened during the Project? Did it produce lasting achievements? What lessons were learned from the Project about systemic reform? First, however, consider the political manoeuvring that was required to set up the Project.

## THE NATIONAL AGENDA

Across Australia during the late eighties there was bitter contestation between state teacher employers and teacher unions over salary claims that climaxed during 1990. Only a supreme optimist would have predicted that in 1991, with the salary battles barely behind them, employers and unions would have formed an alliance to restructure school education without even the inducement of substantial extra funding. This was out of character for both parties.

The reason for the turn-around had more to do with the capturing of education by powerful interests in a nation-wide reform program than the enlightenment of education officials at the time. The Commonwealth Government and the Australian Council of Trade Unions (ACTU) had calculated that if the nation's economic objectives were to be achieved then a massive restructuring of Australian industry was required. Economic recovery depended upon the replacement of long-standing Taylorist work structures which fragmented and compartmentalised work roles with more flexible arrangements based on a mutuality of interest between management and employees. Hence, the education and training 'industry' would have to play a prominent role in upgrading the skills of the workforce, a goal that was unlikely to be achieved without fundamental restructuring of schools and school systems. Implicit in the thinking was the assumption that the fundamental features of flexible and productive work organisation are much the same whether applied to schools or to any other form of organisation or industry. It was further assumed that schools have adopted patterns of work organisation which inhibit the development among teachers initially, and among students consequentially, of the competencies required for industry restructuring. Given these origins it is not surprising that the National Schools Project borrowed the metaphors and language of industry restructuring and applied them to the schools sector.

The Commonwealth Government responded to the industry restructuring demands in a ministerial report, *Strengthening Australia's Schools* (Dawkins, 1988), in which it foreshadowed the Commonwealth's interest in establishing national standards and frameworks for Australian school systems. This was a provocative declaration as far as the states were concerned since in Australia, as is the case in most countries with federal political structures, the powers to undertake school restructuring rest with the state education authorities. The states traditionally resist Commonwealth (federal) intervention in school education unless the conditions are meticulously spelled out so as to leave state sovereignty intact and large sums of Commonwealth funds are committed in advance. The National Schools Project represented a different approach.

Rather than confront the states head-on, the Commonwealth's stratagem was to establish the National Project on the Quality of Teaching and Learning (NPQTL). The NPQTL was more a formal alliance than a 'project' in the usual sense of that word. The basic idea was to persuade the unions and employers to sit around the table and discuss education rather than industrial relations with the hope that good sense would prevail and that sooner or later some worthwhile proposals would emerge. The Commonwealth and ACTU would, of course, be in attendance also. The invitation from the Commonwealth Minister for Employment, Education and Training to form the NPQTL, with its accent on teaching and learning, was cautiously received by all the parties. The idea had some appeal largely because union leaders and teacher employers were tired of the public brawling over salary claims; further, membership of the NPQTL did not oblige any party to subscribe to a course of action agreed to by the others. Beyond a relatively small membership fee to meet the secretariat costs there was nothing to lose by joining up. There was also the unstated possibility that the Commonwealth might later reward participants with generous special purpose grants to continue the work after the NPQTL's official completion. From meetings of these parties under the NPQTL umbrella of committees there emerged the school restructuring project known as the National Schools Project which by 1993 involved nearly 200 schools in all states and territories in the country.[1]

Thus the National Schools Project was one of several initiatives of the NPQTL, directed by a committee drawn from the members of the NPQTL's Governing Board. Under this governance structure it was subject to all of the political currents that swept through the NPQTL – currents that could carry the National Schools Project to a secure landing or sweep it onto the rocks.

## THE POLITICS OF THE ALLIANCE

The Commonwealth Government has used its purse adroitly since its entry into school education in the mid-60s. Although the Commonwealth funds about 11 percent of the operating costs of state school systems it can exercise a disproportionate influence in steering public education in Australia, either by tying its grants to specific objectives or by setting the policy agenda for the states. In the NPQTL, it positioned itself as a kind of umpire or 'third party' to coax and cajole the others along. From the Commonwealth's perspective, holding the alliance together was almost as important as achieving the specific Project goals since as long as there was dialogue there was the prospect of separately negotiated agreements between the NPQTL partners.

The apprehension of state employers towards a Commonwealth takeover of state responsibilities led them to prefer a 'federal' structure for the National Schools Project in which the eight states and territories managed their own state restructuring projects under the umbrella of a working party of the NPQTL. These arrangements sat comfortably with the Commonwealth, cognisant of previous failed attempts to ride over the top of the state departments to reach the schools. State premiers are extremely sensitive to what they perceive to be Commonwealth intrusion into state matters. It was clear to the Commonwealth that unless the state education departments supported the Project, even tacitly, the odds were stacked against schools which tried to pursue the restructuring objectives.

Of equal magnitude to the Commonwealth-state tension was the deeply rooted division between unions and employers. In Australia, the largest employers of teachers are state education departments which must comply with their government's policies and standards. Unions instinctively distrust the motives of governments, non-labor governments in particular. They have sought to maximise working conditions and salary levels for their members through a centralised arbitration system which fixed their agreements with employers in 'awards'. Once agreed in the industrial courts (in most cases established by state legislation) the awards become legally binding for all employers and employees covered by them. While protecting the interests of employees the awards imposed limits on the kinds of restructuring that might be undertaken by the employers. Hence, early discussions in the NPQTL about how to design more flexible work arrangements for the purpose of improving educational productivity were viewed ambivalently by unions who feared the prospect that the across-the-board gains in working conditions, achieved over several decades, might be negotiated away. The employers, for their part, recognised that the Project offered the prospect of breaking away from the strictures of class size regimens, labrynthian promotional systems, and other practices which they deemed 'restrictive'. Further, most state governments were in the throes of school system restructuring of their own making, based on devolving administrative responsibilities from head office to the school site (Harman, Beare, & Berkeley, 1991). Award restructuring offered an opportunity for them to negotiate with unions conditions which might favour the implementation of the devolution agenda, an agenda viewed by unions with either suspicion or downright hostility since it seemed like the thin end of the deregulation wedge (Angus, 1995a).

Into this political potpourri add the spice of sectarian and class divisions of public and private school education. More than a quarter of Australian children of school age attend private schools. Relations between the public and private school sectors are currently quite civil though there remain subterranean undercurrents of competition. Although the religious animosities between the Catholic and government systems have mostly faded there still exists a level of discomfort with the smaller number of 'elite' private schools that serve Australia's middle and upper-middle class. Teachers in the private sector have their own unions. There are various employers, ranging from the large Catholic state offices to the individual school boards. These interests were represented on the NPQTL Governing Board.

As a final touch – the pepper and salt of party politics. The NPQTL was an initiative of a Commonwealth Labor government. Its relations with the states depend to a large extent on the 'hue' of the state governments. Further, it is a fact of Australian politics that the larger states, especially New South Wales and Victoria in which 60 percent of Australians live, exercise considerable influence; if New South Wales declined to participate in the National Schools Project, for example, the Project would hardly be national and, more to the point, the resolve of other states to proceed would most likely be seriously weakened. At the commencement of the NPQTL the majority of the states had Labor governments. The balance changed during the course of the three-year term of the NPQTL as a result of several state elections.

Not surprisingly, national and state political divisions complicated the management of the National Schools Project. Employer representatives on the Governing Board had not only to juggle their personal views about what they thought best for their schools with their State's apprehension of being tricked or railroaded into a Commonwealth scheme but had also to be watchful that they read the party political plays. Distrust of the Commonwealth's intentions is not always a sufficiently powerful unifying force among the states to lead them to a common view. They are more inclined to know what they don't want than what they do. Hence, it proved extremely difficult for the employers to reach shared positions regarding the Project. State union leaders, on the other hand, were able to reach unified positions after caucusing through their national body, the Australian Teachers Union (state employers have no analogous national structure). The net result was that the union side of the Project tended to be more coherent and proactive, while employer representatives, often privately supportive of a Project initiative, were obliged to reserve their position in formal decision making arenas. A considerable portion of Project energy was spent in formulating statements that were sufficiently open ended or bland that they could be endorsed by all parties.

Thus the politics within the Project shifted along different axes, depending on the issue: Commonwealth versus state, local versus national, union versus employer, public versus private, big state versus small state, Labor versus Liberal.

So powerful was the constellation of interests represented on the Governing Board of the NPQTL that providing the issues could be resolved within the Project, the politics of interest groups external to the Project were managed 'after the event'. The question is whether the application of such unprecedented power, applied in a climate of such ambiguity and political sensitivity, could achieve what has eluded more homespun efforts to restructure schools in the past.

## THE FOCUS OF THE PROJECT AND HOW IT WAS TO WORK

At its inception the purpose of the Project seemed clear cut: the National Schools Project would become an action research project designed to identify how changes in the work organisation of schools could lead to improved student learning. A cohort of pilot schools would be encouraged to identify impediments to student learning arising from work organisation and to devise their own solutions to such problems. Significantly, the solutions to be found by schools had to be cost neutral: there would be no large grants to schools to purchase additional staff and other resources. Schools would be authorised to redirect their own resources to new priority areas. It was expected that there would emerge from a synthesis of the trials conducted over several years some new approaches to organising the work of schools. For example, it was conceivable that some of the schools would find a way of re-allocating instructional time in order to allow the whole school staff, or major subgroups, to plan and review their work collaboratively during the school day. These ideas would then be publicised and adopted by other schools. This strategy was preferred to the orthodox, research-driven approach whereby staff were taught in professional development sessions how to adopt practices identified in the research literature as 'superior'.

An assumption underpinning the Project was that many of the constraints faced by schools in designing more effective educational workplaces arise because of outdated agreements between unions and employers, or because of constraining regulations and policies imposed by state departments. The Project had grown out of award restructuring discussions, was governed by the industrial parties, and would conclude with an examination of the appropriateness of existing awards, regulations and policies. From this point of view it might be expected that the principal outcome of the Project would be a new regulatory framework, one that enabled the successful experience of pilot schools to be more widely put into effect. Such an outcome would transform a school reform project into systemic reform.

A small secretariat was located in Canberra, the national capital. However, in keeping with the federal form of governance for the Project, the pilot schools were selected by the state authorities and their restructuring plans approved by state committees. In addition, states appointed coordinators who met regularly and formed the nucleus of an emerging national network. It was via these state coordinators who liaised with the national secretariat, and indirectly with the

NPQTL Governing Board, that the experiences of the pilot schools were to be evaluated and examined for their policy implications.

The national 'glue' that held the whole project together came in the form of a Project 'template' specifying the ground rules for school restructuring which applied to all pilot schools. The template was devised as a means of determining whether the proposals of the pilot schools fitted the intentions and principles underpinning the Project.[2] The template, therefore, became a means of operationalising much of the abstruse thinking and was a key document, in some respects comparable to the manifesto of the Coalition of Essential Schools (Sizer, 1989), though differing in as much as it avoided specifying any ideological preference for particular kinds of work organisation or pedagogy. The employers generally adopted a pragmatic stance, not wanting to foreclose on any ideas that schools might generate providing they would be cost efficient or cost neutral to implement. In general the employers feared that the limits of what they thought was possible were not being pushed hard enough in the Project whereas the union representatives insisted that there must be non-negotiable limits to what schools might trial. However, the non-negotiables were never declared; there is no reference to them on the template. These unspoken rules and understandings within the Project were all the more powerful because of their tacit nature. As an illustration, a pilot school at an early stage indicated its intention to trade the salary entitlement for a teacher's position for a bank of computers and software that would be used for a school-based professional development program. The proposal lapsed because of union opposition to the principle of trading staff for physical resources. The decision was made by the state steering group without reference to the central NPQTL working party; it was within the rules to 'manage' this issue at the state level. The union position on such matters was to acknowledge that as far as possible the school's objective should be supported and alternative means found, if necessary, to put them into effect. In the case of the 'staff trade-off' cited above, the union sought to find 'other ways' of financing the purchase of the computers for the staff's professional development.

Typically, staff members in the pilot schools spent the first year of the Project re-examining their purpose in relation to student outcomes. State coordinators, attached to the Project, would work with groups of school staff members to promote the values and operating principles as well as trouble-shooting in relation to union and departmental politics. The pilot schools were encouraged to network with one another. Most states held occasional meetings of their pilot school representatives to share ideas.

The Project became an odd ideological mix of rationalist economics and progressive education, a kind of 'beauty and the beast'. The economic rationalism, most usually propounded by the Commonwealth and the employers, was countered by the neo-Keynesian views of the unions and the majority of teachers who controlled what actually happened in the pilot schools. They wanted less restructuring and more government spending. The elastic properties of the template allowed the Project to avoid enunciating and debating ideological positions on issues that might fracture the alliances on the Governing Board. The boardroom was reserved for more formal, set-piece performances.

The tolerance of such ambiguity was due not only to the use of the template but also to the style of leadership allowed within the Project. The need to maintain a carefully balanced triad of interests – Commonwealth, employer and union – made the emergence of a 'leader' undesirable. The academic community played only a minor role in the Project. Whether a strength or weakness, the practical consequence was that the Project operated without a charismatic leader to arbitrate internal political or ideological disputes. The Project, after all, began as a coalition of political interests, nominally equal.

## THE SPECIAL FEATURES OF THE NSP REFORM STRATEGY

The combination of several features, in addition to the Project leadership, made the National Schools Project significantly different from other large scale reform programs such as The Coalition of Essential Schools or the Accelerated Schools program in the United States.

First, the Project was genuinely national in so far as all states and territories were formal participants. As well, the Catholic and independent non-Catholic sectors participated. Pilot schools were drawn from all states and sectors. State and Commonwealth Ministers for Education all gave their official support. The membership of the Governing Board for the Project reflected the national character of the reforms.

Second, traditional adversaries – teacher unions and teacher employers – were co-directing the Project according to nationally agreed guidelines with guaranteed funding for three years. This feature was quite unprecedented in Australia.

Third, the Project was designed around the concept of work organisation according to the following logic:

- work organisation frames teaching (and learning);
- work organisation is regulated (whereas teaching is relatively unregulated);
- teacher employers and unions control the regulation of work organisation;
- the National Schools Project should be used to find out which controls over work organisation should be relaxed, tightened, or abolished; and
- at the end of the Project, the employers and unions should recast the regulatory framework in the light of feedback from pilot schools.

The initial focus on work organisation, as defined in the terms of the Project, had never been the subject of a large scale investigation previously.

Fourth, the Project, although initiated by senior officials, provided school staffs with considerable scope to identify problems and target areas for improvement which were independent of any existing corporate constructions of best practice. The Project was not an archetypal top down reform initiative, designed to implement specific improvements to work practices.

Fifth, excepting for a small allocation of start-up funding, school projects had to be conducted from within existing resources.[3]

These features, the qualities that gave the Project its special character and its participants a sense of optimism, were central to its undoing.


## DID IT WORK?

### *The Lack of Dramatic Results*

Early in its life, the absence of dramatic results from the National School Project became a matter of concern to some of the employer members of the Governing Board. They were temporarily mollified by the explanation that it would take the pilot schools most of the first year to develop their restructuring proposals and complete negotiations with their school communities while at the same time satisfying the requirements of the National Schools Project state steering committees. A formal evaluation of the Project was conducted during the second year by an independent evaluation team. Connors (1993) noted that the joint support of unions and employers had provided schools with a chance to explore their options in a relatively open-ended way, free from external sanctions. However nearly all the 'exploration' occurred within the formal regulatory framework; there appeared to be plenty of scope to undertake a great variety of work patterns within existing award conditions.

By the end of the third year of the Project the picture with regard to award restructuring was much the same – there had been a considerable volume of school restructuring of one form or another but most of the school projects did not challenge state education systems by requiring any variation of the regulatory framework. Ladwig, Currie and Chadbourne (1994) conducted an extensive synthesis of National Schools Project restructuring activities based on 127 school reports. They were able to categorise these activities into 375 identifiable 'projects'. Ladwig and his associates reported that most of the projects focused on restructuring the curriculum and the organisation of classrooms. However, the school initiatives were spread over a wide spectrum of work organisation and teaching practices which included, for example, applications of new technology, student assessment, reallocations of time, use of ancillary staff and school management. Ladwig and his associates concluded that the National Schools Project had succeeded in building a network but stopped short of declaring the Project a success. Although the National Schools Project may have stimulated innovative thinking and practice in schools, a conclusion supported by other case studies of pilot schools (Grundy, 1993; McRea, 1993; Louden & Wallace, 1994), the Project appeared to have produced little, if any, restructuring of the regulatory framework leading Ladwig and colleagues (1994) to conclude that 'the habits of mind and historically embedded taken-for-granted practices of schooling are much more restricting than any official demarcations or limits' (p. 35).

In response to the criticism that the Project was unable to generate any fundamental restructuring its supporters argued that it would take perhaps five to ten years before such results could be expected. But a five year time span exceeded the scheduled life span of the NPQTL by two years – a fact which fed growing cynicism in employer ranks that the National Schools Project was essentially a side-show and that the main school restructuring action would take place elsewhere. Some employer representatives held the view that the union interests could claim the National Schools Project as their own if it kept the unions pre-occupied while the employers pressed on with their centrally-controlled devolution and decentralisation agendas.

As the NPQTL drew to a close there was considerable debate over the future of the National Schools Project. The unions wanted to continue it; the employers, predictably, ranged widely in their views. The balance of the Governing Board favoured its continuation in one form or another but overall the support, excepting from a few enthusiasts, was lukewarm. The teacher unions saw the Project as a national initiative in which they had already invested considerable energy and had acquired, as a result of their enthusiasm, a dominant measure of control. The Project would complement the work of the Australian Teaching Council, another initiative which had emerged from the NPQTL and which was also strongly backed by the teacher unions. The employers were inclined to revert to their pre-NPQTL positions and regard school restructuring as a state matter. Why continue with a national structure?

The Commonwealth was locked into a position of continuing to support the unfinished work program of the NPQTL as a result of the deft political manoeuvring of the Australian Teachers Union (ATU) – the federal body to which the state teacher unions belonged. During the 1993 federal election campaign the ATU had forthrightly promoted the interests of the imperilled Labor government. Earlier, the ATU and the Government had signed an 'education accord' in which the parties agreed to promote a school reform agenda consistent with the objectives of the NPQTL and the union movement. Labor managed to win the election and so, in their own way, did the teacher unions. Having nurtured the National Schools Project for three years the ATU made sure that it would continue, with or without the faltering support of the state employers.

The National Schools Project metamorphosed into the National Schools Network, a school reform program almost identical to its predecessor. Promised financial support for a three year term by the Commonwealth, a secretariat was located within the administrative structure of the New South Wales Department of School Education. This was seen as a coup by the Network supporters since New South Wales was the largest and politically most powerful of the Australian states. There was, however, a serious down-side. State education ministers downgraded the level of their representation on the steering group of the Network. The potential of the NPQTL to achieve significant breakthroughs in award restructuring lay in the composition of the Governing Board. For three years the most senior bureaucrats from all teacher unions and government and non-government systems had convened to consider ways of improving the quality of teaching and learning. Although the creation of the National Schools Network kept alive the promise of the National Schools Project, the fold-up of the NPQTL Governing Board and its replacement by a forum of less senior officials limited its prospects of achieving any decisive, systemic breakthrough.

## *Was the Project a Success or Failure?*

Was the Project a success or failure? The answer depends on who you ask and the evaluation criteria that are adopted.

At an individual school level there were many successful projects initiated in the pilot schools and described by Ladwig and associates (1994). Further, the National Schools Network has continued to support school change and the publications from the Network suggest that participating schools have found the framework developed initially by the National Schools to be helpful in managing school change (National Schools Network, 1995). It would be misleading and unfair to the pilot schools to cast the National Schools Project as a failure when viewed from the schools' perspective. Good things have happened and are continuing to happen through the National Schools Network.

From the unions' point of view the Project must be regarded as moderately successful. The national teacher union bodies for public and private sector teachers and several, although not all, of their state counterparts have co-opted the National Schools Network and can represent themselves as credible leaders and national commentators on school reform. This is of considerable strategic significance given the overall decline in membership in Australian trade unions and the tendency of state education departments to promote managerialist agendas for school reform. The rhetoric of the teacher unions on school change is much more in line with the views of teachers than the hard-line, managerial rhetoric of state education departments.

The assessment of the teacher employers must be bleaker. The best that they can claim is that at least for the duration of the Project they were obliged to discuss an educational agenda, as distinct from an industrial agenda with their union officials and there developed a temporary camaraderie which contributed to a period of industrial peace.

Although for the Commonwealth and the ACTU, the Project may not have achieved all that it promised at its inception, they used the Project in conjunction with other initiatives sponsored by the NPQTL to exercise national leadership in school reform. The National Schools Project became a vehicle for promoting national curriculum frameworks, national work-related competencies for students, national teacher competencies and the notion of national employment conditions for teachers. Although not successful in achieving all of these outcomes, the Commonwealth and ACTU nevertheless drove the reform programs of states during the lifetime of the NPQTL.

*Did the Project Achieve its Stated Purposes?*

The primary objective of the National Schools Project was to achieve structural change to the patterns of work organisation in schools by recasting the regulatory framework that was thought to hold them in place. However, the summit on the regulatory framework at the end of the NPQTL's three year term, perhaps naively envisaged to take place in 1993, never occurred. The grand plan never came to fruition. Members of the NPQTL who expected a rush of requests from pilot schools for exemptions from the regulatory framework were destined to be deeply disappointed. There was barely a need to pull any regulatory levers in order to enable the pilot schools to implement their projects.

In a survey of 169 of the Project schools, Angus (1995b) found that only 8 percent both sought an exemption of any kind and received approval to operate outside the official rule system. A further 13 per cent sought approvals and were refused by the state steering committees or were informally advised by Project coordinators that their proposals would not be sanctioned by the union or education department. Some of the exemptions that were granted appear relatively trivial – starting the school 15 minutes ahead of regulation time, re-scheduling professional development days so that they fell back-to-back, and knocking out a wall between classrooms. Several were more challenging – redefining the duties of staff, teacher supervision of students on work placement during school holidays, the conversion of a school's allowance for teacher absence into regular teacher support time. Of the proposals rejected by steering committees, several were relatively straight-forward claims for extra resources and fell outside the terms of reference of the Project. However, a small number were turned down even though they met the espoused purposes of the Project. Three schools sought direct control over the centrally managed staffing process in order to retain current staff due for promotion and also to select staff to fill particular vacancies. One proposed a redefinition of duties that involve the state teachers' union and another union covering non-teaching staff; however, the latter would not agree and felt under no special obligation to do so since it was not represented on the Governing Board of the NPQTL.

The fact that only a small number of schools sought exemptions from regulations and policies suggested to employer and union members of the Governing Board, the latter particularly, that the regulatory system was not restrictive. Where there were regulatory or policy barriers there were ways around the barriers that did not require an official exemption. Unions and employers would help schools do what they wanted without having to test the official rule system. Further, the conventional wisdom that emerged from the Project suggested the school culture was a much more substantial impediment to change than official regulation and that the promotion of cultural change ought to constitute the Project's primary purpose. Cultural change is a softer, more diffuse target than regulatory change.

The results from the National Schools Project corresponded closely with studies of regulatory waivers in the United States. Fuhrman, Fry and Elmore (1992) evaluated a program in which schools in South Carolina were offered regulatory waivers. They found that the majority of schools were able to accomplish school improvement projects without requiring waivers that were nominally available to them. Fry, Fuhrman and Elmore (1992) evaluated a similar program in Washington State and found a similar picture. It appeared that schools had more scope to implement change than was commonly thought possible under the existing regulatory system.

The modest take up of waivers in both U.S. and Australian reform programs suggests that the claim that school regulation restricts good practice is a convenient myth used to justify the status quo. It seemed on the surface, as Moore Johnson (1990) observes of schools in the United States, that teachers are reluctant to use the powers to which they already have access. If there already existed ample opportunity for school staffs to restructure the way their schools operated then perhaps the whole thrust of teacher award restructuring was a misguided enterprise.

This is a premature conclusion, however, since the restrictiveness of the regulatory system was never fully tested by the National Schools Project. It concluded before there could be any formal consideration of whether awards and regulations served to constrain the adoption of new approaches to teaching and learning. From this point of view the Project failed to achieve its primary purpose. Why did this happen?

## WHAT WENT WRONG?

### *The Fragility of the National Alliance*

There are supposed to be propitious moments in time signalled in the heavens when the planets orbit into alignment. There was such a moment in 1991 in Australia when a spectacularly reform-minded Commonwealth Minister for Education, with the support of a majority of Labor state ministers of education, pushed ahead with a national agenda to reform the school sector. By adroit political manoeuvring the Commonwealth Minister, John Dawkins, established the NPQTL and for three years kept state teacher employers and unions at the Governing Board table contemplating, and sometimes expediting, industry restructuring. That in itself was a major achievement.

The problem for the Commonwealth, and for its partner the ACTU, was that the administration of school systems lay in the hands of the states and that regulatory reform of public schools required the initiative of state governments. Most of the employer representatives on the Governing board were content to allow the action research project to continue and involve schools under their jurisdiction but were wary of being positioned, even in the Labor-led states, where they were obligated to follow through in regulatory reform. Also, if by merely participating they could keep the unions off their backs, then they were under little real pressure to do more. Had the Commonwealth produced a hundred million dollars to be shared by the states on condition of adopting an agreed workplace reform policy they might have shown more interest since the states have learned how to respond to the cargo cult funding of school education by the Commonwealth, though whether the policies would have been faithfully implemented is dubious. Such funding was not forthcoming. The Commonwealth, which might have dug into its purse had the early results been more impressive, concluded after three years that the National Schools Project was unlikely to deliver the fundamental industry restructuring that it hoped for. Only the unions continued to believe in the Project. If there had not been a sunset clause of three years the Governing Board, by the third year, would have begun to disintegrate. Three years in politics is a long time to wait for meagre results.

There was little resistance, even from the union side to the dismantling of the Governing Board. The national structure of the NPQTL, presided over by its peak governing body, operating within a finite time-line, produced a kind of pressure-cooker. It is easier to situate national reform projects on the political margins where schools and project officials can set their own agendas without the sophisticated compromising that is required to get warring governments and unions to reach agreement. The question is whether by being quarantined from such political manoeuvring, school reform projects have a substantially diminished prospect of influencing national and state policymaking.

The cohesion of the national alliance was produced by self interest and pragmatism. Well before the end of the three year term of the Project expired most of the parties had decided that it would not deliver quickly enough what they wanted and what they thought they could get by other means.

## *The Dependence of Unions and Employers on Regulation*

Although the employer and union officials on the NPQTL Governing Board were able to develop a collegial relationship between meetings and accepted one another's word when an agreement was reached, the situation changed when they boarded their aircraft and flew home. The senior employer officials recognised that the position they represented at NPQTL meetings could be undone by their Minister or by Cabinet even in union-friendly states. By early 1992, there were several state elections scheduled and union leaders feared that anti-union non-Labor parties might be returned as government, a fear that was realised in three states between 1992 and 1994. The regulatory framework defining teachers' salaries and conditions, and the culture within which the framework was situated, had been built over a century. Union leaders instinctively distrusted governments and never seriously countenanced a complete overhaul of the regulatory system. Regulations may constrain school changes but they also protect working conditions.

For their part, the employers had limited regulatory objectives. They wanted to undo restrictions on class size maxima and ensure that the working hours of teachers would not constrain more flexible scheduling of classes and enable schools to operate with more flexible mixes of teaching and non-teaching staff. Individual states may have had more ambitious restructuring goals but they were never stated.

However, they did not wish to be committed to a national agreement or implementation regime. Nor did they want to share the kudos of a successful outcome with the Commonwealth or the unions.

In fact, it suited both sides to maintain a high level of ambiguity about what they expected from the National Schools Project. This was the price of holding the coalition together. The official rhetoric of the Project counted for little. To have insisted on eliminating the ambiguity would have fractured the NPQTL alliance and returned the parties to their traditional adversarial positions. There was one point of agreement between the unions and employers, however; neither side wanted to devolve entirely to schools the power to make their own restructuring decisions. Although schools were genuinely encouraged to rethink in a fundamental way how they could improve the quality of teaching and learning, employers and unions insisted they retain the centralised decisionmaking frameworks and the right of veto.

Thus the Project rhetoric falsely implied that schools would be guaranteed the support of their state teachers union and state employer to implement a project that fell within the guidelines and which challenged a union or education department position. What was allowed or disallowed was in the hands of state union and employer officials. They had the power to suggest to schools that they reframe their project to avoid confronting a work organisation orthodoxy. Schools, if they accepted this advice, could then get on with their projects. If the objectives of school project could be achieved without seeking an exemption from some rule or policy which challenged the power of central officials, then this should be the preferred course of action.

*The Loss of Focus*

The broadening of the scope of the National Schools Project began during the early stages of its formation. There was a strong and successful push within the Project steering group to extend the focus to incorporate pedagogy as well as work organisation since pedagogy, the act of engaging students in learning within particular work organisation parameters, is what teachers actually do; pedagogy directly influences student learning whereas work organisation is conceptually a step removed and may not.

Pedagogy is not directly controlled by regulation or awards (Angus, 1994). It has been the object of continuing efforts for improvement whereas work organisation has either been regarded as fixed by regulation or perceived to be part of the everyday landscape and therefore taken for granted. By incorporating pedagogy into its conceptual framework the National Schools Project became like other school improvement projects and lost its special cutting edge. This is not to argue that the conceptual expansion was unreasonable. In most cases, if work organisation were to change then pedagogy also would need to change; one needed to be considered in tandem with the other. Also, when engaged in rethinking teaching and learning most teachers began by considering their pedagogy; it was argued that work organisation changes should follow a calculated need to change pedagogy rather than drive a change in pedagogy. These arguments were pressed by the union side and circumvented the move of employers to apply pressure to the pilot schools to trial more radical variations of work organisation, particularly variations that challenged centrally devised parameters governing the deployment of resources.

Although the focus on school reform obfuscated the award restructuring purpose of the Project it broadened the appeal of the Project to schools since any school project designed to improve teaching and learning might qualify for inclusion. The strategy also allowed the Project to appear responsive to ideas initiated by schools rather than the top-down approach to school improvements, widely condemned by academics and union leaders and usually regarded as the stock-in-trade approach of education departments.

The legitimation of this broadening of scope was strengthened by linkages with school reformers in the United States. The principal source was the Coalition of Essential Schools, founded in 1984 by Theodore Sizer (Sizer, 1989). The Coalition consists of a network of several hundred schools, some of which have achieved remarkable success in school restructuring and acquired an international profile. Although the National Schools Project had much to learn from Sizer and his associates, the Coalition of Essential Schools was different in one key respect; it operated 'outside the system'. On the other hand, the National Schools Project was conceived as a tool for systemic reform and, unlike U.S. reform movements such as the Coalition, appeared to have the state education departments, teacher unions, and Commonwealth government locked into supporting the reform process. The primary target was not to enable improvement in the 200 or so pilot schools, but rather to produce systemic changes that would enable the other 9,800 schools in Australia to follow suit. The Project did not have the resources to engage all these schools beyond propagandising newsletters. The members of the Governing Board of the NPQTL did, however, control the regulatory levers.

In this way, using these arguments, the unions captured the Project and recast its purpose. The teacher unions had no interest in overhauling the regulatory framework per se. They believed that to begin a systematic review of regulations might result in the opening of Pandora's box. Instead, required by the ACTU to participate in 'industry restructuring', they were willing to consider amendments to regulations only where there was demonstrable evidence that the amendment would lead to improved productivity without jeopardising the working conditions of their members. As it turned out, the evidence was not forthcoming and, given the time-line for the Project and the quality of feedback from schools, was never likely to be produced in a form that would support decisive, systemic changes. The regulatory framework was not challenged by the NPQTL.

*The Powerlessness of Schools*

In theory, power relations were delicately balanced in the Project. There were equal numbers of union and employer officials in the Governing Board. The Commonwealth chaired the Board and together with the ACTU, had a relatively small number of places on it. The states were equally represented. But what about teachers? The Board's position was that the employers and unions represented teachers even though no member was a practising teacher and several had never been teachers.

The Governing Board appointed from its members a steering committee to direct the Project. The notion that the pilot schools should nominate representatives to form a steering committee was not seriously considered and nor were pilot school representatives nominated to augment the steering committee. The prevailing view of Governing Board members was that the implementation of the Project was so politically sensitive that it could only be managed by members of the Governing Board; it would be unworkable to establish a national steering group that reflected school interests as well as the Project's corporate interests. Further, state officials wanted to retain the capacity to influence schools under their jurisdiction; if they surrendered the powers to a national group of teachers and principals then their interests might be subverted or even overturned; the whole Project might collapse.

The decision about the steering group mechanism meant, in practice, that the Project reflected faithfully the power structures that operated in the centralised state education departments and Catholic school systems. There was no means whereby the pilot schools as a group might contest openly policies relating to the conduct of the Project itself or, or of more importance, the policies of their employing authority and union. To illustrate this point, pilot schools had to apply for a specific exemption from a regulation knowing the employer's or union's attitude towards the regulation and knowing that their request could be denied. The template and public rhetoric were sufficiently ambiguous to require an official interpretation of what it meant. Because it was agreed that the starting point for school project development should be student learning and that regulations would be waived if it could be shown that they were impeding learning, there was no official statement listing the kinds of work organisation regulations that would be waived. Neither were blanket exemptions given to schools. The pilot schools continued to operate in systems in which they were situated in line management structures and bound by all regulations other than those for which they were exempted. In a follow-up of the pilot schools, Angus (1995b) found that 9 percent of the pilot schools did not submit their proposals to the state steering committees because they thought they would not be approved. For example, one school considered setting up a summer school program, a program that would have required a number of complex regulatory exemptions. Others commented on how their projects were modified in discussions with officials before they were forwarded to the state steering committee. Teacher cynicism is understandable in the face of such power.

CONCLUSIONS

The National Schools Project sought to address the problem of rigid and outdated patterns of work organisation. The solution was perceived to be the development in schools of self-managing work teams, with teachers committed to collaborative problem solving and monitoring their achievement of agreed outcomes. The Project assumed that the reforms had to be developed and negotiated in individual work-places. Using an action research strategy involving several hundred schools, the Project attempted to find out what were the barriers to the reform of work organisation practices which impeded improved teaching and learning. On the basis of this action learning in schools, it was anticipated that the Project would be in a position to lead a restructuring of the regulatory framework towards improvements in teaching and learning. As has already been explained, by the end of the Project none of the parties had any appetite for a systematic review of the regulations that were thought to restrict work organisation and pedagogy. If regulation was still perceived to be a problem, it could barely be measured on the Richter Scale of pressing issues to be addressed by union and employer leaders. The opportunity for systemic reform had gone.

For Australia, and perhaps for other countries with a federal political structure, there are lessons to be drawn from the National Schools Project. Ironically, the features of the Project, which at its inception were thought to be its strengths, by the time of its conclusion were found to be among its weaknesses.

*Politics and Systemic Reform*

Unlike most previous school reform strategies in Australia, the Project was truly national. By including all states, both public and private school sectors, and all teacher unions, and by ensuring their participation, the Project retained the possibility of national agreements on regulatory reform. A genuinely national agreement was thought to be a much more dramatic and potentially influential outcome than an agreement between several of the parties. While all the parties were nominally committed to the Project's objectives there existed the possibility of imposing political pressure on any who might want resile from the agreements made by the Governing Board. Whether it would have been better to have allowed the Project to become less politically inclusive is a moot point. Ultimately, the states would have had to make their own decisions about whether to implement any of the Project's findings. From this point of view it could be argued that the alliance would have been strengthened by the withdrawal of members whose position was neutral or even privately hostile. Yet had some of the parties quit the alliance, there may well have been a mass exodus and the Project might have disintegrated well before its scheduled completion date.

This potential benefit of political inclusiveness was offset by the cost of maintaining the alliance and presenting to the public and the profession an image of traditional foes setting aside selfish interests. In practice, the primacy of preserving the alliance meant that principle quickly gave way to compromise. Many of the concerns or fears that were held by participants could only be expressed in a caucus of like-minded colleagues. The Project, to a large extent, was governed by tacit understandings among the members of the Governing Board about what could be raised as an issue and what could not. For example, some of the employers privately thought that at the pilot school level the Project was controlled by the unions who sought to discourage schools from seeking exemption from regulations and award conditions which reflected core union beliefs and were thought to protect their interests. For their part, the employers were perceived by the unions to be uninterested in genuine educational reform and primarily motivated by the cost-cutting agendas of their governments. These kinds of issues were seldom explicitly challenged in the Governing Board since they implied that either the unions or the employers were not playing by the rules; to have pursued the issues publicly would have endangered the alliance.

The inclusiveness generated another problem. At the Project's inception the majority of state governments were Labor. So was the Commonwealth government. Employer representatives from Labor states held the clear balance of power on the Governing Board. However, as a consequence of state elections, during the course of the Project the political division between Labor and non-Labor interests became more evenly balanced. It became evident that the school reform agenda was shifting back to the states. On the surface, this development made no difference to the operation of the Project. However, it was clear that the prospect was fading of pushing through any national agreements at the end of the Project. Instead of becoming stronger as the pilot schools began to implement their projects, the National Schools Project became more anaemic. Powerful coalitions of traditional political enemies are difficult to sustain across electoral cycles yet the history of school reform suggests that deep-seated changes cannot be achieved within such a time frame.

In hindsight, it clear that too much was compromised in order to maintain the alliance. On the other hand, had the Project consisted only of volunteer schools and been managed without the participation of senior officials from the unions and employing authorities, or had the unions participated but not the employers, or vice versa, then the Project would have been politically marginalised from the start. Though there may have been a number of superb demonstration projects in the pilot schools, there would have been little pressure on education officials and little prospect of any systemic reform.

In conclusion, it seems that the National Schools Project was overly ambitious. Even in the Australian federal system with its relatively small number of states and territories (eight in number), achieving a genuine political consensus on school reform, one that could be translated into action at the school system level, was too much to hope for. The odds are stacked against such an outcome. Other national reforms, such as the idea of national curriculum and standards frameworks, where they require more than a rhetorical assent, seem likely to meet the same fate.

*Power and Systemic Reform*

The National Schools Project was a creature of stakeholder politics. Representation on the Governing Board was restricted to peak organisations in the education systems: unions, employers, governments. This was its strength, bringing together the organisations with the power to make bargains and make bargains stick. But it was also a fatal weakness. There was no place at the table for voices able to present other kinds of claims to knowledge about school reform.

Teachers and principals from Project pilot schools were not represented on any of the key committees. Ostensibly, the reason for their absence was that they were already represented by their union leaders and employers. But there were several other reasons. First, none of the Governing Board members wanted to co-opt 'wildcards' – persons who had not been inducted into the culture of industrial relations – who might jeopardise the whole program of the NPQTL. To risk such an outcome was seen as a backward step, particularly as there was no pressure from the pilot schools for representation. They knew their place. Second, no-one was wanted who was unable to commit their political constituency to an agreement at the Governing Board. The pilot school teachers and principals were never seen to constitute a political constituency nor represent one. Finally, and most importantly, though the unions and employers were willing to waive particular rules they were not willing to devolve power. In the final analysis, the maintenance of power was more important than the substance of the reform. Hence, individual rules did not count for much whereas control of the regulatory framework for schools was all-important. In fact, waiving a rule, under the conditions of the Project, actually strengthened the power of the unions and employers vis-a-vis schools since pilot school staff had to ask for exemptions and knew that they might receive a knockback. Alternatively, the officials could turn a blind eye. The waiver process reminded the pilot schools of their place. It was clear where power was vested.

Though rhetorically the Project valued empowerment and could claim that schools could undertake their own restructuring or improvement projects, whatever the schools sought to do required the approval of both their union and employer. In some respects, even with the prospect of waivers, it was more restrictive to change work organisation under the aegis of the Project than to go it alone and either ignore any restrictive regulations or subvert them.

*Regulation and Systemic Reform*

The Project yielded no clear-cut evidence about the efficacy of school reform beyond anecdotal reports that suggested that in some circumstances particular regulations were obstacles to good teaching and learning. To have demonstrated the effect of a specific regulation on teaching and learning, while taking into account its interrelationship with the myriad of other contextual factors, was beyond the resources of the pilot schools, and as it eventuated, beyond the resources of the Project. It is doubtful if any conclusive evidence could have been provided given the limits of educational research. In the absence of this evidence, and given the modest demand for regulatory waivers, the Governing Board came to the conclusion that the regulatory framework was not the problem it was earlier thought to be.

To explain the paucity of examples of where the pilot schools had radically departed from the current patterns of work organisation, a number of reasons were cited: the pilot schools needed more time develop challenging projects; the current patterns of work organisation are basically efficient and effective and therefore waivers were unnecessary; and, the 'problem' is not regulatory but cultural. By the end of the National Schools Project the cultural explanation gained primacy.

Thus, the unofficial conclusion of the Project was that regulations were not a serious impediment to work organisation reform; the real obstacle was the culture of schools which reinforced the status quo. It followed from this conclusion that to promote reform, unions and employers should focus on 're-culturing' schools. In reaching this conclusion, its proponents failed to observe that regulation is itself a cultural phenomenon. The place of regulation in the day-to-day governance of schools, the attitudes of school staff toward official rules, and the power that is ascribed to those who are seen to 'wield' the regulations, are as important as the legal fiat of regulations in explaining how they shape practice (Angus, in press). The shift of focus from regulation to culture, where culture is defined in opposition to regulation, leaves unchallenged the existing power structures which are legally defined by the regulations and symbolically supported by them.

Thus, the elevation of culture as the dominant factor in school reform was a conclusion that suited the unions and employers. Local union officials were reluctant to risk trading away parts of an edifice of regulation which they had erected to protect teachers' working conditions. Similarly, middle managers in school systems were reluctant to devolve to schools power to alter centrally controlled regulations about staffing and finance. Both unions and employers wanted innovation but only on their terms, that is, essentially within the existing regulatory framework. Both wanted to retain the power of exempting schools from regulation but only on individual cases.

Regulatory waivers are unlikely to yield systemic reform. They are an instrument used by central officials to retain power while appearing to support empowerment. Where flexibility and local control are perceived to be essential conditions for school reform then these conditions must be inscribed in legislation in such a way that schools can proceed to restructure their workplaces without fear of arbitrary intervention by either employers or unions. Opportunities for such reforms to the regulatory framework are unlikely to be welcomed by union and employing authorities, judging from the experience of the National Schools Project.

## The Starting Point for Systemic Reform

Initially, the concentration on work organisation gave the Project a unique conceptual edge. In work organisation, a concept that had arisen outside school education, the parties to the Project found a plausible and untried lever for national school reform. The decision to incorporate pedagogy into the conceptual framework made the Project's ideas more accessible to teachers, but it reduced the pressure on the parties to confront the regulatory impediments to systemic work organisation reform.

Where should systemic reform start? One line of argument suggests that the starting point should be the school and, more particularly, the local teachers' beliefs (Elmore, Peterson, & McCarthey, 1996). Until there is a shared understanding and local commitment to introduce changes to pedagogy, then restructuring work organisation may turn out to be a waste of time: existing forms of pedagogy will persist in spite of the structural changes. On the other hand, many of the changes in pedagogy that teachers might want to put in place are contingent upon changes in work organisation and work organisation rules are often inscribed in official regulation. If the possibility of negotiating changes to such regulation seems remote, or likely to provoke some punitive response because the changes that are sought threaten the power structures of union and employer officials, then there is considerable pressure on staff to reformulate their restructuring proposals in narrower, less ambitious terms.

Teachers about to embark on school restructuring projects need firm guarantees that regulatory restrictions are not going to be used as an excuse to veto their proposals for reasons that make sense to system authorities but no sense to individual schools and their local constituencies. However, officials who have systemic management responsibilities will be unable to give unconditional assurances that every request for exemption will be met. There would be no point to the regulatory framework if this were the case. The problem is exacerbated by the invisibility of many of the work organisation regulations. Teachers are generally unfamiliar with the official rule books (Angus, in press). Also many of the regulations that constrain work organisation are several administrative layers removed from the classroom and are entwined with other regulations in complex rule regimes. For example, regulations governing promotion can have an impact on the capacity of a school to retain a key staff member. To waive that regulation might bring into play other regulations governing equal employment opportunity. Thus, the issues of school restructuring, pedagogy and work organisation should be considered together rather than serially. For this to happen, teachers require a wider understanding of the regulatory framework and how it operates so that they can identify at the early stages of a restructuring project what are the regulatory consequences of its implementation. With such knowledge teachers will be better positioned to demand that system authorities – union and employer – match their educational reform rhetoric with regulatory reform.

ENDNOTES

[1]   This account of the National Schools Project is based on the experiences of a Project 'insider' and 'outsider'. Max Angus chaired the National Schools Project Steering Committee of the NPQTL for the first two years of the Project while representing his state department on the Governing Board. After taking a university appointment he continued as a member of the Committee and the Governing Board until the conclusion of the NPQTL. William Louden evaluated the impact of the Project in several Western Australian pilot schools. The descriptions of the dynamics of the Project and the judgments expressed about its efficacy are not necessarily shared by others who served on the Governing Board or by pilot school teachers.

[2]   The 'Template for Developing and Approving Proposals' states that participating schools must articulate how changes in work organisation influence the nature of the work that is done in the school and lead to better learning. The key criteria, which are elaborated in the template document, are:

- **Links to educational outcomes.** How is the proposal designed to improve educational outcomes?
- **Effect on work organisation.** How does the proposal modify work organisation in the school?
- **Stakeholder participation.** Have those responsible for the implementation of the proposed changes participated in their design, and have the stakeholders participated in the decision to go ahead with the changes?
- **Concept of a whole school unit.** Does the proposal demonstrate acceptance by the whole school of responsibility for the learning of all students?
- **Proposal formulation.** Has the proposal fully considered the problem being addressed? Have the implications of the proposed change(s) been thought through?
- **Use of resources.** Is the recurrent cost of implementing and sustaining the proposed change able to be met within the existing recurrent resources available to the school?
- **Monitoring.** How can it be shown that the initiative is having the effect expected of it?

[3]   The level of external support to pilot schools was a contentious issue from the start. Initially, the unions adopted the position that major additional funding would be required of pilot schools in order for them to trial serious modifications of work organisation. Subsequently, they qualified their position by stipulating that 'start up' funds were required to provide staff with additional planning time and access to consultancy support and professional development. The employers were fearful that by agreeing to some formula of extra resources they were locking their governments into a major budget commitment if the Project were expanded. It transpired that the matter was practically resolved variously by the states. For example, one state department allocated $20 000 per pilot school as a direct grant; another maintained a pool of funding within its central office for allocation on request; others expected pilot schools to apply for funds through existing administrative channels and tap into generally accessible resource pools. It would be fair to state that the pilot schools were not awash with Project money and that what ever criticisms might be levelled at the Project it could not be regarded as promoting the cargo cult of school change. The agreed position was finally expressed in the carefully worded template statement which indicated that trials were to be developed 'within existing resources'.

REFERENCES

Angus, M. (1994). The regulation of teaching. *Australian Journal of Teacher* Education, **19** (1), 20–29.
Angus, M. (1995a). Devolution of governance in Australian school systems: Third time lucky? In M. O'Neil & D. Carter (Eds.), *Case studies in educational change: An international perspective*. Lewes: Falmer.
Angus, M. (1995 b). *Waiving the rules goodbye: The impact of regulation on teachers' work*. Technical Report No. 1, Regulatory Frameworks Project. Perth: Edith Cowan University.
Angus, M. (in press). *The rules of school reform*. Lewes, East Sussex: Falmer.
Cohen, D., & Grant, S. (1993). America's children and their elementary schools. *Daedalus*, **122**(1), 177–207.

Connors, L. (1993). *Interim report of the National Review Panel of the National Schools Project*. Canberra: AGPS.

Cuban, L. (1984). *How teachers taught*. New York: Longmans.

Cuban, L. (1990). Reforming again, again and again. *Educational Researcher,* **19** (1), 3–13.

Dawkins, J. (1988). *Strengthening Australia's schools: A consideration of the content and focus of schooling*. Canberra: Australian Government Publishing Service.

Elmore, R. E., Peterson, P. L., & McCarthey, S. J. (1996). *Restructuring in the classroom: Teaching, learning and school organisation*. San Francisco: Jossey-Bass.

Fry, P., Fuhrman, S., & Elmore, R. (1992). *Schools for the 21st Century Program in Washington State: A case study*. New Brunswick, NJ: Consortium for Policy research in Education.

Fuhrman, S., Fry, P., & Elmore, R. (1992). *South Carolina's flexibility through deregulation program: A case study.* New Brunswick, NJ: Rutgers University, Consortium for Policy Research in Education.

Goodlad, J. (1984). *A place called school*. New York: McGraw Hill.

Grundy, S. (1993). *National Schools Project: Overview of schools' research and reform proposals.* Sydney: New South Wales Department of School Education.

Harman, G., Beare, H., & Berkeley, G. (Eds.). (1991). *Restructuring school management: Administrative reorganisation of public school governance in Australia*. Canberra: Australian College of Education.

Ladwig, J., Currie, J., & Chadbourne, R. (1994). *Toward rethinking Australian Schools: A synthesis of the reported practices of the National Schools Project*. Sydney: National Schools Network.

Louden, W., & Wallace, J. (1994). *Too soon to tell: School restructuring and the National Schools Project.* ACEA Monograph Series, Australian Council for Educational Administration.

McRea, D. (1993). *Reforming school work organisation. A report to the Centre for Educational Research and Innovation*. Canberra: DEET.

Moore Johnson, S. (1990). Teachers, power and school change. In W. Clune & J Witte (Eds.), *Choice and control in American education* (Vol. 2). New York: Falmer.

National Schools Network. (1995). *Schools register: Project descriptions*. Ryde, NSW: New South Wales Department of School Education.

Schools Council. (1990). *Australia's teachers: An agenda for the next decade*. Canberra: AGPS.

Sizer, T. R. (1989). Diverse practice, shared ideas: The essential school. In H. J. Walberg and J. Lane (Eds.), *Organizing for learning: Toward the 21st century*. Reston, VA: National Association of Secondary School Principals.

Tyack, D., & Cuban, L. (1995). *Tinkering toward Utopia: A century of public school reform.* Cambridge, MA: Harvard University Press.

# Large-Scale Change: The Comer Perspective

EDWARD T. JOYNER

*Yale Child Study Center, Yale University*

*The School Development Program (SDP) focuses on building caring and effective school communities in situations where communities and schools have been previously mutually alienated. The expansion of SDP from a small pilot project to a nation-wide initiative is considered in terms of the change strategies and assumptions that underlie SDP. A strong emphasis on assessment of the SDP model has resulted in the foundation of a nine step set of guidelines for success.*

## THE AMERICAN CONTEXT FOR SCHOOL REFORM

After nearly three decades of intensive work in schools in the United States and the Caribbean, the School Development Program (SDP) has learned a great deal about school change and the factors that contribute to school effectiveness. There are fundamental problems associated with change efforts in American schools that make change difficult. Our challenge as change agents begins with an understanding of the unique characteristics of American society and its schools, and how these qualities influence reform attempts.

Several factors explain the difficulty of initiating and sustaining meaningful, large scale reform in American schools. They include: (1) inadequate preparation of teachers and administrators for service in schools, particularly those that serve low-income students and students of color; (2) inability of school districts to make informed choices regarding the selection of reform initiatives and purposeful staff development; (3) failure by school districts to create structures and processes to assess, plan, implement, and evaluate education programs; (4) ineffective policy making; (5) school unions that can be part of the solution to school reform, or part of the problem (6) frequent turnover of leadership and school staff; and (7) a deficit rather than developmental orientation with respect to student potential.

These seven factors are the most important for analysis because they are under the control of individuals – college deans, professors, school board members, superintendents, principals, teachers, and school support staff – who exert a direct influence on what happens in schools. Hence, one starting point for large scale school reform is in the higher education system that prepares teachers and administrators to work in schools.

There is a solid body of research documenting the effectiveness of a number of approaches for teaching disadvantaged students and for reorganizing the school

*M. Fullan (ed.), Fundamental Change*, 185-206.

to respond to this challenge (see Comer, 1980; Levin, 1987; Slavin et al., 1989, & Wehlage,1981). Yet few colleges and universities have incorporated this knowledge base into their coursework at meaningful levels.

Preparation of teachers is largely a theoretical, campus based experience with little or no opportunity (beyond a semester of student teaching) to work in real settings to gain meaningful teaching experiences with support from experienced faculty. Much of what is in the curriculum does not address the impact of poverty, race, and language differences on teaching and learning. This content deficit has made it difficult for new teachers to cope with the tremendous changes in the climate and characteristics of schools and communities over the past 25 years.

The preparation of administrators in our schools of education is also largely theoretical and campus based. There is not enough emphasis in these programs on the application of change theory, organization development, action research, instructional leadership, and communication skills. Few programs offer the opportunity for aspiring leaders to work with effective principals and superintendents on authentic problems. And the knowledge base that is critically important – child and adolescent development, and course work that addresses the effects of socio-economic status on school performance, and how these effects are countered – is not rich enough for students to acquire the depth necessary to work effectively on these issues once they become school leaders.

Teacher and administrator preparation programs in the United States have also not kept pace with the growing need for educators in schools to work together in teams, across disciplines, to create a common agenda for change. Little emphasis is directed at preparing future teachers and school leaders to work with parents as partners in the education and development of students. Since many schools are using governance structures like site-based management and interdisciplinary teams, some preparation for managing these interventions would be helpful. Since parents and teachers are demanding a greater voice in the operation of the school, it would also be beneficial if administrators were trained as collaborative leaders.

The inadequate preparation of teachers and administrators in schools and universities places a burden on school districts to provide additional training and development to help teachers and administrators carry out their responsibilities. School and district level staff development should be building on a rich knowledge base acquired in pre-service programs. Unfortunately, much of the staff development delivered to schools is designed to compensate for what has not been learned in pre-service education.

Staff development in the United States has become a multi-million dollar business. In far too many cases, educators are served a buffet menu of profit driven, quick fix interventions claiming to solve such problems as discipline and low self-esteem. *Some of these interventions purport to address the problems of specific targeted groups, such as low-income African-American males who live in high rise housing projects.* Staff are "trained" in the use of these interventions, then they are asked to plug them into a crowded schedule along with everything else that is important.

The quick fix is implemented in isolation from activities in other parts of the system, and teachers and administrators sit back and wait for the miracle to happen. This problem is compounded by the "drive by" variety of staff development or one shot presentations offered to staff with no coaching and follow through to help participants master the requisite skills needed for implementation. Such an approach to staff development is more likely to address symptoms rather than causes, and without follow-up, it is unlikely that transfer of knowledge will take place.

Choosing appropriate reform initiatives is clearly a major challenge for many schools, and often, key staff are not even consulted in the selection process. The result is a poor fit between the reform and the school or district and implementation becomes problematic. When staff are not involved early enough in the selection process, their attitude is often: "You selected it, now you do it." Finally, schools select too many initiatives that are not connected to teaching and learning, that do not have a record of demonstrated effectiveness, or that compete with existing programs. An organizational filtering system is called for to prevent these problems from occurring.

When school districts fail to institute such controls, they often end up with a patchwork of cookie cutter reform programs that create false promises and unrealistic expectations for immediate results. This has resulted in a cynicism from staff that makes it harder to implement any substantive comprehensive change. Each subsequent change is approached with a "this too shall pass" attitude.

Selecting the appropriate reform, identifying the skills and knowledge base needed for implementation, and coupling the reform with appropriate staff development and coaching is essential. Then it is critically important to provide the supportive organizational structure, and to create a mechanism for ongoing monitoring and assessment.

Most school organizations are characterized by structures that are inefficient and loosely connected to the core functions of teaching, facilitating child and adolescent growth, and learning. Teachers and administrators need to be placed in structures that will give them the time to plan together and to interact with students and their families in a way that aids students' learning and personal development. The work of educators in schools should relate directly to this function. Teaching, development, and learning should dictate the structure and organization of schools. Yet many systems are not organized as if their core mission is to support staff who work directly with students. Form does not necessarily follow function in school systems.

The central administration in many districts is characterized by fragmentation and lack of coordination across units and departments. Administrators at this level do not spend enough time in schools and classrooms. This limits their ability to make key decisions based on an understanding of the day to day challenges faced by building staff. The problem is exacerbated by the lack of a unifying structure at the central office (with representation from the school and community) to assess, plan, implement, monitor, and adjust programs and activities that support school buildings and classrooms. Much of what is done is top down management. Generally there is too little input from parents and building staff. The end result is horizontal and vertical fragmentation which stifles the flow of information and energy vital to decision making and planning.

At the school level the school day is not typically structured to allow for coordination of instruction across grades and content areas. Faculty members work in isolation from each other with no systematic efforts to jointly diagnose and solve problems, or use data in planning and decision making. If the school is fortunate to have social service staff, they are not usually engaged in work with teachers to help students cope with factors that limit their academic performance, and few schools have structures that enable them to engage external family service providers in helping at-risk students and families.

In addition to problems related to structure and the organization, policymaking at the district level is a deficient area in school reform. There are at least two reasons for this: there is no system in place to train board members to handle the complexities of policymaking; and many board members do not have sufficient time to acquire the information that is necessary for effective policy development. We feel that school systems should provide training and consultation to school board members. It is also important for systems to institute a formal process that provides board members with the research, information, and expert testimony that provide a rationale for specific policy. And finally, to implement an annual review protocol to assess the impact of policy on practice and to make the necessary adjustments.

Policy development is an important part of school reform because it can be a way to institutionalize best practices and provide legal support for those behaviors deemed to be essential to the operation of schools. Excellence cannot be legislated, but strategic policymaking can provide a supportive context to allow school leaders to press for it.

Pragmatic, district level policy making does not receive enough attention in discussions of school reform, nor does work with unions. Moreover, in the United States, unions are seen as a major stumbling block in the school reform movement. This does not have to be the case. Our work with teacher and administrator unions in Detroit, New York, and the District of Columbia has indicated that it is essential to get union leadership involved in reform efforts as early as possible. Unions exert a powerful influence on their constituents, and it is critically important to work with them in the pre-implementation phase of any reform initiative. This early work is necessary to cultivate the win/win attitude that is so important to the successful resolution of the unavoidable problems that accompany change. Involving union leadership early, and on an ongoing basis, demonstrates respect for professional educators. It provides them with the opportunity to be full partners in the change process.

Involving other critical stakeholders early in the change process is also vital. Unfortunately, in many systems, the players change too frequently. Large urban districts experience high turnover rates that make it difficult for such systems to initiate and sustain change programs. Over a five year period (1991–1996) the New

York City public school system has had three chancellors. Each introduced major change initiatives that were either dropped or given a lower priority by their successors. If large business organizations were faced with similar instability, most experts would agree that their productivity would be severely undermined.

Schools in poor rural communities are beset with similar problems. Staff either leave teaching in these communities or find work in systems perceived to be more attractive. This persistent problem has denied many of these districts the stability that is crucial to the success of large-scale change efforts.

Organizational and structural deficiencies, failure to identify and support meaningful staff development, inadequate preparation of teachers and administrators, and the contentious relationship between unions and school executives, limit school effectiveness. The most dangerous threat to young people in American schools, however, is the education malpractice that grows out of the conviction that some children – the poor and children of color – have limited abilities that are fixed at birth. This deficit orientation is deeply embedded in American society, and ironically, the irresponsible and erroneous scholarship that contributes to this belief is produced at some of our finest universities.

There are those who feel that investing in school reform to create a more equitable learning environment will do nothing to change the probable destinies of students who are deficient-fundamentally flawed. This seemingly intractable belief is the driving force behind teaching and grouping practices in American schools. It has led to a rigid tracking system with poor children and children of color found predominantly in lower tracks (Wheelock,1992). Maintaining a deficit perspective on human potential denies many children access to high quality content, instruction, and assessment. The end result is an unacceptable number of young people who leave school or drop out and find it difficult to secure a place in an economy that demands highly skilled and adaptable employees.

The work of such reformers as James Comer (1996), Howard Gardner (1983), E. D. Hirsch (1996), Daniel Levine and Lawrence Lezotte (1990), Henry Levin (1987), Robert Slavin (1989), and Margaret Wang (1992) has done much to disprove the notion that some children are inherently deficient. Yet these reformers have found institutionalization of their programs to be extremely difficult.

The American reform agenda has not been comprehensive and intense enough to effectively address the broader context factors that have a bearing on improvements in our nation's schools. We seem to have a national learning disability that limits our capacity to see the connections that we must make between the institutions that we have created to develop our most valuable resource – our youth. America needs a reform agenda that works for changes in the larger system of education and in our national human service delivery system. This will provide a more supportive context for changes in schools and classrooms. Establishing such an agenda is admittedly complex and labor intensive, but the School Development Program and other reformers have focused national attention on many of the context barriers that make it difficult to plant the seeds and reap the harvest of school improvement.

## PROGRAM HISTORY

The history of the School Development Program tells the story of the tremendous challenges faced by agents of school change, and offers additional insight into broader national social concerns. We have tried to respond to many of the factors discussed in this section of the chapter, and are admittedly frustrated with the scope and intricacy of the work. We are reminded, however, by Frederick Douglass, the American abolitionist, that: "Where there is no struggle, there is no progress."

The School Development Program (SDP) or "Comer Process," which Dr. James P. Comer founded in New Haven in 1968, focuses on building caring and sensitive school communities. Attention to child and adolescent development undergirds the collaborative work of teachers, administrators, and parents in schools (Comer, 1980). The SDP recognizes that students' academic learning or cognitive development rests on a foundation of development in the physical, psycho-emotional, social, language, and ethical pathways. This development is made possible when significant adults in young people's lives work together to understand the difficulties that face contemporary youth, and begin to respond as a cohesive team to their needs. We believe that consistent school achievement follows good development; and good development is made possible when adults provide good examples, consistently reinforce expectations, and provide support for what, in their collective wisdom, is appropriate behavior. The broad program goal is to create a student-centered, collaborative school with support from the district and community to improve educational practice by addressing the total development of all students along six interlocking pathways.

Between 1968 and 1988 (the pilot and field testing stages of the program) direct service was used to inform, train and support districts and schools that were part of the SDP's relatively small network. Comer's major thrust was to determine if the early work in New Haven could be replicated in other school districts. The districts selected were Benton Harbor, Michigan and Norfolk, Virginia along with expansion of the effort in New Haven. By 1986 outcome data from controlled studies in these three districts showed significant gains in achievement, attendance and behavior for students in SDP schools when compared to students in matched control schools. Analyses of aggregated data (Comer, 1996) in Prince George's County, Maryland also showed impressive gains for students in schools implementing the SDP.

By 1987 the Rockefeller Foundation recognized that a gap existed in the school reform movement and it was attracted to the conceptual views and demonstrated effectiveness of the School Development Program. In a joint effort with the Melville Corporation, the Foundation decided to support an expanded training program through what was called the Comer Project for Change in Education. The idea was to build greater capacity for school districts to sustain SDP implementation by providing Yale based training followed by coaching and consultation in the field. A group of training and development experts with experiences as educators developed a training program that was designed to transfer knowledge and skills to a "Comer Facilitator." The Comer Facilitator would teach and coach the model in schools and be supported with coaching and consultation from SDP staff. Facilitators would be asked to serve on a national faculty of trainers after demonstrating that they could work successfully in schools.

This coincided with another Rockefeller-supported initiative, the formation of school-university and school-state departments of education partnerships. The goal of these partnerships was to use the School Development Program's perspectives, principles and strategies to strengthen school districts' capacity to implement the program, and to work with university staffs to reform teacher education programs. To further disseminate the process as broadly and as strategically as possible, a thirteen-part video series titled "For Children's Sake" was developed under the auspices of the Rockefeller Foundation.

In 1992 the SDP embarked on two additional major initiatives: Systemic Implementation and the development of Regional Professional Development Centers. Having demonstrated that we could work with individual schools to improve achievement for poor children, we felt that our next thrust should be to apply our principles at multiple levels of the school district. Systemic Implementation was based on the view that policies and practices at the board and central office levels had to change to support the implementation of the SDP in buildings. Three districts were selected to begin the systemic drive: New Haven, Connecticut; Washington, D.C.; and Community School District 13 in Brooklyn, New York. The Guilford County School District in North Carolina decided to use the SDP as the organizing governance and management infrastructure for school change across the district without support from Rockefeller.

Our dissemination strategy has always involved requesting public and fiscal support from the school board and superintendent before we enter a district. The systemic initiative, however, presses for changes in the way policy is developed, as well as for changes in central office and school building relationships. The school is embedded in the district, and in a broader community that can either support or oppose its efforts to improve. Consequently, we recognized the need for the district to adopt a systemic view regarding school improvement, and to accept that school reform is a perpetual series of activities that must engage all critical stakeholders.

We also decided to work on other fronts by recruiting allies that shared our philosophy, and could add value to our work. Toward this end, we developed regional centers and strategic alliances. The Regional Training Centers (RTC's) were designed to facilitate regional training and development activities. The selected RTC sites were: Prince George's County, Maryland; Cleveland, Ohio; and San Francisco, California. The SDP established strategic alliances with other significant school reform groups. These alliances include; the Comer-Zigler Initiative (COZI), Authentic Teaching, Learning, and Assessment for All Students (ATLAS), School Development Program-Developmental Studies Center (SDP-DSC) and School Development Program-National Urban Alliance (SDP-NUA).

Research and documentation has played a vital role in the work of the SDP and there was early recognition of the need to strengthen documentation efforts.

Efforts included the quasi-experimental methodologies that traditional social science expects and demands in program evaluations, and the more qualitatively rich ethnographic studies that yield a wealth of information about context and process. SDP's approach to research and evaluation has been to combine context and needs assessments, process documentation, and quality of implementation studies, with quantitative, quasi-experimental methodologies that focus on outcomes. The research unit also evaluates the SDP's training and consultation services to determine if the content, skills and support offered by the organization meet the needs of our clients.

## PROGRAM DESCRIPTION

The SDP is a nine element process that includes three teams, three operations, and three guiding principles.

*The Three Teams:*

1. The School Planning and Management Team (SPMT) serves as the major decision making body allowing representatives from the various constituent groups (staff, parents, and sometimes students) of the school to have input in decisions and comprehensive planning.

2. The Student and Staff Support Services Team (SSST) addresses the psychosocial and health needs of individual students and helps the school to develop a preventive focus by identifying and correcting inappropriate institutional practices. This team also works with family service providers within the broader community, often inviting them to meetings to develop strategies and to create a seamless network of child and adolescent support services for students. It provides clinical feedback to staff who may be struggling to work effectively with students experiencing difficulties.

3. The Parent Team (PT) is intended to involve parents at all levels of school life, especially parents who have typically not been involved in their children's education due to feeling uncomfortable in the school. Level one involves general support activities, including attendance at Parent Teacher Association (PTA), Parent Teacher Organization (PTO), or Parent Teacher Student Association (PTSA) meetings, social events, and other school activities. At the second level, some parents serve in school buildings as volunteers or paid assistants in the library, cafeteria, or classrooms. At the third level, parents are selected by their fellow parents to represent them on the SPMT. As members of the SPMT, parents transmit the views and opinions of the general parent body on issues related to academic, social and staff development needs of the school. The PT bridges the gap between home and school. It reduces the dissonance that disadvantaged students experience as they attempt to adjust from one environment to the other. By empowering parents, schools provide consistency and continuity in children's

lives. Empowerment can also serve to strengthen families and help them become resilient supporters of their children's development. The SDP views parental involvement as the cornerstone for success in developing a school environment that stimulates the total development of its students. Parents are expected to:

1.  Select their representatives to serve on the SPMT;
2.  Review the school plan developed by the SPMT;
3.  Work with staff in developing and carrying out activities of the parent-teacher general membership group (PTA, PTO, PTSA) in line with the overall school plan;
4.  Support the efforts of the school to assist students in their overall development; and
5.  Encourage new parents to become involved in school activities.

### The Three Operations

The SPMT is responsible for managing three operations. It should be noted that this team does not supersede the legal-jurisdictional authority of the principal, but works with school leadership to develop proactive school improvement strategies. Its major responsibility is to develop a one to two year comprehensive school plan that identifies instructional priorities and develops programmatic responses to students' developmental needs. The final plan should reflect the collective wisdom of staff and parents and should include a calendar of important events associated with the plan's life cycle. The plan should contain measurable goals and objectives. As its second operation, it is the SPMT's responsibility to monitor and assess the achievement of these goals. Action research techniques are used to monitor the plan monthly. Staff use data to ask three essential questions regarding expected outcomes: What went well? What did not go as well as expected? What corrective adjustments must we make to achieve desired results?

Staff development is the third operation administered by the SPMT. In a school district there should be three levels of staff development. District level staff development should address needs common to all district staff. School based staff development should arise out of the unique needs of the individual school. Clusters of schools, for instance those in a common feeder pattern facing common needs, should consolidate their resources to develop cost effective staff development strategies for the needs of the cluster.

### The Three Guiding Principles

Collaborative diagnosis and planning, no-fault problem solving, and consensus decision making are the guiding principles of the SDP. *Collaboration* requires that representative stakeholders work together across various roles to make key decisions related to school improvement. This strategy allows participants to develop a comprehensive agenda for change with widespread input from constituents. *No-fault* problem solving allows team members to focus on solving problems instead of looking for someone or something to blame. This tactic channels energy toward solutions instead of toward useless, subversive finger pointing. The drive toward *consensus* encourages teams to reach a decision that can be supported by the whole organization. Decisions reached by a simple majority do not necessarily reflect broad input, and as a consequence do not receive broad support. Working an issue through to consensus gives participants the opportunity for deeper and broader exploration of problems and their causes. It is important for decision making bodies to accept that any decision is subject to modification when new information reveals a more suitable alternative.

The SDP was initially designed to provide schools with structures and processes that would organize educators and parents around the effort to improve the school. As the work progressed, we learned that parallel changes beyond the school building were necessary to build momentum and provide support for change in schools. The history and development of the School Development Program clearly points to the need for systems thinking in school change efforts, and an understanding of how various context factors can affect desired outcomes. This revelation also suggests that reform cannot be limited to the schools. The social institutions that serve children and families, universities, and local, state, and national policy makers must be willing to examine their work as it relates to creating a more supportive context for schools. School reformers must be willing to work in a more collaborative fashion with front line practitioners. Practitioners are on the inside. They must be seen as partners in any change initiative. Reform is not what we do to schools; it is what we do with them.

## THE SDP CHANGE PROCESS

The SDP has responded to the multiple challenges involved in changing American schools by developing a set of principles based on our understanding of organizational development, social science research, staff development, and the social, historical, and current context of American school reform. We believe that:

1.    Successful large scale change begins with a shared assessment of the problem by power groups and stakeholders, and the identification of the specific challenges associated with the change effort.
2.    The proposed change strategy should be selected on the basis of its demonstrated effectiveness.
3.    The change strategy should be morally defensible and governed by ethical principles.
4.    Change requires multiple strategies.

5. Three major stages characterize the change process; these stages are not discrete, and each stage presents specific challenges.
6. Change efforts should be initiated from the top down and bottom up.
7. Change must be supported by leadership, structure, organization, resources, and policy.
8. School change initiatives should focus on support for learning, teaching, and development.
9. Action research is an essential tool for monitoring and adjusting the process and content of change.

*Joint diagnosis of the problem is an essential element of school reform.* Power brokers and stakeholders need to assume collective responsibility for identifying and defining the problem or problems that will be the focus of change efforts. Sharing the problem is a good start toward sharing the responsibility for its resolution. This is best done when teams work together to conduct the deep assessment that allows them to identify problems rather than symptoms. Additionally, participants need to identify the specific challenges that they are likely to face in the various phases of the change process. The merger of the Guilford County Schools in North Carolina, is an example of how a superintendent used this principle and the SDP to initiate a large scale change program.

Dr. Jerry Weast became Superintendent of the school district in July of 1993, and was given the difficult task of merging two city school districts together with one county district into what would become the third largest school district in the state, and one of the largest in the South. Each of the previous districts had its own school board, superintendent, staff, budget, and organizational culture. The county had a history of racial tensions dating back to the antebellum period.

Greensboro, its largest city, was the birthplace of the famous student sit-ins, one of the first attempts in the United States to integrate public accommodations during the Civil Rights Movement of the 1960's. These non-violent actions were led by The Reverend Jesse Jackson, then a student at North Carolina Agriculture and Technical University. It was also the site, in 1979, of an attack by the Ku Klux Klan and the American Nazi Party on an anti-Klan rally held by the American Communist Party in a predominantly Black area of the city. Five demonstrators were killed. The history of race (and class) relations in any American community has always been a factor in the power relationships within school systems. These power relationships determine who gets hired as well as how system resources are distributed to schools. Dr. Weast assumed his position in a contentious community; even the school board was divided along racial lines regarding his selection as the chief executive officer of the school district.

The situation in Guilford County was a challenging one for Weast, an educator who has spent his entire professional life advocating equity. He made it clear to the community that he felt that the poor children in the district needed additional services to help them bridge the developmental gaps associated with poverty. To give substance to his vision of a school system based on equity and quality, Dr.

Weast personally led a series of activities designed to educate the community and to remind the adults in Guilford County of their obligations to children.

Weast's first major activity was to engage the community's major power brokers and stakeholders in a deep assessment of the district's status in the following areas.

- equity
- leadership and management
- instructional effectiveness
- cost effectiveness
- community outreach and alliances with human service providers
- ethical behavior
- effective policy making

The Superintendent and the School Board immersed the business and academic communities, the clergy, various community groups, parents, teachers, administrators and support staff in identifying the critical challenges that had to be faced in transforming three districts into one. This was an inclusive process that embraced some of his most severe critics. When the smoke cleared, Weast had presided over the most complex merger in North Carolina state history. This was done despite vicious personal attacks from an area newspaper, some internal resistance by school staff, and contention from various community activists. Large scale change was accomplished in part because of constructive engagement and inclusive assessment.

The Superintendent and Board demonstrated a high tolerance for the chaos that characterized the change process, and they kept the public discourse on what was best for students. The majority of the community took ownership of the problems associated with the merger, and Weast presented the merger as a means of improving the school district rather than as an end unto itself. This strategy allowed him to reinvent the school district around equity, effective teaching and learning, cost effectiveness, and school/community relationships. The Superintendent used the structures, processes, and guiding principles of the SDP as the vehicle at the school and central office level to make structural changes, and to achieve a student centered focus. The SDP was selected because of its longevity and documented impact.

*A change initiative should be selected on the basis of documented effectiveness, or because collective wisdom suggests that it is the best solution available.* Educators and policymakers should do the necessary background research to assess the soundness and relevancy of proposed reforms, and should develop a process to insure that new initiatives are not duplicating old ones.

For example, the late Edward Meade spent a year working with the Detroit Public Schools and the Skillman Foundation examining national models with the potential to integrate school and family services. The Foundation and school district involved teachers and administrators, leaders of the professional and paraprofessional unions, parent groups, and the school board in the search. They also developed a series of questions to guide the selection process: Could the model be implemented in a city and school system like Detroit? Could it improve the teaching and learning climate in the schools? Did it have a successful track record? Was it cost effective? These guiding questions led the search committee to the School Development Program.

*Any school reform effort should be morally defensible and governed by ethical principles.* Much of what needs to be changed in our schools is the result of practices that are unethical and morally indefensible. The history of American education clearly points out discriminatory treatment of people of color and disproportionate allocation of resources between rich and poor communities. Forty-two years after the 1954 Brown decision some school districts are still under court order to provide equitable schooling for African-American and Latino children.

Labeling, verbal abuse, rigid tracking, discontinuity, low expectations, and the assignment of the most needy students to the least qualified teachers, are all examples of the education malpractice that exists in American schools. Such practices must be changed. In the medical profession the most important ethic is: "First do no harm." As educators we would do well by our students if we adapted this ethical principle to our profession. We should submit any change proposed for our schools to the following questions:

1.   Is the change proposed based on a developmental or deficit paradigm?
2.   Will the benefits of the change be available to the students who need it the most?
3.   Does the proposed change deprive other students of vital resources?
4.   Does it impose a hardship on staff or parents?
5.   Will staff and students receive the time and appropriate resources they need to make the change happen?

There are probably other questions that can guide decisionmakers as they identify reform goals for schools and school systems. The guiding principle, however, should be "First do no harm."

*There is no single strategy that is effective in dealing with the complexities of large-scale change.* Chin and Benne (1976) have identified three basic change strategies: empirical/rational; normative/re-educative; and power/coercive, that are useful in transforming organizations. The School Development Program uses a fourth strategy borrowed from social reform movements, moral suasion. These four change strategies are incorporated into our training, coaching, and consultation activities. The School Development program teaches the theory and application of the strategies in our training program, and provide consultation to facilitators and school leaders as they employ various combinations of the strategies in the field. The chart that follows describes each of the strategies, their underlying assumptions, and their counter assumptions.

The Guilford County merger is an example of the application of all four strategies. Weast developed a change framework grounded in a rational and moral appeal to staff, parents, the business community, clergy, and elected officials. Who could

**Change Strategies**

| | Strategy | Assumption(s) | Counter Assumptions |
|---|---|---|---|
| 1. | Rational/Empirical | People are rational and will follow their rational self-interest when it is revealed. | People do not always act in their self-interest – what is rational to one person may not be rational to another. |
| 2. | Normative/Re-educative | Group norms and values exert a powerful effect on attitudes and behaviors; individual change to conform or to commit to new norms, thus discarding new ones. | A "critical mass" of individuals who support new or different norms is needed in order to produce deep changes. Charismatic individuals may have the ability to counter group influences. |
| 3. | Power/Coercive | Power forces compliance | People actively and passively resist forced change, particularly if it does not involve them in meaningful ways. |
| 4. | Moral Suasion | People will change if the change is "right," "just," or "good." | In a world of unshared meanings, even these terms are relative. |

reasonably argue with his slogan of "costs down, achievement up," or morally oppose his emphasis on equity?

The school board was willing to use policy to drive the system toward accountability for the education and development of its students. And using the SDP, Dr. Weast created a critical mass of staff who have embraced the norms and values that are associated with a learning community of dedicated professionals. They place children first and are willing to work hard to support change designed to improve the physical, cognitive, psycho-emotional, social, language, and ethical development of students. The merger of the three systems was a masterful example of using multiple strategies to constructively engage stakeholders in the assessment, planning, and implementation of large-scale change.

While changes requires multiple strategies, we have found that it also flows through several major non-discrete phases. Change is not linear. It can be characterized by progression and regression. Meaningful progression through change phases is dependent on a number of consistent support factors and specific action steps. We have identified five phases in the SDP implementation cycle.

*Phase One (6 months – 1 year): Planning and Preparation.* Primary activities in this phase are directed at getting support from the school board, superintendent and central office staff, principals, union leaders and relevant community groups. The District Facilitator is selected in phase one.

*Phase Two (1 – 2 years): Foundation Building.* This phase actually marks the beginning of building level involvement. Program schools are selected and trained and schools begin to implement the nine elements with support from the Corner Facilitator and central office staff.

*Phase Three (2 – 3 years): Transformation.* During this phase the schools use the SDP as a vehicle to filter new programs and initiatives, evaluate, refine or eliminate practices based on data feedback. They practice the nine elements consistently and can use qualitative and quantitative assessments for continuous improvement. Staff development reflects building and district needs. There is an instructional focus within the school that is aligned with local, state, and national achievement standards. A collaborative solution oriented climate is part of the school culture and there is a consistent emphasis on putting the needs of students first. Both social and academic programs are culturally sensitive and developmentally appropriate. There is a schoolwide emphasis on all six of the development pathways that is relfected in day-today practice and that can be articulated by staff and parents.

*Phase Four (4 – 5 years): Institutionalization.* The SDP becomes standard operating procedure within the school and common district. Staff and parents use a common Comeresque language. Student achievement and social behavior shows measured improvement. Policy support for the program is evident and staff and program activities are supported by the district budget rather than external funds.

*Phase Five: Renewal.* The program is assessed for faithful replication and adjustments are made. New staff and parents are trained. If necessary board and superintendent will make public commitment to program as the way that schooling is conducted in the district.

An understanding of these phases and their benchmarks helps district staff to prepare for the various challenges that are presented in the movement toward program implementation.

*Effective change is systemic.* At the core of SDP work is the belief that schools need collaborative structures and parent and community support to enhance student performance. This calls for top down and bottom up involvement of implementers and respondents.

French and Bell (1984) have given five important factors to consider when using a systems approach to change:

1.  Issues, forces, incidents, and events are not viewed in isolation; they occur in relationship to other issues, forces, incidents, and events.
2.  A systems approach encourages analysis of events in terms of multiple rather than single causes.
3.  The driving and restraining forces at the time of the event are the relevant forces for analysis. We analyze the contemporary and not the historical forces in order to understand an event.
4.  One cannot change one part of the system without influencing some other parts in some way.
5.  If one wants to change a system one changes the system, not just its component parts.

A systems approach organizes and integrates structure, organization, resources, and policy to support the desired change. There are a number of ways that change agents can apply this concept. The Superintendent of Community School District 13 (CSD13) in Brooklyn, New York, Dr. Lester Young Jr., is using this approach in a five year systemic reform initiative that is being funded by the Rockefeller Foundation. Training and consultation is provided by the SDP. Young has mobilized the school board and the greater community to use the SDP as a vehicle to :

- increase student academic outcomes
- enhance student social development
- improve organizational and staff effectiveness
- strengthen parent effectiveness in improving student outcomes

Young has developed a massive public relations and training program to change the culture of the district by challenging the community and educators to make sacrifices for children. The appeal to adults to "do right" by children, the development of a district-wide training agenda tied to the district's strategic plan, policy that sets standards for selecting school leadership, and the collaborative development of 13 core values that drive the work in CSD13, is an application of a systems approach and the four major change strategies.

All schools in CSD 13 are required to engage parents and staff in developing a comprehensive school plan that addresses the academic and social needs of students. The plan is monitored monthly and each school is required to present an annual report to the school board and it's feeder community. While the superintendent and board provide support to the schools, they also hold the staff accountable for results. The leaders in this district are very deliberate in using education, power, and moral appeals to the adults in the community to support student growth and development. This has led to a cultural transformation of the system that has created a developmental paradigm that is in sharp contrast to the deficit paradigm that exists in other districts in New York City.

*Change should be related to the fundamental purpose of schools to improve learning, teaching, and development.* In America everyone knows what is good for schools and there are a growing number of individuals and organizations that take advantage of the pressure on low achieving schools and districts to raise achievement quickly. Often there is no direct connection to improvements in instruction, or in the capacity of staff and parents to mobilize their efforts to this end.

Several years ago a superintendent asked me to attend a public meeting with the school board to hear a firm give a pitch to privatize some of the schools in the district. Although I thought that having the firm in the district was inviting the fox into the henhouse, I attended the meeting. After a colorful multimedia presentation, and the promise of overnight improvement of test scores, the group received questions from the audience. I asked the following:

1. Who is your curriculum expert and how knowledgeable is he or she about local, state, and national standards and assessments?
2. How do you propose to create a staff development agenda for the schools?
3. What are your plans for underachieving students and what are the underlying theories of those plans?
4. How long have you been in operation and what is your success rate in similar districts?

5.  What are some of your assumptions about urban learners, specifically children of color and bilingual children?

It was clear that the firm's representatives had not anticipated such questions. This organization had put together a group of businessmen, a building and maintenance company, and a computer firm to reform schools. The major initiatives were computer assisted instruction and clean buildings. These are important, but, in the larger scheme of things, insufficient to address the deeply rooted problems in our schools. The proposal was rejected and the superintendent is now delivering the services proposed by the firm within a larger systemic reform plan that has effective teaching and learning as its primary goal.

Superintendents and school boards in the United States spend millions on consultants and staff development programs often without insuring that they connect to teaching and learning. While some are effective, many are not. School leaders should never hesitate to probe deeply when making decisions about school reform. We often take programs at face value, or we select reform initiatives that may not yield a return related to improving teachers' ability to teach and supporting students' capacity to learn. Action research is a helpful tool in identifying and implementing reform.

*Action research is an essential strategy for monitoring the process and content of change but it is the most underutilized.* Corey (1953) defined action research in education as research which practitioners undertake to improve their practices. Action research, therefore, is a both a process and approach for problem solving.


THE ACTION RESEARCH PROCESS

As a process, action research moves through the following stages:

1.  Data collection based on a system need or goal;
2.  Feeding the data back into the system;
3.  Taking action by changing selected practices or factors within the system based on the data and on the hypothese; and
4.  Evaluating the results of the actions taken by collecting more data.

As an approach, the action research model applies the scientific method of fact-finding and experimentation to practical problems requiring action solutions. It allows an organization to find a solution to a problem, and to use the information gained in the pursuit of the solution as a contribution to knowledge and theory.

The Comer Facilitator must work with the school community to help it collect, organize, and use data for diagnostic planning and problem-solving. The data should be used as a tool to aid the change process, not as punishment to enforce certain behaviors. Consistent with the scientific method, data are used to make decisions on the basis of empirical facts rather than on power, position, tradition, or persuasion (French & Bell, 1984). In order to participate with school-based staff in the action research process, the SDP facilitator assumes the role of both researcher and practitioner.

Kurt Lewin (1946) suggested that there should be no action without research, and no research without action. If school organizations are to improve continually, they must develop building and district-based action research strategies that will allow them to determine if they are effectively meeting the needs of their students.

Large scale change is a complex and fragile process. We have discussed several factors that are important to consider when plotting the course of change. While success can never be guaranteed, paying careful attention to these factors can increase the liklihood of goal achievement. Much of what we know is reflected in a document, The SDP Guide to Systemic Reform, that we use with school districts that are interested in using the SDP as the means to focus the school and its community on student-centered reform. It involves nine steps that bring stakeholders together at the beginning of the change process to activate all of the key factors that are critical to successful program implementation.

## THE SDP GUIDE TO SYSTEMIC REFORM

The following nine steps contained in the School Development Program's Guide to Systemic Reform summarize our protocol for working with school districts and incorporates application of what we have learned about large scale change.

*Step 1 – Analyze district context issues.* This is an exploratory process where all of the relevant stakeholders get an opportunity to determine if the conditions necessary for broad change exist. Key contextual elements include:

- Factors related to district leadership: superintendent, school board, central office, unions, principals
- Political stability
- Expected levels of cooperation between the district and the SDP
- What district staff know about current education reform efforts
- Understanding of the Comer Process and its relationship to other reforms
- District's ability and willingness to develop policy to support the change
- Overall administrative capacity
- Fiscal capacity

This step also includes a discussion between the school board, superintendent, and representatives of the SDP staff to determine if the district is willing to make the level of commitment required to initiate and sustain systemic change by applying the School Development Program's structures, philosophy, and particular emphasis on development and academic achievement. Union leadership participation is strongly encouraged. If the respective groups feel that it is appropriate to go ahead, we move on to the next steps.

*Step 2 – Create a District Steering Committee which provides oversight to the change process.* The superintendent and representative leaders from relevant stakeholder groups (which may vary from community to community) make up the membership. This group performs a critical role in the change process. It includes representatives of all the key stakeholders in the system. Their first task is to assist in making the final decision about the feasibility of adopting the program. Should this group agree to adopt the program, they then become the oversight group who meets quarterly to monitor progress and to address major implementation problems. This team, as all teams, commits to using the three SDP guiding principles, "No-Fault," Collaboration, and Consensus.

*Step 3 – Create a Memorandum of Understanding between the District and the School Development Program and establish the position of a Comer Facilitator to serve as the key change agent.* This document clarifies the roles and responsibilities of policymakers, central office staff, union representatives, principals, teachers, support staff, and parents.

*Step 4 – Orient the central office staff and key community members.* This is the stage in which to promote wider understanding of the change and build enthusiasm for it. The facilitator works with Yale staff to move the process along.

*Step 5 – Create an Executive Work Group. Chaired by the Comer Facilitator, this is an executive subcommittee of the District Steering Committee.* It is a small team made up of seven to nine members charged with creating the Comprehensive District Plan to be implemented at the beginning of the following school year. Membership consists of the various heads of departments that have responsibility for the core activities of the system, such as staff development, research and evaluation, curriculum content areas, and pupil personnel. The Comprehensive Plan must address the following areas:

- Building-based expansion: The number and rate of expansion of the School Development Program to individual schools.
- Full staffing and community linkages of the Student Staff Support Services Team.
- Parent and Community Involvement: Identification of key leaders among parents and community organizations.
- Staff Development: Timelines for orientations and training events; time and funding for staff development; and strategies for moving the central office to a service orientation.
- District Integration: Designing an integrative vision using SDP and other system initiatives.
- Curriculum, Instruction and Assessment: Developing an alignment between curriculum, instruction, and assessment. Providing developmentally-appropriate instruction and multiple levels of assessment.
- Supervision: Designing new criteria for evaluation and supervision based on the new, required behaviors.
- Policy: Identifying key policy barriers and making the policy changes that are necessary to support faithful replication of the program.
- Evaluation/Research: Developing monitoring and evaluation procedures; developing an efficient process for collecting data and feeding it back to the system in a user-friendly format.

- Public relations: Developing a public relations campaign to communicate the goals and expectations of the program.

It is important to conceptualize the process of creating the Comprehensive Plan as occurring on two different, but highly coordinated levels. Level I is school by school implementation of the SDP, while Level ll involves restructuring the central office. Each must provide support to the other. For example, a mature SDP school with a well written Comprehensive School Plan can pilot autonomous staff development activities with central office support. The key task for the Executive Work Group is to identify critical action steps and the scope and sequence of work at these two levels for each stage of implementation. The School Development Program's staff act as consultants to this planning process.

Our research unit evaluates the systemic intervention. We are committed to documenting and publishing research findings as a part of our intervention. It is a multi-level form of action research that examines the following areas:

1. Faithful replication of SDP in individual schools
2. School climate
3. Student variables: achievement; self-concept; self-efficacy; behavior; and grade performance
4. Teacher variables: teacher efficacy and job satisfaction
5. Parent variables: efficacy and involvement
6. Demographics
7. Contextual analysis of system variables: funding levels; pupil expenditures; past reform initiatives; union/board relations
8. Analysis of principal leadership behavior
9. District-wide policies and programs

We employ a number of different instruments and methods, such as the SDP Climate Scale, the Piers Harris Self-Concept Scale, the Bandura Efficacy Scale and field ethnographic interviews.

The scope and sequencing of the overall evaluation and research is negotiated as a part of the Memorandum of Understanding. This agreement will outline which data analyses are to be done by the district and which are to be done by the SDP staff.

*Step 6 – Train Comer Facilitator and schedule training events for schools, central office staff, and school board.* These events are designed to transfer the skill and knowledge needed to implement the nine elements of the School Development Program.

*Step 7 – Facilitate the implementation of the SDP.* Monitor, assess and, when necessary, modify implementation based on the Process Documentation Inventory.

*Step 8 – Develop a specific set of desired learning outcomes directly related to local, state and national goals in Mathematics, Science, Language Arts, Social Science, and Fine Arts.* Products might include a written performance-based curriculum and a staff development plan that would support teaching and learning.

The School Planning and Management Team, specifically the Curriculum, Instructional and Assessment sub-committee, would play a key role in addressing school-wide instructional issues related to curriculum, instruction, and assessment. This would be supported by a parallel process at the central office.

*Step 9 – Establish an annual school district retreat to celebrate accomplishments, offer staff development activities that relate to program success, and identify areas of implementation that need further work.*

The nine steps are fundamental to program implementation and success at each phase builds momentum for the various activities that follow. The Guide helps participants engage in constructive dialogue, using the three guiding principles as an ethical foundation to plan the work that must be done to build a supportive environment for students.


CONCLUSION

While organizational change theory has been available to school leaders for at least the past forty years, few have attempted to consciously transform this theory to practice. We owe a great debt to Michael Fullan, the late Matthew Miles, and Seymour Sarason for their contributions to the study and application of change. Dr. James Comer can justifiably be called the Dean of American school reform because he has broadened our nation's definition of education, and shown that all of America's social institutions can and must contribute to the development of our nation's youth. He has shown us how to put complex reforms into practice while maintaining a focus on the developmental needs of children and adolescents. This contribution to American education is unprecedented.

Comer's early work focused primarily on the school as the unit of change, but after nearly 30 years of laboring in the field of school reform he realized that large scale systemic change was needed in education (pre-school through colleges and universities) if schools were to be effective for the majority of American students. He has also pointed out the need for changes in economic and political institutions since these institutions can provide the fiscal, moral, and political support for what happens in schools. The work of the SDP has helped reformers to see the need for collaboration, no-fault problem solving and consensus decisionmaking in the change process, as well as the need for policy support to integrate human services delivery and education. In communities where the two systems are integrated, children, particularly poor children, are provided with a seamless network of support for their education and development.

The work is admittedly complex and demanding, but we recognize that it is a sacrifice that we must make. We are reminded of this every time we walk into a school and see children whose destinies are directly linked to the education and development that they receive there; children who count on adults – parents, teachers, support staff, administrators, and school board members – to validate their worth and to insure that they receive safe passage to a bright future.

# REFERENCES

Chin, R., & Benne, K. (1976). General strategies for effecting change in human systems. In W. G. Bennis, K. D. Benne, R. Chin, & K. E. Corey, (Eds.), *The planning of change* (3rd Ed., pp. 22–45). New York: Holt, Rinehart and Winston,.

Comer, J. P., Haynes, N., Joyner, E., & Ben-Avie, M. (Eds.). (1996). *Rallying the village: The Comer process for reforming education.* New York: Teachers College Press.

Comer, J. P. (1980). *School power.* New York: MacMillan Publishing Co., Inc.

Corey, S. M. (1953). *Action research to improve school practices.* New York: Bureau of Publications, Teachers College, Columbia University.

Dawson, J. A., & Firestone, W.A. (1984). *School context and social change.* New York: Teachers College Press.

French, W. L. & Bell, C. H., Jr. (1984). *Organization development.* Englewood Cliffs, NJ: Prentice Hall, Inc.

Gardner, H. (1983). *Frames of mind.* New York: Basic Books.

Hirsch, E. D. (1996). *The schools we need.* New York: Doubleday.

Levin, H. (1987). *Towards accelerated schools.* Stanford, CA: Center for Accelerated Schools at Stanford (CERAS).

Levine, D., & Lezotte, L. (1990). *Unusually effective schools.* Madison, WI: National Center for Effective Schools Research and Development.

Lewin, K. (1946). Action research and minority problems. *Journal of Social Issues,* 2(4), 34–46.

Slavin, R. E., Karweit, N. L., & Madden, N. A. (Eds.). (1989). *Effective programs for students at risk.* Needham Heights, MA: Allyn and Bacon.

Wang, M. (1992). Adaptive education strategies: Building on diversity. Baltimore, MD: Brookes Publishing Co.

Wehlage, G., Stone, C., Lesko, N., Naumann, C., & Page, R. (1981). *Effective programs for the marginal student.* Madison, WI: Wisconsin Center for Education Research.

Weisbord, M. R. (1983). *Organizational diagnosis.* Reading, MA: Addison Wesley Publishing Co.

Wheelock. A. (1992). *Crossing the tracks: How untracking can save American schools.* New York: The New Press.

# New Roles for Community Services in Educational Reform

ROBERT L. CROWSON
*Vanderbilt University*

WILLIAM LOWE BOYD
*Pennsylvania State University*

*The relationship between community and school reform is experienced from two perspectives: the coordinated professional services model, and the community development or employment model. The chapter compares the strengths and weaknesses of each model with the intent of gaining new insights into the community context of improved urban schooling*

## INTRODUCTION

At the turn of the century in Chicago, people of some twenty-six nationalities lived within three blocks of Jane Addams' famous west-side "settlement," Hull-House. The teeming slums surrounding Hull-House, filled to overflowing with newly arrived immigrants, encased as much misery as human living conditions could engender in early twentieth-century America. Addams and her partner, Ellen Gates Starr, were determined to play an active role in extending "social organization" and bringing "order" to the chaos of these slums (Philpott, 1978, p. 70).

Accordingly, Hull-House established nurseries, day-care centers, free medical clinics, a pure-milk station, a bathhouse, an employment bureau, a cooperative coal yard, a gym, libraries and reading rooms, men's and women's clubs, a children's playground, and "classes" by the score for neighborhood children and their parents (Philpott, 1978). It was a remarkable and courageous step, for its time, in the notion of applying middle-class guidance and resources towards a development of self-help powers among the urban poor.

Many decades later, in 1968, a notable historical event in public education accompanied the use of *power* by the urban poor. A pathbreaking experiment (a "demonstration" project) in school decentralization and community-control, gave New York City's Ocean Hill-Brownsville neighborhood its own governing board. In the spring of 1968, this board decided to dismiss a substantial group of headquarters appointed teachers and administrators – replacing them with hires of their own. A resulting New York teachers' strike went citywide, while the Ocean

*M. Fullan (ed.), Fundamental Change, 207-224.*
© 2005 *Springer. Printed in the Netherlands.*

Hill schools struggled to remain open. Eventually, with state legislative intervention, the strike was settled, and New York's "demonstration" in community-control came to an end. In an analysis of the event, LaNoue and Smith (1973, p. 175) concluded that the demonstration "created potent symbols-among the most polarizing in the city's history."

Developments in the past decade have increasingly brought to the fore these two contrasting strands of community regeneration: coordinated professional services and community development or empowerment. Disturbing social trends have led to the widespread recognition that relationships between schools and their surrounding communities must be strengthened – and that, indeed, communities themselves must be strengthened. Good schooling and the development of children require attention to multiple needs far beyond the narrowly educational; furthermore, many families now require an active investment by society in improving the "social capital" of neighborhoods to support learning. Thus, both the professional "services" of a Hull-House tradition and the community involvement and even "empowerment" of an Ocean Hill tradition are being actively reviewed in many settings today as an introduction into a new brand of "reform" in public education.

Neither the tensions between nor the differing implications of, these two strands have been fully worked out. One strand, settlement-house-like, places an emphasis upon a concerted (and hopefully coordinated) extension of professional services to communities – through connections with the omni-present institution of the public school. Indeed, the development of school-based or school-linked coordinated children's and family services programs (as "full-service schooling") has achieved widespread attention and experimentation in the United States (Dryfoos, 1994). The other strand, oriented toward community empowerment, places greater emphasis upon grassroots efforts to re-establish the larger communal and economic vitality of poor neighborhoods – seeking to strengthen the self-help capacities of individual families by simultaneously developing and strengthening local supports and institutions (Judd & Parkinson, 1990; Garr, 1995).

The two strands need not be at odds. Indeed, Deborah Cohen (1995, p. 35) observes that, "only by working together can schools and communities hope to salvage young lives and fulfill education's promise of literacy and opportunity." Nevertheless, the two approaches can present quite different options in regard to the relationships between schools and their communities, and quite different implications for educational reform. These differing community development strategies (or "strands") have been only minimally examined comparatively to date; thus, the intent of this chapter is to begin such a comparative discussion, in the hope of gaining added insights into the community context of improved urban schooling.

COORDINATED CHILDREN'S SERVICES AND THE SCHOOL-SITE

In a significant broadening of the mission of the public school, the notion of an array of coordinated, non-educational children's and family services has captured widespread interest across America. The central concept is by no means new. Precedents can be found in the Gary Plan of Willard Wirt, in Progressive-era forays by the schools into medical exams and innoculations, in the long-term support of community schooling by Michigan's Mott Foundation, and in a still-lingering residue of many state and local initiatives from the "Great Society" thinking of the 1960's (Tyack, 1992).

Nevertheless, the current expansion of coordinated services experimentation across the United States is unprecedented. Fortuitously, the movement has coincided with a new appreciation and understanding of the learning potential in positive school-community connections (see, Crowson & Boyd, 1993; Rigsby, Reynolds, & Wang, 1995; Yinger & Borman, 1994; Weiss, 1995). In what Goodlad (1987) has labeled "the new ecology of schooling," many today recognize that school, family, and community are vitally interdependent and that the development and learning of children depend heavily upon many supports available to them in their environments (Comer, 1980). Enhancing parental involvement in the learning process, collaboration and "sharing" between families and educators, and much greater attentiveness to the home on the part of educators – are all elements of this new sense of school-community learning connections (Epstein, 1988, 1990). These, along with an array of other supports and services (e.g., health and recreation services, good housing, economic development, libraries), can ideally form "a network of learning environments" (Fantini, 1983).

Coordinated services initiatives have also coincided with growing concerns about the wide disparities in the "social capital" available to children from one family and community to another (Coleman, 1987, 1994). As defined by James S. Coleman (1987, p. 36), social capital encompasses "the norms, the social networks, and the relationships between adults and children that are of value for the child's growing up." Although long aware that the strengths of the home are also strengths in children's learning, many now appreciate that it behooves the schools to seek to reach out, and indeed to "invest" in the very creation of strength (social capital) in their community environments. As Coleman (1994, p. 31) put it:

> Now, confronting newly fragile families and weakened communities, schools find their task to be a different one: to function in a way that strengthens communities and builds parental involvement with children. The school's very capacity to educate children depends upon the fulfillment of this task.

From early on, a key assumption of the coordinated services movement has been that the multiple needs of children and families require a serious effort to somehow link the often disconnected services into a coherent "whole." The long-standing fragmentation of services to children and families has damaged their effectiveness (Kirst & Kelley, 1995). Multiple needs cannot be well addressed in a piecemeal

fashion, so reformers believe that the differing service frameworks and their specialized professionals must be coordinated to benefit at-risk children and families. This
effort to coordinate, to integrate, or to achieve collaboration among disparate
services has been the prime focus of attention in the services movement to date –
far beyond any focusing upon school-community connections or the development
of social capital. However, despite major foundation funding and assistance from
a number of well-crafted handbooks for practitioners, evidence of successful
service-coordination is still limited (White & Wehlage, 1995).

Repeatedly, researchers have found that the main barriers to success lie in
substantial political and organizational constraints surrounding service-
coordination efforts. Differing professional cultures and incentive systems are
thrown together; a sharing of information about a service-receiving clientele is to
replace professionally-valued autonomy; space and "turf" must be renegotiated;
categorical funding is to be redirected toward commingling; the separate "needs"
of children and families (e.g., education, health, welfare) are now to be reoriented
toward the "whole;" and administrative visions of what the school is "all about"
are to be significantly expanded (Crowson & Boyd, 1993, 1996; Smrekar, 1996).
Additional constraints derive from the short-term, foundation sponsored funding
of much experimentation to date, from the limited consensus as to just what government should do for children and families in need, and from a public mood nationally that appears, at this writing, to be far more interested in a contraction rather
than an expansion of government (Cibulka, 1996; Smrekar, 1996).

Interestingly, the coordinated-services movement has coincided with, and has
even contributed to, a renewal of scholarly attention to the "deep structures" of
organizational change. What better opportunity to open organizations to very close
scrutiny than to study them under a microscope of "cooperation"? Accordingly,
instructive research has inquired into such "structural issues" as the deep differences in the professional cultures of varying service providers, the differing
"conventions" and "ordering" of services across human service organizations, the
historical "baggage" that institutional players bring separately to the service
coordination effort, and the close linkages and, at the same time, the discontinui-
ties between systems of professional training and the demands of coordination
(see, Crowson & Boyd, 1996; Tyack, 1992; Adler & Gardner, 1994; Knapp & Ferguson, 1995).

Nevertheless, despite the important windows that have been opened into
organizational and institutional behaviors, it is increasingly apparent that the
"coordinated" aspect of the services movement may not be the most important of
its elements. More significant are the implications of the community services effort
for a reexamination of some key aspects of the school reform movement, writ
large.

Indeed, the services phenomenon helps to identify some important "watershed"
considerations, regarding the school-community relations aspect of educational
reform, and at a time when popular acceptance and the very "legitimacy" of public
education in the U.S. may be in substantial decline (Crowson, Boyd, & Mawhinney, 1996). The family and children's services idea re-opens a long, unresolved

debate about the separate roles of parents and professionals, the roles of professionals other than educators in children's development, the roles of the lay citizenry in school programs and governance, and even the overall institutional role of the school in relation to the modern welfare state (Cibulka, 1996). All of this occur at a moment when such notions as home schooling, voucher style parental choice, the "break-up" of school districts, mayoral and state "takeovers" of city schools, and charter schools ("opting-out," U.S. style) appear to be introducing a far more radical set of solutions to a movement that until recently was content simply to "restructure."

It remains to be seen whether the coordinated services movement will manage to establish "staying-power" among the array of strategies for educational reform. Our contention, in agreement with White and Wehlage (1995), is that the test for community services is less its success in coordinating resources and agencies than it is in reshaping the priorities and practices of schools – toward a closer understanding of, and even partnership with, the families and clientele to be served. Furthermore, the test for community services may be less its case-by-case distribution of added assistance to individual families and children than its capacity for "fostering networks of interdependency within and among families, neighborhoods, and the larger community" – that is, in firmly re-establishing the learning-connection and in building social capital (White & Wehlage, 1995, p. 35).

## COMMUNITY DEVELOPMENT AND THE SCHOOL-SITE

The local school is seen by many as the logical and indeed best situated place of deployment for human-services-oriented community outreach. However, there are observers who argue that our beleaguered and much criticized schools should not be burdened with these additional duties. Some critics continue to raise questions about the appropriateness and legitimacy of "social roles" for the schools beyond the 3R's. The schools and their teachers, they claim, should be left alone to teach.

Other critics see the local school as a very poor choice for leadership in community development – for schools, especially in big cities, simply do not have a very glorious history of "openness" to its families and its neighborhood. Finally, critics note that the central notion of school-linked or school-based "services" outreach to the community fails to address appropriately the more deep-seated problems of urban development. Many of these critics urge a more focused attention to broader, neighborhood revitalization strategies, tackling economic and empowerment issues as a first priority with spill-over into, but less direct dependence upon the schools (Cohen, 1995).

The community development (or neighborhood revitalization) strategy draws much of its strength from a larger conception of the problem than that which typically animates the coordinated services movement. The notion of the neighborhood as an embedded reflection of leadership and regeneration/renewal city-wide is a key concept (Judd & Parkinson, 1990; Gittell, 1992). A parallel idea, offered by Weeres and Kerchner (1996), goes well beyond the local school and its array of "services" to a picture of public education as a fundamental "basic industry" of the city. Schools, as much as other institutions, help to develop cities – and help to serve as agencies of each city's civic and economic growth.

The community development perspective also offers a further and deeper broadening of understandings of child development. Closely linked to the notion of "social capital," a child-development flavor to the coordinated services movement has been reflected in the clear recognition that "care" (e.g., health care, social services) and education must go hand in hand developmentally (Comer, 1980, 1984, 1988). The neighborhood revitalization recognition, however, is that a child's development is also critically affected by "larger" community conditions and investments – in housing quality, parks and recreation opportunities, employment and training, law enforcement, etc. (see, Haveman & Wolfe, 1994). Sadly, the typical size of the public investment in a child-development infrastructure in inner-city neighborhoods falls far short of comparable investments in suburbia (Littell & Wynn, 1989).

There is a grassroots activism about much of the neighborhood-revitalization movement that has yet to penetrate deeply into coordinated services experimentation. The language of "empowerment," enterprise, self-reliance, "indigenous leadership," entrepreneuralism, mobilization, and "restoration" is to be found throughout discussions of community development (Garr, 1995). But this is not typically the language of professional social services providers, including educators, who are likely to find more comfort in a discussion of "meeting needs" than of "enterprise." Additionally, such institutions as neighborhood churches, local banks, welfare rights groups, citizens' action councils, food banks, and community youth centers have been much more likely to date to be cooperating "players" in revitalization than in service coordination.

In the United States, the community revitalization approach has received much of its current impetus from the July, 1995 publication of President Clinton's National Urban Policy Report. Entitled "Empowerment: A New Covenant with America's Communities," this report offers a "Community Empowerment Agenda" – focusing upon family self-sufficiency and independence through employment, a renewed encouragement of private investment in urban communities, and a locally or "grassroots" driven strategy of action.

For the most severely distressed of the nation's urban communities, an Empowerment Zones (EZ) and Enterprise Communities (EC) Program is to generate "strategies for change that combine innovative economic development initiatives with essential human capital and community building investments" (Empowerment, 1995, p. 44). In the EZ/EC program, the heaviest stress is upon a transition into employment, job-training, private-public partnerships in the stimulation of economic activity, and such quality-of-life improvements as better housing and anti-crime initiatives. The focus is also heavily upon self-determination rather than governmental largesse. At the same time, consolidated services efforts are not ruled out in the President's Report; indeed, integrated human services which link health, education, family assistance, and job training are specifically mentioned and encouraged.

The idea of an "enterprise zone" (EZ) is generally credited to a 1978 speech by Sir Geoffrey Howe, a member of the British House of Commons (Butler, 1991). From the start, the focus has been upon the economic improvement of poor neighborhoods through strengthening of indigenous community institutions, through investment incentives and the encouragement of public-private partnerships, and through a preference for market forces above governmental intervention (Green, 1991).

The low regulation block grant and bottom-up strategies of the enterprise zone concept have considerable appeal – in contrast with the earlier, over federalized methods of the Urban Development Action Grant (UDAG) Program for inner-city economic development (Watson, Heilman, & Montjoy, 1994). Nevertheless, many unresolved questions remain about the combination of public and private roles in neighborhood revitalization. As Green and Brintnall (1994) note, little private investment is now found in many distressed communities, and most of the key resources in the lives of community residents continue to derive from public sources – e.g., transfer payments, public education, police protection, public health, public transportation.

Indeed, supporters of focusing upon the schools in community-family connections initiatives point to the omni-presence of the local school as a significant element. The public school is one of the last, ongoing and stable institutions remaining in many distressed neighborhoods. It is an institution of substance, with a modest, if constrained tradition of its own in the game of "development." From the revitalization perspective, however, community development (through investment and "enterprise") has thus far not matched at all well with the work of the public school – even when the school begins to work hard towards "outreach" and "services" beyond the narrowly educational. Furthermore, neither the "social capital" nor the "empowerment" implications of both strategies have been well analyzed comparatively. Consequently, for all intents and purposes, to date the local school-site has been left out of the EZ/EC innovation.

## COORDINATED SERVICES, ENTERPRISE ZONES, AND SCHOOL REFORM

With delightful imagery, Tyack and Hansot (1982) have observed that it was not by accident that our earliest, one room schools resembled churches, complete with steeplelike bell towers. The local schoolhouse was in the very middle of the educational, social, political, and even religious life of its neighborhood. From Fourth of July picnics, to weekly spelling bees, to the occasional revival – the community was schoolhouse centered, and in turn the schoolhouse molded itself around the lives and values of its community.

Arguably, the more modern legacy in public education, over the past fifty years, has been a thrust toward a bit of "disconnection" between schools and their communities (Crowson, 1992). The need to preserve strong norms of professional discretion against private-regarding parents and narrow-minded communities was a theme as early as 1932, in the work of Willard Waller. Generations of school administrators in the U.S. have been trained around the dangers of losing managerial control to the "politics" of their communities (Iannaccone, 1989). Curiously, while parental involvement has been long recognized as essential to successful learning for children, this recognition has not translated into a full "partnership" with the school (Sarason, 1995). Similarly, thoughts of closer relationships with parents and with the local community in the governance of schools have long encountered a "system" of governance that emphasizes "top-down" rather than "bottom-up" decision making (Mann, 1986).

Amidst a wide ranging agenda for reforming American education – from choice, to "standards," to charter schooling, to site-based management – attempts to reverse the "disconnections" strategy are just beginning to gather momentum. Interestingly, while the staying power of the coordinated services idea may be in question,[1] the goal of re-connecting schools to their communities appears to be increasing in appeal. The plight of the American family is a major consideration; a new and widespread interest generally in the power of "community" is involved; decentralization to the grassroots in America continues to receive attention; the parent as a key figure in learning is now more fully respected; and, with or without coordination, the public school as a service rich institution continues to be an appealing notions.

What is to be learned from the two very different strategies for community regeneration we have discussed – about educational reform that will re-connect schools and communities, about the options and possibilities for community oriented changes in public schooling, and about the potential gains and losses from one approach or another? We offer three observations.

*First*, whether "family strategies" are to be focused upon services, opportunities for employment, empowerment or all three, the public school must now consider itself an integral part of the full scale development (economic, social, human-capital, and pedagogical) requirements of its community. More than service, the relationship under reform involves forms of support – from the institution of the school to the remainder of a network of both public and private "investors." The most important consequence of reform could be to fundamentally alter the *direction of interaction* between schools and their neighborhood environments. In terms used by Gary Wehlage and colleagues (1989), the newly reformed role for the schools would be its activation as a "community of support" for the families and children in its orbit.

"Support" is a term long used by educators to describe the responsibilities of parents and of the community (particularly financial support) if the schools are "to do their jobs" effectively. Non-supportive parents and an inadequately supportive community are among the most common of teacher and administrator complaints. Seldom, however, has the profession adequately addressed "the other side" of a support coin – that is, the degree to which the school can be credited with and held responsible for its support of the home and the larger community.

An extended role for the school, in full support of those in its environment (as well as supported by its environment) touches upon and potentially alters some deeply rooted structural features in public education. At a theoretical level, the notion of the school as an exercise in supportive "outreach" to its community connects with the idea of building "social capital," as noted earlier. It also finds strength in a new sense of the school as a central source of its own brand of societal "investment" in families, communities, and in the development of children (Hawley, 1990; Kagan & Neville, 1993).

An initial implication, clearly delineated by Cibulka (1996), is that community re-connection through "outreach" suggests a fundamental reshaping of public schooling – toward the full balancing of both academic *and* social/economic objectives. Far beyond the tentative and somewhat peripheral add-ons of lunches, breakfasts, and nurses, the "full-service school" (as one strategy) envisions a thoroughly changed institution – one that places the public school in a pivotal position in a much reshaped welfare state (Dryfoos, 1994). The evidence thus far, in investigations into coordinated services ventures, is that professional educators have experienced considerable difficulty in "getting their heads around" such a transformed institutional role (see Smylie, Crowson, Chou, & Levin, 1994).

But, there are other options. The local school could maintain its 3R's emphasis but cooperate extensively with community development agencies and other centers of family services. The local school can also be a fully active partner in a developmentally oriented network of public/private community institutions (from banks, to churches, to employers, to "activists"). To date, educators have only minimally understood that they too are part of an "enterprise" – despite the saliency of the school-to-work transition, the school's own role as an employer and purchaser of goods/services, the "products" even the most narrowly defined school contributes to its community (e.g., lunches, health examinations, school age day-care), and the school's accumulation of professionally credentialed "social capital."

*Second*, "empowerment" has been much more clearly recognized in the shaping of enterprise and development strategies than in coordinated services planning. This is not hard to understand. A provision of added professional services to families and communities can very easily proceed (and usually does) with only minimal involvement of the "client" in decision processes. Most of the key issues in service coordination (e.g., questions of professional turf, control of/confidentiality in client information, overcoming fragmented rules/regulations structures, resource-commingling restrictions) are issues of traditional *professions-dominated* service delivery (Crowson & Boyd, 1993). The struggle between professionals know best (for the good of the client) and the client knows best (for his or her own good) constitutes an unresolved battle of values, with deep roots historically in the progressive-era origins of the family-services and school-outreach constructs.

In development-language terms, there has been a cost to this approach. Much of the focus in the children's services movement has been upon the *supply* of added services to a presumably needy community. Much less attention has been paid to the community's *demand* for assistance. From the *supply* side, an array of new options for assistance, added professional expertise, and often some connecting personnel (e.g., family advocates) are made available to a targeted clientele. From the *demand* side, the new service offerings may be somewhat less important than a sense of welcome, a partnership in "development," a celebration of "community," a sense of need from the clients' perspectives, and a communication to families that they are not problems to be "fixed," so much as they are shareholders with the school and its professionals.

From a very similar perspective, White and Wehlage (1995, p. 29) concluded from their examination of the "New Futures" initiatives in collaborative services – that one key impediment to success was "the disjuncture between a specific collaborative policy and the actual social conditions affecting at-risk youth." "Disjuncture," they wrote, "describes bad policy, usually the result of inadequate and inaccurate knowledge about conditions in the communities being served."

The New Futures experimentation began in 1988, in five selected cities in the U.S., with funding from the Annie E. Casey Foundation. White and Wehlage (1995, p. 23) have described it as "one of the earliest and most ambitious attempts to bring about community collaboration." In some concluding remarks, following their evaluation of New Futures, they noted that this experimentation "failed to find ways to involve members of targeted communities in solving their own problems" (White & Wehlage, 1995, p. 36). Furthermore, they contend that the "major issue [in collaboration] is how to get whole communities, the *haves* and the *have nots*, to engage in the difficult task of community development" (White & Wehlage, 1995, p. 37).

The meaningful participation of the client in human services is a theme that has bedeviled community development initiatives through much of this century. From "urban renewal" strategies of the 1950's, which ignored the clientele; to politicization accompanying "maximum feasible participation" requirements in the 1960's; to the Model Cities and Community Development Corporation initiatives of more recent times – the issue of participation (let alone empowerment) has remained largely unresolved. Indeed, the very image of parents and community residents as the "clients" of professionals (who, moreover, may view many as dependent and even pathological "cases") severely limits participatory options. On the other hand, to assume that lay participation (e.g., in policy setting) will automatically improve the need-relevancy of services or even change institutional values – is to assume most naively. Robert Halpern (1995, p. 178) warns that to make participation (and eventually empowerment) work requires very careful anticipation and planning – around "a clear, multistep process, with rules, parameters and objectives jointly set by community members and professionals, and a trust in that process among all the stakeholders."

*Third*, school-based coordinated services to children and families may have limited effects without the assistance of some community-wide revitalization and empowerment. On the other hand, however, enterprise zone and economic development strategies may be seriously weakened if there is no effective liaison with the public schools. Cohen (1995, p. 36) has observed that the schools "have seldom played more than a bit part" thus far in most neighborhood revitalization. Consequently, most of the broad based efforts toward community development seem to be unaccompanied by any significant change in the schools (Cohen, 1995).

To be sure, advocates of community revitalization clearly recognize that the local schools must be central players. Indeed, in federal grant-approval for education, attention is steadily increasing to needs for additional technology allocations, programming incentives (e.g., priority funding for the gifted, bilingual education, parent-training, etc.), and the encouragement of community programs/services (including service integration) within designated "empowerment zones" (Cohen, 1996). The school-to-work transition, job-readiness training, skills training, courses in entrepreneurship and individual self-sufficiency, after school programs, and an array of opportunities for family counseling – are among the further ingredients in economic development and empowerment-zone funding to date (Cohen, 1996).

Nevertheless, the emerging notion that neighborhood initiatives should proceed broadly and holistically, on many fronts simultaneously (e.g., education and human services plus job creation, community development, and community safety, as well as improved physical surroundings), encounters an organizational environment in which little thought has been given to just how thoroughly and deeply institutional reform may be necessary, if community regeneration is to occur. As one "deep structure" example, Skocpol (1992) observed that the public schools have been far more comfortable historically with a "maternal" focus upon children, parent-partnerships, and caring homes than upon the economic well-being of the community. On the other hand, those who have espoused improvements over the years – in such arenas as housing quality, crime prevention, resident participation and empowerment, job creation, and neighborhood "clean-up" – have tended to neglect the regenerative power of the "maternal", of especially committed and caring individuals ("wizards," says McLaughlin), of whom public education historically has had aplenty (see, McLaughlin, Irby, & Langman, 1994; also Halpern, 1995). Many other deeply embedded differences between the institutions serving communities can be found in traditions of bureaucratic control, professional ideologies and training, attitudes toward client and community, reputations for neighborhood responsiveness, and historical patterns of racial/ethnic exclusion.

Of even greater and, indeed, critical significance is the fact that the very logic of family and neighborhood assistance has changed dramatically over the course of this century (Halpern, 1995). Historically, neighborhood institutions such as settlement houses and the local school helped to prepare residents for entry into the nation's economic and social mainstream. For many – particularly poor, minority Americans – however, urban neighborhoods have now become not way-stations but end-points, with little realistic chance of a fulfilled journey into the mainstream (Halpern, 1995, p. 224; Wilson, 1987, 1996). Tightly aligned with the old notion of "preparation" (for the mainstream), the public schools have experienced difficulty in attempting to redefine themselves (in a recognition of urban realities) toward a more "full service" orientation, offering "outreach," family assistance, and "social capital" in the support of improved children's learning (see Smylie, Crowson, Chou, & Levin, 1994).

Yet to be explored at all, to date, in educational reform is the potentially even more difficult transition of the public school, under EZ/EC initiatives, from a "full service school" into an "enterprise school."[2] An enterprise school might be expected to join an array of other neighborhood and city institutions in a much larger than services and a more substantive than preparation participation in the development and regeneration of the school's own neighborhood environment. Services to children and families would be provided, to be sure, but far more fulsome, well planned relationships may also be necessary with neighborhood churches, businesses, community organizers, housing authorities, the parks department, the police, youth organizations, and the city at large.

## CONCLUSION

Extending social organization and bringing "order" to distressed neighborhoods, along with providing hope and "preparation," constitute a role for service organizations with deep roots in turn of the century America. The rediscovery of such a service and outreach role for the public school, not unlike the work of the settlement house, has now become a reform motif in the U.S. of considerable power and appeal. A "full service school," linking education and an array of other supports (e.g., health services; counseling; family advocacy; employment, housing, and welfare assistance) can contribute to the development of much of the "social capital" needed to improve children's learning. There is more than a bit of "professionals know best" to all of this; thus, a key constraint has been how to involve the "clients" meaningfully in the coordinated-services relationship.

While a laudable concept, the full service school conflicts with many twentieth-century traditions of bureaucratization, professional distancing, fragmented and "categorical" programming and, as noted earlier, often only a very tentative partnering between educators and families/communities. Coordinated children's services initiatives are fairly widespread now, not only in the United States but in other nations. However, the results in the U.S. thus far have been mixed – with evidence that the changes in educational lifeways promised by the concept of full service schooling threaten many deeply embedded "institutionalized" features of American schooling (Crowson & Boyd, 1993). The "test" for coordinated services, observe White and Wehlage (1995, p. 35), is in "reshaping the priorities and practices of schools." That is an extremely tall order.

Even more demanding, however, is the newer suggestion for reform – that, where needed, the public schools should now play an active (and even more complex and socially involved) role in the empowerment and economic revitalization of their communities. Important assumptions here are the notions that: (a) added assistance to families and children, while vital, can fail to pay off if the full involvement of parents and the community is not a simultaneous goal; (b) the local school should be recognized as very much a part of the "basic industry" of the city, with economic and community development responsibilities that go well beyond a mere "delivery" of services (Weeres & Kerchner, 1996); and, (c) powerful neighborhood revitalization strategies should proceed from the realization that in poor neighborhoods "physical, economic, and social, individual and collective, adult and child well being are all interconnected" (Halpern, 1995, p. 198). Thus, as noted above, this logic argues that, rather than just "full service schools," local public schools should be transformed into "enterprise schools."

Just what does this mean for practical school reform and policy? Altering schools, even on their own terms, is notoriously difficult; reorienting them toward a community services outreach extending well beyond their traditional activities is still more challenging. The added issues to be addressed in a transition toward "enterprise schools" in urban neighborhoods will be major – going well beyond localized foci upon the "developmental" needs of children and families that have usually been the aim of coordinated-services efforts. Partnering with revitalization forces (as well as family "welfare" forces) in a neighborhood might mean tackling such issues as: economic incentives; employment options and training; a neighborhood's attractiveness to investment capital; and partnering with such "economic" institutions as banks, retail businesses, insurers, and property owners – those persons whom educators tend to regard as "just out to make money." To accomplish such goals will take a serious rethinking of school, community, and family connections, as James Cibulka (1996, p. 429) concludes, along with a "transformation" (not just reform) of the schools, and "a new approach to the welfare state."

In evocative language, Claire Smrekar (1996, p. 31) reaches a similar conclusion, asserting that the new economic revitalization and empowerment press in urban education should:

> . . . force us to penetrate the veneer that has helped slide the issue of children's services to the center of the policy table on the naive and narrow assumption that integrated services will provide more economic and efficient systems for families.
>
> Our responses require us to move beyond the erratic and irregular child-saving impulses that have marked earlier actions, to efforts that understand the complexity of the lives of children and their families . . .

In the final analysis, the issue seems to come down to a question of how to meld together aspects of the two competing strategies – professional coordinated services and community development or empowerment – into workable approaches for schools in partnership with parents, community organizations, and other agencies. Each approach, in isolation from the other, appears likely to produce only limited success. Yet, merging the two approaches presents daunting problems. Community empowerment approaches are inclined to become highly politicized (Alinsky, 1971) and conflict strongly with professional and bureaucratic norms and procedures. Professional services approaches are inclined to be disconnected from, and sometimes disrespectful of, parental and community preferences and values. At the same time, some believe that going very far in either direction will all too easily divert schools from their central and most important function – basic academic instruction (Committee for Economic Development, 1994). Moreover, economic trends toward the "disappearance" of work opportunities, which are most acute in depressed inner cities, conflict with the aspirations of community development approaches (Rifkin, 1995; Wilson, 1996).

What then is to be done? We believe the best answer is to encourage experimentation, especially in ventures led by entrepreneurial educators who are willing to take the risks to try to create "enterprise" schools. To foster this sort of experimentation, we need local, state and national policies that will support and provide incentives for this kind of bold activity. That this kind of school can be created, with the right kind of dynamic leadership, has been proven by the well publicized and dramatic success of Yvonne Chan in transforming the Vaughn Street School in Los Angeles, which serves a disadvantaged Hispanic population (see Freedman, 1995). School principals like Chan have been rare in pubic education, but it is also true that we only recently have begun to encourage this kind of leadership through such means as the creation of "charter schools," which is one of the mechanisms Chan used to transform her school. Clearly, "business as usual" cannot get the job done.[3] We believe that a variety of experiments is needed, to explore the potential of enterprise schools and of alternative approaches to the melding of the two strategies discussed in this chapter.

## ENDNOTES

[1]    A major blow to the coordinated children's services notion occurred in mid-1994, with an announcement by the Pew Charitable Trust that it was terminating its commitment to the development of school-linked family centers. Pew had been a major philanthropic player in the movement (Cohen, 1994). Our thanks for this insight to our colleague at Vanderbilt University, James Guthrie. The truth is that the norms and incentives of "business as usual" in large urban public school districts militate strongly against entrepreneurial behavior and instead reward school principals for "playing it safe" and "going by the book."

[2]    Our thanks for this insight to our colleague at Vanderbilt University, James Guthrie.

[3]    The truth is that the norms and incentives of "business as usual" in large urban public school districts militate strongly against entrepreneurial behavior and instead reward school principals for "playing it safe" and "going by the book."

## REFERENCES

Adler, L., & Gardner, S. (Eds.). (1994). *The politics of linking schools and social services.* Washington, D.C.: Falmer Press.

Alinsky, S .D. (1971). *Rules for radicals, a practical primer for realistic radicals.* New York: Random House.

Butler, S. M. (1991). The conceptual evolution of enterprise zones. In R.E. Green (Ed.), *Enterprise zones: New directions in economic development* (pp. 27–40). Newbury Park, CA: Sage Publications.

Cibulka, J. (1996). Conclusion: Toward an interpretation of school, family, and community connections: Policy challenges. In J. Cibulka & W. J. Kritek (Eds.), *Coordination among schools, families and communities: Prospects for educational reform* (pp. 403–435). Albany, NY: SUNY Press.

Cohen, D. L. (1996, May 1). In the zone: Effort aims to link economic gains, school reform. *Education Week,* 15(32), 1, 8–9.

Cohen, D. L. (1995, May 3). Joining hands. *Education Week,* 35–38.

Coleman, J. S. (August/September, 1987). Families and schools. *Educational Researcher,* 16(6), 32–38.

Coleman, J. S. (1994). Parental involvement: Implications for schools. In R. J. Yinger & K. M. Borman (Eds.), *Restructuring education: Issues and strategies for communities, schools, and universities* (pp. 19–31). Cresskill, NJ: Hampton Press, Inc.

Comer, J. (1988). Educating poor minority children. *Scientific American*, **259**(5), 42–48.

Comer, J. P. (1984, May). Home-school relationships as they affect the academic success of children. *Education and Urban Society*, **16**, 323–337.

Comer, J. P. (1980). *School power: Implications of an intervention project*. New York: Free Press.

Committee for Economic Development. (1994). *Putting learning first: Governing and managing the schools for high achievement*. New York: Author.

Crowson, R. L. (1992). *School-community relations, under reform*. Berkeley, CA: McCutchan.

Crowson, R. L., & Boyd, W. L. (1996, June). Achieving coordinated school-linked services: Facilitating utilization of the emerging knowledge base. *Educational Policy*, **10**(2), 253–272.

Crowson, R. L., & Boyd, W. L. (1993, February). Coordinated services for children: designing arks for storms and seas unknown. *American Journal of Education*, **101**(2), 140-179.

Crowson, R. L., Boyd, W. L., & Mawhinney, H. (Eds.). (1996). *The politics of education and the new institutionalism: Reinventing the American school*. The 1995 Yearbook of the Politics of Education Association. London: Falmer Press.

Davies, D. (1991). Schools reaching out: Family, school, and community partnership for student success. *Phi Delta Kappan*, **72**(5), 376–382.

Dryfoos, J. (1994). *Full-service schools*. San Francisco: Jossey-Bass.

*Empowerment, a new covenant with America's communities: President Clinton's national urban policy report*. (1995). Washington, D.C.: U.S. Dept. of Housing and Urban Development, Office of Policy Development and Research.

Epstein, J. (1988). *Parent involvement*. Baltimore, MD: Johns Hopkins University, Center for Research on Elementary and Middle Schools.

Epstein, J. (1990). School and family connections: Theory, research, and implications for integrating sociologies of education and family. *Marriage and Family Review*, **15**(1), 99–126.

Fantini, M. D. (1983). From school system to educative system: Linking the school with community environments. In R. L. Sinclair (Ed.), *For every school a community: Expanding environments for learning*. Boston: Institute for Responsive Education.

Freedman, J. (1995). *The charter school idea: Breaking educational gridlock*. Red Deer, Alberta, Canada: Society for Advancing Educational Research.

Garr, R. (1995). *Reinvesting in America*. Reading, MA: Addison-Wesley.

Gittell, R. (1992). *Renewing cities*. Princeton, NJ: Princeton University Press.

Goodlad, J. I. (Ed.). (1987). *The Ecology of School Renewal*. Eighty-ninth Yearbook of the National Society for the Study of Education. Chicago: University of Chicago Press.

Green, R. E. (Ed.). (1991). *Enterprise zones: New directions in economic development*. Newberry Park, CA: Sage Publications.

Green, R.E. and Brintnall, M. (1994), "Conclusions and Lessons Learned," in R.E. Green (Ed.), *Enterprise Zones: New Directions in Economic Development*. Newberry Park, CA: Sage Publications, pp. 241–257

Halpern, R. (1995). *Rebuilding the inner city: A history of neighborhood initiatives to address poverty in the United States*. New York: Columbia University Press.

Haveman, R., & Wolfe, B. (1994). *Succeeding generations: On the effects of investments in children*. New York: Russell Sage Foundation.

Hawley, W. D. (1990). Missing pieces of the educational reform agenda: Or, why the first and second waves may miss the boat. In S. B. Bacharach (Ed.), *Educational reform: Making sense of it all* (pp. 213–233). Boston: Allyn & Bacon,.

Iannaccone, L. (1989). Foreword. In F. W. Lutz & G. Merz (Eds.), *The politics of school/community relations* (pp. xi-xiv). New York: Teachers College, Columbia University.

Judd, D., & Parkinson, M. (Eds.). (1990). *Leadership and urban regeneration*. Newberry Park, CA: Sage Publications.

Kagan, S. L., & Neville, P. R. (1993). *Integrating services for children and families*. New Haven: Yale University Press.

Kirst, M. W., & Kelley, C. (1995). Collaboration to improve education and children's services. In L. C. Rigsby, M. C. Reynolds, & M. C. Wang (Eds.), *School-community connections: Exploring issues for research and practice* (pp. 21–43). San Francisco: Jossey-Bass.

Knapp, M. S., & Ferguson, M. (1995). *Integrated services reforms and the front-line professional*. Paper presented at the Annual Meeting of the University Council of Educational Administration (UCEA), Salt Lake City, October.

LaNoue, G. R., & Smith, B. L. R. (1973). *The politics of school decentralization*. Lexington, MA: Lexington Books.

Littell, J., & Wynn, J. (1989). *The availability and use of community resources for young adolescents in an inner-city and a suburban community.* Chicago: University of Chicago, Chapin Hall Center for Children.

Mann, D. (1986). *The politics of administrative representation.* Lexington, MA: Lexington Books.

McLaughlin, M. W., Irby, M. I., & Langman, J. (1994). *Urban sanctuaries: Inner-city youth and neighborhood organizations.* San Francisco: Jossey-Bass.

Philpott, T. L. (1978). *The slum and the ghetto: Neighborhood deterioration and middle-class reform, Chicago 1880–1930.* New York: Oxford University Press.

Rifkin, J. (1995). *The end of work: The decline of the global labor force and the dawn of the post-market era.* New York: Tarcher/Putnam.

Rigsby, L .C., Reynolds, M. C., & Wang, M. C. (Eds.). (1995). *School-community connections: Exploring issues for research and practice.* San Francisco: Jossey-Bass.

Sarason, S. B. (1995). *Parental involvement and the political principle.* San Francisco: Jossey-Bass.

Skocpol, T. (1992). *Protecting soldiers and mothers.* Cambridge: Harvard University Press.

Smrekar, C. (1996). *The organizational and political threats to school-linked integrated services.* Unpublished manuscript. Department of Educational Leadership, Peabody College, Vanderbilt University, Nashville, TN.

Smylie, M. A., Crowson, R. L., Chou, V., & Levin, R. (1994). The principal and community-school connections in Chicago's radical reform. *Educational Administration Quarterly, 30*(3), 342–364.

Tyack, D. (1992, Spring). Health and social services in public schools: Historical perspectives. *Future of Children, 2,* 19–31.

Tyack, D., & Hansot, E. (1982). *Managers of virtue: Public school leadership in America, 1820–1980.* New York: Basic Books.

Waller, W. (1932). *The sociology of teaching.* New York: Wiley.

Watson, D. J., Heilman, J. G., & Montjoy, R. S. (1994). *The politics of redistributing urban aid.* Westport, CN: Praeger.

Weeres, J. G., & Kerchner, C. T. (1996). This time it's serious: Post-industrialism and the coming of institutional change in education. In R. L. Crowson, W. L. Boyd, & H. B. Mawhinney (Eds.), *The politics of education and the new institutionalism: Reinventing the American School* (pp. 135–152). London: Falmer Press.

Wehlage, G. G., Rutter, R. A., Smith, G .A., Lesko, N., & Fernandez, R. R. (1989). *Reducing the risk: Schools as communities of support.* London: Falmer Press.

Weiss, H. B. (1995). *Raising our future: Families, schools, and communities joining together.* A Report. Cambridge, MA: Harvard Family Research Project, Harvard Graduate School of Education.

White, J. A., & Wehlage, G. (1995). Community collaboration: If it is such a good idea, why is it so hard to do? *Educational Evaluation and Policy Analysis, 17*(1), 23–38.

Wilson, W. J. (1987). *The truly disadvantaged, the inner city, the underclass, and public policy.* Chicago: University of Chicago Press.

Wilson, W. J. (1996). *When work disappears: The world of the new urban poor.* New York: Knopf.

Yinger, R. J., & Borman, K. M. (Eds.). (1994). *Restructuring education: Issues and strategies for communities, schools, and universities.* Cresskill, NJ: Hampton Press, Inc.

III: Professional Development for Reform

# Teacher Unions and Educational Reform

NINA BASCIA

*Ontario Institute for Studies in Education, University of Toronto*

*This chapter delineates the contemporary involvement by teacher unions in projects to improve teaching and learning, including but extending beyond the arena of collective bargaining drawing from research on a variety of recent reform efforts by teachers' organizations in Canada and the United States. The challenges of and necessity for unions' current reform work are identified.*

To many North Americans, teacher unions' initiation of and support for educational reform seems like an oxymoron. In the press, in the educational literature, and even among many teachers, teacher unions are characterized as conservative organizations whose preoccupation with teachers' well-being is antithetical to students' educational interests. For some observers, any organization with an overtly "political" role is categorically unable to concern itself with issues of educational substance (Mitchell & Kerchner, 1983). In fact, however, many teachers' organizations across Canada and the U.S. treat their responsibility to improve the quality of teaching and learning as a major, if not *the* major, priority. National-level organizations in the U.S., and many provincial or state and local organizations in both countries, are concerned simultaneously with so-called "bread and butter" and "professional" issues – with improving teachers' material and working conditions, but also with broadening teachers' roles and competence and increasing schools' and school systems' capacities to meet the needs of an increasingly diverse and needy student population. Many of these reform initiatives are relatively new developments; in other cases, political lobbying, collective bargaining, and direct support for the development of new educational practices are seen as complementary strategies. Particularly in the U.S., these projects often are undertaken in partnership with departments of education, philanthropic foundations, universities, district administrators, computer corporations, and other organizations (Bascia, 1996a).

Teacher unions' work toward the reform of public education is largely hidden behind the prevailing rhetoric that insists their purposes are fundamentally obstructive to good educational practice. Media coverage of teacher unions is scant except during episodes of labor conflict; then the union is personified as a tough-talking president and teachers chanting slogans – sound bites that appear to have little connection to classroom or school issues but rather emphasize concerns about teachers' salaries and working conditions, at least implicitly portraying teachers and their organizational effects as selfish or obsessed with minutae. Much of the

*M. Fullan (ed.), Fundamental Change, 225-245.*

educational literature, even that which focuses on educational policy, school governance, and teachers' work, is silent on teacher unions. Research that focuses on various aspects of educational reform – school restructuring, enhancements to teachers' professional development, new roles for teachers – reveals only scant glimpses of union sponsorship or participation (e.g., Lieberman, 1995; Little, 1993); rarer is literature that focuses directly on union involvement in educational reform (but see Bascia, 1994a; Johnson, 1988; Kerchner & Koppich, 1993; Kerchner & Mitchell, 1988; McClure, 1991, 1992; Rauth, 1990). The research that focuses explicitly on teacher unionism typically has been undertaken by researchers whose training, close contacts, and sympathies are with administrators and policymakers from whose perspective unions are anathema, or at best organizational anomalies or puzzles (Bascia, 1997c). Much of the scholarly attention to unions has emphasized bargaining processes and collective agreements – the formal rituals and documentation of labour relations.

Teachers themselves articulate a variety of opinions on the utility of their unions. Because school systems tend to be organizationally complex; activities occurring at one level or location often are invisible or partially obscured at another. Teachers tend to perceive district-level actions (including collective bargaining) in terms of their consequences for their work; and this work engenders complex webs of logistical concerns (Bascia, 1994a; Talbert & McLaughlin, 1994); union strategies, in short, are visible to some teachers, valued by a few, and irrelevant or obstructive to others (Bascia, 1994a). Union-active teachers are uncommon, their union roles, like many other extra-curricular professional activities, unseen by their colleagues and sometimes without obvious collective merit (Bascia, 1997a). Like the biases of media and scholarly coverage, this invisibility to teachers presents serious challenges for teacher unions' reform work.

The obscurity of unions' roles in relation to educational reform can also be attributed to the ambiguity and contested nature of the concept: reform of what, specifically? In whose interests? Toward what ends, and with what consequences? Might there be multiple and divergent reform strategies, and might we disagree on their utility? Andrew Gitlin (1996) has described how, between 1880 and 1920, some teachers' organizations in the U.S. challenged the "professionalism projects" advanced by "normal schools" and schools of education with their own "political professionalism" strategies that attempted to protect and enhance teacher autonomy and authority. Similarly, Dennis Carlson (1992) has provided an illustrative, more contemporary study of how a local union in the Midwestern U.S. reacted against the initiation of a "basic skills" curriculum to which teachers objected in practical and ideological terms. Revelations that local unions rejected proposals for "professional" contractual provisions for "staff development" programs (Retsinas, 1982) suggest that union leaders and teachers at least sometimes believe such provisions are not as relevant, useful, or important as other issues (Cooper, 1988; Freedman, 1987; Malloy, 1987). This research helps explain unions' motives, at times, for deliberately obstructing certain reform schemes advanced by others: for example, when they believe teachers' work is not well-supported, encouraging

teachers to "work to rule" – refuse to perform any duties not contractually specified – and consequently impeding teachers' involvement program and curriculum
planning and development activities; or challenging teachers' assumptions of new
roles and responsibilities out of fear that administrators will be able to demand
increasing amounts and types of work by teachers and teachers will have no legal
recourse. While many "outsiders" see unions' concerns over economic benefits,
job security, and the conditions of teaching as the antithesis of educational innovation, for many teachers collective agreements are inherently, however incrementally
or incompletely, about improving the quality of teaching and learning, or at least
containing the "excesses" of authority by administrators to constrain or obstruct
their work.

This chapter delineates the contemporary involvement by teacher unions in
projects to improve teaching and learning, including but extending beyond the
arena of collective bargaining, drawing from research on a variety of recent reform
efforts by teachers' organizations in Canada and the United States. The first section identifies the variety of motives for unions' reform work, charting the history
union activities, discussing both the enduring relevance of traditional union strategies and the logical links between them and more recent "professionalizing"
projects. The second section describes the substance and structure of current reform
endeavors: teacher development projects, projects to increase schools' capacity for
quality educational programming, and the phenomenon of collaborative sponsorship, or "joint custody" of reform (Kerchner, Koppich & Weeres, 1996). The final
section discusses the challenges of, and the necessity for, unions' current reform
work.

## THE LOGIC OF REFORM

Much of the literature characterizes unions' involvement in educational reform as
a recent phenomenon, a strategic necessity, after a long history of fairly exclusive
attention to teachers' material and security concerns. Some studies, however, both
historical and contemporary, characterize teacher union strategies as consistently
interested in enhancing the professional status of teachers, focusing particularly
on increasing teachers' control over their work and their authority over educational
policy. This section provides an overview of the social and political contexts that
have framed teachers' organizations priorities from their inception until the present.

The literature on teacher unions in both Canada and the U.S. has emphasized
those organizations' enduring focus on teachers' job security and material benefits.
Educational historians describe how teachers organized a century ago in response
to new bureaucratic school systems that established the regulation of teachers'
pay, job security, and teaching assignments – in short, the nature of their daily
work as well as their prospects for longer term careers (Braun, 1972; Larson, 1977;
Murphy, 1990; Smaller, 1991; Tyack, 1974; Urban, 1982). The emerging teachers'
organizations attempted to minimize the detrimental effects of what teachers
experienced as inappropriate, obstructive, and demoralizing regulation. Wayne

Urban (1982) and Harry Smaller (1991) have described how, in both countries, teachers were driven to form and join unions in numbers large enough to persuade administrative authorities to modify some of the employment controls. Smaller and Urban are clear that differences in "backgrounds, values and family/work situations" (Smaller, 1991, pp. 104–105) prevented teachers from finding any fundamental ideological commonality; "bread and butter" issuers were the only broad basis for collective action. McDonnell and Pascal (1988), writing about more recent teacher unions' agendas in the U.S., have described unions' pursuit of, or accommodation to, so-called "professional" agendas as inhibited by teachers' "skepticism and even hostility" (p. viii) toward reform initiatives and their insistence that their organizations focus on traditional issues: job security, material benefits, and working conditions.

Legislation that governs collective bargaining in the U.S. and Canada appears to have reinforced this emphasis on material and job security issues. Labor laws passed in the 1930s and 40s in both countries make a clear distinction between managerial prerogative and the issues over which unions, as employees' legal representatives, could have some influence. These legal provisions were, at the time of their passage, seen as a "great compromise" (Carlson, 1992, p.91): teachers won the right to organized representation (and in many Canadian provinces, teachers' federations won the right to compulsory membership and exclusive right to negotiate contracts) in exchange for severely limited purview over educational issues. Provincial and state legislation passed in the 1960s and 70s follows this pattern, restricting the purview of teachers' organizations to issues of wages, benefits, and working conditions and limiting teachers' organizations' ability to influence educational policy to an "advisory" or informal lobbyist role (Carlson, 1992, pp 91–102; Larson, 1977; Ray, 1991).

The restrictive focus of collective bargaining has been the subject of much scholarly critique. Mitchell and Kerchner (1983), for example, describe how collective bargaining fosters a conception of teaching as labour (rather than art, craft, or professional work), including "time-bounded" rather than "mission-bounded" work, the homogenization of teachers' work roles, an emphasis on rules and compliance rather than the quality of instruction, and an incentive for teachers' passive resistance, rather than active engagement. Myron Lieberman (1988) blames the existence of teacher unions for the absence of a code of ethics among teachers, and by extension, a lack of occupational accountability. Dennis Carlson (1992), writing from a different ideological position, nonetheless reinforces this line of critique, characterizing teacher unions as caught up in a reactive "contract game" in which union leaders focus on negotiating the best power position but are unable to mobilize effective responses to educational policies crafted by powerful but distant legislators and administrators.

Unions' one-down position in terms of educational policy-making and the uncertain nature of educational funding have meant that, in many locales, unions have found themselves renegotiating the same items, or new versions of enduring issues, again and again (Bascia, 1994a; Retsinas, 1982; Russo, 1979). In a comprehensive assessment of collective agreements across the U.S., McDonnell &

Pascal (1988) discovered that after 1975 the majority of teacher unions were unable to negotiate smaller class sizes, assurances that teachers would only be assigned to teach subjects in which they were certified (therefore competent), and teacher involvement in setting instructional policies. According to Rauth, "Unions had gotten so far but no farther with improvements in working conditions," (1990, p. 782).

In the mid-1980s, amid a heightened public rhetoric about the need to improve the quality of education and increasing calls for the "professionalization" of teaching, American teacher unions were criticized for continuing to emphasize bread and butter provisions rather than endorsing "professional items" like staff development. Some writers blamed teachers and others blamed the unions themselves for this "conservatism" and "shortsightedness." In the late 1980s, several researchers noted that some locals were interested in educational reform and theorized an "evolutionary" movement away from an exclusive emphasis on traditional items, not only in terms of what got written into the contract but in terms of a visibly active joint district-union commitment to educational improvement (Johnson, 1987; Kerchner & Mitchell, 1988). In many of these instances, clearly, the ability to "evolve" was contingent upon local economic capacity and political will – the ability to assure and then build upon a basic quality of teaching conditions. In other, less well-documented instances, especially in poor urban districts, sheer desperation led union officials and district administrators to try something new, including suspension of long-standing labor acrimony. There is some evidence that unions' recent attention to educational reform has been driven by union leaders' desires to repair the damages of chronically negative publicity. Researchers have noted that teachers' organizations have had to "respond to escalating pressure to balance a concern with personnel issues with responsible attention to matters surrounding professional practice" (Little, 1993, p. 146), "to emphasize their pursuit of better instructional outcomes and to downplay their demands for higher pay and better working conditions" (Johnson, 1988, p. 746). During the same period, Canadian teachers' federations were feeling some of the same pressures: "Do teachers want more prestige, more money or both? Or are they sincere in the belief that the elevated professional status will lead to better schools, students, and society?" asks Soder (1986, p. 16).

When teachers' political activities by definition are treated as "unprofessional" (Bascia, 1997a; Hargreaves, 1994b), teachers' concerns over working conditions are presumed to be selfish, and even reductions in class size can be characterized as "material benefits" for teachers (see for example McDonnell & Pascal, 1988). It is easy to understand why unions have wanted to reconstitute their public images. There is evidence that some of the major reform initiatives undertaken by teacher unions were deliberately started with this goal in mind: for example, the National Education Association's Mastery in Learning Project, according to a staff insider, was "initially . . . seen exclusively as an opportunity to demonstrate to the public and policy-makers that the Association cared about improving schools" (McClure, 1992, p. 85). Unions' frustration with their minimal impact on educational policy-making also has been an impetus for sponsorship of reform initiatives. For example, in 1992, after the limits of its ability to influence provincial educational policy directions were made frustratingly clear, the Ontario Teachers Federation initiated several linked province-wide projects to help teachers and schools increase their capacity to implement the new policies (Bascia, 1994b).

In the U.S., the recent so-called second wave of school reform has provided the opportunity for many organized groups to legitimately participate in school reform, and teacher unionsunion have been no exception (Bascia, 1996a; Ogawa, 1994). Teachers', administrators' and school board members' organizations, university educators, test developers and textbook publishers, computer and software manufacturers, local and national philanthropic organizations, business leaders, and elected officials all are active participants on the educational reform scene, generating recommendations for educational change and, in many instances, supporting specific site-based programs (Bascia, 1996a). Reform initiatives frequently involve the support and participation of multiple organizations (Harrington-Lueker, 1992; Meade, 1991). Teacher union leaders serve on advisory bodies for major reform efforts; in many cases, unions are the conduits for teachers' involvement as project coordinators, developers, and staff.

According to the evidence reviewed above, then, teacher unions' interest in "professional" or "reform" projects emerges out of a frustration with the limits of their traditional purview and the damaging effects of negative publicity. Repeatedly coming up against the limits of their ability to improve the quality of the conditions of teaching and to influence educational policy more broadly, union leaders have found opportunities in the current restructuring movement to legitimately engage in educational program and policy development in hopes that their efforts will result in improved an public image and enhanced policy leverage. But this line of argument, while predicated on several types of evidence, does not tell the whole story. Research that foregrounds the perspectives of teacher unionists, union-active teachers, and teachers more broadly present a somewhat different picture. While many scholars perceive a disjuncture between union concerns and substantive educational issues, and frame teachers' political and curricular activities as dichotomous, a recent study of teachers' assessments of unions in the U.S. (Bascia, 1994a) reveals how contemporary teachers value union protection because, in their estimation, the conditions of their work, and the vulnerability of teaching and schooling to external regulation and authority, warrant such vigilance. In this study, all the teachers, regardless of their level of union commitment, believed union representation was necessary to enhancing the quality of teaching, or at least minimizing obstructive administrative practices. And according to a recent study of contemporary union-active teachers in both the U.S. and Canada, advocacy work on behalf of students, programs, and colleagues is a common motive for union involvement. Union-active teachers reported using the opportunities provided by their union roles to seek practical support, access to information, and influence over policy decisions toward better teaching and learning conditions (Bascia, 1997a, 1997b).

From these perspectives, not only is a concern with traditional union issues understandable, but it can be consistent with, rather than antithetical to, a number of the arguments and foci of the current educational reform movement. A central tenet of the restructuring movement views teachers as the critical agents for school reform; their roles and responsibilities, and the effects of their practice on students learning are perceived as central to school improvement (Darling-Hammond, Cobb, & Bullmaster, 1995). The quality of conditions of teaching are seen as linked to the quality of student learning (see A. Lieberman, 1988; McLaughlin, 1993; Talbert & McLaughlin, 1994). The "second wave of education reform," in short, legitimates unions' longstanding emphasis on working conditions as well as their enduring position that teachers take a greater role in shaping their own practice. The legitimation of traditional union issues and arguments for teacher union involvement are understood as "common sense" and seen as integral to widespread, systemic reform of the entire educational system – see, for example, the report by National Commission on Teaching & America's Future (1996). Recent events have provided the opportunity to extend the union agenda from the work of a handful of teachers on small-scale curriculum, projects *within* union organizations to the larger, more visible arenas of school, district, provincial and, in the U.S., national educational reform.

These two possible interpretations of teachers' organizations' motives for engaging in educational reform work, one emphasizing disjuncture, dissonance, and political expediency and the other logical coherence and opportunity may, to some extent, represent the different orientations of union outsiders and insiders. Each explanation is, obviously, a generalized simplification constructed in hindsight. It is not appropriate to assign a single, or even a simple cluster of motives across the variety and number of teachers' organizations across the U.S. and Canada. National, state/provincial, and local political economies, variation in legal frameworks, union leadership, local community contexts, public and political sentiment, class and ideological differences among teachers, the nature of teachers' authority as well as their practical needs for information, resources, and influence all colour and contribute to the motives and strategies of organizations who claim to work in teachers' interests in any particular place and time.


REFORM STRATEGIES

This section provides an overview of the reform projects currently sponsored by teachers' organizations in Canada and the U.S., initiatives that mirror some of the projects that have been developed within teachers' organizations for many years but recently have expanded into the larger educational milieu. These initiatives are undertaken by teachers' organizations at all levels – national, state and provincial, and local (district); they range in scope from broad-scale professionalizing efforts (for example, to influence national standards for teaching and teacher education) to medium-scale organizational efforts (for example, supporting a statewide network of districts working on collaborative labor relations) to small-scale reform experiments (for example, sponsoring the restructuring of a single school, or of a peer coaching project across a small number of schools in a single district).

In the U.S., both national teachers' organizations, the American Federation of Teachers and the National Education Association, have provided technical assistance for number of local projects. Subunits within the organizations – sometimes longstanding staff development groups, sometimes new units with flashy new names, and sometimes an individual or group whose formal job titles require their attention on more traditional union activities, like grievances – take particular responsibility for the reform projects, negotiating resources and support, providing direct training, coordinating the deployment of other staff, and so forth.

This section organizes the broad range of reform strategies sponsored by teachers' organizations under three general headings. The first section describes the most comprehensive cluster, of reform initiatives that focus on various aspects of the teacher development continuum. The second describes the combination of experimental and structural efforts to transform school programs. The third delineates the partnership arrangements in which teachers' organizations participate that govern the reform projects. The examples are intended to be illustrative but are not exhaustive.

These particular initiatives, like the partnerships that sponsor them, are new – none more than a decade old – but there is also a logical continuity between the kinds of work unions have been engaged in for longer periods of time. The relative paucity of cited references in the text of this section is due to the minimal attention to union sponsorship in the literature. At the same time, because of similarities with efforts initiated or sponsored by other organizations – schools of education, philanthropic foundations, provincial ministries and state departments of education, corporations, and so forth – the nature of these projects will be familiar to those knowledgeable about the current reform context. In many instances, in fact, teachers' organizations undertake these projects in partnership with other organizations, partly funded by public educational jurisdictions or private foundations and involving advisory groups that bring together not only union leaders and administrators but also such disparate members teachers, academics, legislators, community members, and business representatives. These partnerships represent a relatively new national infrastructure of reform groups that encourage sustained interactions among formerly disassociated individuals and organizations as well as the rapid dissemination of ideas and information about educational ideas and strategies (Bascia, 1996a).

*Teacher Development*

*Teacher training.* While states and provincial agencies maintain legal authority for the terms of teacher licensure, teachers' organizations have made it their business to participate in new structures that have been established to regulate teachers' initial and ongoing formal training. In the U.S., the NEA and the AFT are members of the National Council for Accreditation of Teacher Education (NCATE) and on the National Board of Professional Teaching Standards, and each has been a conduit for teachers' involvement in developing standards in particular subject areas. In Canada, where educational reform in the main is not a national-level phenomenon, British Columbia and Ontario have each established Colleges of Teachers, independent bodies that accredit provincial teacher training programs and require and monitor teachers' ongoing professional learning, as well as disciplining teachers and decertifying those found to be incompetent; while the Colleges were deliberately set up to be independent of the teachers' federations (in Ontario, promotional material touts the College as "teachers' *real* professional organization" and argues that the federations are in a "conflict of interest" if they both discipline and defend teachers), the federations so far have ensured that they have significant representation in the College by electing their own slates of teachers to the governing boards (see Glegg, 1992).

Teachers' organizations have made claims on teacher training and development by developing and coordinating a variety of experimental projects. Many unions have special units or staff devoted to teacher preparation. In both countries, some local teachers' organizations work with colleges of education to develop new teacher education programs, many of them predicated on a professional development school model; for example, the AFT, in partnership with Michigan State University and Apple Computer have piloted a new, technology-rich teacher training program in a number of Michigan school districts. The Chicago Teachers Union has established its own teacher training academy; the teacher union in Dade County (Florida) has developed a teacher education center in collaboration with district administration.

Concerns that initial teacher preparation programs and over-worked school administrators are not sufficient supports for a teacher's first years on the job have prompted unions in school districts including Scarborough, Ontario; Cincinnati and Toledo, Ohio; and Poway and Lompoc, California to sponsor induction, peer assistance, and mentoring programs for beginning teachers. In many of these programs, small numbers of veteran teachers are released from all or part of their classroom duties to spend time observing, providing resources and informal feedback, demonstrating lessons, advocating with administrators, and otherwise assisting new teachers. In some locales, these teacher consultants also work with more seasoned teachers identified as having difficulties in the classroom. In such cases, the teacher consultants may be responsible for making formal recommendations to district administration for teachers' promotion or dismissal; unions place such a high value on such support that they are willing to waive their usual practice of automatic defense for teachers whose classroom performance shows little improvement (Bascia, 1994a; Gallagher, Lanier, & Kerchner, 1993; Kerchner et al., 1996; Phillips, 1993; Rauth, 1990). Mentoring and peer coaching programs focus on providing practicing teachers with observational skills and a vocabulary that enables discussion of classroom practice. Like induction programs, they are intended no only to encourage instructional improvement in isolated cases but to foster teachers' greater willingness and ability to work with colleagues, to discuss classroom problems as well as successes, and ultimately to change the culture of teaching in schools toward ongoing improvement of educational practice (Bascia, 1994a; Cole & Watson, 1991).

*Ongoing professional development.* Beyond the special opportunities available to selected teachers through induction and mentoring programs described above, union organizations have maintained professional development units over many decades that provide workshops, courses, materials, and curriculum development projects for practicing teachers more broadly (Levin & Young, 1994; McClure, 1992). In recent years, unions' efforts have expanded markedly and in a number of different directions. In some school districts, unions co-sponsor district professional development offerings with district administrators. These programs may focus on the topics that leaders jointly decide are of local import, but often these programs are organized around issues identified by polled teachers. Some professional development projects look like traditional staff development – workshops of short duration, delivered by "experts" – but increasingly these initiatives recognize local teachers' expertise and provide opportunities for teachers to learn with and from each other over the longer term and focus on addressing practical problems identified by the teachers themselves (see Bascia, 1994b; Cochran-Smith & Lytle, 1992; Little, 1993; McLaughlin, 1993 for more general discussion of these issues). These "professional communities" of educators work within a variety of possible venues: Some teacher unions provide funding to teachers to conduct research in their classrooms or in other educational settings toward the development of curriculum or new programs or services in their schools. In Petaluma, California, all district employees, including non-teaching staff, are required to participate in monthly, district-wide study groups organized around topics of interests to participants. The National Education Association and Ontario Teachers Federation each have established computer networks that allow educators dispersed across long distances to discuss curricular issues, school restructuring plans, books they're reading, critiques of educational policy directions, as so forth (Bascia, 1994b; McClure, 1991, 1992). Teachers' organizations also sponsor symposia and conferences so practitioners can share educational ideas and strategies. The American Federation of Teachers and several state AFT affiliates host "Quest" conferences, at which educators working on a variety of educational reform initiatives present their ideas, network with far-flung colleagues, and listen to offerings by academics, technology gurus, and others (Bascia, 1996a; Goldsberry et al., 1995).

*Teacher leadership.* Unions have a long history of providing opportunities for teachers to assume organizational as well as curricular development roles – by identifying potential "teacher leaders" and providing focused training, support, and opportunities for their involvement in union and school system affairs, with the hope that they will not only contribute to the union but enrich the school system more broadly. Summer and weekend "leadership institutes" or "academies" for union-active teachers cover a wide range of topics from collective bargaining and grievance proceedings to conflict mediation, school reform, and school-community relations. Traditional union roles, such as school representative, may provide such teachers with useful access to school and district decision making arenas and new kinds of relationships with colleagues and administrators –

opportunities to practice "teacher leadership" in the service of students, colleagues, and programs (Bascia, 1994a, 1997a). Where shared decision making is a district priority, teachers in traditional union representative roles often serve as co-chairs of school governance committees and work more directly with school administrators in shaping school policies. The kinds of teachers who are targeted as leaders or attracted to union work, it should be noted, are often those who have already distinguished themselves as organizational players. Some unions, however, make concerted efforts to increase the diversity of local teacher and administrative leadership: Ontario's Federation of Women Teachers employs a variety of strategies to encourage women teachers to become administrators, and because women have been so underrepresented in administrative ranks, such training is in itself a sort of educational reform (Bascia, 1997b). Other teachers' organizations, like the Cleveland Teachers Union, maintain programs to increase the influence and number of teachers of colour in the educational system.

The new generation of union-sponsored reform projects provides opportunities for teachers to develop curricular, pedagogical, process, organizational, and other skills and to serve colleagues, students, and their schools in new ways. The new leadership academies are intended "to produce people who can advance the agendas of restructuring and professionalization and can sustain the union's role in keeping up this momentum" (Rauth, 1990, p. 790). The American Federation of Teachers and Ontario Teachers Federation each have trained and deployed a cadre of teacher "facilitators" who work with groups of educators to develop new school projects or solve educational problems and, in the process, practice new collaborative working skills (Bascia, 1994b). In California, unions have helped create and shape the roles of state-funded "mentor teachers" who provide various kinds of curricular guidance to their school or district colleagues; Pittsburgh's union-district alliance has established "instructional teacher leaders" (Kerchner, 1993).

*Increasing school capacity*

While many of union reform projects focus on improving teachers' competence and expanding their involvement to new educational arenas, other union-led initiatives treat schools as the unit of change and focus on reconfiguring the structure and cultures of the organizations in which teaching and learning occur. Emphasizing innovation and local experimentation, many union-sponsored restructuring initiatives take the form of technical assistance, small grants, and opportunities for educators engaged in restructuring to research, plan, discuss, and learn together. The hallmark of many of school restructuring initiatives is an absence of any prescribed plan; school staffs are expected to take major responsibility for design and implementation.

Many of these initiatives emphasize the process by which educators come to consensus about the fundamental purposes of a school, construct a plan, and continue to meet and solve problems. Teacher-facilitators trained and mobilized by the Ontario Teachers Federation and the American Federation of Teachers visit schools to do such group-process work (Bascia, 1994b). Other organizations, like the teachers' unions in Chicago and Louisville, Kentucky, sponsor or co-sponsor "academies" and other physical environments where school staffs or teams of educators can "retreat" to study, be trained, reflect, and plan, away from the pulls and demands of daily school work. Other initiatives emphasize the role of teachers' professional development as central to school improvement. The National Education Association's Mastery in Learning is intended to help schools become "centers of inquiry," begins with assistance toward establishing initial priorities, contains elements of shared decision making, but is most concerned with encouraging teachers to use research and create and share new understandings about teaching and learning by creating skills and inclinations for sustained inquiry (McClure, 1991, 1992). The National Education Association's KEYS initiative is a diagnostic process to help school staffs understand where their organizational strengths and limitations are. Other organizations dispense small grants that teachers can apply toward new school projects, typically curriculum, program, or professional development strategies.

Teacher unions increasingly step in to develop school programs where teachers have noted a crucial need for additional services for students. For example, in Ontario, the Secondary School Teachers' Federation's "Stay in School" program is a six-school, multi-year pilot drop-out prevention project. With support from the Ontario Teachers Federation's "Creating a Culture of Change" initiative, a teacher in London, Ontario, established a community-based mentoring program for high school students. A district-wide peer mediation and violence prevention program for youth is one of a dozen teacher-initiated projects sponsored by the Joint Committee for Educational Reform, a new collaborative venture between the Cleveland Teachers' Union and the Cleveland Public School District.

Some initiatives work most directly on fostering teachers' greater involvement in school decision making. In conjunction with district administration, for example, Petaluma Federation of Teachers provides training and direction on a variety of shared decision making strategies. While the collective agreement, as well as district personnel, make it clear that some degree of staff participation is expected, the actual form – who is responsible for what kinds of decisions, to what degree, using what decision-making methods – is left to school staffs' discretion. Written into many district agreements are provisions for teachers', students', parents', and staffs' involvement in decisions of organizational import such as the selection of administrators, teachers, and other staff; some organizations have instituted procedures so that teachers and other educational community members participate in the regular performance assessments of administrators. Finally, some teacher unions have agreed to suspend some collective agreement provisions to allow school staffs more flexibility in structuring teachers' work.

*Partnerships*

While many of the previously described initiatives are independently administered and directed by teachers' organizations, many others are initiated and governed by cooperative relationships between teacher unions and other groups, an arrangement that is a system-level reform in and of itself. Especially in the U.S., teachers' organizations support and participate in initiatives to help foster collaborative management relationships – between local unions, district administrators, teachers, and community members (Bascia, 1991, 1994a; Kerchner & Koppich, 1993). A network of a dozen California districts received small amounts of foundation funding and technical assistance to establish "trust agreements" to sit alongside collective bargaining as non-adversarial alternative arenas for union-district administration interaction (Bascia, 1991; Kerchner & Koppich, 1993); the NEA has sponsored nearly thirty local collaboratives across the U.S. through its Learning Laboratory initiative. The idea of collaborative labor relations has expanded beyond unions' own efforts: for example, the Panasonic Corporation, which has funded district-level reform initiatives in a dozen and a half districts across the U.S. since 1987, names "teachers unions and other professional associations as important system components" in its emergent model of "successful system change" and requires "mutual respect, a belief in shared decision making, and regular leadership dialogue" as a tenet of involvement in its reform assistance program (Panasonic Foundation, 1996). In the early 1990s, Kerchner and Caufman (1993) estimated that several hundred districts across the U.S. were engaged in union-management partnerships.

Collaborative labor relations and local educational reform frequently occur in tandem, in intentional as well as emergent ways. Alongside the substantive focus (e.g., school restructuring) of many of these reform initiatives stand more overt examinations of union roles in district affairs, teacher participation, the impact of contractual provisions and the conditions of teachers' work on the nature of educational programs. A close examination of local collaborative ventures suggests that the motives for partnership and its relationship with the substance of the reform varies from one context to another. In some instances, union and district leadership together develop and promote a comprehensive plan intended to reshape educational practice at all levels; here, the emphasis is on systemic change, and "joint stewardship" is seen as a necessary foundation. In other instances, union and district administration or school board trustees focus on changing an adversarial working relationship to a more cooperative and collaborative one; a project is selected to provide the focus to "practice" the new working relationship but is understood to be of lesser importance (Bascia, 1994a). In still other locales, the project is of paramount importance; participation in a reform partnership or network is merely a necessary step toward establishing a new program or service (Bascia, 1996a). Such different motives and priorities have different consequences for the success and impact of these and subsequent reform efforts, particularly insofar as they shape the sensitivity and permeability of the new leadership team to district conditions and needs.

Ideally, entering into new relationships with administrators, philanthropic foundations, and other co-sponsors allows teachers' organizations to broker greater resources, to exert greater systemic influence, and to link and strengthen their own projects (Bascia, 1994a; Kerchner & Koppich, 1993). Union leaders' and teachers' participation in discussions about new teacher roles, professional development, or increased school capacity may also heighten organizational sensitivities – both union and school system – about what is required to support teaching and learning. Union involvement in district decision making may be quite deep and broad, involving increased participation by union officials but also by teachers and other practitioners in many aspects of district organization; or it may remain confined to certain realms, issues, and arenas, sitting alongside practices and assumptions of longer standing. Changes in one aspect of educational practice may lead to changes in many more aspects or they may be restricted by a variety of local or environmental conditions.

CHALLENGES

This section delineates some of the conundrums and disjunctures teachers' organizations face in their educational reform efforts. Some of these challenges are endemic to the current generation of reform efforts, irrespective of organizational sponsorship, because of the the magnitude of change they represent, the effort and cost required, and the pervasiveness and resilience of traditional norms and structures. Other challenges are particular to unions themselves, given their internal organizational capacity, their responsibility to represent a diverse body of teachers working under a variety of conditions, and their power relative to other entities in the larger educational milieu. This section closes by arguing that, despite these difficulties, teachers' organizations must find ways to champion and participate in the reform of education.

*The magnitude of reform*

In some ways, teachers' organizations encounter many of the same challenges as other organizations – university research and development centers, foundations, school districts, and reform networks, to name a few obvious ones – in terms of the relative success of their efforts. For example, teachers' organizations must contend with teachers' unequal opportunities to benefit from the new generation of teacher development projects; teachers' personal obligations may constrain their ability to participate in after-school activities, and their differential roles and locations engender unequal access to professional opportunities within school settings (see Little, 1992; Robertson, 1992). The Ontario Teachers Federation has discovered that,in many schools, teachers lack access to the equipment necessary for participation in its provincial computer conferencing system, or lack the time to use them during their school days; as a consequence, nearly all participating teachers do so via their personal equipment at home, outside the regular teaching hours. These conditions have organizational as well as individual consequences: where computer access is limited and where there are few opportunities to share network discoveries with colleagues, this form of professional development is a private rather than a shared good, and its impact on practice is restricted to (some teachers') classroom practice rather than enriching school programs more generally (Bascia, 1994b).

The new roles for teachers engendered by union-sponsored reforms face many of the same dilemmas and ambiguities inherent to teacher leadership work more generally. Teachers whose work extends beyond the classroom often find that they must invent their jobs and that there are no clear boundaries in terms of time or activities (see Wasley, 1991). Often they work in contexts where the traditional hierarchical authority structure is alive and well; their ability to advocate for teachers or students is dependent on administrators' willingness to share power, and their own daily movements and authority are restricted by assumptions that teachers' only rightful place is in classrooms with students (Bascia, 1997a, 1996b). Especially in their own schools, teacher leaders often find it difficult to broach professional norms of privacy and autonomy when it comes to issues of classroom practice (Lichtenstein, McLaughlin, & Knudsen, 1992; Little, 1990a, 1990b, 1992). The complexity of teachers' work in schools often may make extra-classroom activities logistically difficult (Bascia, 1994a, 1997a). Such challenges not only require great skill and tact but place significant limits on teacher leaders' ultimate influence and efficacy (Bascia, 1996a, 1997c; Wasley, 1991).

While school-based collegial "professional communities" can be sites where educators work together to solve real and compelling educational problems (see Cochran-Smith & Lytle, 1992), such communities can also isolate teachers from the rest of a school program, from more holistic views of and relationships with students, and from important professional development opportunities (Hargreaves, 1994a). Where resources are scarce or perceived as scarce, and where there is a general lack of support for teachers' work, teachers tend to "retreat" from the larger organization into "balkanized" groups. Emerging small-scale programs can actually create new divisions within staffs, leading to exacerbated differences in teacher knowledge and engagement and fragmenting rather than enhancing and integrating students' educational experiences (Bascia, 1996c; Finley, 1984; Muncey & McQuillan, 1993). More challenging are efforts to engage all staff in comprehensive program overhaul. Finding and maintaining constructive ways to engage in dialogue when staff are not in consensus is both crucial and extremely challenging (Little, 1993).

At an organizational and inter-organizational level, jointly sponsored reform projects are often precarious, predicated as they are on the incorporation of multiple perspectives, authority locations, and ideologies. Rarely are collaborative efforts accompanied by a clear understanding that institutional relationships, like shared decision making in schools, require the deployment of new skills and a willingness to work through the unavoidable conflicts that arise (see A. Lieberman, 1988; Zeichner, 1991). Values, goals, and understandings about what constitutes evidence of success may be more difficult to match with multiple partners. By its very nature, the restructuring process can unearth previously hidden differences on fundamental issues (Timar, 1989). Good will and a faith in process may not be sufficient: whatever the intentions of the players, these unexplored assumptions and differences in goals can lead to an incremental adding on, rather than a fundamental rethinking of, school programs (Timar, 1989). There often is little opportunity to directly confront differences in goals and values, or the assumptions about relative power, among the partners (Bascia, 1996a). At the same time, reforms that focus primarily on changing relationships among organizational leaders without attending sufficiently to the conditions of teaching and learning are doomed to failure (Bascia, 1994a; Kerchner et al., 1996).

There are few precedents or referents for the magnitude of the reform efforts in which teachers' organizations are engaged; innovation and invention have been the rule of the day. The projects are fragile and require much energy and political and fiscal support (Darling-Hammond, 1995). They are subject to multiple influences, and may take on a variety of different forms; it is difficult if not impossible to extrapolate from them a blueprint to guide future projects with any success. The kinds of projects in which unions are engaged take many years to institutionalize; many are not well-suited to the kinds of evaluation methods and instruments that have been used with other programs in the past. They require fundamental changes in activities, responsibilities, skills, and relationships – among teachers but also among administrators, students and parents; not only among individuals but among schools, universities, businesses, foundations, as well as teachers' organizations. These projects have been established in an educational system still overwhelmingly structured in ways that inhibit all of these new practices, a system where much of the "business as usual" continues (Kerchner & Koppich, 1993), but they require more comprehensive changes in the nature of support for teaching and learning. In all of these ways, teacher union-sponsored reforms are representative of other organizationally-sponsored efforts that focus on discrete aspects of educational practice, rather than on a comprehensive agenda for reform.

*Challenges for teachers' organizations*

Teacher unions also face challenges unique to their organizational type. The dichotomy between "traditional" union issues and educational reform is played out between the political and professional development units within many teachers' organizations (McClure, 1992). While the traditional organizational structure is dysfunctional in this era of reform, the limits of unions' political and legal authority make this enduring internal disjuncture understandable. The legal limits to unions' role in making policy, locally, provincially and nationally, are a serious and significant restriction on their actions. A good portion of their efforts must necessarily fall under the category of damage control. With educational funding uncertain and teachers' participation in decision making minimal, unions must continually focus their efforts on securing educational resources and minimizing the damage of policies crafted by those with divergent priorities about schooling (Bascia, 1994a). These tensions and challenges were recently exemplified in Ontario, where sharp decreases in provincial funding for education resulted in loss of time for teachers' non-classroom activities, including professional development and new program planning; this, along with a loss of support staff and threats of widespread teacher layoffs prompted the Ontario Teachers' Federation to suspend its sponsorship of its school-based facilitated change initiative out of concerns that it would be "unfair" to ask teachers to continue taking on "extra" work with so little support.

Studies of local teachers' organizations' reform attempts reveal how labor law recognizes only the authority of administrators and policy makers and how teachers' organizations participate or advise only under particular conditions. The reform innovations initiated by a number of National Education Association locals have been stalled or suspended altogether not only by new state standardized testing requirements but by changes in local district leadership. The recently established Colleges of Teachers in British Columbia and Ontario have further circumscribed the limited purview of the provincial teachers' federations. Such events suggest both the vulnerability of teachers' organizations to legislative amendment and the suspicion with which other members of the educational establishment continue to regard them.

### The need for reform

Despite their good intentions and good works, the positions of teachers' organizations and their reform efforts are as precarious as ever – from without as legislative bodies erode their authority, from within as they attempt to wrestle with the competing (and necessary) agendas of damage control and educational reform; and among the ranks of teachers, many do not directly benefit from the reform projects or, if they do, see them as "temporary aberrations" to unions' business as usual (Kerchner et al., 1996) and fail to recognize their practical utility in terms of their own work (Bascia, 1994a).

But despite these formidable challenges, teachers' organizations have an imperative to survive, to transform themselves, and to be active partners in educational reform. The recent report of the National Commission on Teaching and America's Future (1996) argues that teacher recruitment, preparation and development, and restructuring schools to "create the conditions in which teachers can teach, and teach well . . . [are] an entire tapestry that is tightly interwoven. Pulling on a single thread will create a tangle rather than tangible progress" (pp. vi-vii). Teachers' organizations have worked on all of these dimensions, and teachers require union presence, vigilance, and representation because no other entity in the educational system pays serious attention to the conditions of teaching. No organizations other than teachers' organizations have responsibility for representing teachers in discussions about educational practice. If teachers' organizations disappeared, they would have to be reinvented.

It is necessary that teachers' organizations find ways to articulate the relevance of the conditions of teaching to the quality of learning – the fundamental logical of the relationship between many of their "traditional" and "reform" strategies; that they develop a conceptual understanding, too, of the logical relationships among, and necessity for, many changes in educational policy and practice at many levels of the system at once – in the recruitment and preparation of teachers, the conditions of schooling that shape teaching, and in how and on what basis programmatic decisions are made in schools and school districts. It is necessary that teachers' organizations develop the capacity to work on many of these dimensions of the educational enterprise, to extend reform efforts by engaging in collaborative relationships with other organizations, but to weigh the risks and costs of such ventures honestly and carefully. It is necessary that while teachers' organizations attend to the "big" picture of systemic reform, they also attend to the "little" picture by providing services and programs that are meaningful and necessary to teachers in their local context (Bascia, 1994a), to creating avenues within their organizations for greater and more varied forms of teacher participation, representation, and innovation (Bascia, 1997a, 1997c). And finally, it is important that teachers' organizations seek changes in labor law that increase the purview of their authority over educational policy making and practice (see Kerchner et al., 1996). These recommendations, admittedly, require mammoth effort, coordination, intelligence, perseverance, and fortitude. The challenges facing teacher unions are immense. To survive, to enhance their own authority and to improve the quality of teaching and learning, require nothing less.

## REFERENCES

Bascia, N. (1991). *The trust agreement projects: Establishing local professional cultures for teachers.* Paper presented at the American Educational Research Association annual meeting, April 3–7, Chicago, Illinois.

Bascia, N. (1994a). *Unions in teachers' professional lives: Social, intellectual, and practical concerns.* New York: Teachers College Press.

Bascia, N. (1994b). *Evaluation Report: Creating a Culture of Change Initiative.* Report prepared for Ontario Ministry of Education and Training and the Ontario Teachers' Federation, June.

Bascia, N . (1996a). Caught in the crossfire: Restructuring, collaboration, and the "problem" school. *Urban Education* 31(2).

Bascia, N. (1996b). Teacher leadership: Contending with adversity. *Canadian Journal of Education*, 21(2), 155–169.

Bascia, N. (1996c). Inside and outside: The experiences of minority immigrant teachers in Canadian schools. *Qualitative Studies in Education*, 9(1).

Bascia, N. (1997a). Invisible leadership: Exploring the roles of teacher union representatives in schools. *Alberta Journal of Educational Research.*

Bascia, N. (1997b). *The politics of gender in teacher union dynamics.* Toronto, Ontario: Ontario Institute for Studies in Education at the University of Toronto.

Bascia, N. (1997c). Teacher unions and teacher professionalism: Rethinking a familiar dichotomy. In B. Biddle, T. Good, & I. Goodson (Eds.), *International handbook of teachers and teaching.* The Netherlands: Kluwer Academic Publishers.

Braun, R. J. (1972). *Teachers and power: The story of the American federation of teachers.* New York: Simon & Schuster.

Carlson, D. (1992). *Teachers and crisis: Urban school reform and teachers' work culture.* New York: Routledge.

Cochran-Smith, M., & Lytle, S. (1992). Communities for teacher research: Fringe or forefront? *American Journal of Education,* May.

Cole, A., & Watson, N. (1991). *Support for beginning teachers.* Toronto: Ontario Teacher Education Council.

Cooper, M. (1988). Whose culture is it anyway? In A. Lieberman (Ed.), *Building a professional culture in schools.* New York: Teachers College Press.

Darling-Hammond, L. (1995). Policy for restructuring. In A. Lieberman (Ed.), *The work of restructuring schools: Building from the ground up* (pp. 157–176). New York: Teachers College Press.

Darling-Hammond, L., Cobb, L. V., & Bullmaster, M. (1995). Rethinking teacher leadership through professional development schools. *Elementary School Journal,* spring.

Finley, M. (1984). Teachers and tracking in a comprehensive high school. *Sociology of Education,* **57,** 223–43.

Freedman, S. (1987). Who will care for our children? Removing nurturance from the teaching profession: Three teachers' views of the Carnegie Report. *Democratic Schools,* 3(1), 7–15,

Gallagher, J., Lanier, P., & Kerchner, C. (1993). Toledo and Poway: Practicing peer review. In C. T. Kerchner & J. E. Koppich (Eds.), *A union of professionals: Labor relations and educational reform* (pp. 158–176). New York: Teachers College Press.

Gitlin, A. (1996). Gender and professionalization: An institutional analysis of teacher education and unionism at the turn of the twentieth century. *Teachers College Record,* **97**(4), 588–624.

Glegg, A. R. L. (1992). Five years of teacher self-governance: The British Columbia College of Teachers. *Journal of Education Administration and Foundations,* 7(2), 46–61.

Goldsberry, L. (with A. Holt, K. Johnson, G. Macdonald, R. Poliquin, & L. Potter). (1995). The evolution of a restructuring school: The New Suncook case. In A. Lieberman (Ed.), *The work of restructuring schools: Building from the ground up,* pp. 136–156. New York: Teachers College Press.

Hargreaves, A. (1994a). *Changing teachers, changing times: Teachers' work and culture in the postmodern age.* London and New York: Cassell and Teachers College Press.

Hargreaves, A. (1994b). Development and desire: A postmodern perspective. In T. Guskey & M. Huberman (Eds.), *New paradigms and practices in professional development.* New York: Teachers College Press.

Harrington-Luecker, D. (1992). Firmer foundations – Good news: Many foundations are expanding their giving to include K-12 education. *American School Board Journal.* February, 29–31.

Johnson, S. M. (1987). Can schools be reformed at the bargaining table? *Teachers College Record,* **89**(2). 269–80.

Johnson, S. M. (1988, June). Pursuing professional reform in Cincinnati. *Phi Delta Kappan,* **69**(10), 746–751.

Kerchner, C. T. (1993). Pittsburgh: Reform in a well-managed public bureaucracy. In *A union of professionals: Labor relations and educational reform* (pp. 43–60). New York: Teachers College Press.

Kerchner, C., & Caufman, K. (1993). Building the airplane while it's rolling down the runway. In C. T. Kerchner & J. E. Koppich (Eds.), *A union of professionals: Labor relations and educational reform* (pp. 1–24). New York: Teachers College Press.

Kerchner, C. T., & Koppich, J. E. (1993). *A union of professionals: Labor relations and educational reform.* New York: Teachers College Press.

Kerchner, C. T., Koppich, J. E., & Weeres, J. (1996). *United mind workers: Representing teaching in a knowledge society.* San Francisco: Jossey-Bass.

Kerchner, C. T., & Mitchell, D. E. (1988). *The changing idea of a teachers' union.* London: Falmer.

Larson, M. S. (1977). *The rise of professionalism: A sociological analysis.* Berkeley: University of California Press.

Levin, B., & Young, J. (1994). *Understanding Canadian schools: An introduction to educational administration.* Toronto: Harcourt, Brace.

Lichtenstein, G., McLaughlin, M. W., & Knudsen, J. (1992). Teacher empowerment and professional knowledge. In A. Lieberman (Ed.), *The changing contexts of teaching* (pp. 37–58). Chicago: University of Chicago Press.

Lieberman, A. (1988, May). Teachers and principals: Turf, tensions, and new tasks. *Phi Delta Kappan,* **69**.

Lieberman, A. (Ed.) (1995). *The work of restructuring schools: Building from the ground up.* New York: Teachers College Press.

Lieberman, M. (1988). Professional ethics in public education: An autopsy. *Phi Delta Kappan*, **70**(2), 159–60.

Little, J. W. (1990a). The mentor phenomenon and the social organization of teaching. *Review of Research in Education*, **16**, 648–653.

Little, J. W. (1990b). The persistence of privacy: Autonomy and initiative in teachers' professional relations. *Teachers College Record*, **91**(4), 509–535.

Little, J. W. (1992). Opening the black box of teachers' professional communities. In Lieberman, A. (Ed.), *The changing contexts of teaching* (pp. 157–178). Chicago: University of Chicago Press.

Little, J. W. (1993). Teachers' professional development in a climate of educational reform. *Educational Evaluation and Policy Analysis*, **15**(2).

Malloy, C. (1987, January). The Carnegie Commission report: A dangerous utopia for teachers. *Radical Teacher*, 23–5.

McClure, R. (1991). Individual growth and institutional renewal. In A. Lieberman & L. Miller (Eds.), *Staff development for education in the '90s: New demands, new realities, new perspectives* (pp. 221–241). New York: Teachers College Press.

McClure, R. (1992). A teachers' union revisits its association roots. In Lieberman, A. (Ed.), *The changing contexts of teaching*. Chicago: University of Chicago Press.

McDonnell, L. M., & Pascal, A. (1988). *Teacher unions and educational reform*. Washington, D.C.: RAND Corporation.

McLaughlin, M. (1993). What matters most in teachers' workplace context? In J. Little & M. McLaughlin (Eds.), *Cultures and contexts of teaching*. New York: Teachers College Press.

Meade, E. J., Jr. (1991, October). Foundations and the public schools, an impressionistic retrospective, 1960–1990. *Phi Delta Kappan*, 1–12,.

Mitchell, D. E., & Kerchner, C. T. (1983). Labor relations and teacher policy. In L. Shulman & G. Sykes (Eds.), *Handbook on teaching and policy* (pp. 214–238). New York: Longman.

Muncey, D. E., & McQuillan, P. J. (1993, February). Preliminary findings from a five-year study of the Coalition of Essential Schools. *Phi Delta Kappan*.

Murphy, M. (1990). *Blackboard unions: The AFT & the NEA 1900–1980*. Ithaca, NY: Cornell University Press.

National Commission on Teaching and America's Future (1996). *What matters most: Teaching for America's future*. New York: Teachers College, Columbia University.

Ogawa, R. T. (1994). The institutional sources of educational reform: The case of school-based management. *American Educational Research Journal*, **31**(3), 519–548.

Panasonic Foundation, Inc. (1996). Panasonic foundation's framework for school system success. *Panasonic Partnership Program Newsletter*, **5**(1), (pp. 4–5). Secaucus, N.J.: Panasonic Foundation, Fall.

Phillips, L. (1993). Miami: After the hype. In C. T. Kerchner & J. E. Koppich (Eds.), *A union of professionals: Labor relations and educational reform* (pp. 116–135). New York: Teachers College Press.

Rauth, M. (1990, June). Exploring heresy in collective bargaining and school restructuring. *Phi Delta Kappan*, 781–790,.

Ray, D. (1991). Professional associations view current teaching. In R. Ghosh & D. Ray (Eds.), *Social change and education in Canada* (2nd edition). Toronto: Harcourt Brace Jovanovich.

Retsinas, J. (1982). Teachers: Bargaining for control. *American Educational Research Journal*, **19**(3), 353–96.

Robertson, H. J. (1992). Teacher development and gender equity. In A. Hargreaves & M. Fullan, *Understanding teacher development*. New York: Teachers College Press.

Russo, J. B. (1979). Changes in bargaining structures: The implications of the Serrano decision. *Education and Urban Society*, **11**(2), 208–18.

Smaller, H. (1991). A room of one's own: The early years of the Toronto Women Teachers' Association. In R. Heap & A. Prentice (Eds.), *Gender and education in Ontario: An historical reader*. Toronto: Canadian Scholars' Press.

Soder, R. (1986). *Professionalizing the profession*. (Occasional Paper No. 4). Seattle: University of Washington Center for Educational Renewal.

Talbert, J. E., & McLaughlin, M. W. (1994, February). Teacher professionalism in local school contexts. *American Journal of Education*, **102**, 123–153.

Timar, T. (1989). The politics of school restructuring. *Phi Delta Kappan*, **71**(4), 264–275.

Tyack, D. (1974). *The one best system: A history of American urban education*. Cambridge, Mass.: Harvard University Press.

Urban, W. J. (1982). *Why teachers organized*. Detroit: Wayne State University Press.

Wasley, P. A. (1991). *Teachers who lead: The rhetoric of reform and the realities of practice.* New York: Teachers College Press.

Zeichner, K. (1991). Contradictions and tensions in the professionalization of teaching and the democratization of schools. *Teachers College Record, 92*(3).

# Teacher Development and Educational Reform

MARILYN COCHRAN-SMITH
*Boston College*

*This chapter is based on the claim that we need a theory of teacher education for social change, one that is grounded in the relevant educational scholarship as well as grounded in the practice of school-based teachers. The components of the grounded theory include: knowledge and interpretation frameworks, ideology and political frameworks, K-12 pedagogy for social change, and teacher education as inquiry across the life span. Implications for policy, practice and research are identified.*

There is overwhelming evidence that we need change in the social and economic structure of American society. One percent of the population owns more than 30% of the wealth, the next nine percent owns another 36%, and income inequalities are widening not narrowing (Stevenson, 1996). The circumstances are particularly dire in cities where there are widespread poverty, curtailed social and economic services, the growth of a permanent underclass, severely diminished opportunities for employment and mobility, and staggering disparities between the circumstances of not only those with and without advantages but also of those with and without hope.

Nested within this brutal picture of American reality is the widely-documented fact that the educational system is failing large numbers of children who are not part of the racial, language, cultural, and economic mainstream – particularly poor children and children of color, who are located disproportionately in urban centers, border states, and areas with large segments of Native American peoples (Beckum, 1992; Darling-Hammond, 1995; Darling-Hammond, 1995; Delpit, 1988; DeVillar & Faltis, 1994; Heath, 1983; Kozol, 1991). The failure of the educational system is due in part to disparities in the allocation of resources to urban, suburban, and rural schools and schoolchildren (Kozol, 1991) – resources ranging from equipment, supplies, and physical facilities to books, access to computer technology, and class size. There are also major disparities across schools and school systems in teacher expertise and in students' opportunities to learn (Darling-Hammond, 1995; Dreeben, 1987; Oakes, 1990). Furthermore, despite mounting disconfirming evidence, deficit theories about non-mainstream values, practices, and beliefs persist as explanations for school failure (King, 1994), and school discourse patterns and expectations continue to be most congruent with White mainstream socialization practices (Cazden & Mehan, 1989).

In short, in the last moments of the twentieth century, the dilemma of American education is not the lack of universal access to schooling, but what DeVillar and Faltis (1994) refer to as the lack of access to "universal quality schooling" (p. 2),

*M. Fullan (ed.), Fundamental Change, 246-281.*
© 2005 *Springer. Printed in the Netherlands.*

or what Bastian and colleagues (1985) referred to more than a decade ago as the mainstream's deep resistance to institutional reforms that would guarantee the "inalienable right of all Americans [to] equality in education" (p. 5). I have proposed elsewhere that in order to alter an educational system that is deeply dysfunctional, we need teachers who regard teaching as a political activity and embrace social change as part of the job, teachers who enter and remain in the teaching force not expecting to carry on business as usual but prepared to join other educators, community activists, and parents in major social reforms as well as local enterprises (Cochran-Smith, 1991, 1995a, 1995b). This is not to suggest that teachers alone – collectively or individually – can transform the conditions that conspire to make the American educational and economic scenes so bleak. But it is to suggest, following Gramsci and others (cited in Cochran-Smith, 1991), that teachers are critical actors in those scenes and that, no matter how apparently powerless, they are accountable for the roles they play or fail to play in the larger struggle for social change. Teaching and teacher education for social change are not neutral nor conservative activities. To the contrary, they are explicitly political and radical in intention. The goal is to teach all teachers and students to contribute knowledgeably and ethically to an increasingly diverse society, to recognize and challenge inequities, to confront racism, and to work for a more democratic society.

In this chapter I submit that we need a theory of teacher education[1] for social change, one that is grounded in the relevant educational scholarship conducted primarily by university-based researchers as well as in the data of practice, particularly in the inquiries and experiences of school-based teachers who work as both educators and activists. A theory of this sort has the potential to guide but also challenge the ways teachers, teacher educators, policy makers, school administrators, and others make decisions about how best to prepare and enhance the work of prospective and experienced teachers.

This chapter is arranged in six major sections. In the first, I discuss the idea of a grounded theory of teacher education for social change and analyze its bases, purposes, and questions. In the next four sections, I identify the components of a grounded theory, arguing for a particular conception of each and linking each to the relevant conceptual and empirical literature: knowledge and interpretive frameworks, ideology and political frameworks, K-12 pedagogy for social change, and teacher education as inquiry across the lifespan. I conclude with a discussion of the implications of a grounded theory of teacher education for policy, practice, and research.

## TOWARD A GROUNDED THEORY

A theory of teacher education for social change is not intended only for those who prepare teachers for diverse student populations. Rather it is intended to provide a conceptual framework that has the potential to help all teachers prepare students to live productive and ethical lives in an increasingly diverse society, to work actively for equity and against racism, and to contribute to a more just society.

This is not a small task or a simple one. Although the problem is both theoretical and practical, it is decidedly not a problem of method, especially if we understand method in the narrow sense sometimes used in the teacher education field as something that can be divorced from content, theory, and perspective.

I have argued elsewhere that what we need in the teaching profession are not better generic strategies for "doing multicultural education" or "teaching for diversity" nor more lesson plans about basket making, piñatas, and other customs in non-Anglo cultures (Cochran-Smith, 1995a). By the same token, I am arguing here that what we need in teacher education are not particular classroom or field activities, readings, or exercises that teacher educators and staff developers can use to turn "culturally un-responsive," "monocultural," or "politically neutral" teachers into responsive, multicultural, and politically-committed ones. Rather, I submit that we need a theory of teacher education for social change that begins with the premise that teaching and teacher education are political and intellectual as well as practical activities that occur within complex historical, economic, and social contexts. Such a theory, grounded in the data of both research and practice, has the potential to guide, suggest critiques, and, most importantly, suggest ways of implementing, understanding, and researching teacher education for social change.

Arguably the most well-known proponents of what has come to be called "grounded theory" in qualitative research, Glaser and Strauss (1967) suggest that in sociology, theory that is most relevant to research and practice is theory that is grounded in data "systematically obtained and analyzed in social research" (p. 2). As Glaser and Strauss point out, the basic purpose of theory in sociology is to "fit" the situation being researched to explain a given behavior or set of behaviors. They summarize the various roles of theory in sociology as follows: allowing for predictions and explanations of behavior, advancing other social theories, providing practitioners with useful understandings and ways of predicting situations, suggesting a "stance" or perspective on the data being explored, and guiding ways of researching particular behaviors (p. 3). Unlike the process of generating theory through logical deduction based on a priori assumptions, Glaser and Strauss argue that the process of discovering or generating theory from the comparative analyses of bodies of evidence produces the most useful and understandable sociological theory – theory that is "suited to its supposed users" (p. 3), sociologists and lay persons alike.

To promote the idea of a grounded theory of teacher education for social change,[2] three basic considerations need to be addressed. First, what would this theory be "grounded" in? Second, what uses and purposes would it serve in teacher education? And third, in order to serve those purposes, what questions, issues, and aspects of teaching, learning, and schooling would it need to address?

*The "Grounds" for a Grounded Theory*

The theory I am working toward in this chapter is grounded in the relevant university-based research as well as in the data of teachers' and other insiders' experiences and inquiries. Relevant university-based research includes work in multicultural education, urban and minority education, culturally responsive curriculum and pedagogy, and related sociological, linguistic, and anthropological research on schools, classrooms, and community cultures. Selected research in teacher education, professional development, the school as workplace, and the cultures of teaching conducted by those located both within and outside of particular program or project contexts is also relevant. As much as possible, I build in this chapter on the thoughtful syntheses that already exist in these areas[3] to discuss and analyze the grounds for a grounded theory. A unique feature of this chapter, however, is that in addition to the standard academic literature, I also take as relevant and attempt to integrate the inquiries of school-based teachers and program-based teacher educators about K-12 classrooms as well as professional development contexts across the lifespan. I use the writing of practitioners, although some of it is unpublished and hence less generally accessible, in order to argue for the importance of what insiders[4] know about teaching for social change, particularly in urban areas, as well as what they know about the contexts in which professional development occurs and the conditions that support and constrain their efforts.

To establish both university-based and school-based research as grounds for a grounded theory, I draw heavily on the conclusions and findings of my recent synthesis of empirical and conceptual research related to the knowledge, skills, and experiences of effective teachers of diverse populations in urban areas (Cochran-Smith, 1997, in preparation). This synthesis includes university-based research as well as teachers' inquiries and analyses of teachers' inquiry groups. Since it is obviously impossible to locate and synthesize all of the writing by and/or about teachers and teachers' groups, I elected to concentrate on inquiries that grew out of four different contexts within which teachers and teacher educators have been doing some of the most visible work for social change – one school (Central Park East), one city (Philadelphia), one state-level project (The California Tomorrow Immigrant Students Project), and one national professional development network (The Urban Sites Network of the National Writing Project). Details about these projects and the individual pieces of published and unpublished practitioner inquiry that serve as grounds for the theory proposed here are available in the synthesis article (Cochran-Smith, 1997).

*The Purposes of a Grounded Theory*

Not unlike grounded theory in sociology, grounded theory in teacher education needs to "work" in particular practical situations and "fit" the contexts being explored. That is, it needs to be relevant and useful to practitioners, researchers, and policy makers who work for social change in the various contexts of teacher education across the professional lifespan, including preservice certification and degree programs in colleges and universities; inservice professional development projects, courses, degree programs, seminars, and workshops located in or sponsored by school districts, colleges and universities, school-university partnerships, regional and national networks, educational foundations, or professional associations; and various teacher-initiated inquiry, action, and community groups not affiliated with colleges and universities or with other professional associations or institutions.

To be useful in each of these contexts, grounded theory in teacher education needs to play a number of roles. These include but are not limited to:

- Providing guidelines for designing, implementing, and evaluating programs, projects, curricula, coursework, fieldwork, and community experiences across the lifespan
- Providing a stance for predicting and understanding program or project events, outcomes, dilemmas, and situations with individual student teachers, experienced teachers, and groups of teachers at particular moments in time and over time
- Generating research questions and agendas, interpretive frameworks, and analytic strategies for research in teacher education for social change as well as other topics of research and theory-formation
- Guiding recruitment and retention procedures and strategies
- Suggesting guidelines for credentialing and other procedures and policies.

It is important to note that what are intentionally absent from the above list are roles such as prescribing social, intellectual, and organizational arrangements for teacher education or designating particular policies and practices. In other words, none of the roles of a theory of teacher education is to stipulate precisely "how to do" preservice teacher preparation or inservice professional development for social change.

### The Questions Addressed by a Grounded Theory

Based on the lines of argument I have outlined so far, it follows that a theory of teacher education for social change must offer a way to conceptualize fundamental questions about the knowledge, interpretations, and political commitments that guide teachers' and teacher educators' actions, social relationships, and questions as well as the practices, experiences, and strategies that inform and influence those perspectives[5]. The theory I am proposing here does so by posing and considering the four fundamental questions that follow. Taken together, these are intended to function as an analytic framework or theory within which teacher educators, policy makers, and researchers may design, construct, critique, and participate in teacher education programs, projects, networks, and other contexts across the professional lifespan.

- *The "Knowledge" Question*: What knowledge and interpretive frameworks guide the work of new and experienced teachers who teach for social change?
- *The "Politics" Question*: What ideologies and political frameworks guide the work of new and experienced teachers who teach for social change?
- *The "Practice" Question*: What are the features of pedagogy and practice in K-12 schools and classrooms where teachers are committed to teaching for social change?
- *The "Training" Question*: What are the characteristics of preservice teacher education programs and/or inservice professional development programs that enhance teachers' efforts to teach for social change?

These four question areas are suggested by the four outer circles of Figure 1, "Teaching for Social Change: Toward a Grounded Theory of Teacher Education." Each of the circles is linked to one another by double-ended arrows to indicate that knowledge, politics, practice, and professional preparation are interconnected in teacher education. Particular teacher education programs or

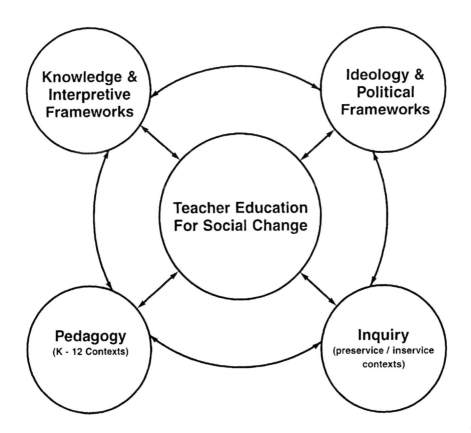

Figure 1

projects are influenced – either explicitly or implicitly – by the ways decision makers conceptualize these four questions, and thus in a certain sense, any given teacher education program or project may be thought of as an instantiation or reflection of particular answers to each of these questions.

It is important to note that even if the four questions are conceptualized and answered in similar ways, however, the details of particular teacher education programs and projects will differ from one another. This is the case because the questions of teacher education for social change are in constant interaction with the history, culture, and traditions of individuals, groups, and institutions as well as with the ways they and others have constructed knowledge, practice, and research paradigms at given moments in time and over time. As indicated inside the center circle in Figure 2, the particularities of local contexts include but are not limited to: variations in school, school-district, regional, and state initiatives in curriculum, instruction, and assessment; state and national certification, recertification, and professional development standards and requirements; local, regional, and national reform and restructuring movements and histories; institutional politics, commitments, traditions, and priorities; and available resources, facilities, and funding opportunities.

Some of the features that distinguish local contexts are listed in Figure 2. This list helps to clarify the distinction I wish to make in this chapter between a theory of teacher education, proposed here, and a "model" of teacher education, an idea often implied if not specified in the rhetoric of reform reports and national evaluations. A model advocates an explicit and pre-determined prescription for doing teacher education, one that is to a great extent to be superimposed onto any given context regardless of the circumstances and conditions. A model, for example, might stipulate that teacher preparation should be offered only at the post-undergraduate level or that all student teachers should work in professional development schools (National Commission Teaching and America's Future, 1996; Holmes, 1985, 1995). A theory, on the other hand, suggests a way to conceptualize the major questions underlying teacher education (in this case the major questions related to teacher education for social change) and thus offers guiding principles within which multiple ways of doing teacher education are possible and desirable.

## KNOWLEDGE AND INTERPRETIVE FRAMEWORKS

As I have conceptualized it in this chapter, a theory of teacher education for social change must conceptualize but also offer answers for four major questions. The first has to do with teachers' knowledge. In this section, I frame the "knowledge" question from a constructivist perspective and based on an epistemology that contests the formal-practical dualism (Lytle and Cochran-Smith, 1994). I then suggest that five aspects of knowledge and interpretation support teaching for social change. These are indicated by Figure 3.

Across the disciplines related to education, it is now widely understood that

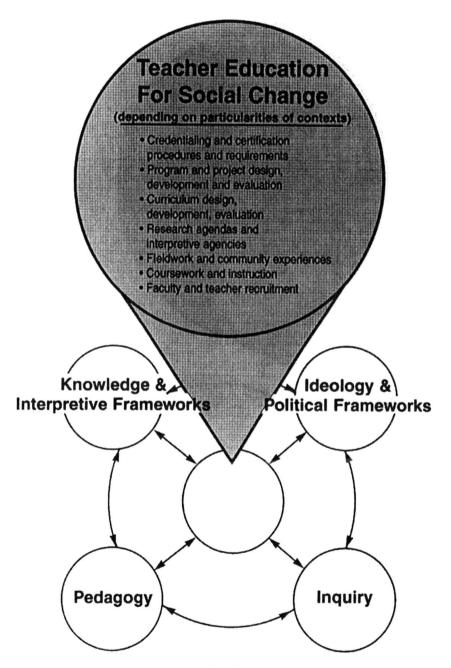

**Teacher Education
For Social Change**
(depending on particularities of contexts)

• Credentialing and certification
  procedures and requirements
• Program and project design,
  development and evaluation
• Curriculum design,
  development, evaluation
• Research agendas and
  interpretive agencies
• Fieldwork and community experiences
• Coursework and instruction
• Faculty and teacher recruitment

**Knowledge &
Interpretive Frameworks**

**Ideology &
Political Frameworks**

**Pedagogy**

**Inquiry**

Figure 2

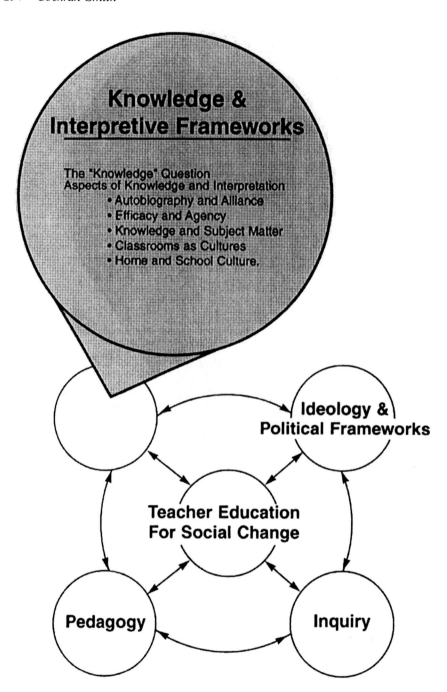

Figure 3

knowledge is socially and culturally as well as psychologically constructed. In his recent volume on the culture of education, Bruner (1996) summarizes this position by explaining what he refers to as "the constructivism tenet" of a psychocultural approach to education:

> The 'reality' that we impute to the 'worlds' we inhabit is a constructed one. . . . Reality construction is the product of meaning making shaped by traditions and by a culture's toolkit of ways of thought. In this sense, education must be conceived as aiding young humans in learning to use the tools of meaning making and reality construction, to better adapt to the world in which they find themselves and to help in the process of changing it as required. (pp. 19–20).

Applied to a theory of teacher education for social change, the constructivist view suggests that knowledge is fluid, shared, changing, situational, and open to critique (Cochran-Smith, 1991b; Giroux, 1984, 1985; Ladson-Billings, 1995; Lytle & Cochran-Smith, 1992; Padilla & Lindhold, 1995). This view of knowledge has enormous implications for the ways teacher education programs are designed and implemented.

*The "Knowledge" Question*

There is widespread agreement that teachers' beliefs, attitudes, values, knowledge frames, and images are not only connected to the ways they teach (Clark & Peterson, 1986; Richardson, 1996) but also deeply entrenched despite instructional reform efforts (Cuban, 1970; Hargreaves, 1994; Irvine, 1990; Ladson-Billings, 1995; Little & McLaughlin, 1993; Sleeter, 1992). In the following section, I pose the question, "What knowledge and interpretive frameworks guide the work of new and experienced teachers who teach for social change?" intentionally avoiding the simpler form sometimes asked in teacher education, "What do teachers know or need to know?" I use "knowledge and interpretive frameworks" to emphasize that teachers' work is indeed guided by knowledge, but also to point out that knowledge is an integral part of complex and evolving frameworks for reflection, interpretation, and action. This conceptualization of knowledge contrasts with a view of "objective knowledge," generated in one location and directly usable in another.

Although a constructivist view of knowledge is largely accepted in the teacher education field, it may not be clearly understood. For example, Cochran-Smith and Lytle (1995), point out that The Holmes Group (1986, 1990, 1995) calls for the relocation of educational research and development in "real" K-12 schools and classrooms, a stance that would seem to value teachers' knowledge. However, the group also advocates that education schools ought to "devote themselves to producing knowledge and putting it into the heads, hands, and hearts of educators" (Holmes Group, 1995, p. 27). "Constructions like these clearly connote a knowledge transmission model of professional development which does little to alter fundamental relationships of schools to universities" (Cochran-Smith and Lytle, 1995, p. 6). Donmoyer (1996) makes a different but related critique, suggesting that while the AACTE knowledge base books (Reynolds, 1989; Murray, 1996) largely reject the idea that there are teaching "formulae" and emphasize instead that teachers need to be flexible, the books (particularly Murray's introductory chapters) continue to regard knowledge as the primary source of professional expertise and reflect a fundamental faith in objective or "true" knowledge for teaching.

I am arguing here that one of the four major pieces of a grounded theory of teacher education for social change is "knowledge and interpretive frameworks" rather than simply "knowledge," "the knowledge base," or "what teachers need to know," all phrases commonly found in the recent rhetoric of teacher education reform. My insistence here is not simply semantic. "Knowledge and interpretive frameworks" emphasizes that teaching is an intellectual as well as a practical activity and hence that teacher education must address the ways teachers use various kinds of knowledge to make sense of what is going on in the local contexts of their own schools and classrooms and to make decisions about practice but also to build theories, develop perspectives, pose questions, and construct dilemmas.

## *Aspects of Knowledge and Interpretation*

There are five aspects of knowledge and interpretation that emerge from the academic literature related to teaching for social change and from accounts of teachers and teacher groups who have been committed to this work over the long haul. In the section that follows, I have space only to identify these five areas and refer readers to the literature that provides details and support for my arguments.

- *Autobiography and Alliance.* Teachers who work for social change understand their own life histories (Bullough, Knowles, & Crow, 1991; Clarke & Zellermayer, 1995; Grant, 1991; Grumet, 1991; Ladson-Billings, 1990; Witherell & Noddings, 1991), especially how their lives are structured by race, class, culture, ethnicity, language, and gender vis a vis those of the prevailing groups and the structures of power in school and society (Florio-Ruane, 1994; King & Ladson-Billings, 1990; Rosenberg, 1994). These teachers work to examine their assumptions about the motivations and behaviors of "other people's children" and about the pedagogies deemed most appropriate for learners (Delpit, 1988, 1995; Kozol, 1991). Most important is the teacher's image of self as connected to, or disengaged from, her students as individuals and as members of groups and larger communities (Ballenger, 1992; Brown, 1993; Dillon, 1989; Foster,1989, 1991; Hollins, 1982; Ladson-Billings,1994). Although there is some evidence that teachers from the same backgrounds as their students are more easily able to support their learning, it is less important what a teacher's actual racial, cultural, or ethnic identity is and more important how she constructs knowledge of "self," "other," and "otherness" (Foster, 1993; Ladson-Billings, 1994; Tatum, 1994; Waff, 1994).

• *Efficacy and Agency.* Teachers who work for social change function as decision makers in their classrooms and believe in and act on their own efficacy (Irvine, 1990; Ladson-Billings, 1994; Villegas, 1991). A sense of efficacy is interdependent with a teacher's image of knowledge, on the one hand, and her belief in the efficacy of her students, on the other. Teachers who work for social change know that all students are capable of learning at high intellectual levels – gathering information, understanding complex material, posing and solving problems, critiquing and questioning conflicting information, constructing alternative perspectives, and synthesizing, comparing, and analyzing evidence (Hilliard, 1989; King, 1994; Knapp, 1995; Meier, 1995; Moll, 1988; Zeichner, 1993). They do not "dumbdown" the curriculum (Haberman, 1991; Irvine, 1990; Zeichner, 1993), settling for poor quality work or no work at all from certain individuals or groups of students, nor do they act as if some students are simply not capable of learning very much.

• *Knowledge and Subject Matter.* To teach for social change, teachers continuously invent and reinvent both pedagogy and curriculum, co-constructing knowledge with students based on the cultural and linguistic resources students bring to school with them and on students' varying transactions with complex subject matter (Erickson, 1986; Lieberman & Miller, 1991). In this way, teachers work from a view of knowledge as neither static nor infallible (Ladson-Billings, 1994), but instead socially constituted in particular contexts and hence open to critique, challenge, and alteration (Giroux, 1984, 1985; Ladson-Billings, 1994; Lytle & Cochran-Smith, 1992; Padilla & Lindhold, 1995). McDiarmid (1991) rightly points out that most analyses of what teachers need to know about cultural diversity have paid little attention to subject matter. However, teaching for meaning with diverse populations requires deep knowledge of subject matter as well as a view of students as active participants in learning (Knapp, 1995; Kennedy, 1991; McDiarmid, 1991).

• *Classrooms as Cultures.* Teachers' conceptions of culture, their knowledge of cultures different from their own, and their images of schools and classrooms as social and cultural contexts influence the ways they construct and act upon "difference" in schooling (Erickson, 1986; Erickson & Mohatt, 1982; Heath, 1995; Hilliard, 1992; Mehan, Lintz, Okamoto, & Wills, 1995; Villegas, 1991). Foremost is the concept that culture is not captured in lists of "the characteristics" of "others" (Florio-Ruane, 1994; Zeichner, 1993), but rather encompasses expected norms, values, attitudes, and modes of knowing, behaving, interacting, and interpreting daily life (Cazden & Mehan, 1989; Heath, 1983; King, 1994; Mehan, Lintz, Okamoto, & Wills, 1995). A broad concept of culture allows teachers to realize that classrooms are not neutral sites for the transmission of information but are instead culturally and socially constructed contexts with deeply interactive, embedded, and political layers of meaning (Cazden & Mehan, 1989; Erickson, 1986; Hollins, King & Hayman, 1994; King, 1994).

• *Home and School Culture.* It is well documented that the discourse patterns and cultural norms and expectations of the school are most congruent with White mainstream patterns of language and socialization (Cazden & Mehan, 1989). This understanding is the basis of the widespread explanation for the gap in achievement between White middle class students and primarily poor students of color, referred to as "cultural incompatibility" or "cultural difference" between home and school (King, 1994; Villegas, 1991). However, incompatibility theories fail to emphasize the structural and institutional reasons for the school failure of students not from the mainstream (McCarthy, 1993; Villegas, 1991; Zeichner, 1993). It is critical that teachers not interpret cultural difference as deficit or deprivation and hence make wrong judgments about minority students' intellectual potential and language abilities (Hilliard, 1989; Irvine, 1990) and that they are caring rather than resentful of students who are not like them (Irvine & York, 1995).

## IDEOLOGY AND POLITICAL FRAMEWORKS

The second question that a theory of teacher education must offer to answer has to do with the politics or ideological commitments associated with teaching for social change. In this section, I pose the "politics" question from a critical perspective, suggesting that an apolitical view of teaching and teacher education is both untenable and not persuasive. I then suggest, as Figure 4 indicates, that two major understandings form an ideological or political framework that supports the enterprise of teaching for social change.

It is widely agreed that teachers cannot fix the problems of society and that teachers alone, whether through group or individual efforts, cannot alter the life chances of the children they teach (Anyon, 1994; Cochran-Smith, 1991; Cuban, 1987). Weiner (1989) makes this point with clarity when she argues that the "Herculean task" of teaching in urban schools, for example, is the result of complex school bureaucracies, the isolation of schools from the families and communities they are supposed to serve, and the large numbers of students in urban classrooms whose families have neither the resources nor the will to affirm and support school values. Weiner points out that teachers can only deal with the students and situations they find in their classrooms; they cannot "substitute for social movements" (p. 153). McCarthy (1993) makes a different but related point in his criticism of multicultural education claiming that by ignoring "the crucial issues of structural inequality and differential power relations" (p. 243), advocates of multicultural education place enormous and unrealistic responsibility on the shoulders of classroom teachers.[6]

### The "Politics" Question

It is correct of course that teachers cannot substitute for social movements just as it is correct that "teaching better" (whether more "multiculturally" or more some other way) without addressing issues of structural and institutional racism and inequity will not lead to social change. But in another sense the criticisms above do not adequately acknowledge the fact that teaching is always a political activity

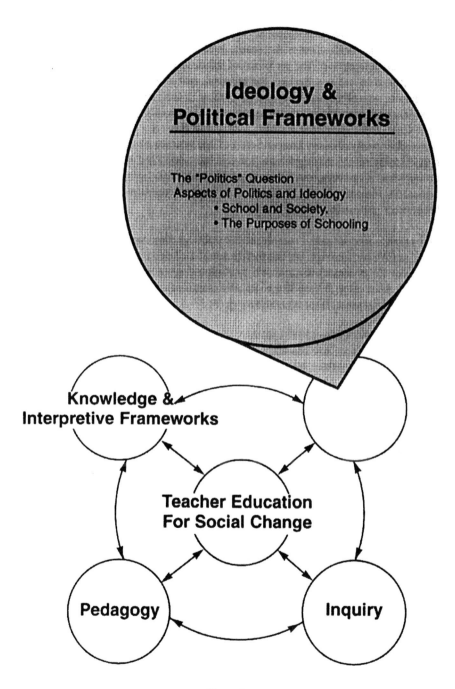

Figure 4

and that it is impossible for teachers to teach in ways that are *not* political and *not* value-laden (Aronowitz & Giroux, 1985; Cochran-Smith, 1991; hooks, 1994; Ladson-Billings, 1995; Sleeter & Grant, 1987; Zeichner, 1986). For this reason, how teachers conceive of the purposes of schooling for mainstream students and for students who are not part of the cultural, racial, language, and/or economic mainstream, as well as how they see their roles in that enterprise are critical.

Like teaching, teacher education is also a political activity (Ginsberg, 1988; Ginsberg & Clift, 1990; Zeichner & Gore, 1990), and there is a conception (or multiple and possibly contradictory conceptions) of the politics of schooling embedded in any particular set of arrangements for teacher education whether intentional or unintentional. Ginsberg and Lindsay (1995) make this point persuasively in their provocative volume on the politics of teacher education in "developed" and "developing" countries around the world:

> This means that we need to examine the political dimension of teacher educa-
> tors' action (or inaction) at the institutional and program levels as well as to
> consider the processes through which students in teacher education programs
> acquire or develop their political identities and orientations which may influ-
> ence their future actions as teachers (p. 8).

As Zeichner and Gore (1990) point out, the socialization of prospective and experienced teachers into the teaching profession is a process that is complex and contradictory, individual but also situated in broader social, institutional, and historical contexts.

In trying to construct a theory of teacher education for social change, then, I include attention to the politics of schooling, a topic that is usually omitted from discussions of how teacher education should be reinvented to meet the needs of society, particularly corporate society. I use the phrase "ideology and political frameworks" to emphasize that the work of teachers and teacher educators is guided by ideological commitments as well as knowledge and is in this sense fundamentally and inevitably political. This is not to suggest that we politicize teaching but rather, following Ginsberg and Lindsay (1995) as well as Bruner's (1996) recent argument about education in general, that we recognize "that it is already politicized and that its political side needs finally to be taken into account more explicitly, not simply as though it were 'public protest'" (p. 29).

Part of teaching for social change is deliberately and publicly claiming the role of activist as well as educator based on political consciousness and ideological commitment to diminishing the inequities of American life. The major idea that animates teaching for social change is that teachers and teacher educators need political lenses or analytic frameworks through which they can see injustices in school and society and then struggle with others in larger arenas to try to do something about them. Teachers and teacher educators who teach for social change, then, do not substitute for social movements but work as part of them (Cochran-Smith, 1995a, 1995b; Foster, 1993; Grant, Sleeter & Anderson, 1986; Hooks, 1994; Ladson-Billings, 1995; Zeichner, 1993).

*Aspects of Politics and Ideology*

Two aspects of politics and ideology are most apparent in the academic literature and in the inquiries of teachers and other practitioners who work for social change.

- *School and Society.* Teaching for social change is supported by several critical perspectives on the social, historical, and political contexts of schooling and the location of the work of teaching within these larger contexts (Giroux, 1984; Irvine, 1990; Sleeter & Grant, 1987; Sleeter & McLaren, 1995; Zeichner, 1993). Most salient are teachers' understandings of: the school not as neutral ground but as a site for contestation and as a place where power struggles are played out (Delpit, 1988, 1995; McCarthy, 1993; Villegas, 1991); the dynamics of power, privilege, and economic oppression in the school and home lives of majority and minority Americans (Delpit, 1988; hooks, 1994; McCarthy, 1993; McIntosh, 1989; Zeichner, 1993); the history of racism in America and the ways "race" has been constructed in society (Hilliard, 1989; Kailin, 1994; Ladson-Billings, 1994; Zeichner, 1993); and especially, the structural inequities that are embedded in the social, organizational, and financial arrangements of schools and schooling and the ways these perpetuate dominance for dominant groups and oppression for oppressed groups (Aronowitz & Giroux, 1985; Asante, 1991; Darling-Hammond, 1995; Kozol, 1991; McDermott, 1974; Villegas, 1991).

- *The Purposes of Schooling.* Underlying the notion of teaching for social change is what some would consider a radical view of the purposes of schooling-that is, preparing all students to live in and contribute to a diverse society but also preparing them to recognize and work to alter the economic and social inequities of that society. King (1994) argues that teaching for social change needs to include "liberating educational purposes that are in the interest of African American survival and in the interest of a more democratic, just, and culturally diverse society" (p. 26). She calls for "culture centered perspectives" on pedagogy and curriculum that honor the integrity and value of indigenous cultures and foreground social critique as well as academic skill. Ladson-Billings (1994) also emphasizes academics along with critique; she frames her discussion of culturally relevant pedagogy for African American students by contrasting it with a more common pedagogy she terms "assimilationist" because it promotes accommodation of minority children into White culture (1995). Ladson-Billings asserts forcefully that education is a negative force when it leads to academic skills but also alienates students from their own cultures, invalidates their identities as African Americans, and tells them that success means leaving their own communities. She calls instead for education that empowers all students by enabling them to critique the current arrangements of school and society and develop the skill and will to make their communities what they want them to be. Bell Hooks (1994) makes a similar point when she calls for teaching that is emancipatory or "transgressive."

## PEDAGOGY FOR SOCIAL CHANGE IN K-12 CONTEXTS

In addition to addressing questions of knowledge and politics, a theory of teacher education for social change must pose and offer answers for questions about practice and pedagogy in K-12 classrooms. In this section, I pose the "practice" question, arguing that practice is practical but also interpretive, political, and theoretical. As Figure 5 indicates, I identify six major aspects of K-12 pedagogy that characterize the work of teachers who teach for social change.

Teachers' knowledge and politics guide and are guided by the practices they develop to meet the current and future intellectual, social, and emotional needs of the diverse learners they encounter in particular schools and classrooms. Because teachers' practices are not discrete from, but profoundly interdependent with, their beliefs and interpretations, these practices cannot be understood as "models" of effective teaching or, as they are sometimes referred to in the reform literature, "best practices." Given all we know about the diversity of teachers' and students' cultures, experiences, and ways of knowing and all that we know about the diversity of classrooms themselves as cultures, it is extremely unlikely that there will ever be specific effective practices that are transportable – full-blown and whole – from one classroom and school site to another.

### The "Practice" Question

It should be emphasized, then, that this chapter is in no way intended to suggest that there are specific practices typical of teachers working for social change (particularly in urban settings) that are generalizable from one context to another. By the same token, I wish to make it clear that the structure of this chapter does not follow from, and is in no way intended to bolster, formal/practical (Fenstermacher, 1994) or theory/practice distinctions in teacher knowledge and/or the activity of teaching. Rather, the intent of this section is to contribute to the argument that teachers' work for social change is fundamentally interpretive, political, and theoretical as well as strategic, practical, and local. Lytle & Cochran-Smith (1994) make a similar point about teacher research, or the systematic and intentional inquiries that teachers do about their own schools and classrooms:

> Teacher research is not about how, when, and where to do things. Rather it is about how students and their teachers construct the curriculum. . . how teachers' actions are infused with complex and multi-layered understandings . . . [and] how teachers develop and alter their questions and interpretive frameworks (p. 4).

To pose the practice question, then, I intentionally use the phrase, "K-12 pedagogy," and avoid phrases like "best practice," "essential teaching skills," or "what teachers need to be able to do," in order to link pedagogy with knowledge and interpretive frameworks, on the one hand, and politics and ideologies, on the other. In doing so, I am arguing that teaching for social change is not so much a

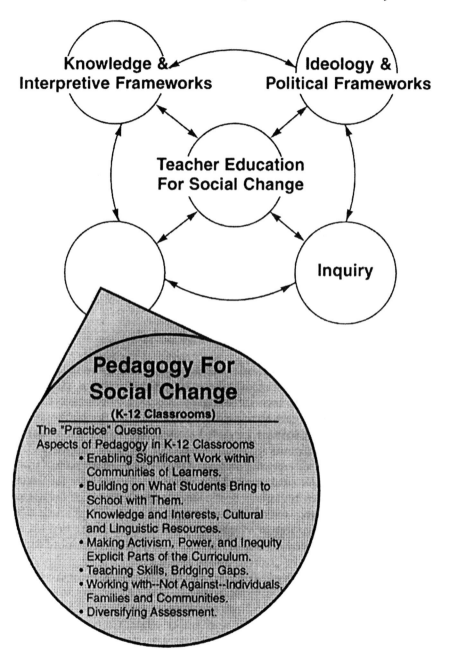

Figure 5

matter of method or practice, but is, to use Lather's words (1986) a matter of praxis, or, "the interactive, reciprocal shaping of theory and practice" ( p. 258) in teaching [7] that is openly committed to a more just social order (Freire, 1970; Nieto, 1996).

Ladson-Billings (1990, 1992, 1994, 1995) provides some of the most coherent ideas about pedagogy as praxis in K-12 contexts, particularly for the successful teaching of African American students.[8] She offers "a grounded theory of culturally relevant pedagogy" that focuses on teachers' beliefs and ideologies, particularly their conceptions of self and others, their conceptions of knowledge, and their social relations with students, families, and communities (1994, 1995). Other conceptions of teaching for social change describe pedagogies that are appropriate for any group. Particularly useful are conceptions such as, "critical pedagogy" (Aronowitz & Giroux, 1985; Shor, 1980), "anti-racist pedagogy" (Sleeter, 1992; Tatum, 1992), and pedagogy that is "multicultural and socially reconstructionist" (Sleeter & Grant, 1987; Sleeter & McLaren, 1995). As Gay (1995) suggests, many of the concerns and goals of multicultural education are analogous with those of critical pedagogy. Along with Sleeter & McLaren (1995), Gay calls for linking these two liberatory movements, a marriage that has great potential.

## *Aspects of Pedagogy for Social Change in K-12 Classrooms*

Although not synonymous, frameworks such as Ladson-Billings' culturally relevant pedagogy and Sleeter and colleagues' conceptions of multicultural education are alike in that they attempt to theorize pedagogy as praxis, or pedagogy for social change. In what follows, I have attempted to pull out and synthesize the common features of this pedagogy that are grounded in university-based scholarship and in the inquiries and accounts of practitioners. In the brief discussions that accompany each of the six aspects I mention below, I have simply named the key features of this work and cited some of the literature that provides the grounds for my claims. The space limitations of the current chapter prohibit inclusion of the details of this pedagogy and/or the empirical evidence that supports it. These are located in the many examples of university-based and school-based research that I cite below. (Interested readers are also directed to the much more detailed synthesis of this literature in Cochran-Smith, 1997).

• *Enabling Significant Work.* Teachers who teach for social change engage all students in significant academic work as members of communities of learners. This is closely linked with teachers' high expectations for students and with their sense of efficacy. Enabling significant work means emphasizing rigorous subject matter understanding as well as critique and consideration of alternative perspectives (Cohen, McLaughlin, & Talbert, 1993; Darling-Hammond, 1995; Haberman, 1991; Hilliard, 1992; Kennedy, 1991; Knapp, 1995; Meier, 1995). This kind of pedagogy depends on interactive, rather than didactic, teaching styles (Irvine, 1992); strong and personal relationships (Irvine, 1990; Ladson-Billings, 1994); joint responsibility rather than individual competition (Mehan, Lintz, Okamoto & Wills,

1995; Villegas, 1991); and collaboration (Johnson & Johnson, 1994; Slavin, 1985) rather than homogeneous groups or tracks (Anyon, 1994; Cummins, 1994; Haberman, 1991; Oakes, 1984; Zeichner, 1993).

• *Building on What Students Bring to School with Them.* Teachers working for social change build on the cultural and linguistic resources as well as the interests and knowledge of all students (Delpit, 1995; Gay, 1995; Ladson-Billings, 1994; Mehan et al., 1995; Villegas, 1991; Zeichner, 1993). Sometimes this means altering social participation structures and/or narrative and questioning styles (Au & Jordan, 1981; Cazden & Mehan, 1989; Erickson & Mohatt, 1982; Irvine, 1990). It also means using more multicultural and inclusive texts (Brown, 1993; Cohen, 1994; Olsen & Mullen, 1990; Waff, 1994) and widening the range of school topics (Fine, 1994; Powell, 1994). These strategies increase all students' opportunities to achieve higher order thinking skills and rigorous academic content (Foster, 1994; Hollins, 1982; Irvine, 1990; Moll & Diaz, 1987) at the same time as they decrease teachers' misinterpretations of students' interactions and abilities (Hilliard, 1992).

• *Making Activism, Power, and Inequity Explicit Parts of the Curriculum.* Pedagogy for social change involves making issues of power and language, equity and inequity, access and learning opportunity, and race and racism explicit parts of the curriculum – part of what is "discussible" in schools and classrooms and part of what is modeled or demonstrated in teachers' work lives (Aronowitz & Giroux, 1985; Cochran-Smith, 1991; Ladson-Billings, 1994; Shor, 1980; Sleeter, 1992; Sleeter & McLaren, 1995; Tatum, 1992). Public discussions like these help students think critically about the information to which they are exposed, take on activist roles at local, national, and global levels, and confront individual instances of prejudice as well as structural and institutional inequities (Feldgus, 1993; Cochran-Smith, 1995a; Ladson-Billings, 1994; Olsen & Mullen, 1990). They allow teachers and students to work together as activists, often with the teacher modeling activism in the community, school, or more globally (Cone, 1990; Cohen, 1994; Fecho, 1993, 1994, 1996; Sheets, 1995; ).

• *Teaching Skills, Bridging Gaps.* When teachers teach for social change, they scaffold students' learning by helping them connect what they know to what they don't know and helping them use present skills to learn new ones (Delpit, 1986, 1995; Irvine, 1990). Specifically, this means helping students who may not come to school with tacit knowledge of the mainstream language and interactional skills – what Delpit (1988) calls the codes of power – needed to negotiate the system. There is some controversy here, particularly with regard to questions about whether explicitly teaching skills is too assimilationist and alienating (King, 1995). But particularly in descriptions that stay very close to observation and practice, it is clear that teachers who work for social change can teach language and discourse skills at the same time that they teach students how to critique the codes of power (Cone, 1990; Cohen, 1995; Fecho, 1996; King, 1995; Ladson-Billings, 1995).

• *Working with – Not Against – Individuals, Families and Communities.* When teachers work for social change, they draw on family histories, resources, and stories, demonstrating respect for all students' family and cultural values (Banford, 1996; Bernal et al., 1994; Miller, 1996; Resnick, 1996; Teachers Learning Cooperative, 1984). They also consciously avoid functioning as a wedge between students and their families (Meier, 1995; Snyder, Lieberman, Macdonald & Goodwin, 1992) or giving students the idea that to succeed is to escape from, ignore, or rise above their own communities rather than learning ways to critique the system and work to make communities what they want them to be (Fecho, 1995; Ladson-Billings, 1995; King, 1995).

• *Diversifying Assessment.* There is significant research that indicates that standardized testing practice perpetuate inequities in the educational opportunities of various groups (Beckum, 1992; Darling-Hammond, 1995). Teaching for social change involves what Beckum (1992) calls "diversifying assessment" by using a wider variety of evaluation strategies and not relying simply on standardized tests as the sole criterion of students' abilities and achievement (Carini, 1986; Letgers & McDill, 1992; Meier, 1995; Philadelphia Teachers Learning Cooperative, 1984). Over time assessment and instruction blend into one another.

## TEACHER EDUCATION AS INQUIRY

I have argued so far in this chapter that a theory of teacher education for social change must address questions of knowledge, politics, and pedagogy. The fourth question required of such a theory has to do with teacher education itself and with the nature of the learning opportunities new and experienced teachers need to prompt and/or enhance their work for social change. In this section, I pose the "training" question, arguing that dominant models of staff development are inadequate to the enterprise of social change and suggesting instead that teachers need to work with others in inquiry communities. As Figure 6 indicates, I identify nine key elements of teacher education as inquiry.

### The "Training" Question

To work as both educators and activists, most new and experienced teachers need professional experiences powerful enough to interrupt long-held and sometimes unexamined assumptions about the purposes of schooling, the values and experiences of people unlike themselves, and the implications of subtle as well as overt curricular, instructional, and community practices. In the following section, I pose the question, "What are the characteristics of teacher education that enhances teachers' efforts to teach for social change?" In framing the question this way, I carefully avoid the word, "training," and all other phrases that connote that teachers' knowledge is primarily practical, teachers' work primarily technical, and teacher education primarily the demonstration and reinforcement of specific classroom skills.

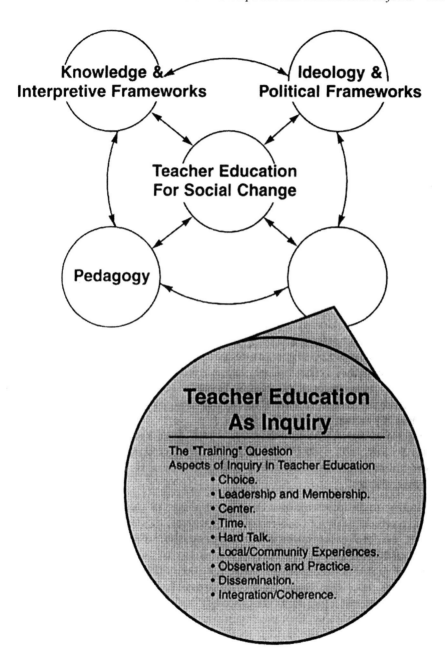

Figure 6

Training models of preservice education and staff development hinge on the assumption that there is a codified body of knowledge that can be transmitted to teachers in the form of skills development and training/retraining (Cochran-Smith & Lytle, 1992; Hargreaves & Fullan, 1992; Lytle & Fecho, 1991). There is mounting recognition, however, that training models are inadequate to the major tasks of teaching for social change and school reform (Little, 1993; Lytle et. al, 1994; Lytle & Fecho, 1991; McLaughlin, 1994). As McLaughlin (1993) points out, we now know that "decontextualized, disembodied, and discrete professional development activities are of only limited use to teachers," and indeed research on multicultural teacher education indicates that most interventions have been weak (Grant & Tate, 1995; Sleeter, 1992).

Further, teaching and learning are increasingly understood as co-constructed practice rather than transmitting and receiving information (McLaughlin, 1994), and teachers' workplaces are understood as constructed cultures rather than simply locations for classroom teaching (Lieberman & Miller, 1994). Teacher education for social change, then, is about "culture-building" not skills training (Lieberman & Miller, 1994).

Explorations of teachers' work and workplaces (Hargreaves & Fullan, 1992; Lieberman & Miller, 1994; Little, 1993; Little & McLaughlin, 1993; McLaughlin, 1993) suggest that the most promising teacher education practices are those that provide opportunities for teachers to identify, reconsider, bolster, or alter classroom beliefs and practices that support or undermine their students' learning opportunities and life chances. This will not happen through skills training, but instead through "close scrutiny of established practice" (Little, 1993, p. 131) by groups and individuals in local situations where they "grapple with what broad principles look like in practice" (p. 133).

With my colleague Susan Lytle, I have written extensively in this area (Cochran-Smith & Lytle, 1990, 1991, 1992, 1993, 1995; Lytle & Cochran-Smith, 1990, 1992, 1994), linking inquiry-based teacher education across the lifespan with teaching for social change:[9]

> Inquiry ought to be regarded as an integral part of the activity of teaching and a critical basis for decisions about practice. . . This argument is based in part on the assumption that the increasing diversity of America's schoolchildren and the increasing complexity of the tasks educators face render global solutions to problems and monolithic strategies for effective teaching impossible. Hence what is required in both preservice and inservice teacher education programs are processes that prompt teachers and teacher educators to construct their own questions and then begin to develop courses of action that are valid in their local contexts and communities (Cochran-Smith and Lytle, 1993, pp. 63–64).

In the following section, I draw on overviews of professional development (Hargreaves & Fullan, 1992; Lieberman & Miller, 1994; Little, 1993; Little & McLaughlin, 1993; McLaughlin, 1993) and multicultural teacher education (Grant & Secada, 1990; Ladson-Billings, 1995; Zeichner, 1993) as well as on the writing of teachers and teacher educators about their own work (e.g., Buchanan et al., 1994; Cochran-Smith, 1991, 1995 a, b, c; Cochran-Smith & Lytle, 1993; Lytle et al., 1994; Meier, 1994; Larkin & Sleeter, 1995; Sleeter, 1995a, b).

*Aspects of Inquiry in Teacher Education*

As in the prior section on pedagogy in K-12 classrooms, the following section is limited to identifying the characteristics of powerful teacher education for social change that emerge from a synthesis of the university literature and the inquiries of teachers. Due to space limitations, I do not attempt in this chapter to provide the full evidentiary warrant or to offer examples. Interested readers should consult the many citations provided and/or review the detailed synthesis located in Cochran-Smith (1997). Although these apply somewhat differently at the preservice and inservice levels, I suggest several aspects or guidelines[10] for teacher education that cut across the professional lifespan.

• *Choice.* The most powerful teacher education experiences for social change are voluntary. They are based on prospective and experienced teachers' choices to participate and, particularly at the inservice level, to exercise to a considerable extent their autonomy and/or significant voice in constructing the issues that are important. This includes participation and choice in project governance and program structures – planning, timing, topics, strategies, speakers, evaluation procedures, and dissemination activities ((Buchanan et al., 1994; Cochran-Smith & Lytle, 1993; Lytle & Fecho, 1991; Lytle et al., 1994; Philadelphia Teachers Learning Cooperative, 1984). At the preservice level, this means recruiting prospective teachers who are already committed to social change and to school reform (Zeichner, 1993).

• *Leadership and Membership.* Powerful teacher education experiences for social change are facilitated by leaders who participate as fellow learners and researchers rather than simply as experts (Cochran-Smith, 1991b; Lytle & Fecho, 1991; McDiarmid, 1990). Alternative structures such as cross-visitations, school-site inquiry groups, self-study projects, and teachers' collaboratives are utilized (Buchanan et al., 1994; Cochran-Smith & Lytle, 1993; Lytle & Fecho, 1991; Philadelphia Teachers Learning Cooperative, 1984; Zeichner, 1993). This kind of teacher education requires diversity among members with deliberate efforts to recruit faculty and teachers of color into membership and leadership roles (Lytle et al., 1994; Muncey, Uhl, & Nyce, 1994; Chinn & Wang, 1992; Dilworth, 1992; Gollnick, 1992; Grant & Secada, 1990; Irvine, 1992; Zimpher & Ashburn, 1992).

• *Center.* Often programs and projects that are supposed to promote cultural diversity, anti-racist teaching, or social change revolve around a "white" center, or, a goal – often unexamined – of helping White teachers and student teachers learn to teach students who are not like them (Cochran-Smith, 1995a). This implies – although almost never explicitly states – that all teachers of color are like each other, like their students of color, and already able to teach all students effectively, assumptions that are, in and of themselves, racist. Teacher education for social change is designed to help all student teachers, experienced teachers, and teacher educators interrogate their experiences and construct practices that are effective in an increasingly multiracial and multicultural society (Nieto, 1996).

• *Time.* Teacher education for social change is an ongoing process that occurs over relatively long periods of time, at least over a school year and often on an ongoing basis wherein groups are stable although membership changes from time to time (Buchanan et al., 1994; Cochran-Smith & Lytle, 1992; Meier, 1995; Muncey, Uhl & Nyce, 1994; Lytle et al., 1994; Philadelphia Teachers Learning Cooperative, 1984; Snyder et al., 1992). Concepts such as staff development "half-days" or twice yearly "auditorium events" are meaningless as are single experiences such as "the multicultural workshop" or "the diversity course" not integrated with ongoing programmatic themes. (This is elaborated below in the section on "integration and coherence.")

• *Hard Talk.* Teacher education for social change includes serious considera- tion of diversity, race and racism, and schooling from multiple, critical, personal, and professional perspectives. Urban Sites Network teachers (Muncey, Uhl & Nyce, 1994) use the expression "hard talk" as a shorthand for this kind of talk among teachers. I borrow their phrase here as a metaphor for serious, thoughtful, sometimes painful, and even graphic (Sleeter, 1995a, b) talk, writing, and reading about diversity, equity and access, privilege and oppression, and the roles of teach- ers and schools in all of these. The point of hard talk is not to come to consensus or closure but to allow the perspectives of other teachers, readers, and writers to challenge assumptions and underscore the need for change (Cochran-Smith, 1995b). It is especially critical that teacher educators engage in hard talk so they can help new and experienced teachers do the same (Agre et al., 1996; Albert et al., 1997; Grant & Secada, 1990; Nieto, 1996; Zimpher & Ashburn, 1992).

• *Local/Community Experiences.* Teacher education for social change is played out differently depending on school cultures, local or state school reform efforts, and the resources and opportunities available. There are no "models" for effective teacher education that cut across all contexts. At the inservice level, this means that local conditions coupled with larger commitments and subject matter under- standings are interdependent with any particular professional development project (Buchanan et al., 1994; Fine, 1994; Lytle et al., 1994). At the preservice level, this means that students are placed in schools with diverse populations where experienced teachers are working "against the grain" (Cochran-Smith, 1991a) and also have experiences in local community groups and cultural events (Dilworth, 1992; Milk, 1994; Sleeter, 1995a; Tellez et al., 1995; Zeichner, 1993).

• *Observation and Practice.* Powerful teacher education for social change involves rich observations of classroom life, pays careful attention to students' understandings, and considers ways to accommodate individual learners and groups of learners. School and classroom life are documented to explore students' understandings, reconsider assumptions underlying school practices, describe themes and patterns in children's work, and reflect on terms common to educational policy and procedure (Carini, 1986; Himley & Carini, 1991; Kanevsky, 1993;

Philadelphia Teachers Learning Cooperative, 1984). New and experienced teachers work along with teacher educators to consider specific recommendations for practice – altering classroom routines, establishing new patterns of interaction, augmenting classroom texts and materials (Banford, 1996; Fecho, 1996), and altering instruction and curriculum to build on students' interests (Cziko, 1996) and connect with family history and culture (Chin, 1996; Miller, 1996; Resnick, 1996).

- *Dissemination.* Teacher education for social change includes dissemination of teachers' knowledge through systematic and intentional inquiries in many different contexts. Inquiry is not simply an avenue for professional development but is also a way to generate a grounded theory of teaching for social change based on teachers' knowledge in practice and on teachers' research about their own efforts (Cochran-Smith & Lytle, 1993). At the inservice level, this making visible teachers' struggles to teach for social change (Olsen & Mullen, 1990) and to disseminate teachers' research at national, state, and local conferences and publications (Brown, Fecho, Buchanan, Kanevsky, Sims, Joe, Harris, Jumpp, Strieb, Feldgus, Pincus, and Farmbry in Cochran-Smith & Lytle, 1993; Buchanan et al., 1994; Lytle et al., 1994; Lytle & Fecho, 1991; Muncey, Uhl & Nyce, 1994; Vanderslice, Farmer, Fecho, and Waff in Fine, 1994). At the preservice level, this means including this work as part of prospective teachers' coursework reading and writing (Cochran-Smith & Lytle, 1995).

- *Integration/Coherence.* Emphasis on social change is not a supplement to teacher education, but is instead, as Larkin (1995) and others (Irvine, 1992; Ladson-Billings, 1995; Zeichner, 1993) have suggested of multicultural education, "an alternative way of conducting teacher education" (Larkin, 1995, p. 2). This means that teacher educators themselves must develop shared understandings of teaching and learning (Zimpher & Ashburn, 1992), the purposes of schooling (King, 1994), and the meanings of concepts and issues such as equity, diversity, multicultural education (Larkin, 1995; Sleeter & Grant, 1988), social change and social justice (Albert et al., 1997), and disability.[11] It also means that these issues cannot be relegated to one segment of a project or program (Larkin, 1995; Larkin & Sleeter, 1995; Nieto, 1996). To develop such shared understandings, teacher educators will have to engage in "hard talk," as suggested above and then significant fieldwork and coursework revision (Larkin & Sleeter, 1995; Rios & Gonzales, 1995) so that social change can become an integral part of a coherent curriculum (Albert et al., 1997).

CONCLUSION: TEACHER EDUCATION FOR SOCIAL CHANGE

This chapter begins with the premise that teaching and teacher education are political enterprises and are, in that sense, value-laden and socially-constructed. Over time they both influence and are influenced by the histories, economies, and cultures of the societies in which they exist, particularly by prevailing views of the purposes of schools and schooling. Throughout the chapter, I have taken the position that as researchers, practitioners, and policy-makers, we ought to acknowledge the inevitable political dimensions of our work in teaching and teacher education. But I have taken this line of reasoning well beyond a call for simple recognition. I have proposed that we ought to operate from the radical perspective that among the most important goals of teaching and teacher education are social change and social justice. It follows, then, that within our own spheres of influence in teacher education – whether those spheres are local, regional, or national – we ought to enact policies, invent teacher preparation programs, establish professional development contexts, construct research agendas, and write papers and position statements that challenge inequities, confront racism and other forms of oppression, and prepare all teachers and students to contribute knowledgeably and ethically to a diverse and democratic society.

A second premise of this chapter is that teacher education is fundamentally a theoretical as well as a practical activity that is (or can be) guided by a theoretical framework. I have submitted that four major questions are central to such a framework: What knowledge and interpretations guide the work of teachers who teach for social change? What values and political commitments animate their work? What practices and strategies do they develop, use, and alter in their schools and classrooms? What teacher education experiences help them develop, reflect on, and act on all of these over time?

In this chapter, I have suggested that particular ways of posing and answering these questions are implicit in the social, organizational, and intellectual contexts of any preservice or inservice teacher education program or project even though the questions themselves may never be addressed explicitly. In this sense, as I have pointed out in previous sections, any particular teacher education program is a reflection or instantiation of the ways decisions makers pose and answer the four questions. Throughout this chapter, however, I have also suggested that there are particular ways of posing the four questions that are most consistent with the ultimate goals of teaching and teacher education for social change. Drawing on the relevant university-based research as well as the data of practice and of teachers' school-based inquiries, I have thus attempted to argue for certain ways both to pose and answer the questions.

Taken together, these questions and answers are intended to function as an analytic or theoretical framework within which teachers, teacher educators, policy makers, school administrators, and others may design, construct, critique, and participate in teacher education programs, projects, networks, and other contexts across the professional lifespan. As I noted in the first section of this chapter, the purposes of this theory are to provide guidelines for designing, implementing, and evaluating professional development experiences across the lifespan; to provide a stance for predicting and understanding program or project events, outcomes, and dilemmas; to generate research and policy questions, perspectives, and agendas; to suggest interpretive frameworks and analytic strategies for research and theory-formation in teaching and teacher education generally and with regard to social change specifically; and, to guide the development of procedures, policies, and strategies for the recruitment, retention, and credentialing of teachers.

As in the previous sections of this chapter, the language used to describe each of the purposes in the above paragraph was carefully chosen to emphasize that a theory offers guiding principles within which multiple ways of doing teacher education are possible rather than offering recommendations for specific practices or model programs. This is the case because of a third premise underlying this paper: the structures of particular teacher education programs or projects are embedded in and interact with the social and historical contexts in which they occur and with the traditions, goals, and values of their institutional hosts. For this reason, structural, curricular, and organizational variation in the arrangements of teacher education programs and projects is inevitable (and desirable) even if the aims of social change and social justice are similar.

## ENDNOTES

[1]   Throughout this chapter, I use the term "teacher education" to mean the preparation and ongoing professional development of school-based and university-based teachers and teachers educators across the lifespan rather than the narrower meaning, often used in the literature, which refers only to the initial preparation of prospective teachers during the preservice period.

[2]   The powerful work of Gloria Ladson-Billings (1990, 1992, 1994, 1995) comes closest to what I am arguing for here. Although the theory Ladson-Billings suggests is a theory of teaching as opposed to a theory of teacher education, these two are clearly related. She makes the case that there is a need to develop a coherent theoretical framework for teaching culturally diverse students, or what she refers to as "a grounded theory of culturally relevant pedagogy" (1995).

[3]   See especially provocative and useful syntheses by Au & Kawakami (1994), Banks (1995), Cazden & Mehan (1989), Darling-Hammond, 1995; Grant, Sleeter, & Anderson (1986), Grant & Secada (1995), Irvine (1995), King (1994), Little & McLaughlin (1993), Sleeter (1995), Sleeter & Grant(1987), Villegas (1991), Zeichner (1993), Zeichner & Liston (1990).

[4]   See Cochran-Smith and Lytle (1991, 1993) for a discussion of the need for insiders' as well as outsiders' perspectives on teaching, learning, and schooling.

[5]   Ladson-Billings (1995) attends to some of these. Her theory, based on case studies of eight successful teachers of African American children, focuses on teachers' beliefs and ideologies, particularly their conceptions of self and others, their conceptions of knowledge, and their social relations with students, families, and communities.

[6]   Sleeter (1995) offers a thoughtful response to this criticism, pointing out problems with critiques of multicultural education that do not draw adequately on the multicultural literature itself and discussing the ways in which multicultural education and critical pedagogy do overlap.

[7]   Although Lather (1986) was describing social science "research as praxis" rather than teaching as praxis, her conceptualization is appropriate here.

[8]   Also see Hale (1994), Irvine (1990), and Irvine & York (1995).

[9]   Also see Cochran-Smith (1991, 1994, 1995a, 1995b, in press).

[10]   The idea of guidelines is in keeping with Judith Warren Little's (1993) notion of "design principles" for professional development that may be adequate to the current climate of school reform and in terms of which teachers' professional development might be evaluated.

[11]   Although this chapter does not deal explicitly with issues of disability, inclusion, and special education, I am convinced that these issues (particularly the ways they are entangled with issues of race, equity and access, and social change/social justice) need more attention in the teacher education literature. With my new colleagues in general and special teacher education at Boston College, I am embarking on a faculty self-study research and curriculum project intended to explore these interrleationships (Albert et al., 1997).

# REFERENCES

Agre, J., Cochran-Smith, M., Delcollo, L., DiLucchio, C., Ebby, C.B., Feinberg, P., Klausner, E., Massey, A., Mitchell, W., Perloff, Schatz, L., M., Stone, P., & Williams, E. (1996). *Supervision as inquiry.* Paper presented at the Ethnography and Education Research Forum. Philadelphia: University of Pennsylvania.

Albert, L., Cochran-Smith, M., Dimattia, P., Freedman, S., Jackson, R., McGee, L., Mooney, J., Neisler, O., Peck, A., & Zollers, N. (1997). *Seeking social justice: A teacher education faculty's self-study.* Paper presented at the American Educational Research Association. Chicago.

American Association of Colleges for Teacher Education. (1987). *Teaching teachers: Facts and figures.* Washington, DC: Author.

Anderson, C. W. (1991). Policy implications of research on science teaching and teachers' knowledge. In M. M. Kennedy (Eds.), *Teaching academic subjects to diverse learners* (pp. 5–30). New York: Teachers College Press.

Anyon, J. (1984). Social class and the hidden curriculum of work. *Journal of Education,* **162,** 67–92.

Anyon, J. (1994). Teacher development and reform in an inner-city school. *Teachers College Record,* **96**(1), 14–34.

Aronowitz, S., & Giroux, H. (1985). *Education under siege.* New York: New World Foundation.

Asante, M. K. (1991). The Afro-centric idea in education. *Journal of Negro Education,* **62,** 170–180.

Au, K. H., & Jordan, C. (1981). Teaching reading to Hawaiian children: Finding a culturally appropriate solution. In H. T. Trueba, G. P. Guthrie, & K. H. Au (Eds.), *Culture and the bilingual classroom: Studies in classroom ethnography* (pp. 139–152). Rowley, MA: Newbury House.

Au, K. H., & Kawakami, A. J. (1994). Cultural congruence in instruction. In E. R. Hollins, J. E. King, & W. C. Hayman (Eds.), *Teaching diverse populations: Formulating a knowledge base* (pp. 5–23). Albany: State University of New York Press.

Ballenger, C. (1992). Because you like us: The language of control. *Harvard Educational Review,* **62**(2), 199–208.

Banford, H. (1995). The blooming of Maricar: Writing workshop and the phantom student. In A. Peterson (Eds.), *Cityscapes: Eight views from the urban classroom.* San Francisco: The National Writing Project Publications.

Banks, J. (1991). Teaching multicultural literacy to teachers. *Teaching Education,* 4(1), 135–144.

Banks, J. A., & Banks, C. A. M. (Eds.). (1995). *Handbook of research on multicultural education.* New York: Macmillan.

Bastian, A., Fruchter, N., Gittel, M., Greer, C., & Hashkins, K. (1985) *Choosing equality: The case for democratic schooling.* Philadelphia: Temple University Press.

Beckum, L. C. (1992) Diversity assessment: Always factoring in the reform equation. In M. Dilworth (Ed.), *Diversity in teacher education.* San Francisco: AACTE/Jossey Bass.

Bernal, Y., DonKonics, A., Good, D. L., Jeter, V., Paikoff, M., Reisner, T., Robinson, M., Sosa, M., Sullivan, L., & Wallach, R. (1994). *Somewhere between silence and voice: Student teachers on learning to teach.* Paper presented at the Ethnography in Education Forum, Philadelphia.

Bloome, D., & Green, J. (1984). Directions in the sociolinguistic study of reading. In P. D. Pearson (Ed.), *Handbook of reading research* (pp. 395–421). New York: Longman.

Brophy, J. E., & Good, T. L. (1986). Teacher behavior and student achievement. In M. C. Wittrock (Ed.), *Handbook of research on teaching* (pp. 328–375). New York: Macmillan.

Brown, S. P. (1993). Lighting fires. In M. Cochran-Smith & S. Lytle, (Eds.) *Inside/Outside: Teacher research and knowledge* (pp. 241–249). New York.: Teachers College Press.

Bruner, J. (1996). *The culture of education.* Harvard University Press: Cambridge.

Buchanan, J. (1993). Listening to the voices. In M. Cochran-Smith & S. Lytle, *Inside/Outside: Teacher research and knowledge* (pp. 212–220). New York.: Teachers College Press.

Buchanan, J. (1994). Teacher as learner: Working in a community of teachers. In T. Shanahan (Ed.), *Teachers thinking, Teachers knowing.* Urbana: NCTE-NCCRE Press.

Buchanan, J., Check, J.,Eidman- Aadahl, E.,Sterling, R., & Tateishi, C. (1994). *Final report: The urban sites network of the national writing project.* San Francisco: The National Writing Project Publications.

Bullough, R. V., Jr., Knowles, J. G., & Crow, N. A. (1992). *Emerging as a teacher.* London: Routledge.

Carini, P. (1986). *Prospect's documentary processes.* Bennington, VT: The Prospect School Center.

Castenell, L. A., & Pinar, W. (1993). *Understanding curriculum as racial text: Representations of identity and difference in education.* Albany: State University of New York Press.

Cazden, C., & Mehan, H. (1989). Principles from sociology and anthropology: Context, code, classroom, and culture. In M. Reynolds (Ed.), *Knowledge base for the beginning teacher* (pp. 47–57). Oxford: Pergamon Press.

Chin, C. (1995). Are you the teacher who gives parents homework? In A. Peterson (Ed.), *Cityscapes: Eight views from the urban classroom.* San Francisco: The National Writing Project Publications.

Chinn, P. C., & Wang G. Y. (1992). Recruiting and retaining Asian/Pacific American teachers. In M. Dilworth (Ed.), *Diversity in teacher education.* San Francisco: AACTE/Jossey Bass.

Clark, C., & Peterson, P. (1986). Teacher thinking. In M. Wittrock (Ed.), *Handbook of research on teaching.* New York: Macmillan.

Clark, C., & Zellermeyer, M. (1995). *Being and becoming: Thoughtful teacher education and the self.* Unpublished manuscript: Michigan State University.

Cochran-Smith, M. (1997). Knowledge, skills, and experiences for teaching culturally diverse learners: A perspective for practicing teachers. In J. Irvine (Ed.), *Constructing the Knowledge Base for Urban Teaching.* Washington: AACTE.

Cochran-Smith, M. (1991a). Learning to teach against the grain. *Harvard Educational Review,* **61**(3), 279–310.

Cochran-Smith, M. (1991b). Reinventing student teaching. *Journal of Teacher Education,* **42**(2), 104–118.

Cochran-Smith, M. (1995a) *Blind vision: Preservice curriculum as racial text.* Paper presented at AERA, San Francisco.

Cochran-Smith, M. (1995b). Color blindness and basket making are not the answers: Confronting the dilemmas of race, culture and language diversity in teacher education. *American Educational Research Journal,* **32**(3), 493–522.

Cochran-Smith, M. (1995d). Uncertain allies: Understanding the boundaries of race and teaching. *Harvard Educational Review.*

Cochran-Smith, M., & Lytle, S. L. (1990). Research on teaching and teacher research: The issues that divide. *Educational Researcher,* **19**, 2–11.

Cochran-Smith, M., & Lytle, S. L. (1992). Interrogating cultural diversity: Inquiry and action. *Journal of Teacher Education,* **43**(2), 104–115.

Cochran-Smith, M., & Lytle, S. L. (Eds.) (1993). *Inside/outside: Teacher research and knowledge.* New York: Teachers College Press.

Cochran-Smith, M. & Lytle, S. L. (1995). *Teacher research and the constructive disruption of university culture.* Paper presented at the Ethnography in Education Forum, Philadelphia.

Cohen, D. K., McLaughlin, M. W., & Talbert, J. E. (1993). *Teaching for understanding: Challenges for policy and practice.* San Francisco: Jossey-Bass.

Cohen, J. (1994). "Now everybody want to dance": Making change in an urban center. In M. Fine (Eds.), *Chartering urban school reform* (pp. 5–30). New York: Teachers College Press.

Comer, J. P. (1988). Educating poor minority children. *Scientific American,* **259**(5), 24–30.

Cone, J. (1990). Untracking advanced placement English: Creating opportunity is not enough. In *Research in writing: Working papers of teacher researchers* (pp. 712–717). Berkeley, CA: Bay Area Writing Project.

Cuban, L. (1970). *To make a difference: Teaching in the inner city.* New York: Free Press.

Cummins, J. (1994) The socioacademic achievement model in the context of coercive and collaborative release of power. In R. A. Devillar, C. J. Faltis, & J. P. Cummins (Eds.), *Cultural diversity in schools: From rhetoric to practice.* New York: SUNY Press.

Cziko, C. (1995). Dialogue journals: Passing notes the academic way. In A. Peterson (Eds.), *Cityscapes: Eight views from the urban classroom.* San Francisco: The National Writing Project Publications.

D'Armaline, W., & Sfalen, K. (1992). *Developing social and cultural foundations from a multicultural perspective.* In M. Dilworth (Ed.), *Diversity in teacher education.* San Francisco: AACTE/Jossey Bass.

Darling-Hammond, L. (1995). Inequality and access to knowledge. In J. A. Banks & C. A. M. Banks (Eds.), *Handbook of research on multicultural education* (pp. 465–483). New York: Macmillan.

Delpit, L. (1986). Skills and other dilemmas of a progressive black educator. *Harvard Educational Review,* **56**(4), 379–385.

Delpit, L. (1988). Power and pedagogy in education other people's children. *Harvard Educational Review,* **58**(3), 280–298.

Delpit, L. (1995). *Other people's children: Cultural conflict in the classroom.* New York: The New Press.

Devillar, R. A., & Faltis, C. J. (1994). Reconciling cultural diversity and quality schooling: Paradigmatic elements of a socioacademic frameworks. In Devillar, R.A., Faltis, C.J., & Cummins, J. P. (Eds.), *Cultural diversity in schools: From rhetoric to practice* (pp. 25–56). New York: SUNY Press.

Devillar, R. A., Faltis, C. J., & Cummins, J. P. (Eds.). (1994). *Cultural diversity in schools: From rhetoric to practice.* New York: SUNY Press.

Dill, D. (Ed.). (1990). *What teachers need to know: The knowledge, skills and values essential to good teaching.* San Francisco: AACTE/Jossey Bass.

Dillon, D. R. (1989). Showing them that I want them to learn and that I care about who they are: A microethnography of the social organization of a secondary low-track English-reading classroom. *American Educational Research Journal,* **26**(2), 227–259.

Dilworth, M. (Ed.). (1992). *Diversity in teacher education.* San Francisco: AACTE/Jossey Biss.

Donmoyer, R. (1996). The concept of a knowledge base. In F. Murray (Ed.), *The teacher educator's handbook: Building a knowledge base for the preparation of teachers* (pp. 92–119). SanFrancisco: Jossey Bass Publishers.

Dreeben, R. (1987). Closing the divide: What teachers and administrators can do to help black students reach their reading potential. *American Educators,* **11**(4) 28–35.

Erickson, F. (1981). Taught cognitive learning in its immediate environments: A neglected topic in the anthropology of education. *Anthropology and Education Quarterly,* **13**(149–180).

Erickson, F. (1986). Qualitative methods in research on teaching. In M. Wittrock (Ed.), *Handbook of research on teaching* (pp. 119–161). New York: Macmillan.

Erickson, F., & Mohatt, G. (1982). Cultural organization of participation structures in two classrooms of Indian students. In G. B. Spindler (Ed.), *Doing the ethnography of schooling: Educational anthropology in action* (pp. 133–174). New York: Holt, Rinehart & Winston.

Evertson, C. M., & Green, J. L. (1986). Observation as inquiry and method. In M. C. Wittrock (Eds.), *Handbook of research on teaching* (pp. 162–213). New York: Macmillan.

Fecho, R. (1993). Reading as a teacher. In M. Cochran-Smith & S. L. Lytle, (Eds.) *Inside/outside: Teacher research and knowledge* New York: Teachers College Press.

Fecho, B. (1994). Language inquiry and critical pedagogy: Co-investigating power in the classroom. In M. Fine (Eds.), *Chartering urban school reform* (pp. 180–191). New York: Teachers College Press.

Fecho, B. (1995). Learning from Laura. In A. Peterson (Eds.), *Cityscapes: Eight views from the urban classroom.* San Francisco: The National Writing Project Publications.

Feldgus, E. (1994). Rethinking phonics: *Graphophonemic awareness in a kindergarten classroom.* Unpublished doctoral dissertation, University of Pennsylvania.

Fenstermacher, G. (1994). The knower and the known: The nature of knowledge in research on teaching. In L. Darling-Hammond (Ed.), *Review of research in education* (Vol. 20, pp. 3–56). Washington: American Educational Research Association.

Fine, M. (Ed.). (1994). *Chartering urban school reform: Reflections on public high schools in the midst of change.* New York: Teachers College Press.

Florio-Ruane, S. (1994). Future teachers' autobiography club: Preparing educators to support literacy learning in culturally diverse classrooms. *English Education,* **26**(1), 52–66.

Foster, M. (1989). Its cookin' now: A performance analysis of the speech events of a Black teachers in an urban community college. *Language in Society,* **18**(1), 1–29.

Foster, M. (1991). The politics of race through African-American teachers' eyes. *Journal of Education,* **172**(3), 123–141.

Foster, M. (1993). Educating for competence in community and culture: Exploring the views of exemplary African-American teachers. *Urban Education,* **27**(4), 370–394.

Foster, M. (1994). Effective black teachers: A literature review. In E. R. Hollins, J. E. King, & W. C. Hayman (Eds.), *Teaching diverse populations: Formulating a knowledge base* (pp. 225–241). Albany: State University of New York Press.

Freire, P. (1970). *Pedagogy of the oppressed.* New York: Seabury Press.

Garibaldi, A. M. (1992). Preparing teachers for culturally diverse classrooms. In M. Dilworth (Ed.), *Diversity in teacher education.* San Francisco: AACTE/Jossey Bass.

Gay, G. (1988). Designing relevant curricula for diverse learners. *Education and Urban Society,* **20**(4), 327–340.

Gay, G. (1995). Mirror images on common issues: Parallels between multicultural education and critical pedagogy. In C. E. Sleeter & P. L. McLaren (Eds.), *Multicultural education, critical pedagogy, and the politics of difference* (pp. 155–189). Albany: State University of New York Press.

Ginsburg, M. B. (1988). *Contradictions in teacher education and society: A critical analysis.* Philadelphia: Falmer.

Ginsburg, M. B., & Clift, R. T. (1990). The hidden curriculum of preservice teacher education. In R. W. Houston (Ed.), *Handbook of research on teaching* (pp. 3–20). New York: Macmillan Publishing Company.

Ginsburg, M. B., & Lindsay, B. (Eds.). (1995a). *Comparitive perspectives on policy formation, socialization, and society.* Falmer Press.

Ginsburg, M., & Lindsay, B. (1995b) The political dimension in teacher education. In M. B. Ginsburg & B. Lindsay (Eds.), *Comparative Perspectives on Policy Formation, Socialization, and Society.* London: Falmer Press.

Giroux, H. (1984). Rethinking the language of schooling. *Language Arts*, **61**, 33–40.

Giroux, H. (1985). Intellectual label and pedagogical work: Rethinking the role of teachers as intellectuals. *Phenomenology and Pedagogy*, **3**(20–31).

Glaser, B. G. & Straus, A.S. (1967). *The discovery of grounded thery: Strategies for qualitative research.* New York: Aldine De Gruyter.

Gollnick, D. (1992) Understanding the dynamics of race, class, and gender. In M. Dilworth (Ed.), *Diversity in teacher education.* San Francisco: AACTE/Jossey Bass.

Grant, C. A. (1991). Culture and teaching: What do teachers need to know? In M. M. Kennedy (Eds.), *Teaching academic subjects to diverse learners* (pp. 237–256). New York: Teachers College Press.

Grant, C. A., & Secada, W. (1990). Preparing teachers for diversity. In M. C. Wittrock (Ed.), *Handbook of research on teaching.* New York: Macmillan.

Grant, C. A., Sleeter, C. E., & Anderson, J. E. (1986). The literature on multicultural education: Review and analysis. *Educational Studies*, **12**(1), 47–71.

Grant, C. A., & Tate, W. F. (1995). Multicultural education through the lens of the multicultural education research literature. In J. A. Banks & C. A. M. Banks (Eds.), *Handbook of research on multicultural education* (pp. 145–166). New York: Macmillan.

Griffin, G. A. (1991). Interactive staff development: Using what we know. In A. Lieberman & L. Miller (Eds.), *Staff development: New demands, new realities, new perspectives* (pp. 243–258). New York: Teachers College Press.

Grumet, M. (1991). The politics of personal knowledge. In C. Witherell & N. Noddings (Eds.), *Stories lives tell.* New York: Teachers College Press.

Haberman, M. (1991). The pedagogy of power versus good teaching. *Phi Delta Kappan*, 290–294.

Hale, J. E. (1994). *Unbank the fire: Visions for the education of all children.* Baltimore: Johns Hopkins University Press.

Hargreaves, A. (1994). *Changing teachers, changing times: Teachers' work and culture in the postmodern age.* New York: Teachers College Press.

Hargreaves, A., & Fullan, M. G. (Eds.). (1992). *Understanding teacher development.* New York: Teachers College Press.

Heath, S. B. (1983). *Ways with words: Language, life, and work in communities and classrooms.* New York: Cambridge University Press.

Heath, S. B. (1995). Ethnography in communities: Learning the everyday life of America's subordinated youth. In J. A. Banks & C. A. M. Banks (Eds.), *Handbook of research on multicultural education* (pp. 114–128). New York: Macmillan.

Hilliard, A. G., III (Ed.). (1987). Testing African American students. *Negro Educational Review*, **38**(2/3).

Hilliard, A. G. (1989). Teachers and cultural styles in a pluralistic society. *NEA Today*, **7**(6), 65–69.

Hilliard, A. G. (1992). Behavioral style, culture, and teaching and learning. *Journal of Negro Education*, **61**(3), 370–377.

Himley, M., & Carini, P. (1991). Deep talk as knowing. In *Shared territory: Understanding children's writing as works.* New York: Oxford University Press.

Hollins, E. R. (1982). The Marva Collins story revisited: Implications for regular classroom instruction. *Journal of Teacher Education*, **33**(1), 37–40.

Hollins, E. R., King, J. E., & Hayman, W. C. (Eds.). (1994). *Teaching diverse populations: Formulating a knowledge base.* Albany: State University of New York Press.

Hollins, E. R., & Spencer, K. (1990). Restructuring schools for cultural inclusion: Changing the schooling process for African American youngsters. *Journal of Education*, **172**(2), 89–100.

Holmes Group. (1986). *Tomorrow's teachers.* East Lansing, Michigan: Holmes Group.

Holmes Group. (1990). *Tomorrow's schools.* East Lansing, Michigan: Holmes Group.

Holmes Group. (1995). *Tomorrow's schools of education..* East Lansing, Michigan: Holmes Group.

hooks, B. (1994). *Teaching to transgress: Education as the practice of freedom.* New York: Routledge.

Irvine, J. J. (1990). *Black students and school failure: Policies, practices, and prescriptions.* New York: Greenwood Press.

Irvine, J. J. (1992). Making teacher education culturally responsive. In M. Dilworth (Ed.), *Diversity in teacher education.* San Francisco: AACTE/Jossey Bass.

Irvine, J. J., & York, D. E. (1995). Learning styles and culturally diverse students: A literature review. In J. A. Banks & C. A. M. Banks (Eds.), *Handbook of research on multicultural education* (pp. 484–497). New York: Macmillan.

Johnson, D. W., & Johnson, R. T. (1994). Cooperative learning in the culturally diverse classroom. In R. A. Devillar, C. J. Faltis, & J. P. Cummins (Eds.), *Cultural diversity in schools: From rhetoric to practice* (pp. 37–74). New York: SUNY Press.

Kailin, J. (1994). Anti-racist staff development for teachers: Considerations of race, class, and gender. *Teaching and Teacher Education*, **10**(2), 169–184.

Kanevsky, R. D. (1993). Descriptive review of a child: A way of knowing about teaching and learning. In M. Cochran-Smith & S. L. Lytle, (Eds.) *Inside/outside: Teacher research and knowledge* (pp. 150–162). New York: Teachers College Press.

Kennedy, M. M. (Ed.). (1991). *Teaching academic subjects to diverse learners*. New York: Teachers College Press.

King, J. E. (1994). The purpose of schooling for African American children: Including cultural knowledge. In E. R. Hollins, J. E. King, & W. C. Hayman (Eds.), *Teaching diverse populations: Formulating a knowledge base* (pp. 25–56). Albany: State University of New York Press.

King, J., & Ladson-Billings, G. (1990). The teacher education challenge in elite university settings: Developing critical perspectives for teaching in a democratic and multicultural society. *European Journal of Intercultural Studies*, **1**(2), 15–30.

Knapp, M. (1995). *Teaching for meaning in high-poverty classrooms*. New York: Teachers College Press.

Kozol, J. (1991). *Savage Inequalities*. New York: Harper.

Ladson-Billings, G. (1990). Culturally relevant teaching: Effective instruction for black students. *The College Board Review*, **155**, 20–25.

Ladson-Billings, G. (1992). Liberatory consequences of literacy: A case of culturally relevant instruction for African American students. *Journal of Negro Education*, **61**(3), 378–391.

Ladson-Billings, G. (1994). *The dreamkeepers: Successful teachers of African-American children*. San Francisco: Jossey-Bass.

Ladson-Billings, G. (1995a). Multicultural teacher education: Research, practice, and policy. In J. A. Banks & C. A. M. Banks (Eds.), *Handbook of research on multicultural education*. New York: Macmillan.

Ladson-Billings, G. (1995b). Toward a theory of culturally relevant pedagogy. *American Educational Research Journal*, **32**(3), 465–491.

Larkin, J. M. (1995). *Current theories and issues in multicultural teacher education programs*. In Larkin, J. M., & Sleeter, C. E. *Developing muticultural teacher education curricula*. Albany: SUNY Press.

Larkin, J. M., & Sleeter, C. E. (1995). *Developing muticultural teacher education curricula*. Albany: SUNY Press.

Lather, P. (1986). Research as praxis. *Harvard Educational Review*, **56**(3), 257–277.

Letgers, N., & McDill, E. L. (1994). Rising to the challenge: Emerging strategies for educating youth at risk. In R. J. Rossi (Ed.), *Schools and students at risk* (pp. 23–50). New York: Teacher's College Press.

Lieberman, A., & Miller, L. (1994). Revisiting the social realities of teaching. In A. Lieberman & L. Miller (Eds.), *Staff development: New demands, New realities, new perspectives* (pp. 92–109). New York: Teachers College Press.

Liston, D. P., & Zeichner, K. M. (1991). *Teacher education and the social conditions of schooling*. New York: Routledge.

Little, J. W. (1993a). Professional community in comprehensive high schools: The two worlds of academic and vocational teachers. In J. W. Little & M. W. McLaughlin (Eds.), *Teachers' work: Individuals, colleagues, and contexts* (pp. 137–163). New York: Teachers College Press.

Little, J. W. (1993b). Teachers' professional development in a climate of educational reform. *Educational Evaluation and Policy Analysis*, **15**(2), 129–151.

Little, J. W., & McLaughlin, M. W. (1993). *Teachers' work: Individuals, colleagues, and contexts*. New York: Teachers College Press.

Lytle, S., Christman, J., Cohen, J., Countryman, J.,F echo, R., Portnoy, D., & Sion, F. (1994). Learning in the afternoon: Teacher inquiry as school reform. In M. Fine (Eds.), *Chartering urban school reform: Reflections on public high schools in the midst of change* (pp. 157–179). New York: Teachers College Press.

Lytle, S., & Cochran-Smith, M. (1990). Learning from teacher research: A working typology. *Teachers College Record*, **92**, 83–104.

Lytle, S. L., & Cochran-Smith, M. (1992 Teacher research as a way of knowing. *Harvard Educational Review*, **62**(4), 447–474.

Lytle, S. L., & Cochran-Smith, M. (1994). *Teacher Research: Some questions that persist.* Paper presented at the Ethnography in Education Forum, Philadelphia.

Lytle, S., & Fecho, R. (1991). Meeting strangers in familiar places: Teacher collaboration by cross-visitation. *English Education*, **23**, 5–28.

McCarthy, C. (1993) In L. A. Castenell, & W. Pinar *Understanding curriculum as racial text: Representations of identity and difference in education.* Albany: State University of New York Press.

McCarthy, C., & Crichlow, W. (Eds.). (1993). *Race, identity, and representation in education.* New York: Routledge.

McDermott, R. P. (1974). Achieving school failure. In G. Spindler (Ed.), *Education and cultural-process* (pp. 82–118). New York: Holt, Rinehart, & Winston.

McDiarmid, G. W. (1991). What teachers need to know about cultural diversity: Restoring subject matter to the picture. In M. M. Kennedy (Ed.), *Teaching academic subjects to diverse learners* (pp. 257–269). New York: Teachers College Press.

McIntosh, P. (1989). White privilege: Unpacking the invisible knapsack. *Peace and Freedom*, 10–12.

McLaughlin, M. W. (1991). Enabling professional development: What have we learned? In A. Lieberman & L. Miller (Eds.), *Staff development: New demands, New realities, new perspectives* (pp. 61–82). New York: Teachers College Press.

McLaughlin, M. W. (1994). What matters most in teachers' workplace context? In J. W. Little & M. W. McLaughlin (Eds.), *Teachers' work: Individuals, colleagues, and contexts* (pp. 79–103). New York: Teachers College Press.

Mehan, H., Lintz, A., Okamoto, D., & Wills, J. S. (1995). Ethnographic studies of multicultural education in classrooms and schools. In J. A. Banks & C. A. M. Banks (Eds.), *Handbook of research on multicultural education* (pp. 129–144). New York: Macmillan.

Meier, D. (1995). *The power of their ideas: Lessons for America from a small school in Harlem.* Boston: Beacon Press.

Michaels, S. (1981). "Sharing time": Children's narrative styles and differential access to literacy. *Language in Society*, **10**, 423–442.

Milk, R. (1994 ). Responding successfully to cultural divisions in our schools: The teacher connection. In R.A. Devillar, C. J. Faltis, & J. P. Cummins (Eds.), *Cultural diversity in schools: From rhetoric to practice.* New York: SUNY Press.

Miller, C. (1995). Utilizing race, language and culture to promote achievement and understanding. In A. Peterson (Eds.), *Cityscapes: Eight views from the urban classroom.* San Francisco: The National Writing Project Publications.

Moll, L. C. (1988). Some key issues in teaching Latino students. *Language Arts*, **65**(5), 465–472.

Moll, L. C., & Diaz, S. (1987). Change as the goal of educational research. *Anthropology and Education Quarterly*, **18**(4), 300–311.

Muncey, D. E., Uhl, S. C., & Nyce, J. M. (1994). *Urban Sites Network evaluation* (Unpublished). New York: Urban Sites Network.

Murray, F. B. (1989). Explanations in education. In M. C. Reynolds (Ed.), *Knowledge base for the beginning teacher.* Oxford: Pergamon Press.

Murray, F. (1996). *The teacher educator's handbook: Building a knowledge base for the preparation of teachers.* SanFrancisco: AACTE/Jossey Bass.

National Commission on Teaching and America's Future. (1996). *What matters most. Teaching for American's future.* New York: Teachers College Columbia.

Nieto, S. (1996). *Affirming diversity: The sociopolitcal context of multicultural edcucation.* New York: Longman.

Noffke, S. E., & Stevenson, R. B. (Ed.). (1995). *Educational action research: Becoming practically critical.* New York: Teachers College Press.

Oakes, J. (1988). *Keeping track: How high-schools structure inequality.* New York: Yale University Press.

Oakes, J. (1990). *Multiplying inequalities: The effects of race, social class, and tracking on opportunities to learn math and science.* Santa Monica, CA.: Rand Corporation.

Olsen, L., & Mullen, N. A. (1990). *Embracing diversity: Teachers' voices from California classrooms.* San Francisco: California Tomorrow.

Padilla, A. M., & Lindholm, K. J. (1995). Quantitative educational research with ethnic minorities. In J. A. Banks & C. A. M. Banks (Eds.), *Handbook of research on multicultural education* (pp. 97–113). New York: Macmillan.

Peterson, A. (Ed.). (1995). *Cityscapes: Eight views from the urban classroom.* San Francisco: The National Writing Project Publications.

Phelan, P., & Davidson, A. L. (Eds.). (1993). *Renegotiating cultural diversity in American schools.* Teacher's College Press, N.Y.

Philadelphia Teachers Learning Cooperative. (1984). On becoming teacher experts: Buying time. *Language Arts,* 61(7), 731–736.

Pincus, M. (1993). Conversion of a skeptic. In M. Cochran-Smith & S. L. Lytle, (Eds.) *Inside/outside: Teacher research and knowledge* New York: Teachers College Press.

Popkewitz, T. (1991). *A political sociology of educational reform.* New York: Teachers College Press.

Powell, L. (1994). Interpreting social defenses: Family group in an urban setting. In M. Fine (Eds.), *Chartering urban school reform* (pp. 112–121). New York: Teachers College Press.

Resnick, M. (1995). Making connections between families and schools. In A. Peterson (Eds.), *Cityscapes: Eight views from the urban classroom.* San Francisco: The National Writing Project Publications.

Reynolds, M. C. (Ed.). (1989). *Knowledge base for the beginning teacher.* Oxford: Pergamon Press.

Richardson, V. (1996). The case for formal research and practical inquiry in teacher education. In F. Murray (Ed.) *The teacher educator's handbook. Building a knowledge base for the preparation of teachers* (pp. 715–738). SanFrancisco: Jossey Bass Publishers.

Rios, F. A., & Gonzales, G. M. (1995). Psychology and developmental perspectives in a multicultural framework: Exploring some possibilities. In J. M. Larkin & C. E. Sleeter (Eds.), *Developing muticultural teacher education curricula.* Albany: SUNY Press.

Rosenberg, P. (1994). *Underground discourses: Exploring whiteness in teacher education.* Paper presented at the annual meeting of the American Educational Research Association, New Orleans.

Sheets, R. H. (1995). From remedial to gifted: Effects of culturally relevant pedagogy. *Theory Into Practice,* 34(3), 186–193.

Shor, I. (1980). *Critical teaching in everyday life.* Boston: South End Press.

Shulman, L. (1987). Knowledge and teaching: Foundations of the new reform. *Harvard Educational Review,* 51, 1–22.

Slavin, R. E. (1985). Cooperative learning: Applying contact theory to desegregated schools. *Journal of Social Issues,* 41, 45–62.

Sleeter, C. E. (1992). Restructuring schools for multicultural education. *Journal of Teacher Education,* 43(2), 141–148.

Sleeter, C. E. (1995a). An analysis of the critiques of multicultural education. In J. A. Banks & C. A. M. Banks (Eds.), *Handbook of research on multicultural education.* New York: Macmillan.

Sleeter, C. E. (1995b). Reflections on my use of multicultural and critical pedagogy when students are white. In C. E. Sleeter & P. L. McLaren (Ed.), *Multicultural education, critical pedagogy, and the politics of difference.* Albany: SUNY Press.

Sleeter, C. E. (1995c). White pre-service students and multicultural education coursework. In J. M. Larkin & C. E. Sleeter (Eds.), *Developing muticultural teacher education curricula.* Albany: SUNY Press.

Sleeter, C. E., & Grant, C. A. (1987). An analysis of multicultural education in the United States. *Harvard Educational Review,* 57, 421–444.

Sleeter, C. E., & McLaren, P. L. (Ed.). (1995). *Multicultural education, critical pedagogy, and the politics of difference.* Albany: SUNY Press.

Snyder, J., Lieberman, A., Macdonald, M. B., & Goodwin, A. L. (1992). *Makers of meaning in a learning-centered school: A case study of Central Park East 1 Elementary School.* New York: National Center for Restructuring Education, Schools, and Teaching.

Stevenson, R. W. (1996, March 12). "Rich are getting richer, but not the very rich." *New York Times*

Tatum, B. D. (1992). Talking about race, learning about racism: The application of racial identity development theory in the classroom. *Harvard Educational Review,* 62, 1–24.

Tatum, B. D. (1994). Teaching white students about racism: The search for white allies and the restoration of hope. *Teachers College Record,* 95, 462–476.

Tellez, K., Hlebowitsh, P., Cohen, M., & Norwood, P. (1995). Social service field experiences and teacher education. In J. M. Larkin & C. E. Sleeter *Developing muticultural teacher education curricula.* Albany: SUNY Press.

Villegas, A. M. (1991). *Culturally responsive pedagogy for the 1990s and beyond* (Trends and Issues Paper No. 6). Washington, DC: ERIC Clearinghouse on Teacher Education.

Waff, D. (1994). Romance in the classroom: Inviting discourse on gender and power. *The Voice of the Philadelphia Writing Project,* 3(1), 15–18.

Weiner, L. (1989). Asking the right questions: An analytic framework for reform of urban teacher education. *The Urban Review*, **21**(3), 151–161.

Witherell, C., & Noddings, N. (Eds.). (1991). *Stories lives tell*. New York: Teachers College Press.

Zeichner, K. M. (1986). Preparing reflective teachers: An overview of instructional strategies which have been employed in preservice teacher education. *International Journal of Educational Research*, **7**, 565–575.

Zeichner, K. M. (1993). *Educating teachers for cultural diversity*. East Lansing, MI: Michigan State University.

Zeichner, K. & Gore, J. (1990). Teacher socialization. In W. R. Houston (Ed.), *Handbook of research on teacher education*. New York: Macmillan Publishing Company.

Zeichner, K. M. & Liston, D. (1990). Traditions of reform in United States teacher education. *Journal of Teacher Education*, **41**(2) 3–20.

Zimpher, N. & Ashburn, E. (1992). Countering parochialism in teacher candidates. In M. Dilworth (Ed.), *Diversity in teacher education*. San Francisco: AACTE/Jossey Bass.

# Norms and Politics of Equity-Minded Change: Researching the "Zone of Mediation"

JEANNIE OAKES

*Graduate School of Education, University of California at Los Angeles*

KEVIN WELNER

*Graduate School of Education, University of California at Los Angeles*

SUSAN YONEZAWA

*Graduate School of Education, University of California at Los Angeles*

RICKY LEE ALLEN

*Graduate School of Education, University of California at Los Angeles*

*This chapter applies literature on the politics of education to data from a recent study of ten racially mixed secondary schools that were attempting to alter their grouping practices to illuminate how macro social, political and economic forces shaped the struggles these schools faced. The study found that unless reforms seek to achieve parity in opportunity and achievement across diverse groups of students, reformers face enormous challenges.*

Most educational change literature focuses on normatively and politically neutral, technical school reforms and neglects to address the unique attributes of reforms that aim specifically to benefit students who hold less powerful positions in schools and communities[1]. Behind this omission lies an implicit assumption that school systems are filled with well-meaning educators who simply need some centralized assistance or prompting to help their bottom-up efforts to achieve more equitable and efficacious pedagogies. As Hochschild (1984) explains, this assumption is grounded in the premise that racist beliefs are at odds with basic American values, and (therefore) Americans will, if given the opportunity, naturally move away from past racist practices. However, the struggles faced by equity-minded reformers over the past three decades suggest that this rarely happens. This paper attempts to clarify the exceptional barriers that change agents encounter as they attempt to initiate and implement equity-minded school reforms, and it also aims to push research and theory on school change to better account for these barriers.

Some change literature does acknowledge the socio-political nature of the change process and the need to alter past assumptions and beliefs (Fullan, 1991; Sarason, 1990). Much of this same literature notes that community support, resistance, or apathy plays an important role in change (Fullan, 1991; Sarason, 1990). Rarely, however, does the discussion move beyond a neutral analysis to examine the actual

*M. Fullan (ed.), Fundamental Change, 282-305.*
© 2005 *Springer. Printed in the Netherlands.*

assumptions and beliefs which underlie the support, resistance, or apathy that creates and sustains inequitable practices and policies.

Instead, the literature mostly focuses on the need for schools to become "learning organizations" where teachers and administrators become "change agents" who are experts at dealing with change as a normal part of their work lives (Fullan, 1994; Louis & Miles, 1990). Consequently, the lessons that educators learn from the change literature are overwhelmingly in the nature of neutral – albeit essential-advice such as, educators must see themselves as in the business of making improvements, and to "make improvements in an ever changing world is to contend with and manage the forces of change on an ongoing basis" (Fullan, 1994, p. 4).

In the following analysis, we apply literature on the politics of education to data from a recent study of ten racially mixed secondary schools that were attempting to alter their grouping practices, to illuminate how macro- social, political and economic forces shaped the struggles these schools faced. We argue that if we conceive of schools as "mediating institutions," themselves situated within locally constructed "zones" of normative and political mediation that embody larger cultural patterns, we can better understand that equity-minded reforms differ from other change efforts in profound ways. In other words, we find that when reforms seek to achieve parity in opportunity and achievement across diverse groups of students, reformers face enormous challenges. These challenges differ from those of other reform efforts, first, because they create a struggle between individuals over resources that are perceived to be scarce, and second, because they entail an ideological struggle over the meaning of culture as it is enacted in schools. These struggles take place within reforming schools as well as between schools and resistant communities, and they entangle schools in larger cultural patterns related to race, class, and gender. We believe this analysis can help us identify the barriers that equity-minded change agents face and the strategies they might employ to confront these barriers more successfully.

## HOW A NEUTRAL CHANGE LITERATURE FALLS SHORT

Over the past three years, we studied how powerful actors in ten racially and socio-economically mixed secondary schools voluntarily pursued alternatives to traditional tracked structures.[2] Specifically, we were interested in understanding what happens when someone with significant power within a racially and economically diverse school setting decides to attempt detracking – a reform that calls on educators to find more equitable ways to distribute resources and educational opportunities. We posited that the educators in the schools would need to address the technical, normative, and political dimensions of detracking and that these dimensions might manifest themselves differently within each school's unique local context (Oakes & Wells, 1991; Oakes, 1992).

When we entered our schools in the fall of 1992, we found that many of the educators at the school sites were reasonably well-versed in the change literature and, understandably, fairly optimistic about their reforms' prospects for success.

Depending on their fluency with the literature, these educators knew that change would likely not go forward precisely as planned (Elmore & McLaughlin, 1988; Sarason, 1990); that school reform is a process, not an event (Fullan 1991); that change involves mutual adaptation (McLaughlin, 1976; Tyack & Cuban, 1995); that reforms will differ depending on the unique culture of each school (Sarason, 1982); that the change process is non-rational and non-linear (Louis & Miles, 1990; Wise, 1977); that successful policymakers set the conditions for effective administration but refrain from predetermining how those decisions will be made and, instead, charge local practitioners with the development of solutions (Elmore & McLaughlin, 1988; Firestone & Corbett, 1989); that schools are "bottom heavy" and "loosely coupled" (Elmore, 1983; Weick, 1976); and, of course, that we cannot mandate what matters (Elmore & McLaughlin, 1988; McLaughlin, 1976).

These school leaders saw themselves as change agents spearheading an ongoing process of improvement. Moreover, in accordance with the change literature, the detracking reforms had a healthy "bottom-up" beginning in all ten schools. Initially, at least, this "bottom" comprised only a fraction of each school's faculty and community; however, all of the schools' reform leaders understood the importance of establishing a culture of change (see Sarason, 1990). Thus, they did not plan merely to tinker with the technical but, rather, to create enabling structures which would help them to eliminate tracking and support their schools' ongoing quest for inquiry and improvement. We watched as these powerful and efficacious change agents (typically a school administrator or respected teacher) worked to create cultures of change within their schools, and we were encouraged by their apparent progress.

For example, in the midwest, Bearfield Middle School's charismatic principal, Ben McCall, told us that before detracking could occur at his school, he would have to create a positive attitude among the faculty towards change in general and detracking specifically (Yonezawa, 1995). Going directly to the heart of change, Ben explained to us, *You wanna change the school? Change the norm.* He whetted his faculty's appetite for general reform – and detracking specifically – by exposing the faculty to films and inspirational talks that stressed the importance of remaining open to new ideas and innovations, and he encouraged teachers to discuss and debate with him and among themselves. In response, Bearfield's already cohesive and generally open-minded faculty grew increasingly willing to detrack.

A rockier road to cultural change occurred at Central High School, an urban school on the West Coast, where faculty sub-cultures included ambivalence and outright hostility (Datnow, 1995). For many years, most Central teachers refrained from voicing their opinions. A silence was typical at Central faculty meetings – a silence only punctuated by the voices of a few of the more outspoken and, at times, downright rude Central teachers. Within this divisive culture, Central's reform leaders purposefully and painstakingly worked to alter the general culture of their school.

Knowing the importance of attending to school culture, and feeling that they could not accomplish this alone, Central's reformers (aided by a state restructuring grant) hired a restructuring "coach." This outside expert prodded Central's usually quiet teachers to speak out against their colleagues' rudeness. The reformers also engaged in other useful activities, such as staff development designed to establish new norms for relating to one another. During one of these staff development activities, entitled "Bridging Group Differences," we witnessed the "silent majority" finally begin to speak out about their beliefs, including detracking.

Principal Foster noted at the end of Central's first year of reform,

> The major difference that we have made that has affected students more than anything else has been the way in which people are treated on this campus. . . . I think that I would see that as the major success, that people are starting to treat other people the way they deserve to be treated.

Central's reform leaders' attention to cultural norms created an environment within which most Central teachers now feel empowered to speak, and the norms of rational discourse predominate.

Although we have used only two cases – Bearfield and Central – to illustrate our point, comparable stories of attentiveness to school culture can be found in each of the other eight schools studied. These educators clearly understood the process of change as generally portrayed in the change literature, and they faithfully tried to apply the lessons from the literature to their unique sites.

At a structural level, these efforts all must be judged a success. Each of the ten schools in our study reduced some, if not all, of their basic or remedial courses, most provided all students with access to the schools' most challenging or "honors" curriculum, and several developed a common curriculum for all students in key academic subjects at some grade levels. All became far more attentive to providing greater curricular access and richer learning opportunities to low-income students and to students of color.

However, none of the change agents, as skillful as they were, even approached the extent of detracking they sought, and several worried that old patterns of inequality were being replicated within their schools' new, "detracked" structure. Most felt battered and bruised by their efforts to reform, and some did not survive as school leaders. They know now that they missed important lessons not taught by the change literature – a literature that generally neglects the unique problems encountered by reform efforts designed to give more to our least powerful citizens – low-income and non-white students – in a societal culture that usually demands that they receive less. Most of the change agents that we observed were caught unprepared when the process and the shape of their equity-minded reforms were profoundly affected by global, societal, regional, local and individual norms and politics concerning race, gender, sexual orientation, language and socio-economic status.

For example, Central High School faculty proposed a new "custom calendar" so that students could earn course credit at a more individualized pace. The school year would be divided into nine-week quarters, followed by two-week intercessions. During the intercessions, students could make up lost credits or repeat classes. The custom calendar was touted as complementing detracking because it would allow lower achieving students to make up work or get ahead during the intercession. Central's principal reasoned,

> The paradigm here is that it takes every student . . . 180 days to learn Algebra 1, and my question is, how valid could that be? Aren't there some students who might need a couple more days to do that? Now is it better to tell that student that they're a failure and can't learn because they can't learn it in 180 days, or is it better to give them a few extra days to do it?

While most Central faculty favored the custom calendar, the proposal was denounced by powerful parents in the community and more conventional teachers. After a year of intense battling, the school board voted it down. An assistant principal realized only later that, although the calendar was not a redistributive policy on its face, it was seen as a symbol of policymaking aimed at helping students traditionally disadvantaged by the system (at this school low-income, limited-English-speaking Latino students) and taking from those who benefit from the status quo. He felt the custom calendar was used as a symbol of a liberal ideological effort *to take away from the haves and [to give] to the have nots.* Thus what reformers saw as a technical change in the school's schedule triggered a response grounded in larger cultural norms and politics around race and social class.

Similarly, a "gifted education" teacher at Explorer Middle School was severely criticized by parents of identified "gifted" students for not offering their children separate enrichment classes – classes not available to other students (Hirshberg, 1996). Concerned that nearly all of the identified students were white and wealthy, the teacher had opted to offer "challenge" courses that both gifted and "non-gifted" students could select. She responded to the criticism by explaining to parents how this reform made sense – given the schools' efforts to provide all students with rich and challenging curriculum – and reassuring them that the "gifted" curriculum was not being compromised by being more inclusive:

> I was prepared to tell them what we do in class, and here's an example. I had course outlines. I send objectives home with every class and goals and work requirements.

However, what caught this teacher off-guard was that the parents' anger was not based on objectives or curriculum. Rather these parents of white students were insistent that their children be singled out and treated differently. They resented losing the high status associated with more exclusive classes.

> And they didn't ask, 'Well what are our kids learning in your classes?' Nobody asked that. I just found that real dismaying . . . [N]obody asked me anything about [the curriculum]. . . . to me it's like I'm dealing with their egos, more than what their kids really need educationally.

In nearly all of the schools, race and class were salient issues as midtoupper income, white parents of hightracked students regularly opposed detracking efforts. As the Central and Explorer examples suggest, these parents (and occasionally their children as well) perceived detracking as an attempt to divert resources away from their children and towards groups they characterized as lessthan-deserving (see Wells & Serna, 1996), for a fuller discussion of this point). Such parental concerns were compounded and reflected within all ten schools by resistance from those educators least willing to problematize stereotypical links between race, gender, class and intelligence (Oakes, Wells, Datnow & Jones, 1997).[3] We should also note that key change agents' abilities to operate were profoundly influenced by the agents' own race, gender, and, in at least one case, sexual orientation (Oakes, Yonezawa, & Wells, 1996). Gender issues came through strongly in at least two of our schools, where faculty cultures split along gender lines-with women teachers actively supporting detracking and their male counterparts battling it (Datnow, 1995).

Of course, the majority of change agents in our schools had little reason to suspect that deeply held beliefs and ideologies about intelligence, racial differences, social stratification, white supremacy, and elite privilege would penetrate their local discussions of educational reform. As they came facetoface with these contentious issues, many of our primary change agents, who admirably turned to the literature, found little to guide them. Thus, these educators struggled as they tried to use their "new and improved," yet neutral, change strategies as wedges to penetrate fierce local opposition to reforms. Most naively proceeded as if support for equity reforms would emerge if only they could provide "evidence" that detracking enhanced the achievement of struggling students without harming their traditionally successful peers. While the most savvy among them worked mightily to establish a culture that would support reform processes, few were even warned (not to mention provided with strategies) about reform-killing ideologies that support race and class exclusivity.

These educators failed to realize that intense opposition against mixing lower and higher achieving students would be influenced as much by lower achieving students' "status" in society signalled in part by physical and behavioral characteristicsas by any risk to hightrack students' opportunities and achievement (Jankowski, 1995). Lacking a real critique of their opposition, many of our change agents found it increasingly difficult to effectively challenge their disputants and to, thereby, compel deep normative changes in how their peers conceptualized issues of race and class.

## EQUITY-MINDED REFORMS CONFRONT SCHOOLS' "ZONES OF NORMATIVE AND POLITICAL MEDIATION"

To understand why these equity-minded change agents encountered such difficulty, we offer a non-neutral change framework that builds on two ideas from existing literature in the politics of education. One idea is the "zone of tolerance." The other is that of "mediating institutions." The zone of tolerance is the area within which a local community will allow policy to be changed and developed. A mediating institution is an organized social setting (e.g., a school system) that channels macro- political and economic forces into particular "sites" (e.g., individual schools) to mediate (i.e., shape, structure, and constrain) the interactions between individuals within those sites. It is in the context of these mediating institutions, then, that these larger social forces actually impact the lives of individuals (Lamphere, 1992). But, we maintain, change agents in schools require conceptual support to develop strategies that unabashedly confront the active ideologies that resist equity-minded change.

We find it helpful, then, to bridge these two ideas to expand the concept of the zone of tolerance into a new construction that we call the "zone of mediation." The zone of mediation (i.e., policy latitude) becomes shaped for any particular site (e.g., a school) as local and societal forces intersect around particular issues, including new policy proposals. As explained in more detail below, we find the "zone of normative and political mediation" and "mediating institutions" to be useful conceptual tools as we struggle to understand the difficulties faced by the ten detracking schools.

*Zone of Normative and Political Mediation.* Schools are situated in particular, local enactments of larger cultural norms, rules, values, and power relations, and these cultural forces promote either stability or change. Accordingly, they set the parameters of policy, behavior, beliefs, and actions in schools. McGivney and Moynihan (1972) introduced the concept of a "zone of tolerance" to describe the cultural boundaries within which schools operate. They define the zone of as "the latitude or maneuverability granted (or yielded) to the leadership of the schools by the local community," and use the concept to explain local resistance to reforms proceeding from conflicting social policy agendas (McGivney & Moynihan, 1972, p. 221). If policymakers or educators introduce policies that fall outside this zone, the community will object (Boyd, 1976; McGivney & Moynihan, 1972). Since schools answer to both their local communities and their larger society, these authors argue, it is not unlikely that proposed policies will fall outside this zone. This double-layered context means that the educational policy agenda may conform to norms of either the local community or the larger society, and, at times, the two may conflict. For example, national policymakers might set a more "cosmopolitan" agenda – say, the need for AIDS education – than a more parochial local community may be willing to accept.

Boyd (1976) used essentially the same definition of the zone of tolerance in his analysis of who effectively governs our schools (school boards, the public, or professional educators). He suggested that the zone of tolerance is constructed through the interaction of the particular characteristics of a local school com-munity and the type of issue or policy question faced. Consequently, each issue produces its own unique zone. Boyd further contended that issues perceived by the community to be redistributive are the most likely to produce conflict and to, therefore, "immobilize" policy makers. Boyd concluded that, even though profes-sional "educators tend to dominate local educational policy making, they usually operate within significant, and generally neglected or underestimated, constraints imposed by the *local* community and school board – not to mention those imposed by state and national forces" (Boyd, 1976, p. 572, emphasis in original).

Other scholars have presented variations on this same theme. For example,

Charters (1953) introduced the "margin of tolerance," which he described as boundaries, composed of values dear to a particular community, within which citizens of the community delegate to school personnel the freedom to educate. Similarly, Barnard (1938), Simon (1947), Bridges (1967) and Bolman and Deal (1984) describe a "zone of indifference." Barnard (1938) explained that administrators' decisions will be accepted unquestionably by subordinates if they fall within the zone. Bridges (1967) specifically applied the Barnard zone to the relationship between teachers and principals.

Our mediation zone shares many characteristics with these earlier concepts. Like McGivney and Moynihan (1972), we look to the zone to help build our understanding of the change process in its local context. Like Boyd (1976) and Bolman and Deal (1984), we believe that a community's level of indifference to an issue is a major determinant of the breadth of the zone. Finally, like each of these authors, we perceive the zone as limiting the boundaries of debate. However, our notion of a zone of mediation also differs from these earlier concepts in several important ways.

First, unlike these earlier zones, whose boundaries are defined solely by the community, the boundaries of the zone of mediation are shaped by forces originating at societal and global levels as well as forces originating in the community. We believe that each school exists within a unique context and that, while this context may be defined directly by the local community, the context is ultimately defined by a myriad of normative and political forces at the local, regional, national and global levels. All these forces interact with one another to create a zone of mediation.

Second, while the mediation zone defines the boundaries of community tolerance, it concomitantly defines the boundaries of the normative and political mediation process within schools. Moreover, the zone's boundaries are not simply set by outside forces-they are largely created by people mediating among themselves and between themselves and those outside forces. Boyd touches on this idea when he acknowledges that "persuasive and skillful [educators can use] public relations techniques [to] modify the community zone of tolerance to some degree to reduce the extent to which it constrains them" (Boyd, 1976, p. 552).

Third, while we agree with McGivney and Moynihan (1972) and Boyd (1976), who stated that the zone of tolerance is always in flux, we also envision the boundaries of the mediation zone as depending on each person's perception or standpoint. Thus, the zone changes with time and with identity and place. (For a related discussion of the zone of mediation see Welner, 1997.)

*Mediating Institutions.* While the zone of mediation helps to clarify the fact that each school is both impacted by and limited by outside structures, ideologies, and politics, the idea of "mediating institutions" helps us recognize that all of these forces are perpetually active inside the school as well. To understand how these forces operate *within* schools as well as *on* schools, it useful to view school systems as mediating institutions and individual schools as "sites of interaction" within these mediating institutions (Lamphere, 1992). According to Lamphere, mediating institutions channel larger social, economic, and political forces (i.e., forces which help create the zone of mediation) into particular sites where they impact individuals. Moreover, if we consider schools as "sites of interaction," we can more easily recognize that larger social forces have their impact as they shape, structure, and constrain the interaction among diverse groups of people who come together to work, learn, and participate within the sites. Because schools, like other mediating institutions, are formally organized settings, interactions within them are defined and limited by well-established roles and relationships. Because they are hierarchically organized settings, members of dominant groups in the community usually also hold positions of power within schools.

This "mediating" activity within "sites of interaction" explains the difficulty that schools experience when they try to navigate around outside forces. It also explains the need for change agents in these schools to confront these forces inside their institutions and inside themselves, in addition to the limited and commonly perceived challenges of convincing "them" – those outside the school. Moreover, because individuals' ways of making sense and acting sensibly are influenced by their own positions in and experiences with political, economic, and social structures, educators – especially those from dominant groups in the community – are as likely to recreate dominant structures and ideologies within schools as community members are to press for them.

*What Forces Shape the Zone of Mediation?* Cuban (1992) explains that policy making around curriculum reform involves "power, control, coalitions, bargaining, and compromise among and between groups and individuals operating inside and outside a decentralized system of governing schools" (p. 224). Among those external factors, Cuban cites (1) social movements (such as the progressive movement at the turn of the century and the changes connected with the Cold War beginning in the early 1950s); (2) legislative and judicial decisions (such as *Brown v. Board of Education*); and (3) influential groups (such as publishers, foundations, accrediting and testing agencies, and professional associations). Inside school systems, Cuban notes that groups and individuals, including students, parents, teachers, principals, curriculum specialists, and superintendents, can play significant roles in curricular change. But, he also warns that the "historical curriculum" presses school and individuals inside them to maintain curriculum stability.

These are among the many forces which combine to shape the zone. When we consider which policies and changes are within the realm of the probable or the possible in a given school or community, we consider – explicitly or implicitly, directly or indirectly – these forces. An understanding of the role played by these forces is therefore vital to an understanding of the equity-minded change process. However, we can deepen this understanding if we consider an additional force which arguably underpins most, if not all, of the factors listed by Cuban: the global political economy.

When analyzing the forces that act upon our schools and communities, we generally do not look beyond the immediate forces and ask how those forces were shaped. For example, we may speak in terms of the forces exerted by a teachers' union or a textbook publisher or a legislative body, but we are unlikely to speak in terms of the larger forces which shape those immediate forces. The global political economy constitutes one such force (see Hargreaves, 1994; Harvey, 1990; Soja, 1993; Torres, 1995; Wallerstein, 1979) and is particularly relevant to equity-minded reforms since it powerfully shapes the role and status of low-income and low-status persons within particular societies.

Scholars of political economy generally acknowledge that a global restructuring of capitalism has been occurring since the late 1960's or early 1970's (Best & Kellner, 1991; Hargreaves, 1994; Harvey, 1990; Soja, 1993). Concurrently changes have occurred concerning the role of government within core capitalist countries. Faced with the economic pressures resulting from capitalism's restructuring, powerful political actors have reduced and weakened those aspects of the government that place controls on the market and the welfare state. In particular, socalled "neoconservatives" have attacked the welfare state as a wasteful and inefficient system that interferes with the crucial free market trade that, they contend, will overcome economic crisis. Their efforts push for deregulation, decentralization, and localization of political power. Moreover, in the U.S., a large branch of liberals, dubbed "neoliberals," have joined these efforts (Torres, 1995).

Torres (1995) notes that in a liberal capitalist democracy like the U.S., the government must, on the one hand, support capitalism – because it is the dominant economy. On the other hand, such governments must also protect citizens from the inequalities that capitalism produces. Thus, capitalist countries have often spawned welfare states in reaction to inequalities that result from the economy. These welfare states tend to come under attack when their surrounding economies are in crisis, but they grow when the economy grows.[4] Importantly for our purposes, the welfare state in the U.S., public education included, is currently losing ground in its role as an oppositional force to the inequalities produced by capitalism. When government decentralizes and deregulates, private market forces penetrate into spaces once solely part of the public domain. As the welfare state shrinks, institutions such as public schools are left unprotected.

The influence of the global political economy can be seen in many of the recent reforms in education: deregulation efforts such as vouchers, open enrollment, and charter schools; decentralization of policymaking such as sitebased management; and corporate pedagogy such as cooperative learning that is geared to prepare workers for the new flexible/specialized high tech industries. Wells and Oakes (forthcoming) describe this conceptual shift to the "market metaphor" of education. Schools, confronted with the same decentralization and deregulation that is occurring in the private sector, are pressured to be efficient, competitive, and have standards and measures of excellence (quality control). Sitebased management schemes are established with the idea that teachers will better meet goals of quality. The ideal of creating a democratic citizenry has arguably been almost completely replaced by the goal of creating good entrepreneurial or corporate citizens.[5]

Schools are thus mediating sites for the influence of global capitalism into our daily lives. As schools draw the market metaphor deep into the heart of everyday activities and meanings, this metaphor (and the beliefs, values, and norms attached to it) becomes a central and dynamic feature of the schools' zone of mediation. In this sense, the local cultural politics are not "natural" conditions; they are partially shaped by previous interactions with the global political economy, among other things (Gupta & Ferguson, 1992).

Acknowledging larger forces such as the global political economy should not lead us to devalue local forces. School location and context clearly do matter. However, these factors are not separable from their own local, regional, national, and global context. When we think about the zone of mediation, we try to keep all of these factors in mind.

## DETRACKING REFORMS STRUGGLE WITHIN THE "ZONES"

Using this framework, we can better understand the struggles that the ten detracking schools experienced both with their communities and among their own faculties. First, differences among the schools' experiences make clear that the zone of normative and political mediation is defined by forces originating both in the community as well as at larger societal and global levels. For example, consider the contrast between the local "zone" around Plainview High School with that around Liberty High. Both schools functioned as sites of mediation that reproduced the status quo of power and privilege among racial and social class groups, but each adhered to quite different community norms about the form and tenor of that mediation.

More than ninety percent of Plainview's residents were white and middle-to upper-middle-class. Nevertheless, about thirty percent of the school-age population in the Plainview district attended private (religious and independent elite) schools. Most of the white families who sent their children to Plainview recognized it as a topnotch suburban high school; and the school's rigorous college-prep curriculum and its excellent extracurricular programs became a drawing card for many whites who might otherwise select private schools. Plainview High's community had little tolerance for progressive school reforms (Wells 1996). Politically they were fairly conservative, with a growing religious right contingent among the younger families. However, progressive reform was thrust upon them. In 1983, a federal court ordered Plainview and other mostly white suburban school districts to accept African-American transfer students from the city as part of an urban-suburban school desegregation plan. However, the above-mentioned award-winning activities and the most advanced college-prep courses remained racially segregated, with only a handful of African-American students participating.

This climate, which was highly adverse to risk taking, thwarted the attempts of Plainview educators to implement changes to serve African-American students. So, at the same time as reform-minded educators eliminated most of the lower track (remedial) courses in all subject areas, the number of high-track students taking Advanced Placement courses dramatically increased. The push for more AP courses cames from some white parents in the community, who voiced their concern about their children's access to competitive universities. Thus, the mantle of an irreproachable parental interest in their children's competitiveness for college admission also sustained their children's edge over, and separation from, the school's African-American students. In Plainview, then, the zone of normative and political mediation was shaped by a federal court desegregation order, institutionalized religion, and market forces, such as the availability of elite private schools and university competitiveness.

In start contrast to Plainview, Liberty City struggled openly for decades to achieve racial equality in its schools and civic life (Cooper, 1995). Led by committed, activist faculty and students at Liberty University, citizens of Liberty voluntarily undertook citywide school desegregation, detracked its most racially diverse middle school, and mounted less formal multicultural activities to acknowledge their city's extraordinary diversity. The university community and the well-to-do, mostly white families in the Liberty Hills neighborhoods were confident that the high school's stable and intellectual faculty and the college-like atmosphere would serve their children well academically, at the same time that they learned to value racial diversity. Nevertheless, educators and many community members chafed at the realization that, for all Liberty High's successes, there were equally impressive failures among its 2,500 students, and these failures were linked quite visibly to race and social class. As Principal Evan Payne put it, *If you're in the 'haves' group, it's one of the best places in America to go to high school. If you're in the 'have nots', it's like a lot of places – it's full of failure.*

Even so, Liberty High's detracked ninth grade classes were not won easily, and their future status remained tenuous. Strongly held norms and political traditions in the Liberty culture posed enormous challenges: the assumed prerogatives of powerful parents and pervasive racial stereotyping and tension that sees minority students as a threat to the Liberty image as an elite – if progressive – academic institution. Many liberal white families understood and were sympathetic to the press for detracking. In the end, however, these parents, just like the more conservative Plainview parents, balked at equity-driven policies that they feared might compromise their children's future educational advantages. As one parent told us,

> . . . people will say, "I believe in this social engineering. I believe in this experiment. I will let my kid stay in this heterogeneous class K-8. But, by the time he gets ready for college, I have got to make sure that he has had what he needs in order to be successful in college, and I don't want you to play around with my kid any longer." I think that's a bargain that a lot of people in Liberty make. . . .

To accommodate this widespread concern, Liberty limited its detracking reforms to the ninth grade.

In contrast to Plainview, Liberty's zone of mediation was shaped by the historical image of the school as an elite academic institution, a highly salient university community, as well as competition for college entrance. But at Liberty, just as at Plainview, reform managed only to raise the bottom of the tracking hierarchy without toppling the top tier, striking a delicate and locally-determined balance between change and the status quo (Wells, 1996). The contrast among the two schools points clearly to locally-constructed differences in the schools' zones of mediation around detracking.

This conceptual framework also highlights the fact that the boundaries of these mediating zones are not set only by forces outside the school. They are largely created by people interacting among themselves within schools and by those same people interacting with outside forces. For example, inside Central High School, two faculty factions struggled bitterly for control over the reform. The most active members of the "Idea Team" – white, highly experienced women teachers in their forties – worked diligently and quietly though a newly established set of "study groups" to change tracking's traditions and structures at Central. At the same time, the self-described "Good Old Boys," a group of entrenched, male teachers-most of whom had been athletic coaches at one time – loudly and staunchly defended the school's status quo, including tracking. (See Datnow, 1997.)

The gulf between the Idea Teams' conviction that all students can learn given the right opportunities and the Good Old Boys' adherence to a conventional view of intelligence was strikingly revealed by veteran Good Old Boy science teacher Walter Brown: *Some of that may just be simple intellectual ability. Some kids are just born with . . . Some kids have got it, and some kids don't.* In response to the Idea Team's interest in restructuring the school in ways that would provide more time and support to less successful students, Ted Kowals, a social studies teacher, made clear the Good Old Boys' opposition: *We do everything we can to help the low end of the scale. Why do we always want to punish the top end of the scale?* Moreover, members of the two groups placed blame for the low achievement among the schools' non-white students in very different places. Members of the Idea Team contended that the school must bear some responsibility: *. . . in the last few years everything around us has changed, except the schools, and that can't be right.* In contrast, one of the Good Old Boys countered, *I don't care what anybody tells you, it's the family structure that's causing the schools to fail.* This internal debate, even while it took place within the zone of mediation, helped to shape this same zone.

Our conceptual framework also focuses attention on how the zone of mediation at the schools depended on the perception or standpoint of different persons. Recall that the zone changes with time and with identity and place. At Rollinghills Middle School, for example, activist, reform-minded white teachers tended to blame the community for constraining detracking reform. According to one such Rollinghills teacher, *You could very often read into the conversation that they [the community] had their own agenda that wasn't about instruction. That agenda was about racially integrated classrooms and personal biases.* Another told us, *Part of their agenda is 'I want a challenging academic program for my child,' but part of the agenda is that it can't be that way if there are twelve black children in the classroom with them.* However, one of their African-American teacher colleagues saw things quite differently. She believed that some Rollinghills teachers were also a source of significant resistance,

> We have members of the faculty . . . who have a mindset – and I know this for a fact from racist remarks that teachers make – that we [African Americans] are not capable of performing at a high academic level. . . . I think they're comfortable as long as the ratio of African Americans in the classroom is kept very low. . . .

A teacher who perceives part of the faculty as contributing to the resistance to the reform is likely to view the zone of mediation quite differently than a teacher who sees that resistance as coming only from the outside.

Complicating matters further at Rollinghills, the external reform context included activist African-American community groups that monitored closely the implementation and impact of school reform. However, these community groups differed considerably in what they viewed as reasonable reform goals in a city deeply divided by two decades of court-ordered desegregation and racial tension. Partly this difference in viewpoint was a function of generational differences between the two groups. One, a highly organized, racially-mixed group, Vision, active since the late 1960s, focused its attention – and that of the city's major newspaper – on tracking's segregative impact and supported detracking as a reasonable alternative for the city's schools. In contrast, a small, but also well-organized group, Rescue, comprised of mostly younger African-American clergy and community leaders-including some of the sons and daughters of Vision's African-American members – had abandoned hope that even the city's liberal whites would ever support desegregated schools that benefited African-American children. They pressed instead for high-quality, if racially separate, schools in African-American neighborhoods.

Finally, the conceptual framework helps us see how the current condition of the global political economy influenced the shape of reform at the schools. Our schools, confronted with the same decentralization and deregulation that is occurring in the private sector, were pressured to appeal to the most privileged segment of their "consumers" with demonstrable evidence of their efficiency, competitiveness, and excellence (see Wells and Oakes, forthcoming, for a fuller treatment of this issue). This press often conflicted with schools' detracking efforts. So, for example, Plainview's principal argued that touting students' high AP scores was essential to keeping the school competitive with private schools, despite the philosophical clash between the school's broader reform effort and the specialized, test-prep curriculum of AP classes. He told us, *I guarantee you private schools aren't scrapping AP. I am competing with private schools, and I've got to have those kids.* Likewise, at Explorer Middle School, district administrators pressed teachers to keep the separate challenge classes for "gifted students" as a way to maintain public confidence in the school.

At Bearfield Middle School, high scores on the state achievement test were the currency that bought the school a zone of mediation in which detracking advocates could operate. When Bearfield's test scores suffered a slight drop in some subject areas, the change was noticed immediately by vocal members of Bearfield's white community who began questioning the school's "excellence." In response, the superintendent expressed his displeasure with what he called Bearfield's *touchy-feely* approach, and he pressured the principal, Ben McCall, to focus on issues of *learning* and *academic excellence.* McCall, increasingly on the defensive, summed up his goals for the next academic year with*, We gotta get the test scores up. Gotta get those test scores up."* English teacher Beth Fleming recalled,

> [T]hey were riding Ben last year. We could feel it when we came back to school this year that the stress was there. . . . And we spent so much of this year worrying about tests, standardized tests. You know . . . it's unfortunate. It's unfortunate because that's not what we're about, and that's not what we should be about.

## REFRAMING THE CHANGE LITERATURE TO BETTER ACCOUNT FOR EQUITY-MINDED REFORMS

The above discussion of zones of mediation and of mediating institutions demonstrates the complex forces that influenced the schools in our study when reforms threatened to redistribute precious resources and renegotiate the meaning of high-status culture. As important, this discussion demonstrates the need for a reframing of the change literature to better account for the course these equity-minded reforms followed. We will now consider some specific ways the change literature might be modified in light of this new perspective (see Welner, 1997 for a more complete discussion).

*Top-down mandates.* The change literature generally advocates a strong bottom-up component as a precondition for successful reform, downplaying the role of top-down mandates. However, the zone of mediation highlights the importance of top-down mandates as a tool to re-shape the zone. Bottom-up, equity-minded reform efforts simply could not survive in many schools unless the zone of mediation is first made more receptive – and top-down mandates are sometimes the only feasible means of radically shifting the zone.

Consider the example of an African-American child placed in a remedial track. This child arguably owes her predicament, in part, to the indirect influence of negative societal normative beliefs about race and intelligence. These beliefs help to shape the zone of mediation in which her school operates and help to form the foundation of this tracking system. What happens if a top-down mandate to detrack is overlaid on this child's school? We know from the change literature that the mandate is unlikely to be implemented as planned. Site-level forces will probably resist the external pressure for change and will try to marginalize the reform by making it a superficial add-on to the existing school culture and school structures. However, this mandate would also, we predict, help to shift the zone of mediation at this school such that those supporting detracking reform would now be much less marginalized. Thus, while it is true that we may not be able to ascertain in advance the ultimate impact of the mandate on the school, this mandate would nonetheless – even given imperfect implementation-still be a positive force in the direction of greater equity (Welner & Oakes, 1996).

This example also demostrates that top-down and bottom-up reforms need not be view as dichotomous. If a hypothetical teacher at this school had wanted to move her school toward detracking, she would have (before the mandate) been told by her fellow teachers that they like the present tracked system and have no interest in change. After the top-down mandate, however, this teacher and others at the school site (and community) level, who before were unable to mount an effective reform effort, can confidently move forward with their *bottom-up* ideas. The opponents of detracking may persist in their opposition, but their strategic position has been moved by the court. The zone has shifted to bring the fringe closer to the center (see Thompson, 1984 for an elaborated discussion of this point).

Thus, we question the axiom that successful policy makers set the conditions for effective administration but refrain from predetermining how those decisions will be made and, instead, charge local practitioners with the development of solutions (Elmore & McLaughlin, 1988; Firestone & Corbett, 1989). The bottom-up focus of the change literature looks to local educators and community members as the primary generators of school change. However, at the local level, equity issues rarely emerge as primary concerns of the political majority. As a result, decentralization of policymaking authority to these local communities may lead to a severe neglect of the equity concerns of the politically less powerful (Elmore, 1993). Under normal circumstances, "local elites" can (and often do) block reforms which they perceive as grounded in values different from their own (Fullan, 1991; Wells & Serna, 1996).

History has shown that more central authorities are sometimes able to advance equity policy goals to a much greater extent than local authorities (Peterson, 1981). Some local schools are unwilling or unable to solve some equity-minded problems, and, in such cases, central authorities are more likely to be successful (Wise, 1982). Thus, community resistance to practices perceived by politically powerful local residents as harmful to their personal interests (i.e., those perceived as substantively redistributive policies) usually will require top-down mandates and monitoring (Peterson, 1981).

These researchers point to what can be termed an "equity exception" to the general recommendations against strong reliance on top-down mandates requiring specific changes. This exception arises because equity-minded reforms differ from other reforms in kind, not merely in magnitude. A central policy-making body desiring to promote an equity reform would, for example, be ill-advised to merely set forth some general equity principles, because resistance and political opposition by local elites would undermine any anticipated bottom-up aspect to the reform. Instead, the central body must craft a more specific mandate, sufficient to substantially shift the zone of mediation and thereby to overcome such local resistance. As Boyd (1989) has explained, we need a balanced approach to educational improvement using elements of top-down and bottom-up reform judiciously, "according to the characteristics and needs of the given policy problem" (Boyd, 1989, p. 517).

*Mutual Adaptation.* The neutrality of the change literature also becomes problematic when we attempt to apply it to the nuts and bolts of implementation. This literature largely fails to acknowledge the normative foundation of many inequitable policies, and, as we have seen, it advises a neutral process of changing those policies that fail to confront those beliefs. But if reforms are not grounded in a critique of norms and politics, they will likely be disappointing.

As another example of the difficulties we encounter if we try to apply extant change theory to equity-minded reforms, consider Berman and McLaughlin's (1978) well-known finding about mutual adaptation. Variability, they say, is both inevitable and desirable. They tell us that the most successful reforms come about when both the project (reform) and the setting (school) are changed. Following this logic, Tyack and Cuban (1995) advise that policymakers should not design reforms to be implemented as planned, but rather view their plans as "hypotheses" that will be transformed as they are implemented.

However, if the project or plan is an equity-minded reform, the adaptation that occurs as the reform makes its way into the pre-existing school culture will almost always be in the direction of less equity. In other words, the pressures from the school and the community are likely to favor the dominant societal actors (the local elites) at the expense of the reforms' beneficiaries (Apple, 1993; Popkewitz, 1991; Wells & Oakes, 1996; Wells & Serna, 1996). Looked at from this perspective, variability and mutual adaptation can be enemies of equity-minded reform. The greater the variability and the greater the adaptation, the less that will be accomplished for those in the greatest need (see Huberman & Miles, 1984).[6]

*Third Order Changes.* Unfortunately, the unique status of equity-minded reforms has not been recognized in the models we use to think about change. Cuban (1992), for instance, distinguishes only between changes of different magnitudes in his two-part typology for educational change. Changes which simply improve the efficiency and effectiveness of current practices are categorized as "first-order" or "incremental" changes, and those changes which seek to alter the basic ways that organizations function are "second-order" or "fundamental" changes (Cuban, 1992).

Perhaps it would be helpful to consider equity-minded reforms such as detracking as "third-order changes," defined as fundamental changes which also seek to reform core normative beliefs about race, class, intelligence, and educability held by educators and others involved with our schools. By so expanding Cuban's model, we highlight the need to think about equity-minded reforms as different in kind from their less factious cousins.

In considering this idea of third-order changes, keep in mind our earlier discussion of the forces that combine to help shape the zone of normative and political mediation. Given these forces both inside and outside the school, school reform can be understood as divisible along different lines than those drawn by Cuban. Some reforms can be viewed as efforts to improve how schools carry out their work in areas that do not actually challenge the larger, external forces. These changes would include most school improvement efforts aimed at "effectiveness" i.e., new curricula and restructuring. (While most of such reforms would be classified by Cuban as first-order changes, some may fall within the scope of second-order changes.)

A second class of reforms can be viewed as efforts to fundamentally renegotiate the terms of the mediation with the external forces. These reforms involve an attempted alteration of the impact of the larger forces on particular groups of individuals and families; they challenge those larger forces. This conceptual model helps us understand why equity-minded reforms demand different adoption and implementation strategies than most other reforms. These third-order changes can be thought of as those changes which most directly oppose and confront the prevailing external forces and which, therefore, most often fall outside the zone of mediation.

## INQUIRY FOR EQUITY-MINDED REFORMERS: PROMISING NON-NEUTRAL DIRECTIONS

Change theorists' and researchers' desire to adopt a neutral stance is somewhat understandable. Most successful change is viewed as pragmatic and politically savvy. When speaking of change, most are ever-mindful of the conventional wisdom that garnering a much needed "buy-in" requires that reformers don't offend. Consequently, researchers and change agents find themselves in wholly unfamiliar territory: Whites usually squirm at the sound of the "r-word"; mid-to-high income researchers feel a hidden guilt when discussing issues of poverty; men hesitate to talk about gender issues; and only the bravest few traverse the taboo grounds of sexual orientation. Even in some of our best efforts, we huddle behind allinclusive and nonspecific words like "equity", "diversity", and "heterogeneity" – words that, without greater explication, may become little more than "window dressing for the same old beliefs and practices" (Oakes, 1995, p. 3). We, too, are inevitably constrained by the zones of normative and political mediation that bound education research. Consequently, equity-minded reformers must fend these issues for themselves.

Left standing in a theoretical vacuum, a few reform leaders at each school were able to begin deconstructing the hidden ideologies driving their opposition and to operate accordingly. These educators were able to unmask their opposition, often because they held particular standpoints (Harding, 1993; Banks, 1994) making them acutely aware that rational thought alone did not drive detracking's opposition – nonrational "symbolic politics" also played a role (Sears & Funk, 1991). These educators, often because of past experiences, and sometimes because of their own social status, had reached a level of "individual consciousness," enabling them to interpret their situation differently and allowing for a more penetrating critique of their opposition (Hill Collins, 1991).

Jane Griffen, Rollinghills Middle School's assistant principal who counseled the school's most alienated youngsters, often visited the South Side homes of the school's bussed-in African-American students. Because Griffen believed that most discipline problems derived from these students' separate and often inferior school learning opportunities, she chafed at the white community's efforts to exclude the school's African-American students from the higher level classes,

> Part of my responsibility is to be respectful, but I have a hard time dealing with a racist. . . Sometimes I want to say [to white parents] ". . . you dare to sit there and put down children who may not have all the advantages that your child has but who are here working despite their disadvantages. You're sitting here telling me that they are not worthy to be in class with your child." This is a real personal issue with me.

And Ben McCall at Bearfield told us,

> Detracking could fail because those coming from the "innate intelligence" perspective really believe that it's in the best interests of kids to be separated by some sort of perceived cognitive ability. We all know that that's been a masquerade sometimes for institutional racism and classism . . .

*and*

> The struggle is not about Blacks; it's about us. It's about what we as humanity will to each other and will tolerate. That's why I get passionate about this stuff, I get excited about this stuff. This is where it's at.

However, even these educators who had moved beyond a neutral perspective of reform have few tools to help them consider what their critique implies for the reform process.

Little has been done toward developing particular strategies for equity-minded change. However, some promising beginnings do exist in scholarship on the moral purposes of schools and teaching and on critical inquiry as a route to realizing those moral purposes in democratic societies. We briefly introduce these ideas here.

One line of potentially helpful work begins to frame teaching and school change as a moral, rather than technical, enterprise. Goodlad and his colleagues' study of teacher education highlights schools' unique moral responsibility of enculturating all of the young into a political democracy (Goodlad, 1990). This charge requires a commitment to social justice and caring, as well as knowledge and competence (Sirotnik, 1990). Teaching and organizational planning become moral decisions. Moreover, as both Sirotnik (1990) and Fullan (1993) emphasize, while individual commitments and actions are essential, the moral commitments of schooling must also be institutional imperatives that "go to the very heart of the moral ecology of the organization itself." (Sirotnik, 1990, p. 298ff).

While this work does not suggest particular strategies for accomplishing equity-minded changes, it does help establish a non-neutral standard or grounding for educators' reform decisions. This moral grounding may bolster educators when their efforts to enact equity-minded change is inconsistent with majority preferences in their schools and communities. It provides principled arguments for seeing equity issues as a "special case" that may – unlike more technical reforms- justify or require mandates.

Another strand of work is located in the so-called "critical" tradition not typically considered part of the school change literature. However, it may provide a theoretical head-start toward ways educators might come to understand and grapple more systematically with equity-minded reforms within their schools' zones of mediation. This line of work distinguishes itself from more mainstream work on change in its refusal to see change as neutral. Scholars in the critical tradition are intensely interested not only in the process of change per se – e.g., whether teachers have time to think, talk, and plan together-but on the substance of what those discussions are about. Accordingly, if changes are to be more than a mere refinement of the status quo – in terms of fundamental school goals and norms – then the status quo needs to be critically examined as part of the change process, so that very different ideas will begin making sense to site-level educators.

In work around the idea of "critical inquiry," Sirotnik and Oakes (1986, 1990) posit that through a site-based critical inquiry process, educators bent on reform can more systematically come to understand and critique deeply held beliefs and ideologies about intelligence, racial differences, social stratification, white supremacy, and elite privilege as powerful forces to be reckoned with inside and outside of schools. The need to delve deeply into these contentious issues is pushed even further by a group of social theorists doing work sometimes identified as "post-colonial" (hooks, 1992; West, 1993). These scholars-writing both inside and outside the realm of education – tell us that social constructions such as race and class are not simply elements of society that are more pronounced in some institutions than others, but that these elements actually help constitute our personal, societal, national, and international worlds (West, 1995).

The proposition underlying this critical stance is that an active and forthright confrontation of these beliefs would greatly enhance the ability of the school actors to overcome obstacles such as those we witnessed in our study. For example, participants in critical inquiry continually remind themselves that the problems they face have a current and historical context and that routine problems of schooling – using time effectively, staff communication, grouping students for instruction, and the like – must be situated in these contexts in order to be understood. What are we doing now? and How did it come to be that way? are questions that help frame this discussion. Such critical inquiry also asks participants to recognize and contend with embedded values and human interests in school practices, by asking "Whose interests are (and are not) being served by the ways things are?"

A critical perspective on change also demands that knowledge of all types – results of research, newly developed professional practices, participants' own experiences – be brought to bear upon matters under discussion. Moreover, new information can be produced in the context of the inquiry through the use of surveys, interviews, observations, document analyses, and other tools. The central question here is, "What information and knowledge do we have (or need to get) that bear upon the issues?"

Sirotnik, Heckman, and others argue that critical inquiry is based on the premise that fundamental, democratic change is possible when people are accountable to each other, express themselves authentically, and negotiate common understandings that support collective action (Sirotnik & Oakes, 1986, 1990; Heckman, 1995; Heckman, Confer, & Peacock, 1995). As Sirotnik (1995) notes, "participants must continually remind themselves that all is not talk; that, notwithstanding the omnipresent ambiguity in educational organizations like schools, actions can and must be taken, reviewed, revised, retaken, reviewed . . ." The questions to ask at every opportunity are "Is this the way we want things to be?" and "What are we going to do about it?" While critical inquiry was not widely employed or even considered by most of the change agents in the detracking schools, its power is clearly evident in the words of one of Central's teachers who shared how dialogue and soul searching related to the larger macro-societal issues enabled them to push the school's zone of normative and political mediation around detracking:

> We need to start thinking about the students and the parents and the people we serve and in the larger sense of the world . . . We can see the turmoil and the strife and the process that the world is taking and who better than a group of people who can deal with the academic education . . . who better to create an internal world structure that should be the model for the external world
>
> (Datnow, 1995, p. 41).

As a radical "bottom-up" strategy, a critical approach may prove to be a helpful accompaniment to mandates that force schools to conform to principles of equity and fairness. However, efforts to explore the promise of a more critical and moral stance toward change remains in its infancy, and far more theorizing and research is needed on its problems and possibilities. In particular, the power of such an approach to reshape the zone of mediation – for good or for ill – has not been tackled systematically.

Certainly, research will never identify a single approach to change – even critical inquiry – as a "silver bullet" for equity-minded reform. However, educators would benefit from the provision of a wide range of ideas and strategies, including critical inquiry, top-down mandates and resources, and more efficacious ways to work with less powerful school constituents. What is nonetheless clear is that these different approaches must be as part of a consistent theme: the non-neutral context of equity-minded reforms requires that change agents employ strategies that directly address the inevitable normative and political resistance they will encounter.

## ENDNOTES

[1]   Typically, we think of such reforms in the U.S. as those benefiting African-Americans, Latinos, and the poor. However, we extend this category to include women, gays, and those that schools identify as of lower ability.

[2]   This study was funded by the Lilly Endowment. Jeannie Oakes and Amy Stuart Wells were the co-principal investigators. Research associates were Robert Cooper, Amanda Datnow, Diane Hirshberg, Martin Lipton, Karen Ray, Irene Serna, Estella Williams, and Susie Yonezawa. For details about the study's methodology and approach, see Oakes and Wells, 1995.

[3] At three of our schools with significant language-minority populations, language was also used as a proxy linking race with intelligence.
[4] See Oakes 1986, for a analyses of such forces in post-World War II education policy in the U.S..
[5] See Hargreaves (1994) for a rare example in the change literature of linking the global political economy to the local culture of schools.
[6] Please see Welner (1997) for a more complete critique of the change literature's treatment of mutual adaptation.

# REFERENCES

Apple, M. W. (1993). *Official knowledge: Democratic education in a conservative age.* New York: Routledge.
Barnard, C. (1938). *The functions of the executive.* Cambridge, MA: Harvard University Press.
Berman, P., & McLaughlin, M. W. (1978). *Federal programs supporting educational change: Implementing and Sustaining Innovations* (Vol. VIII). Santa Monica, California: RAND Corporation.
Banks, J. (1995). The historical reconstruction of knowledge about race: Implications for transformative teaching. *Educational Researcher*, 24(2), 15–25.
Best, S., & Kellner, D. (1991). In search of the postmodern. In S. Best & D. Kellner (Eds.), *Postmodern theory: Critical interrogations* (pp. 1–33). New York: The Guilford Press.
Bolman, L. G., & Deal, T. E. (1984). *Modern approaches to understanding and managing organizations.* San Francisco: Jossey-Bass.
Boyd, W. L. (1976). The public, the professionals, and educational policy making: Who governs? *Teachers College Record*, 77, 539–577.
Boyd, W. L. (1989). Policy analysis, educational policy, and management: Through a glass darkly? In N. Boyan (Ed.), *Handbook of research on educational administration* (pp. 510–522). New York: Macmillan.
Bridges, E. (1967). A model for shared decision making in the school principalship. *Educational Administration Quarterly*, 3(1), 49–61.
Brown v. Board of Education. (1954). 347 U.S., 483.
Charters, W. W., Jr. (1953). Social class analysis and the control of public education. *Harvard Educational Review*, 24(4), 268–283.
Cooper, R. (1995). *Liberty high school.* Los Angeles: Research for Democratic School Communities, UCLA Graduate School of Education & Information Studies.
Cuban, L. (1992). Curriculum stability and change. In P. Jackson (Ed.), *Handbook of research on curriculum* (pp. 216–247). New York: Macmillan.
Datnow, A. (1995). *Central high school.* Los Angeles: Research for Democratic School Communities, UCLA Graduate School of Education & Information Studies.
Datnow, A. (1997). Using gender to preserve tracking's status hierarchy: The defensive strategy of entrenched teachers. *Anthropology & Education Quarterly*, 28(2), 1–26.
Elmore, R. F. (1983). Complexity and control: What legislators and administrators can do about implementing public decisions. *Political Science Quarterly*, 94(4), 601–616.
Elmore, R. F. (1993). School decentralization: Who gains? Who loses? In J. Hannaway & M. Carnoy (Eds.), *Decentralization and school improvement: Can we fulfill the promise?* (pp. 33–54). San Francisco: Jossey-Bass Publishers.
Elmore, R. F., & McLaughlin, M. W. (1988). *Steady work: Policy, practice, and the reform of American education.* Santa Monica: RAND.
Firestone, W. & Corbett, H. D. (1989). Planned organizational change. In N. Boyan (Ed.), *Handbook of research on educational administration* (pp. 321–340). New York: Macmillan.
Fullan, M. G. (1991). *The new meaning of educational change.* New York: Teachers College Press.
Fullan, M. G. (1993). *Change forces: Probing the depths of educational reform.* London: Falmer Press.
Fullan, M. G. (1994). Coordinating top-down and bottom-up strategies for educational reform. In R. Elmore & S. Fuhrman (Ed.), *The governance of curriculum. The 1994 ASCD yearbook* (pp, 186–202). Alexandria, Virginia: ASCD.
Goodlad, J. I. (1990). *Teachers for our nations schools.* San Francisco: Jossey Bass.
Gupta, A., & Ferguson, J. (1992). Beyond "culture": Space, identity, and the politics of difference. *Cultural Anthropology*, 7(1), 6–23.

304   *Oakes*

Hargreaves, A. (1994). *Changing teachers, changing times: Teachers' work and culture in the postmodern age*. New York: Teachers College Press.
Harding, S. (1993). Rethinking standpoint epistemology: "What is strong objectivity?" In L. Alcoff & E. Potter (Eds.), *Feminist epistemologies*. New York: Routledge.
Harvey, D. (1990). *The condition of postmodernity*. Cambridge, MA: Blackwell Publishers.
Heckman, P. (1995). *The courage to change*. Newbury Park, CA: Corwin Press.
Heckman, P., Confer, C., & Peacock, C. (1995) A demonstration of democracy: The education and community change project. In J. Oakes & K. Quartz (Eds.), *Creating new educational communities*. Yearbook of the National Society for the Study of Education. Chicago: University of Chicago Press
Hill-Collins, P. (1991). *Black feminist thought: Knowledge, consciousness, and the politics of empowerment*. New York: Routledge, Chapman, and Hall, Inc.
Hirshberg, D. (1996). *Explorer middle school*. Los Angeles: Research for Democratic School Communities, UCLA Graduate School of Education & Information Studies.
Hochschild, J. L. (1984). *The new American dilemma: Liberal democracy and school desegregation*. New Haven, CT: Yale University Press,
hooks, B. (1992). *Black looks: Race and representation*. Boston, MA: South End Press.
Huberman, M., & Miles, M. (1984). *Innovation up close: How school improvement works*. New York: Plenum.
Jankowski, M. S. (1995). The rising significance of status in U.S. race relations. In M. P. Smith & J. Feagin (Eds.), *The bubblingcauldron: Race, ethnicity, and the urban crisis*. Minneapolis, MN: University of Minnesota Press.
Lamphere, L. (1992). Introduction: The shaping of diversity. In L. Lamphere (Ed.) *Structuring diversity: Ethnographic perspectives on the new immigration* (pp. 1–34). Chicago: University of Chicago Press.
Louis, K. S., & Miles, M. B. (1990). *Improving the urban high school*. New York: Teachers College Press.
McGivney, J. H., & Moynihan, W. (1972). School and community. *Teachers College Press*, **74**(2), 317–356.
McLaughlin, M. W. (1976). Implementing a mutual adaptation: Change in classroom organization. *Teachers College Press*, **77**(3), 339–351.
Mann, D. (Ed.). (1978). *Making change happen?* New York: Teachers' College Press.
Oakes, J. (1992). Can tracking research inform practice? Technical, normative, and political considerations. *Educational Researcher*, **21**(4), 12–22.
Oakes, J. (1995). *Rollinghills middle school*. Los Angeles: Research for Democratic School Communities, UCLA Graduate School of Education & Information Studies.
Oakes, J., & Wells, A. S. (1991). *Beyond sorting and stratification: Creating alternatives to tracking in racially mixed secondary schools*. Research proposal.
Oakes, J., Wells, A., Datnow, A., & Jones, M. (1997). Detracking: The social construction of ability, cultural politics and resistance to reform. *Teachers College Record*.
Oakes, J., Yonezawa, S., & Wells, A. S. (1996). *Race, class, and change agentry: Lesson from detracking schools*. New York: Paper presented at the Annual Meeting of the American Educational Research Association, 1996.
Peterson, P. E. (1981). *City limits*. Chicago: Univ. of Chicago Press.
Popkewitz, T. S. (1991). *A political sociology of educational reform: power/knowledge in teaching, teacher education, and research*. New York: Teachers College Press.
Sarason, S. (1982). *The culture of the school and the problem of change* (2nd ed.). Boston: Allyn & Bacon.
Sarason, S. (1990). *The predictable failure of educational reform*. San Francisco: Jossey-Bass.
Simon, H. A. (1947). *Administrative behavior*. New York: Macmillan.
Sirotnik, K. (1995). Personal communication.
Sirotnik, K. (1990). Society, schooling, teaching, and preparing to teach. In J. I. Goodlad, R. Sodor, & K. Sirotnik (Eds.), *The moral dimensions of teaching*. San Francisco: Jossey Bass, pp. 296–327.
Sirotnik, K., & Oakes, J. (1986). Critical inquiry. In K. Sirotnik & J. Oakes (Eds.), *Critical perspectives on the organization and improvement of schooling*. Boston: Klewer.
Soja, E. W. (1993). Postmodern geographies and the critique of historicism. In J. P. J. III, W. Natter, & T. R. Schatzki (Eds.), *Postmodern contentions: epochs, politics, space*, (pp. 113–36). New York: The Guilford Press.
Thompson, F. J. (1984). Policy implementation and overhead control. In G. C. Edwards, III (Ed.), *Public policy implementation*. Greenwich, CT: JAI Press.

Torres, C. A. (1995). State and education revisited: Why educational researchers should think politically about education. *Review of Research in Education*, **21**, 255-331.

Tyack, D., & Cuban, L. (1995). *Tinkering toward utopia*. Cambridge, Massachusetts: Harvard University Press.

Wallerstein, I. (1979). *The capitalist world-economy*. New York: Cambridge University Press.

Weick, K. E. (1976). Educational organizations as loosely coupled systems. *Administrative Science Quarterly*, **21**, 1-19.

Wells, A. S. (1996). *Plainview high school*. Los Angeles: Research for Democratic School Communities, UCLA Graduate School of Education & Information Studies.

Wells, A. S., & Oakes, J. (in press). Tracking, detracking, and the politics of educational reform: A sociological perspective. In C. A. Torres (Ed.), *Emerging issues in the sociology of education: Comparative perspectives*. Albany, NY: SUNY Press.

Wells, A. S., & Serna, I. (1996). The politics of culture: Understanding local political resistance to detracking in racially mixed schools. *Harvard Educational Review*, **66**(1), 93-118.

Welner, K. (1997). *Mandating equity: Rethinking the educational change literature as applied to equity-minded reforms*. Ph.D. dissertation, UCLA.

Welner, K. & Oakes, J. (1996). (Li)Ability grouping: The new susceptibility of school tracking systems to legal challenges. *Harvard Educational Review*, **66**(3), 451-470.

West, C. (1993). *Race matters*. Boston, MA: Beacon Press.

Wilson, W. J. (1987). *The truly disadvantaged*. Chicago: The University of Chicago Press.

Wise, A. (1977). Why educational policies often fail: The hyperrationalization hypothesis. *Curriculum Studies*, **9**, 43-57.

Wise, A. (1982). *Legislated learning: The bureaucratization of the American classroom* (2nd ed.). Berkeley, CA: University of California Press.

Yonezawa, S. (1995). *Bearfield middle school*. Los Angeles: Research for Democratic School Communities, UCLA Graduate School of Education & Information Studies.

# Restructuring Schools for Improving Teaching

MARK A. SMYLIE

*University of Illinois at Chicago*

GEORGE S. PERRY, JR.

*University of Illinois at Chicago*

*This chapter focuses on the complicated relationship between school restructuring and the improvement of classroom teaching. The analysis examines the causal mechanisms linking restructuring and classroom change, reviews empirical research on the impact of restructuring of teaching, and concludes with an assessment of the potential for improving instruction.*

Since the mid-1980s, much of educational change has been about school "restructuring." Restructuring emerged, in large part, as a critical response to the regulatory reforms that preceded it. These earlier reforms targeted existing structures and practices and sought to make them better through prescription, intensification, and control (Rowan, 1990). To critics, these reforms were inadequate and wrongheaded. In their view, the system itself was fatally flawed and trying to improve it better would make little meaningful difference. To them, the system required a major overhaul – a restructuring (Murphy, 1990).

While plausible arguments exist that school restructuring can improve teaching and learning, there is not much empirical evidence to support them. Scholars point to a "slippery and unreliable" relationship between changing structures and improving teaching (Elmore 1995a; Murphy, 1993). Structure certainly matters. It presents opportunities for and impediments to teaching and learning. At the same time, changing structures is not synonymous with changing the beliefs, knowledge, and skills that undergird teachers' instructional practice. As Newmann and Wehlage (1995) contend, the effectiveness of any restructuring initiative depends on how well it organizes and develops these capacities.

This chapter focuses on the complicated relationship between school restructuring and the improvement of classroom teaching. Our analysis begins with an overview of the logic of restructuring and a close look at the causal mechanisms that could link restructuring to classroom change. It proceeds to a review of empirical research on the impact of restructuring on teaching and concludes with an assessment of the potential of restructuring for improving instruction. Before we begin, we look briefly at some of the characteristics of the literature.

*M. Fullan (ed.), Fundamental Change, 306-335.*
© 2005 *Springer. Printed in the Netherlands.*

## CHARACTERISTICS OF THE LITERATURE

The literature on school restructuring is relatively young but expanding rapidly. Its growth is illustrated vividly in the listings of the Educational Research Information Clearinghouse (ERIC). A general search of these listings reveals 2,100 papers, articles, and technical reports written on school restructuring between 1986 and mid-1996. Over 80 percent of this literature has been produced since 1990.

Despite its growth, the literature on restructuring is limited in several ways. First, most of it is descriptive and promotional of particular programs or elements of restructuring. It pays little attention to variation in implementation or outcomes and is typically atheoretical, providing little insight into why initiatives may achieve their objectives. Second, much of the research consists of cross-sectional studies of initiatives in their early stages of implementation. Very little longitudinal research exists. Finally, much of the empirical research considered part of the restructuring literature is not about restructuring at all. A substantial portion of it focuses on extant organizational conditions of schools, often associated with restructuring agendas. Another portion of the research examines new schools established around particular pedagogical principles and organizational structures. Studies of new schools or of extant conditions are not about change. They do not consider going from one organizational form to another. In fact, very little research to date has examined directly the processes of consequences of changing organizational structures.

Our review focuses on a relatively small subset of the literature which consists of systemic investigations of organizational restructuring and classroom teaching. By systemic investigations, we mean original empirical research characterized by (a) an identifiable, orienting question for inquiry, (b) a specified methodology, (c) collection of original data, and (d) efforts to address issues of validity and reliability (see Malen, Ogawa, & Kranz, 1990). We focus primarily on studies of changes in school organization and their relationships to teaching. Where relevant, we draw upon studies of extant organizational conditions as well as studies of newly-created schools. While these studies do not provide direct evidence of the effects of structural change, they do provide some useful insights. Our selection of literature is not exhaustive, however, it represents the primary works on the subject.

## THE LOGIC OF RESTRUCTURING

The concept of restructuring has deep historical roots, but no consensus has formed around its meaning (Tyack, 1990). To many scholars, restructuring encompasses changes in structural elements of school organization, including roles and rules that define working relationships among professional staff, administrators, students, and parents; authority relations and governance; and connections between the school and its environment (Kahne, Goren, & Amsler,

1991). Other scholars add that restructuring goes beyond altering structures to rethinking the basic values and assumptions that underlie them (David, Purkey, & White, 1987).

While restructuring means different things to different people, its espoused goals are to enhance organizational performance and productivity. While restructuring can be pursued for political or economic reasons, most observers agree that its ultimate purpose is to improve teaching and student learning (Newmann & Wehlage, 1995). But how is school restructuring to achieve this ultimate purpose?

The logic of restructuring is grounded in an assumption that the problems of education can be ascribed to the basic structure of schooling. Restructuring's advocates point to a litany of organizational problems that compromise teaching and student learning (Sirotnik, 1986). This litany includes bureaucratic governance, isolation of schools to families and communities, fragmentation of services, insufficient support of teachers' work, inadequate standards and accountability mechanisms, and inappropriate groupings of students and allocations of time for instruction. If these and other structural elements are the primary sources of our problems, the logic goes, it makes sense to develop programs and policies to alter them. Restructuring rests fundamentally on a belief in the power of organizational structure over human behavior. This belief asserts that organizing schools differently will cause teachers to teach more effectively. Restructuring will introduce new teaching practices and remove organizational barriers to their implementation. When teaching improves, student learning will increase.

This logic projects a path between school-level restructuring and classroom teaching that is long, complex, and loosely-linked (Murphy, 1991). It says little about how restructuring may lead to changes in teacher behavior. It does not explain why changes in certain aspects of school organization might lead to improved teaching.

## THE DRIVERS OF RESTRUCTURING

Miles (1993) argues that the effectiveness of reforms depends on the efficacy of their underlying functional mechanisms, what he calls "engines" or "drivers." To understand what the drivers of restructuring might be, we start at the level of the teacher and consider the organizational mechanisms that might affect a teacher's practice. We posit that three types of mechanisms may influence classroom teaching: (a) controls; (b) incentives; and (c) learning opportunities (Smylie, 1994). Theory and research on these mechanisms are extensive and offer many different and sometimes inconsistent perspectives. For this analysis, we define controls as mechanisms that seek to compel individual action through some external source (Katz & Kahn, 1978). Incentives seek to motivate and promote specific voluntary actions (Deci, Vallerand, Pelletier, & Ryan, 1991). Learning opportunities aim to develop knowledge and skills that may lead to new behavior (Merriam & Caffarella, 1991).

*Control Mechanisms*

One way that school restructuring might affect teaching is through new bureaucratic and professional-cultural controls. These include goal structuring, new authority relationships, specification of work roles and activities, and new systems of accountability. Because of the largely nonroutine, autonomous, context-specific nature of teaching, bureaucratic controls are considered largely inappropriate and ineffective in school settings (Bucher & Stelling, 1980). They can be influential, however, when focused and applied intensively (Rowan, 1990).

More effective forms of control in schools are professional and normative (Etzioni, 1964). Influence is more likely to be exercised through "face-to-face" interactions, organizational symbols, and collective negotiations than through standard work rules, procedures, and accountability systems (Blankenship, 1980). Even these forms of control may lack potency. Their effectiveness depends on communication and normative cues and their potential to influence is weakened in settings, such as schools, that are characterized by low rates of interaction among employees (Bacharach & Aiken, 1976; Little, 1990).

*Incentives*

Restructuring may introduce a variety of incentives to motivate change in teacher behavior. The primary issue is whether these incentives are actually motivational. One of the most widely accepted theories of motivation in work is the job characteristics model (Hackman & Oldham, 1980). This model postulates that the motivating potential of work is associated with experienced meaningfulness of the job, responsibility for work outcomes, and knowledge of how effectively a person is performing his or her job. These psychological states are related to core job characteristics. Skill variety, task identity, and task significance are thought to promote experienced meaningfulness of work. Autonomy and feedback in work promote knowledge of and responsibility for results.

Among the many factors that affect motivation, individual autonomy or self-determination is particularly important. As one of several innate psychological needs, it is itself a motivating condition. Thus, motivation will be promoted within social contexts that provide persons the opportunity to satisfy their need for autonomy. Further, self-determined behavior may be motivational because it allows individuals to attribute their success to their own efforts (Bandura, 1986). If behavior is compelled, individuals may attribute their success or failure to the controlling force.

The job characteristics model and related perspectives on autonomy suggest two motivational elements in the relationship between school restructuring and teaching. First, while teaching has many rewards (Feiman-Nemser & Floden, 1986), a substantial amount of evidence indicates that students' learning and attachment provide teachers' most valued rewards and most potent incentives for change. Restructuring may be motivational to the extent that it promotes teachers' success with students. Second, autonomy to make decisions for their own classrooms has also long been a valued aspect of teachers' work (Lortie, 1975). Where restructuring leads to new authority relations between teachers and administrators and to greater "upward influence" in the organization, the motivational potential of restructuring may increase. On the other hand, restructuring may introduce new controls, such as goal and task structures and accountability systems, that reduce motivation, not only by constraining autonomy and self-determinism, but by linking the outcomes of teachers' work to an external source. Furthermore, where restructuring reduces teacher isolation and increases teacher collaboration, work group pressures may constrain individual autonomy. This too may reduce the motivational potential of restructuring. Or, it may increase it by shifting the source of motivation from individual to collective self-determinism.

*Learning Opportunities*

Most restructuring initiatives claim to create new learning opportunities for teachers, either through formal staff development programs or opportunities for workplace learning. Social learning, incidental learning, and organizational socialization theories identify several workplace conditions associated with restructuring that may promote teacher learning. One of the most salient conditions is the opportunity for individuals to work with and learn from others (Marsick & Watkins, 1990). Collective learning opportunities increase exposure to new ideas and experiences. They provide access to additional sources of feedback and referents for self-assessment (Bandura, 1986). Of further importance is open communication and collective examination of taken-for-granted beliefs and assumptions (Argyris & Schön, 1974). Such interaction encourages critical reflection and innovation. Another condition concerns power and authority. Learning is enhanced by opportunities to work with and learn from others of similar position and status. Egalitarianism encourages openness of expression for critical thinking and analysis.

In sum, these mechanisms – controls, incentives, and learning opportunities – provide some of the missing pieces of restructuring's logic. They suggest possible explanations of relationships between school restructuring and classroom teaching. We now turn to research that examines these relationships.

## RESEARCH ON RESTRUCTURING AND CLASSROOM TEACHING

Our review of research is presented in three major sections, each focusing on distinct groups of studies. The first section discusses several major programs of school restructuring in the United States. These programs, which are guided by specific philosophies about teaching and learning and contain distinctive configurations of restructuring strategies, include Accelerated Schools, the Coalition of Essential Schools, the Comer School Development Program, Professional Development Schools, and Success for All. The second section examines four specific restructuring strategies – standards and assessments; small schools; detracking and special education inclusion; and participative decisionmaking. These initiatives represent some of the most basic elements of restructuring – organizing subject matter; grouping of students and assigning teachers for instruction; assessing student progress; and distributing authority and influence (Elmore, 1995b). The third section reviews a growing number of case studies of specific examples of successful restructuring. Many are of single schools adopting idiosyncratic approaches to restructuring. These are often presented as "best cases," where relationships between restructuring and teacher should be apparent.

*Major Restructuring Programs*

Accelerated Schools

The Accelerated Schools Project was founded in 1986 by Henry Levin and a team of educators at Stanford University. Beginning in two pilot elementary schools, it has expanded to include over 700 schools in 37 American states (Levin, 1996). This project aims to bring low-achieving, at-risk students up to grade level by the end of elementary school so that they can succeed in secondary education. This calls for changing schools in ways that advance children's academic and social development, not to slow it down. This goal is to be accomplished through an integrated approach to restructuring curriculum, instruction, and school organization. The preferred curriculum focuses on higher-order skills and interdisciplinary content related to students' lived experiences. Instruction is to be student-centered and experiential. Group activities, peer tutoring, and cooperative learning are encouraged. The school organization is to be restructured around participative decision making and the broad-based parent and community involvement. The school day is to be extended to provide students with rest periods, physical and arts activities, and time for independent assignments (Levin, 1987). Upon entry into the project, schools are provided intensive training. A coach provides follow-up training and implementation support.

The primary empirical research on Accelerated Schools consists of a small number of case studies of a limited number of schools, conducted almost exclusively by researchers affiliated with the project. Each case documents how groups of teachers expanded their knowledge and instructional repertoires. Each attributes these improvements, in some part, to accompanying organizational changes.

Keller's (1995) case study of Thomas Edison Elementary School documents the school first established participative planning groups to involve teachers in curriculum decision making. It also established a schoolwide steering committee and system of work groups to provide additional opportunities for teachers, parents, and other community members to participate in decision making. By its third year as an Accelerated School, Edison's curriculum and instruction shifted toward constructivist pedagogy. Students became more involved in learning through hands-on and open-ended problem solving activities. Keller attributes these changes in large part to the new committee and planning group structures, which reduced isolation and provided new learning opportunities for teachers. Some staff members assumed new leadership roles, attended workshops outside the school district, and brought back information to share with others. Keller concludes that as teachers worked together, they were exposed to new ideas about curriculum and instruction. As a result, they expanded their knowledge and improved their classroom practices.

In a case study of Hollibrook Elementary School, McCarthy and Levin (1992) report that after several years as an Accelerated School, instructional practices changed considerably. Where once this school's classrooms were dominated by lectures, drills, and recitation, cross-age peer tutoring, flexible grouping and scheduling, integrated thematic learning activities, and hands-on instruction became commonplace. There was evidence of authentic instructional tasks and stronger ties between the curriculum and students' real-world experiences. McCarthy and Levin attribute these changes to collaborative inquiry, staff development, and problem solving associated with participative planning and governance. They also attribute these changes to shared responsibility generated from participation. Similar findings are reported in McCarthy and Still's (1993) and Chasin and Levin's (1995) studies of this school.

Knight and Stallings (1995) also document improvements at an unnamed Houston-area Accelerated School. Upon entry to the project, teachers and administrators joined in an intensive summer training session. Throughout the first year, teachers participated in weekly cadre meetings. They planned and participated in workshops on whole language, process writing, and the use of alternative grouping arrangements, which led to new instructional programs. Knight and Stallings report that teams of teachers developed cross-grade thematic units of instruction, instituted a cross-age student tutoring program, and used more cooperative grouping in their classrooms. Teachers relied less on texts and more on authentic instructional materials.

*The Coalition of Essential Schools*

The Coalition of Essential Schools, founded by Theodore Sizer in 1986, is a national network that advocates restructuring as part of a broader agenda to improve secondary schooling. This agenda focuses first on enhancing classroom teaching and learning. Structural changes in school organization follow from this priority. The Coalition is organized around nine common principles of teaching and learning: (1) maintain an intellectual focus; (2) concentrate on academic essentials; (3) acknowledge and meet the diverse needs of all students; (4) personalize learning; (5) make students active learners; (6) judge mastery by demonstrated exhibition, (7) promote trust and decency; (8) view teachers as generalists; and (9) limit total teaching load per teacher to 80 students. Each Coalition school is to interpret these principles within its own context and develop programs and practices accordingly.

Like the research on Accelerated Schools, the research on Essential Schools is limited to a few studies of a limited number of sites. Most of this research consists of single or multiple case studies of individual schools. Unlike the research on Accelerated Schools, much of the research on Essential Schools has been conducted by researchers unaffiliated with the Coalition.

In a five-year ethnographic study in eight of the 12 original Coalition schools, Muncey (1994) found wide variation in structural and programmatic reforms. She discovered that the usual starting points for change were those common principles that individual or small groups of teachers could address without disrupting the whole school. This approach spawned a host of relatively independent initiatives, such as altering class-level instructional emphases and creating schools-within-schools. Without strong school-level leadership, these initiatives rarely expanded into a coherent school-wide reform strategy.

Muncey's (1994) research indicates that Coalition activity often led teachers to become more reflective about their work. However, because of the idiosyncratic nature of this activity, its impact rarely extended beyond a core group of faculty. While Coalition activity promoted some change at the classroom level, it introduced obstacles to broader improvement. Political divisiveness among faculty groups often arose around reform goals, resource distribution, and new instructional arrangements such as schools-within-schools. Subsequent disillusionment, coupled with increased workloads brought on by Coalition activities, led some initially innovative teachers to return to previous practices or disengage from Coalition activity. Political problems isolated teachers into like-minded groups, reducing opportunities for collaboration and collegial learning (McQuillan & Muncey, 1991).

Prestine's longitudinal analyses of four Coalition schools in Illinois made similar findings. At the midpoint of a five-year restructuring project, two schools had begun only modest curricular projects that were seen as too small and fragmented to develop momentum for school-wide change (Prestine & Bowen, 1993). The other two schools made more substantial progress. One had restructured a grade level into teams. The other began a whole-school reorganization to establish a core team or "house" structure. Prestine (1994) found that by the last year of the project, the most radical initial changes had eroded to resemble more traditional organizational forms and practices. Coalition activities had generally run along side of the "regular" school. While new organizational structures had been built, they failed to challenge or penetrate the instructional core of these schools. This general finding of pedagogical persistence is also made in Prestine's (1993) case study of a junior high school that was one of the first Essential Schools in Illinois.

More positive findings are found in Wasley's (1991) comparative case studies of three experienced teachers who worked in different Essential Schools. Each of these teachers initially described herself as a good "conventional" teacher. Each used teacher-centered methods, where lectures, recitations, and textbooks were central. Their schools made several structural changes when they joined the Coalition. Interdisciplinary teaching teams and participative decision making structures were introduced. As a result, Wasley reports, all three teachers altered their teaching substantially. Each began to organize instruction around basic questions and problems from students' daily lives. They made more interdisciplinary connections among academic subjects. Instruction shifted from content coverage to in-depth learning. Each teacher placed less emphasis on textbooks, using them as one of many instructional resources. Assessments became more performance-based, and were used more for diagnosis than for grading.

Wasley (1991) attributes these changes to new collegial relationships fostered by interdisciplinary teaching teams and participative decision making. All three teachers saw these relationships as sources of professional learning. While they pointed to the potential for tension and strain, they saw collegiality as a positive source of collective responsibility and accountability. They believed that being a member of the Coalition, a network extending beyond their schools, bolstered their confidence and motivation.

Wasley's cases do not look far beyond the three teachers under investigation, and it would be improper to infer any conclusions regarding broader instructional impact. Indeed, her cases point to several factors that might mitigate schoolwide instructional improvement, including weak administrative support and faculty tensions surrounding the adoption and implementation of Essential School principles. These factors are similar to those reported by Muncey and Prestine.

### The Comer School Development Program

The School Development Program was developed by James Comer in 1968. It began in two elementary schools as a collaborative effort between the Yale University Child Study Center and the New Haven, Connecticut school system. This program has now been adopted by over 100 schools in places such as Washington, DC, Chicago, Detroit, New York, Dallas, San Diego, New Orleans, Miami-Dade County (Squires & Kranyik, 1995–1996).

This program was designed to help schools become more responsive to the needs of children from diverse backgrounds. It creates three structures that bring together teachers, principals, mental health professionals, parents, and community members to foster student learning and development (Comer, 1980). The first is a school planning and management team that establishes guidelines for curriculum and instruction, helps coordinate school operations, and monitors school conditions and program effectiveness. The second structure is a mental health team whose functions are to improve school climate and address problems among students and teachers. The third structure is a parents program that involves them in different aspects of school life.

Most research available on the School Development Program was conducted by program staff at Yale and focuses on the program's two pilot sites (Comer, 1980, 1984; Squires & Kranyik, 1995–1996). These studies document the first five years of implementation and examine most closely the development and function of teams, parent involvement, changes in school climate, and student outcomes. Comparatively little attention is paid to changes in classroom instruction. This research shows that curriculum and instruction received more attention after an initial period when most emphasis was placed on improving school climate and parent-school relations (Comer, 1980, 1984). The program employed curriculum specialists and consultants who provided staff development for teachers, introduced demonstration teaching, and encouraged teachers to visit one another's classrooms. By their fourth and fifth years in the program, teachers had introduced a number of changes in their classrooms, including new programs for language and social skill development. They increased curricular integration, using art to advance the regular academic curriculum. Teachers instituted new team teaching structures with flexible scheduling; they followed students from one grade level to a second for continuity in student-teacher relations. Finally, teachers developed new thematic units which were typically taught during elective time in students' schedules.

This research notes the difficulty these schools experienced trying to change teachers' orientations and day-to-day practices (Comer, 1980). Comer (1984) attributes the gradual changes that were observed to programs of staff development, the curriculum specialists and consultants, participative planning and governance, and teaching teams. Similar findings were made by Ramirez-Smith (1995) in a more recent case study of a Comer School in Newport News, Virginia.

*Professional Development Schools*

Professional Development Schools (PDSs) are partnerships between schools and universities created to support the learning of prospective and experienced teachers while simultaneously restructuring schools and schools of education (Darling-Hammond, Bullmaster, & Cobb, 1995). There are many ways to define PDSs but most definitions embody the following concepts and goals: (a) improve the quality of student instruction, the preparation of prospective teachers, and the continuing education of professional educators; (b) provide a research base that informs the teaching profession; (c) encourage the school to undergo a structural reform that promotes collaboration between teachers and university faculty; and (d) develop exemplary practices and disseminate knowledge about them to the profession (Book, 1996). In constructing environments where novices can learn from experts, veteran teachers may assume new roles as mentors, university adjuncts, and school leaders. They can join university educators in research and rethinking practice. By the mid-1990s, more than 200 PDSs had been established across the United States (Darling-Hammond, 1994).

Most of the research on PDSs focuses on the development of new roles and relationships among schools and universities and among veteran teachers, novice teachers, and university faculty. There are some studies about collaborative processes, how veteran teachers respond to their new responsibilities, the experiences of novice teachers, and the role of teacher inquiry. However, little research examines classroom teaching in PDSs.

The greatest proportion of research on instruction consists of case studies of individual PDSs or of individual teachers who work within them. Several of these cases were conducted through the National Center on Restructuring Education, Schools, and Teaching (NCREST) at Teachers College, Columbia University (Darling-Hammond, 1994). These studies examined seven "mature" PDSs, representing "best cases" of relatively long-standing partnerships between schools and universities. These cases present teacher testimony that working in PDSs enhanced their pedagogical knowledge and teaching practices. In Berry and Catoe's (1994) case of a South Carolina PDS, over 70 percent of the teachers reported that they changed the way they reflect on practice. Fifty-five percent reported that they changed the way they teach and their conception of what needs to be known by teachers to teach well. Lemlech and her colleagues (1994) describe how teachers in a Los Angeles PDS worked in teams to plan and implement thematic units after first requesting help from university participants on how to develop these units. Similarly, Lythcott and Schwartz (1994) document how teachers in a New York City PDS implemented interdisciplinary, student collaborative projects in their classrooms. These projects were planned and supported by teams of student teachers, experienced PDS teachers, and university faculty.

These studies attribute instructional innovation to new opportunities for teacher learning from collegial sharing, participative planning and decision making, and relations with student teachers and university faculty. Change is also attributed to various incentives associated with self-determinism in participative decision making, meaningfulness of work that involves preparing novice teachers, and responsibility for developing and sustaining the profession through teacher education. Finally, these cases point to accountability from joint work as an impetus for classroom change.

Other studies of PDSs report similar findings. In a study of a Louisville, KY PDS, Kerchner (1993) found that joint planning and shared decision making gave rise to a number of classroom initiatives, including interdisciplinary teaching teams and a four-teacher, cross-grade team. In two studies of a Michigan PDS, Roth and his colleagues (1993a, 1993b) documented changes in teachers' thinking and classroom practices that were attributed to collaboration among teachers, university professors, and doctoral students working in the school. Peterson's (1992) study showed how a 3rd grade PDS teacher altered her math instruction through discourse with and modeling by a university professor. McCarthey and Peterson's (1993) study of two PDS teachers also provide evidence of collaboration's effects on classroom practice. Finally, Stallings and Kowalski (1990) found that by participating in workshops with preservice teachers and university faculty, PDS teachers changed their patterns of classroom interaction with students. Like the NCREST cases, these studies attribute changes in teachers' practices to the motivational value of increased autonomy and meaningfulness of work in PDSs.

They also attribute changes to learning opportunities associated with collaboration, joint study and planning, working with university faculty, and helping prepare preservice teachers.

*Success for All*

The Success for All (SFA) program was developed by Robert Slavin and his colleagues at Johns Hopkins University. SFA began as a pilot project in one Baltimore elementary school in 1987. Since then, it has expanded to more than 300 schools in 24 states across the United States country (Slavin et al., 1996). SFA is designed to address school failure among students in inner-city schools, focusing particularly on the early development of reading and language skills. The program is grounded in principles of failure prevention; immediate, intensive intervention; and persistence in working with individual children until they succeed. SFA embodies a combination of specific instructional components and school organizational changes. The instructional components include an intensive pre-reading and reading program begun in kindergarten and 1st grade; one-to-one daily student tutoring in reading by certified teachers; flexible ability and heterogeneous instructional grouping; cooperative learning; regular student assessments with individual academic learning plans; a half-day preschool and full-day kindergarten program; and special education inclusion into the regular classroom. New organizational structures include advisory committees of administrators, teachers, and SFA staff, and family support teams of non-teaching professional and paraprofessional staff. Advisory committees monitor the program's progress and solve problems that arise. Family support teams provide parent education, help families obtain social services, and encourage parents to support their children's learning. These teams meet with grade-level teams of teachers to discuss problems and develop solutions. School personnel are trained by program staff before and throughout the first year of implementation. Teachers are given manuals detailing instructional components of the program. A facilitator provides teacher staff development and promotes program implementation.

Studies of SFA have been conducted by its developers and independent evaluators in both initial implementation sites and other districts. This research consists primarily of longitudinal evaluations of student achievement outcomes (Madden, Slavin, Karweit, Dolan, & Wasik, 1993; Slavin, Madden, Shaw, Mainzer, & Donnelly, 1993). Relatively little attention has been paid to changes in teachers' instructional practice. The most direct evidence on the effects of SFA on classroom teaching comes from a two-year study of a precursor program, the Cooperative Elementary School Model (Stevens & Slavin, 1995). This program contained most SFA elements. The study found that by the second year of implementation, teachers began to introduce cooperative learning in a number of subject areas. Special education pull-out remediation had been discontinued. Special educational teachers taught learning disabled students in regular classrooms in team-teaching arrangements with regular classroom teachers. Learning disabled students were also integrated with other students in learning teams. Teachers within and sometimes across grade levels met regularly to plan instruction. They served on building committees to plan and evaluate the school's progress in the program. Similar changes in instructional practices were documented in three subsequent case studies of SFA schools (Slavin et al., 1993).

Studies of SFA generally attribute classroom changes and student outcomes to the specific instructional foci of the program and to the comprehensive nature of its change mechanisms. With regards to teaching, these mechanisms include teacher learning opportunities provided through training, program facilitators, and collaborative planning and decision making. They also include incentives and accountability mechanisms associated with the collective autonomy, monitoring, and problem-solving in participative decisionmaking.

*Specific Restructuring Strategies*

In this section we examine research on several specific restructuring strategies. We begin with studies of standards and assessments and proceed to research on small schools, detracking and special education inclusion, and participative decision making.

*Standards and Assessments*

In recent years, new efforts have been made in the United States and Europe to develop centralized systems of learning outcome standards and assessments. These systems seek to improve teaching by identifying common goals and specific standards for student learning. Typically, these systems contain indicators and assessment procedures, including standardized tests and alternative assessments. They may be accompanied by curriculum frameworks and promotion requirements. Unlike the minimum competency testing programs of the mid-1970s and early 1980s, these systems typically aim toward higher levels of cognitive attainment. Unlike the "teacher proof" curriculum projects of the 1970s, they focus more on articulating and assessing student learning outcomes than on identifying specific pedagogical processes to achieve them. Little research is available on the most recent of these initiatives. However, some insight may be gained from studies of earlier centralized curriculum and testing policies.

Cross-national research consistently finds that central curriculum control is related positively to consistency in subject matter coverage (Cohen & Spillane, 1992). There is less evidence, however, that curriculum control changes the basic nature of teachers' classroom practice. Most evidence suggests that while teachers make accommodations, change in practice occurs at the margins. This general conclusion was reached by Archbald and Porter (1994) in their study of high school teachers in high and low control districts in California, Florida, and New York. High control districts required high schools to offer the same courses, provided detailed guidelines on course topics and sequences, mandated particular textbooks, and administered course-based testing to monitor attainment of districtwide achievement standards. Low control districts had not adopted these types of policies. This study found that teachers in high control districts reported having significantly less control over the content they would teach in their classrooms than teachers in low control districts. However, teachers in high control districts did not differ significantly from their counterparts in the discretion they maintained over instructional strategies.

More detailed effects are documented by Darling-Hammond and Wise's (1985) study of teachers in three mid-Atlantic school districts. This study found that standardized tests tied to new learning standards substantially altered teachers' curricular emphases. Some teachers reported that testing forced them to focus instruction on tested knowledge. These teachers focused on the precise topics appearing on the tests rather than the concepts underlying them. They reported that they changed their instruction to teach skills that would be tested rather than skills that students might need. Many teachers in this study chafed under the tests, viewing them as constraints on their ability to address the most important needs of their students. They complained about dilution of their professional autonomy.

Smith's (1991) study of the effects of statewide mandatory testing in two Arizona elementary schools made similar findings. Teachers in this study also reduced the range of teaching methods used in their classrooms. They complained that their work had been "deskilled." Teachers felt compelled to make their teaching consistent with the testing program. Many believed that if they resisted, or if their students did not score well on the tests, they would suffer sanctions and additional loss of autonomy.

This research suggests that the influence of standards and assessments may depend a great deal on the stakes attached to them. In a study of school districts in eastern Massachusetts, Johnson (1990) found that teachers were more likely to alter their instruction, at least for a time, under high stakes conditions than under low stakes conditions. Wilson and Corbett's (1990) study of teacher responses to high and low stakes testing programs in Pennsylvania and Maryland made similar findings. Maryland, a high stakes state, required students to pass tests in reading, writing, math, and citizenship in order to graduate from high school. Pennsylvania, a lower stakes state, required testing in reading and math but attached relatively minor consequences to scores. On the average, Pennsylvania teachers reported only minor impact of the tests on their work, however, teachers in Maryland reported moderate to major impact on their professional discretion, time demands, and pressure to improve student performance. Yet, this study found that basic instruction was hardly affected, even under high stakes conditions. While teachers felt a need to respond to these tests, most saw them as "just one more add-on," something that must be addressed along with what they would ordinarily do in the classroom (Wilson & Corbett, 1990, p. 255).

Black's (1994) study of the national testing component of Britain's 1988 Education Reform Act also found that teachers made adjustments in their teaching to fit the reform. But they too considered the "new curriculum" of the tests to be extra, to be added to "normal" teaching. Teachers conducted extra summative assessments to satisfy demands of the reform, but for most teachers, these assessments had little to do with the basic processes of teaching and learning in their classrooms.

The limits of instructional change evoked by standards and assessments are further illustrated in case studies of California's Mathematics Framework, a statewide standards, curriculum, and assessment program (Cohen & Ball, 1990). These cases portray teachers as active agents, adapting elements of the Framework to their classrooms. Teachers in these cases responded differently to the new program; their responses were shaped by individual conceptions of teaching and learning, knowledge and skills, and beliefs and interests. In one particularly cogent case, Cohen (1990) describes a teacher who considered herself successful in implementing the Framework. The case shows that many elements of the Framework were present in her classroom, but these elements existed along side of and in some conflict with her established practices.

Several explanations are offered for the generally weak relationship between standards and assessments and change in teachers' practice. Most studies indicate that these policies are adopted with scant attention to developing the requisite knowledge and skills for teachers to implement them effectively (Cohen & Spillane, 1992; Koffler, 1987). In addition, while these policies suggest new directions for instruction and contain accountability mechanisms for teacher and student performance, standards and assessments often create disincentives to change. The research identifies overload, value and role conflicts, and reduction in self-determinism as common by-products of these policies (Porter, 1989). The incentive value of these programs may be diminished further if, as reported in several studies, teachers gain little useful knowledge about their students' learning needs and how to address them (Johnson, 1990; Wilson & Corbett, 1990).

*Small Schools*

Small schools are just that – schools that have limited the size of their student populations. Proponents seek an alternative to the post-World War II trend to educate students in larger institutions. Larger schools were thought to increase program comprehensiveness, expand equality of student opportunity, and create fiscal economies of scale. Yet, as schools and districts across the United States steadily increased in size, arguments mounted against this logic. Lee and her colleagues (1993) suggest that in large schools, benefits from economies of scale may be undercut by stratification of student learning opportunities, and by problems of alienation and detachment from school. They contend that large schools compromise organizational cohesion, communication, and social relations that are instrumental to teaching and learning. On the other hand, small schools are thought to foster community. Small school advocates contend that reducing school size will help overcome the problems of student alienation and detachment. It will provide greater opportunities for supportive adult-student relations, flexibility in curriculum, and more personalized instruction.

Research on school size focuses primarily on differences between large and small schools in curricular comprehensiveness; student attitudes, discipline, and participation; and academic achievement (Fowler, 1995). Little research has examined differences in classroom instruction. Further, little research exists on the effects of reducing school size on teaching. Some studies describe instruction in newly-established small schools, however, these studies are typically conducted without comparisons to other schools. They are also conducted without due consideration that these schools are generally formed around particular philosophical principles and pedagogical practices. Teachers who work within them are most often self-selected or chosen for their compatibility with those principles and practices. It is difficult to determine whether smaller schools foster the development of instructional practices seen within them or whether they simply reflect the practices people bring to them. Further, these studies do not distinguish the contribution of size relative to the contributions of other factors, such as curricular coherence, shared vision and values, and selective staffing, in explaining how these schools function.

The few studies that examine instructional differences in large and small schools present mixed findings. Mortimore and his colleagues' (1988) study of British primary schools found few differences between large and small schools in classroom instruction. When compared to teachers in smaller schools, teachers in larger schools tended to give pupils less individual feedback and used more whole-class instruction. Several studies suggest more significant, but indirect, relationships between school size and instructional practice. In their analysis of Chicago school reform, Bryk and his colleagues (1993) found that small elementary schools were more likely than larger elementary schools to have strongly democratic governance processes and over twice as likely to be engaged in systemic approaches to improvement. In schools with systemic approaches to improvement, the greatest proportions of students were reported to be engaged in cooperative learning, writing across the curriculum, and hands-on math and science activities. It was also in these schools that this study found most reports of "authentic " teaching involving deep engagement of students in subject matter, active student participation in the learning, and assessment of student knowledge production.

Similarly, analyses by Lee and Smith (1995) point indirectly to relationships between school size and authentic pedagogy. Using data from the National Education Longitudinal Study (NELS), they found that students in smaller schools posted significantly higher achievement gains than students in larger schools, and those gains were more equitably distributed. They also found that the main predictors of achievement gains-common curriculum, academic press, and responsibility for student learning-were more likely to be found in schools with the greatest preponderance of organizational conditions associated with restructuring, including schools-within-a-school. Higher levels of authentic instruction were found in schools with these organizational characteristics than in schools without them.

This study suggests that school size may be related in some way to instruction, but overall, that size may be less important than the academic focus and motivational commitments of teachers.

Several studies document instructional practices in newly-founded small schools. One example is Ancess' (1995) case of Urban Academy, an ungraded alternative school located within a large comprehensive New York City public high school. This study is discussed in more detail below. Here, it is sufficient to note that instruction in this small school was organized by teachers in block-schedules and seminar format rather than in traditional class periods. It emphasized group work, problem-based learning, student-centered discourse, and reflection. Meier's (1995) description of Central Park East, a cluster of four alternative schools in New York City's East Harlem, presents a similar picture of instructional organization. Both cases show teachers responsible for school-level instructional planning and decision making and assessment of student progress.

Finally, the few studies that examine changes in classroom practice that occur when schools reduce their size paint a less positive picture than studies of newly-created schools. In one study, Christman and Macpherson (1996) examined instructional change associated with the first seven years of restructuring Philadelphia's 22 comprehensive high schools into small "charter" learning communities. In their five-school sample, these researchers found a highly variable array of schools-within-schools, ranging from "empty shells" to "vibrant and resilient" units. Some small learning communities developed coherent and stimulating curricula and staff succeeded in meeting students' personal and academic needs. However, these settings were relatively few. Most students in other small school settings reported that their classes were "uninspired" and their teachers "don't teach." Only a small minority of students were in charters that offered "real connection and caring" along with rigorous course work.

In a second study, Levine (1992) examined changes associated with a district-wide, 9th grade schools-within-a school (SWAS) program in Kansas City, Missouri. This program was established to help students with low reading scores succeed at subsequent grade levels. Operating in all but one of the district's senior high schools, this program assigned 60 to 100 students to teams of four or five different subject matter teachers. Teachers were selected for their willingness and ability to work with at-risk students. This program included common planning periods for teachers, teacher selection of texts and grading policies, intensive staff development, and a concerted emphasis on reading comprehension. Levine's research concludes that about half of the SWASs functioned well while the others functioned sporadically. Observational data reveal substantial variation in teachers' use of instructional strategies that were encouraged by program.

It is not clear from this evidence that reducing school size promotes change in instruction. Some studies suggest that creating small schools may impede the development of practice. Workloads may increase for teachers who assume responsibility for developing and administering small schools (Christman & Macpherson, 1996). Small schools may also isolate and create political divisiveness among faculty groups (McQuillan & Muncey, 1991). Most research contends, however, that small schools create conditions conducive to instructional improvement. Several studies suggest a relationship between small school size and strength of teacher professional community (Newmann & Wehlage, 1995). Professional community can be defined by shared purpose for student learning, collaborative activity to achieve that purpose, and collective responsibility (Louis & Kruse, 1995). Small schools may promote group loyalty and cohesion that increase collegial influence over individual behavior. Increased authority and responsibility for the success of small school units may prompt improved teacher performance, as may new sources of accountability that derive from more intimate groups of colleagues and students. Finally, smallness may provide new learning opportunities for teachers through collaborative activity.

While these effects seem theoretically sensible, there is not much empirical evidence for them. Indeed, several studies suggest that the relationship between school size and strength of professional community may not be strong (Louis, Marks, & Kruse, 1996). This research indicates that human-social factors such as trust and respect, principal leadership, and formal socialization of new teachers are more strongly associated with the strength of professional community than structural conditions, including school size (Bryk et al., 1996). Once more, the literature suggests that structure may create opportunity but is an insufficient condition to promote change in classroom practice.

*Detracking and Special Education Inclusion*

Grouping students by academic ability has been a long-standing practice in American schools. Ability grouping occurs in many forms within and between classrooms at both elementary and secondary levels. While there is mixed evidence on the academic and social outcomes of ability grouping (Oakes, Gamoran, & Page, 1992), efforts are increasing to eliminate or at least minimize its practice (Gamoran & Hallinan, 1995). These efforts, popularly called "detracking," aim to change the norms and practices that reinforce inequalities in learning opportunities available to students of different academic abilities. They call for schools and classrooms to be restructured so that students can be taught alongside of classmates of varying ability.

Special education inclusion, a related restructuring strategy, is also intended to improve learning opportunities for students with physical and learning disabilities. Inclusion derives from the concept of least restrictive learning environments. Rooted in Public Law 94–142, now the Individuals with Disabilities Education Act, and in the U.S. Department of Education's 1986 Regular Education Initiative, it calls for new structures and strategies for teaching special education students in general education classrooms (Falvey, Givner, & Kimm, 1995).

Detracking and inclusion are unlikely to succeed without concurrent changes in curriculum, instruction, assessment, and counseling. Both require teachers to develop new knowledge and skills to provide appropriate learning opportunities for a broader range of students. In inclusion classrooms, teachers must learn new prereferral intervention strategies. They must modify traditional approaches to disciplining students with handicaps and they must learn how to make their classrooms socially hospitable to disabled students.

Very little research examines the effects of detracking and special education inclusion on teaching. Most studies focus on student academic and social outcomes and find, or infer, that effects are largely attributable to teachers' ability to adapt their teaching to increased classroom heterogeneity (Baker, Wang, & Walberg, 1994). Regular education teachers often express significant differences in their perceived ability to serve both regular and special education students. In one study, O'Connor and Jenkins (1996) directly attributed unsatisfactory learning experiences for special needs students to teachers' inability to conduct cooperative learning groups effectively.

The few studies that examine changes in classroom instruction stress the importance of systematic professional development and support systems. Without them, regular classroom teachers are likely to merely extent their current teaching strategies to new students (Allsop, 1980). In a study of detracking in two elementary schools, Hall and her colleagues (1995) show how teachers implemented new multimethod, multi-level instructional and assessment strategies to accommodate the inclusion of special education and Chapter I students in their classrooms. The impetus for these changes came primarily from two sources – targeted staff development and informal learning opportunities associated with new collaborative planning and development activities. In another study, Stevens and Slavin (1995) documented how teachers in a school implementing the Cooperative Elementary School Model adopted new cooperative strategies that integrated learning disabled students with other students on learning teams. These strategies were supported by new teacher collaborative planning structures and by ongoing staff development.

A final example is MacKinnon and Brown's (1994) study of inclusion in two secondary schools in Nova Scotia. Teachers in these schools began dealing with high needs students in regular classrooms as if they were no different from other students. After an initial period of uncertainty, fear, and frustration, teachers moved from "hit and miss" efforts to accommodate these students to more systematic, innovative changes. Like the findings of other research, this study attributes these changes not to inclusion per se but to new collaborative structures and teacher learning opportunities. In addition to formal staff development, teachers received assistance from a resource team and a facilitator. They also gained substantial technical and emotional support from exchanging ideas with one another during regularly-scheduled team meetings.

*Participative Decisionmaking*

Teacher participation in school-based decisionmaking has become a key component of recent efforts to restructure schools. A substantial amount of research exists on the general subject of participation. While it is generally acknowledged that participative decisionmaking is related positively to teachers' attitudes about work, research examining the instructional outcomes reports generally equivocal findings.

Some studies indicate that participation is related positively to school improvement planning and to the adoption of curricular and instructional innovations. For example, Bryk and his colleagues (1993), in their survey and case study research on the early implementation of parent and community-dominated participative structures in Chicago, found that schools with the most democratic governance processes were most likely to engage in systemic approaches to curricular and instructional innovation. Similarly, Jenkins and his colleagues (1994) found that when compared with similar schools, schools with participative decisionmaking were more likely to enhance instructional programs and support services, in this case for special education students. Likewise, Wohlstetter, Smyer, and Mohrman (1994) found in their comparative study of more and less actively restructuring schools that schools making the most significant changes in curriculum and instruction were those that had the most developed mechanisms for teacher participation in school governance. These were schools that also invested heavily in team process training and instructional staff development and had more effective systems for sharing information with a broad base of constituents.

Other studies indicate that teacher participation is related to implementation of programmatic decisions. Mortimore and his colleagues' (1988) large-scale survey of British schools found participation related to consistency in classroom implementation of curricular and instructional programs. Weiss (1993) also found that teachers in schools with participative decisionmaking were more likely to support implementation of curricular decisions than teachers in non-participative schools.

While the research suggests that participation may create opportunities for curricular and instructional improvement and support implementation of innovations, it also suggests that participation may do little to promote meaningful change in day-to-day classroom practice (David & Peterson, 1984). In a recent study, Griffin (1995) showed how participative decisionmaking promoted substantial changes in school-level programs but also how those changes had little impact on teachers' daily work with students. Teachers in Sebring and her associates' (1995) study reported that the most positive effects of Chicago's participative decisionmaking bodies had occurred in school-community relations and parent involvement in schools, not in curricular quality or teaching effectiveness. However, in a longitudinal study of teacher-dominated decision making bodies, Smylie, Lazarus, and Brownlee-Conyers (1996) found that classroom instructional improvement and gains on student standardized achievement test scores were greatest in schools with the most collaborative and inclusive participative processes.

While the literature is equivocal in its findings, it suggests that classroom change occurs when participation promotes self-determinism and collective accountability among teachers (Smylie et al., 1996). It also occurs when participative structures create new opportunities for teacher learning (Smylie et al., 1996). Adoption of participative structures does not automatically trigger mechanisms for classroom change, as is shown in research examining variations among participative schools (Smylie et al., 1996; Wohlstetter et al., 1994). However, these structures have the potential to do so.

### Cases of Successfully Restructured Schools

We conclude this review with a few examples of case studies of successfully restructured schools. These examples come from three national research centers – the Consortium for Policy Research in Education (CPRE) at the University of Pennsylvania; the Center for the Organization and Restructuring of Schools (CORS) at the University of Wisconsin-Madison; and the National Center for Restructuring Education, Schools, and Teaching (NCREST). Additional case studies may be found in Lieberman (1995) and Murphy and Hallinger (1993). [See related work conducted at the Center for the Study of the Context of Teaching at Stanford University; e.g., Cohen, McLaughlin, & Talbert, 1993.]

### The CPRE Cases

The CPRE cases were conducted between 1988 and 1991 in three elementary schools (Elmore, Peterson, & McCarthey, 1996). According to Elmore and his colleagues (1996), all three schools looked like "models of enlightened practice" (p. 222). Each provided supportive collegial environments for teachers. Teachers participated actively in deciding how their schools would be organized and what their responsibilities would be. Each school held shared beliefs about the importance of all children learning at high levels. Teachers were willing to make significant changes in how students were grouped for instruction, how teachers related to each other in their daily work, and how time was allocated among academic subjects.

  These cases found that teaching in two of the three schools varied substantially. Some teachers enthusiastically pursued new ways of teaching but demonstrated a lack of understanding of how to make new practices successful. Others thought they were teaching in bold new ways, when in fact they made only minor modifications in the strategies they had previously used. The third school was different. There, teachers and students were engaged in ambitious teaching and learning with far greater consistency. Some variability was evident at this third school, but it was largely related to teachers grappling with dilemmas of constructivist teaching. For the most part, teachers at this school held a strong, shared set of norms about what constitutes good teaching. They had substantial success translating these norms into practice.

  Elmore and his colleagues (1996) are careful to point out that this third school was a new school which had recruited its own staff around a set of commonly-held principles about teaching and learning. It had established from the beginning strong patterns of teacher interaction outside the classroom that sustained shared beliefs about teaching. This school promoted systematic opportunities for teacher learning. In contrast, the other two schools had undergone structural change with their current personnel. The opportunities for teacher learning were less systematic than those in the new school.

This research reached several related conclusions. First, the relationship between structural change and changes in teaching is mediated by school norms and teachers' knowledge and skills. Second, structural change has less to do with teachers' instructional practices than the vision, beliefs, and social relations that exist within those structures. Third, the problem of changing classroom teaching is a problem of developing teachers' knowledge and skills, not merely a problem of altering organizational structure.

*The CORS Cases*

Between 1991 and 1994, researchers at CORS conducted case studies of 24 "significantly" restructured elementary, middle, and high schools in 16 states (Newmann & Associates, 1996). These schools shared combinations of the following organizational characteristics: (a) school-based management and participative decision making; (b) team organization of teachers and students; (c) common planning time for teachers; (d) student membership in multi-year instructional or advisory groups; (e) heterogeneous grouping of students for instruction in core subject areas; and (f) student enrollment based on student and parent choice rather than residential location. They included new schools as well as schools undergoing major structural changes. Schools were studied during one year; they were not tracked longitudinally. An important focus of this research was teachers' use of authentic pedagogy, defined as instruction emphasizing higher-order student thinking, in-depth understanding, and application of academic learning to important, realistic problems.

These cases reveal that the 24 schools varied substantially in the practice of authentic pedagogy. The most significant factor related to the presence of authentic pedagogy (and higher student academic achievement) was the strength of teachers' professional community (Louis & Marks, 1996). In schools with strong professional communities, principals and teachers developed new knowledge and skills through joint learning and problem solving, and through a continuous improvement cycle of innovation, feedback, and redesign of curriculum, instruction, and student assessment. Stronger professional communities were found in schools that had more time for collaborative planning, and in schools with smaller student enrollments.

While the CORS cases do not distinguish newly-established schools from schools that underwent restructuring, they are similar to the CPRE cases in that they identify only weak and second-order relationships between organizational structure and classroom teaching. Like the CPRE cases, the CORS cases emphasize the importance of intermediate factors, such as professional community, that mediate the relationship between structure and instruction. Collaborative activity provides opportunities for teachers to develop new knowledge and skills. Shared purpose and collective responsibility provide incentives that direct teachers' actions.

### *The NCREST Cases*

In addition to its PDS cases, NCREST conducted a number of case studies that document various aspects of teaching and learning in successfully restructured schools. In one group of cases, Jervis and Wilson (1995) describe the professional development and instructional practices of teachers participating in IMPACT II, a nationwide network supporting classroom innovation. These teachers worked in schools, some new and some restructured, that were organized around collaborative work and participative governance. They were typically members of grade-level or cross-grade-level teams and participated with other teachers in instructional planning groups. They worked in house structures or schools-within-schools with smaller groups of students. Their schools had scheduled time for them to work together regularly. In addition to IMPACT II, most teachers worked with teachers from other schools or from other educational projects and organizations.

These cases show how collaboration so structured became an important source of teacher learning and development. It created opportunities to share ideas and solve problems. It provided incentives, support, and a new sense of accountability for individual practice. The cases suggest that for most teachers, these mechanisms led to higher levels of professional commitment and innovation in teaching. For other teachers, particularly those hired into new schools, these mechanisms served to sustain initially innovative practice.

Ancess' (1995) case of Urban Academy provides a detailed picture of relationships between the structural elements of a new school-within-a-school and teachers' work with students. Urban Academy is a new school, founded around a particular set of pedagogical and organizational principles; it hired its own teachers whose orientations and teaching methods reinforced these principles. The school is organized around the concept of a "caring community." Its small size is intended to promote regular, personalized relationships among teachers and students. Teachers' work is structured according to undifferentiated staffing patterns. Schedules and course assignments are made on the basis of student and school needs and the interests and talents of teachers. There are strong systems for student academic, social, and emotional support. Teachers have substantial autonomy and make collective decisions about curriculum and instruction. Regularly scheduled time is built into teachers' work week for meetings and collaborative work.

Ancess (1995) describes instruction at Urban Academy as innovative and flexible. Most classes are organized as seminars and scheduled for extended periods several times a week. They are characterized by discourse and reflection, student group work, and problem-based learning. Students participate in structured learning experiences outside the school. Ancess associates these instructional practices with the school's collaborative structures, which she considers sources for teacher learning, motivation, and accountability.

## CONCLUSIONS

Across the literature, we see how school restructuring and classroom instruction are linked by different functional mechanisms. The literature suggests that restructuring has the strongest influence on teaching when it introduces new incentives, controls, and learning opportunities for teachers. It has less influence on teaching when these mechanisms are weak or absent.

Perhaps the most salient mechanism at work in the relationship between restructuring and instruction are new learning opportunities for teachers. Consistent with theory and research on learning in organizations, the restructuring literature points to the importance of work groups, planning teams, and team teaching as sources of exchange, collegial problem solving, and learning. It also suggests that teacher learning and change can be constrained by relational and political problems that impede the development of these structures. The importance of teacher learning is evident in studies of most every form of restructuring.

It is important to note that the effectiveness of restructuring may be enhanced additionally by staff development programs. These formal learning opportunities seem particularly salient for initiatives that do not aim directly to promote teacher collegial relations. For example, the pedagogical changes documented in research on Accelerated Schools, Comer Schools, and Success for All schools are attributed largely to initial training, ongoing staff development, and facilitators who support implementation. The importance of staff development is also seen in literature on standards and assessments and detracking and inclusion.

Of further importance is the introduction of new incentives. The literatures on participative decisionmaking and inclusion suggest that collective responsibilities and team structures create incentives for teachers to act in ways consistent with the group. These incentives are also highlighted in the literature on Professional Development Schools where teachers attach new meaning to their roles in preparing preservice teachers and developing new knowledge for the profession. Finally, the literature suggests that professional learning opportunities created by restructuring may introduce new incentives when teachers perceive these opportunities as means of increasing their success with students.

The literature also points to several disincentives that could impede instructional change. Increased responsibilities outside the classroom that often accompany restructuring may create disincentives if they detract from teachers' work with students. Likewise, political divisiveness may be a disincentive to risk-taking and change. Other disincentives derive from constraints on teachers' classroom autonomy. Such disincentives are seen most clearly in literature on standards and assessments. These policies, particularly those that carry high stakes, may increase teachers' sense of responsibility and accountability and thus serve as an impetus for change. At the same time, they may introduce disincentives for change if they reduce teacher creativity and discretion and direct instruction toward processes and outcomes teachers believe do not serve their students well.

Finally, the literature illustrates how restructuring can introduce bureaucratic and professional controls. The effects of bureaucratic controls are seen most clearly in specific restructuring programs, such as Success for All, and in standards and assessment policies. These initiatives set external goals and foci for instruction. In varying degrees, they also impose external accountability mechanisms on teachers' performance. The literature indicates that these controls can influence teachers' practice. They seem most influential when they are intense and consistent with teachers' perspectives and values (see Rowan, 1990). They are also influential when accompanied by new incentives and opportunities for teacher learning. Still, teachers may do little more than accommodate or give symbolic representation to instructional goals and processes they deem inappropriate to their students. Even when teachers find new standards and assessments compatible with their own goals, instructional change may be limited in the absence of learning opportunities that help teachers adopt new content and teaching strategies.

Like theory and research on control in organizations, the restructuring literature points to the strength of professional controls associated with collaborative work and shared decisionmaking. Studies of Professional Development Schools and participative decisionmaking, as well as a number of cases of successfully restructured schools, illustrate how collective responsibility from joint work and decisionmaking can increase accountability among teachers. It also shows how new decisionmaking authority can increase teachers' accountability to those who share a stake in their decisions.

The literature suggests that the relationship between restructuring and classroom instruction is strongest when new learning opportunities, incentives, and control mechanisms work in concert. This confluence is best illustrated in the most systemic restructuring initiatives, such as Professional Development Schools and the creation of new schools, particularly new small schools. It is also well illustrated in research on the most comprehensive forms of participative decisionmaking and teacher professional community.

The purpose of this chapter was to examine the relationship between school restructuring and improvement in classroom teaching. We found that the relationship is much more complex and problematic than the logic of restructuring suggests. There are many programs and strategies for restructuring that differ in design and implementation. And, the research on restructuring is relatively young and varies considerably in its focus and rigor. While it is extremely difficult to judge the efficacy of any particular program or strategy for restructuring on the basis of the available evidence, we can have some confidence in the relatively consistent patterns of findings across studies of different restructuring initiatives.

In conclusion, the research indicates that structural change is important in that it can create occasions for instructional improvement. At the same time, it argues strongly that restructuring is an insufficient strategy. Changing the organizational structures of schools will do little to promote instructional improvement without concurrent attention to the motivation, knowledge, and skills of teachers who work within them.

# REFERENCES

Allsop J. (1980). Mainstreaming physically handicapped students. *Journal of Research and Development in Education*, **13**(4), 37–44.

Ancess, J. (1995). *An inquiry high school: Learner-centered accountability at the Urban Academy*. New York: National Center for Restructuring Education, Schools, and Teaching, Teachers College, Columbia University.

Archbald, D. A., & Porter, A. C. (1994). Curriculum control and teachers' perceptions of autonomy and satisfaction. *Educational Evaluation and Policy Analysis*, **16**, 21–39.

Argyris, C., & Schön, D. A. (1974). *Theory in practice: Increasing professional effectiveness*. San Francisco: Jossey-Bass.

Bacharach, S. B., & Aiken, M. (1976). Structural and process constraints on influence in organizations: A level-specific analysis. *Administrative Science Quarterly*, **21**, 623–641.

Baker, E., Wang, M., & Walberg, H. J. (1994). The effects of inclusion on learning. *Educational Leadership*, **52**(4), 33–35.

Bandura, A. (1986). *Social foundations of thought and action: A social cognitive theory*. Englewood Cliffs, NJ: Prentice-Hall.

Berry, B., & Catoe, S. (1994). Creating professional development schools: Policy and practice in South Carolina's PDS initiatives. In L. Darling-Hammond (Ed.), *Professional development schools: Schools for developing a profession* (pp. 176–202). New York: Teachers College Press.

Black, P. J. (1994). Performance assessment and accountability: The experience in England and Wales. *Educational Evaluation and Policy Analysis*, **16**, 191–203.

Blankenship, R. L. (1980). Toward a theory of collegial power and control. In R. L. Blankenship (Ed.), *Colleagues in organizations: The social construction of professional work* (pp. 394–416). Huntington, NY: Krieger.

Bryk, A. S., Easton, J. Q., Kerbow, D., Rollow, S. G., & Sebring, P. B. (1993, July). *A view from the elementary schools: The state of Chicago school reform*. Chicago: Consortium on Chicago School Research, University of Chicago.

Bucher, R., & Stelling, J. G. (1980). Four characteristics of professional organizations. In R. L. Blankenship (Ed.), *Colleagues in organizations: The social construction of professional work* (pp. 121–144). Huntington, NY: Krieger.

Chasin, G., & Levin, H. M. (1995). Thomas Edison Accelerated Elementary School. In J. Oakes & K. H. Quartz (Eds.), *Creating new educational communities, schools, and classrooms where all children can be smart* (pp. 130–146). Chicago: University of Chicago Press.

Christman, J. B., & Macpherson, P. (1996). *The five school study: Restructuring Philadelphia's comprehensive high schools*. Philadelphia: Philadelphia Education Fund.

Cohen, D. K. (1990). A revolution in one classroom: The case of Mrs. Oublier. *Educational Evaluation and Policy Analysis*, **12**, 311–329.

Cohen, D. K., & Ball, D. L. (1990). Relations between policy and practice: A commentary. *Educational Evaluation and Policy Analysis*, **12**, 331–338.

Cohen, D. K., McLaughlin, M. W., & Talbert, J. E. (Eds.). (1993). *Teaching for understanding: Challenges for policy and practice*. San Francisco: Jossey-Bass.

Cohen, D. K., & Spillane, J. P. (1992). Policy and practice: The relations between governance and instruction. In G. Grant (Ed.), *Review of Research in Education* (Vol. 18, pp. 3–49). Washington, DC: American Educational Research Association.

Comer, J. P. (1984). Home-school relationships as they affect the academic success of children. *Education and Urban Society*, **16**, 323–337.

Darling-Hammond, L., Bullmaster, M. L., & Cobb, V. L. (1995). Rethinking teacher leadership through professional development schools. *Elementary School Journal*, **96**, 87–106.

Darling-Hammond, L., & Wise, A. E. (1985). Beyond standardization: State standards and school improvement. *Elementary School Journal*, **85**, 315–336.

David, J. L., & Peterson, S. M. (1984). *Can schools improve themselves? A study of school-based improvement programs*. Palo Alto, CA: Bay Area Research Group.

David, J. L., Purkey, S., & White, P. (1987). *Restructuring in progress: Lessons from pioneering districts*. Washington, DC: National Governors Association.

Deci, E. L., Vallerand, R. J. Pelletier, L. G., & Ryan, R. M. (1991). Motivation and education: The self-determination perspective. *Educational Psychologist*, **26**, 325–346.

Elmore, R. F. (1995a). Structural reform and educational practice. *Educational Researcher*, **24**(9), 23–26.

Elmore, R. F. (1995b). Teaching, learning, and school organization: Principles of practice and the regularities of schooling. *Educational Administration Quarterly*, **31**, 355–374.

Elmore, R. F., Peterson, P. L., & McCarthey, S. J. (1996). *Restructuring in the classroom: Teaching, learning, and school organization*. San Francisco: Jossey-Bass.

Etzioni, A. (1964). *Modern organizations*. Englewood Cliffs, NY: Prentice-Hall.

Falvey, M. A., Givner, C. C., & Kimm, C. (1995). What is an inclusive school? In R. A. Villa & J. S. Thousand (Eds.), *Creating an inclusive school* (pp. 1–12). Alexandria, VA: Association for Supervision and Curriculum Development.

Feiman-Nemser, S., & Floden, R. (1986). The cultures of teaching. In M. Wittrock (Ed.), *Handbook of research on teaching* (3rd ed., pp. 505–526). New York: Macmillan.

Fowler, W. J. (1995). School size and student outcomes. In H. J. Walberg (Ed.), *Advances in educational productivity: Organizational influences on educational productivity* (Vol. 5, pp. 3–26). Greenwich, CT: JAI Press.

Gamoran, A., & Hallinan, M. T. (1995). Tracking students for instruction: Consequences and implications for school restructuring. In M. T. Hallinan (Ed.), *Restructuring schools: Promising practices and policies* (pp. 113–131). New York: Plenum.

Griffin, G. A. (1995). Shared decision making: Influences on school and classroom activity. *Elementary School Journal*, **96**, 29–45.

Hackman, J. R., & Oldham, G. R. (1980). *Work redesign*. Reading, MA: Addison-Wesley.

Jenkins, J. R., Rank, J. Schrag, J. A. Rude, G. G., & Stowitschek, C. (1994). Effects of using school-based participatory decision making to improve services for low-performing students. *Elementary School Journal*, **94**, 357–372.

Jervis, K., & Wilson, N. (1995). *Collaboration: Looking beneath the surface*. New York: National Center for Restructuring Education, Schools, and Teaching, Teachers College, Columbia University.

Johnson, S. M. (1990). *Teachers at work: Achieving success in our schools*. New York: Basic Books.

Kahne, J., Goren, P., & Amsler, M. (1991, September). *Restructuring: Where are we and where are we going*. San Francisco: Far West Laboratory for Educational Research and Development.

Katz, D., & Kahn, R. L. (1978). *The social psychology of organizations* (2nd ed.). New York: Wiley.

Keller, B. M. (1995). Accelerated Schools: Hands-on learning in a unified community. *Educational Leadership*, **52**(5), 10–13.

Kerchner, C. T. (1993). Louisville: Professional development drives a decade of school reform. In C. T. Kerchner & J. E. Koppich (Eds.), *A union of professionals: Labor relations and educational reform* (pp. 25–42). New York: Teachers College Press.

Knight, S. L., & Stallings, J. A. (1995). The implementation of the Accelerated Schools Model in an urban elementary school. In R. L. Allington & S. A. Walmsley (Eds.), *No quick fix: Rethinking literacy programs in America's elementary schools* (pp. 236–251). New York: Teachers College Press.

Koffler, S. L. (1987). Assessing the impact of a state's decision to move from minimum competency testing toward higher level testing for graduation. *Educational Evaluation and Policy Analysis*, **9**, 325–336.

Lee, V. E., Bryk, A. S., & Smith, J. B. (1993). The organization of effective secondary schools. In L. Darling-Hammond (Eds.), *Review of research in education* (Vol. 19, pp. 171–267). Washington, DC: American Educational Research Association.

Lee, V. E., & Smith, J. B. (1995). Effects of high school restructuring and size on gains in achievement and engagement for early secondary school students. *Sociology of Education*, **68**, 241–270.

Lemlech, J. K., Hertzog-Foliart, H., & Hackl, A. (1994). The Los Angeles professional practice school: A study of mutual impact. In L. Darling-Hammond (Ed.), *Professional development schools: Schools for developing a profession* (pp. 156–175). New York: Teachers College Press.

Levin, H. M. (1987). Accelerated schools for disadvantaged students. *Educational Leadership*, **44**(6), 19–21.

Levin, H. M. (1996). Empowerment evaluation and Accelerated Schools. In D. M. Fetterman, S. J. Kaftarian, & A. Wandersman (Eds.), *Empowerment evaluation: Knowledge and tools for self-assessment and accountability* (pp. 49–64). Thousand Oaks, CA: Sage.

Levine, D. U. (1992). Implementation of an urban school-within-a-school approach. In H. C. Waxman, J. W. de Felix, J. E. Anderson, & H. P. Baptiste, Jr. (Eds.), *Students at risk in at-risk schools* (pp. 233–249). Newbury Park, CA: Corwin.

Lieberman, A. (Ed.). (1995). *The work of restructuring schools: Building from the ground up*. New York: Teachers College Press.

Little, J. W. (1990). The persistence of privacy: Autonomy and initiative in teachers' professional relations. *Teachers College Record*, **91**, 509–536.

Lortie, D. C. (1975). *Schoolteacher*. Chicago: University of Chicago Press.

Louis, K. S., Kruse, S. D., & Marks, H. (1996). School-wide professional community: Teachers' work, intellectual quality and commitment. In F. M. Newmann & Associates (Eds.), *Authentic achievement: Restructuring school for intellectual quality* (pp. 179–203). San Francisco: Jossey-Bass.

Louis, K. S., & Marks, H. (1996, April). *Does professional community affect the classroom? Teachers' work and student experiences in restructuring schools*. Paper presented at the annual meeting of the American Educational Research Association, New York.

Louis, K. S., Marks, H., & Kruse, S. (1996). Teachers' professional community in restructuring schools. *American Educational Research Journal*, **33**, 757–798.

Lythcott, J., & Schwartz, F. (1994). Professional development in action: An idea with visiting rights. In L. Darling-Hammond (Ed.), *Professional development schools: Schools for developing a profession* (pp. 126–155). New York: Teachers College Press

MacKinnon, J. D., & Brown, M. E. (1994). Inclusion in secondary schools: An analysis of school structure based on teachers' images of change. *Educational Administration Quarterly*, **30**, 126–152.

Madden, N. A., Slavin, R. E., Karweit, N. L., Dolan, L. J., & Wasik, B. A. (1993). Success for All: Longitudinal effects of a restructuring program for inner-city elementary schools. *American Educational Research Journal*, **30**, 123–148.

Malen, B. Ogawa, R. T., & Kranz, J. (1990). What do we know about school-based management? A case study of the literature – A call for research. In W. H. Clune & J. F. Witte (Eds.), *Choice and control in American education, Vol. 2: The practice of choice, decentralization and school restructuring* (pp. 289–342). New York: Falmer.

Marsick, V. J., & Watkins, K. (1990). *Informal and incidental learning in the workplace*. New York: Routledge

McCarthey, S. J., & Peterson, P. L. (1993). Creating classroom practice within the context of a restructured professional development school. In D. K. Cohen, M. W. McLaughlin, & J. E. Talbert (Eds.), *Teaching for understanding: Challenges for policy and practice* (pp. 130–163). San Francisco: Jossey-Bass.

McCarthy, J., & Still, S. (1993). Hollibrook Accelerated Elementary School. In J. Murphy & P. Hallinger (Eds.), *Restructuring schools: Learning from ongoing efforts* (pp. 63–83). Newbury Park, CA: Corwin.

McQuillan, P. J., & Muncey, D. E. (1991, May). *School-within-a-school restructuring and faculty divisiveness: Examples from a study of the Coalition of Essential Schools* (Working Paper #6). Providence, RI: School Ethnography Project, Brown University.

Meier, D. (1995). *The power of their ideas: Lessons for America from a small school in Harlem*. Boston: Beacon Press.

Merriam, S. B., & Caffarella, R. S. (1991). *Learning in adulthood*. San Francisco: Jossey-Bass.

Miles, M. B. (1993). Forty years of change in schools: Some personal reflections. *Educational Administration Quarterly*, **29**, 213–248.

Mortimore, P., Sammons, P., Stoll, L., Lewis, D., & Ecob, R. (1988). *School matters*. Berkeley: University of California Press.

Muncey, D. E. (1994, April). *Individual and schoolwide change in eight Coalition schools: Findings from a longitudinal ethnographic study*. Paper presented at the annual meeting of the American Educational Research Association, New Orleans.

Murphy, J. (1990). The educational reform movement of the 1980s: A comprehensive analysis. In J. Murphy (Ed.), *The educational reform movement of the 1980s: Perspectives and cases* (pp. 3–55). Berkeley, CA: McCutchan.

Murphy, J. (1991). *Restructuring schools: Capturing and assessing the phenomena*. New York: Teachers College Press.

Murphy, J. (1993). Restructuring: In search of a movement. In J. Murphy & P. Hallinger (Eds.), *Restructuring schooling: Learning from ongoing efforts* (pp. 1–31). Newbury Park, CA: Corwin.

Murphy, J., & Hallinger, P. (Eds.) (1993). *Restructuring schools: Learning from ongoing efforts*. Newbury Park, CA: Corwin.

Newmann, F. M., & Wehlage, G. G. (1995). *Successful school restructuring*. Madison: Center on Organization and Restructuring of Schools, University of Wisconsin.

Oakes, J., Gamoran, A., & Page, R. N. (1992). Curriculum differentiation: Opportunities, outcomes, and meanings. In P. W. Jackson (Ed.), *Handbook of research on curriculum* (pp. 570–608). New York: Macmillan.

O'Connor, R. E., & Jenkins, J. R. (1996). Cooperative learning as an inclusion strategy: A closer look. *Exceptionality*, 6, 29–51.

Peterson, P. L. (1992). Revising their thinking: Keisha Coleman and her third grade mathematics class. In H. H. Marshall (Ed.), *Redefining student learning* (pp. 151–176). Norwood, NJ: Ablex.

Porter, A. C. (1989). External standards and good teaching: The pros and cons of telling teachers what to do. *Educational Evaluation and Policy Analysis*, 11, 343–356.

Prestine, N. A. (1993). Feeling the ripples, riding the waves: Making an Essential School. In J. Murphy & P. Hallinger (Eds.), *Restructuring schools: Learning from ongoing efforts* (pp. 32–62). Newbury Park, CA: Corwin.

Prestine, N. A. (1994, April). *Sorting it out: A tentative analysis of Essential School change efforts in Illinois*. Paper presented at the annual meeting of the American Educational Research Association, New Orleans.

Prestine, N. A., & Bowen, C. (1993). Benchmarks of change: Assessing Essential School restructuring efforts. *Educational Evaluation and Policy Analysis*, 15, 298–319.

Ramirez-Smith, C. (1995). Stopping the cycle of failure: The Comer model. *Educational Leadership*, 52(5), 14–19.

Roth, K. J., Hasbach, C., Hazelwood, C., Hoekwater, E., Ligett, C., Lindquist, B., Beasley, K., & Rosean, C. L. (1993a, February). *Entry-ways into science and science teaching: Teacher and researcher development in a professional development schools* (Series No. 84). East Lansing: Institute for Research on Teaching, The Center for the Learning and Teaching of Elementary Subjects, Michigan State University.

Roth, K. J., Ligett, C., Kerksen, J., Hasbach, C., Hoekwater, E., Masters, J., & Woodhams, P. (1993b, February). *Many voices: Learning to teach social studies* (Series No. 86). East Lansing: Institute for Research on Teaching, The Center for the Learning and Teaching of Elementary Subjects, Michigan State University.

Rowan, B. (1990). Commitment and control: Alternative strategies for the organizational design of schools. In C. B. Cazden (Ed.), *Review of research in education* (Vol. 16, pp. 353–389). Washington, DC: American Educational Research Association.

Sebring, P. B., Bryk, A. S., Easton, J. Q., Luppescu, S., Thum, Y. M., Lopez, W., & Smith, B. (1995, August). *Charting reform: Chicago teachers take stock*. Chicago: Consortium on Chicago School Research, University of Chicago.

Sirotnik, K. (1986). *Critical perspectives on the organization and improvement of schooling*. Boston: Kluwer.

Slavin, R. E., Madden, N. A., Dolan, L. J., Wasik, B. A., Ross, S., Smith, L., & Dianda, M. (1996). Success for All: A summary of research. *Journal of Education for Students Placed at Risk*, 1, 41–76.

Slavin, R. E., Madden, N. A. Shaw, A., Mainzer, K. L., & Donnelly, M. C. (1993). Success for All: Three case studies of comprehensive restructuring of urban elementary schools. In J. Murphy & P. Hallinger (Eds.), *Restructuring schools: Learning from ongoing efforts* (pp. 84–112). Newbury Park, CA: Corwin.

Smith, M. L. (1991). Put to the test: The effects of external testing on teachers. *Educational Researcher*, 20(5), 8–11.

Smylie, M. A. (1994). Redesigning teachers' work: Connections to the classroom. In L. Darling-Hammond (Ed.), *Review of research in education* (Vol. 20, pp. 129–177). Washington, DC: American Educational Research Association.

Smylie, M. A., Lazarus, V., & Brownlee-Conyers, J. (1996). Instructional outcomes of school-based participative decision making. *Educational Evaluation and Policy Analysis*, 18, 181–198.

Squires, D. A., & Kranyik, R. D. (1995, 1996). The Comer program: Changing school culture. *Educational Leadership*, 53(4), 29–32.

Stallings, J. A., & Kowalski, T. (1990). Research on professional development schools. In W. R. Houston (Ed.), *Handbook of research on teacher education* (pp. 251–263). New York: Macmillan.

Stevens, R. J., & Slavin, R. E. (1995). The cooperative elementary school: Effects on students' achievement, attitudes, and social relations. *American Educational Research Journal*, 32, 321–351.

Tyack, D. (1990). "Restructuring" in historical perspective: Tinkering toward Utopia. *Teachers College Record*, 92, 170–191.

Wasley, P. A. (1991). Stirring the chalkdust: Changing practices in Essential Schools. *Teachers College Record, 93*, 28–58.

Weiss, C. H. (1993). Shared decision making about what? A comparison of schools with and without teacher participation. *Teachers College Record, 95*, 69–92.

Wilson, B. L., & Corbett, H. D. (1990). Statewide testing and local improvement: An oxymoron? In J. Murphy (Ed.), *The educational reform movement of the 1980s: Perspectives and cases* (pp. 243–263). Berkeley, CA: McCutchan.

Wohlstetter, P., Smyer, R., & Mohrman, S. A. (1994). New boundaries for school-based management: The high involvement model. *Educational Evaluation and Policy Analysis, 16*, 268–286.

# Teaching Standards: Foundations for Professional Development Reform

LAWRENCE INGVARSON

*Monash University*

*This chapter argues that teaching standards have the potential to reform radically the profes-sional development system for teachers, and to move control into the hands of the profession. It proposes a standards-based professional development system. Goals for the standards are determined in the main by educational policy. Profession-defined standards provide the basis on which the profession can establish expectations for professional development and account-ability.*

Over the past ten years the teaching profession has begun to demonstrate a capac-ity to develop a consensus around standards for highly accomplished teaching. Perhaps the best known examples are those produced by the National Council for the Teaching of Mathematics (NCTM) and the National Board for Professional Teaching Standards (NBPTS) in the U.S. These standards provide exciting and challenging descriptions of high quality teaching in specific teaching areas. They go far deeper into the nature of what it means to teach well than the lists of criteria and competencies typical of most managerial models for teacher appraisal and evaluation (Darling-Hammond, 1986). Most important for this chapter, these emerging examples of teaching standards indicate that the profession has the capac-ity to lay down its own long-term directions and goals for the professional develop-ment of its members.

This chapter argues that teaching standards have the potential to reform radi-cally the professional development system for teachers and move its control into the hands of the profession. It proposes a *standards-guided professional develop-ment system* as an alternative to, not a substitute for, traditional models of in-service education. Goals for the latter are determined, in the main, by changes in employer policy or the priorities of universities. In the standards-guided model, profession-defined standards provide the basis on which the profession can lay down its own agenda and expectations for professional development and accountability.

Professional learning communities, networks and collaboratives are now seen to be characteristic of more effective contexts for teacher development (Little, 1993; Lieberman & McLaughlin, 1992). Standards provide a necessary foundation for the evaluative work of these groups. They need reference points for reviewing their practice that go beyond the local school community or employing authority. Profes-sional communities, by definition, are bonded by a mutual interest in helping each other move their practice toward higher levels of profession-defined standards.

336

*M. Fullan (ed.), Fundamental Change, 336-361.*
© 2005 *Springer. Printed in the Netherlands.*

Standards provide an indispensable basis for deliberation and reflection within professional communities. They articulate the deep structure of educational values embodied in good practice – what it means, for example, to develop autonomy in student thinking, or what it means to engage in modes of inquiry characteristic of particular disciplines.

Despite major advances in our understanding of teacher development, much of what is provided in the name of in-service education still fails to engage or excite the majority of teachers. Several reasons for this failure have been identified in the literature (Fullan, 1995). One, which this chapter explores, is that the profession rarely exercises the major responsibility for the professional development of its own members; in particular key decisions about the long term aims and methods of professional development. The typical course mode of delivery, despite the best intentions of providers, often leaves teachers passively following someone else's agenda for change or development, not an agenda they have developed themselves. It rarely focuses on them as persons, as teachers, or as workgroups – where they are now, what they want to become, and, perhaps, what the profession believes they should become. As a result, levels of teacher commitment to, or engagement in in-service education are often disappointingly low.

An assumption underlying this paper is that this failure is not because we do not know much about conditions for effective in-service education and teacher learning. While there is always more to learn, we do know a great deal about how to engage a small proportion of teachers deeply in exciting forms of professional learning. Rather, the failure is because teachers do not see the professional development system – its goals, its knowledge base, its incentives, its methods and its modes for giving professional recognition to teachers who attain high standards – as a collective responsibility of their profession. One mark of a highly skilled occupation is that those who gain entry and career advancement should have attained standards set by practitioners themselves. Another is that the continuing development of its members should largely be the responsibility of the profession. This has not been a characteristic of teaching.

## THE IDEA OF A "PROFESSIONAL DEVELOPMENT SYSTEM"

The argument here is that radical reform of professional development is contingent upon steps that enhance the leadership and responsibility that teachers exercise over the professional development system. What is meant by the "professional development system".

Every country develops some kind of support system to enhance the quality of teaching and the implementation of educational reforms in its schools. Key functions of such systems are to generate ideas for improvement, to keep these ideas circulating, and to provide opportunities for teachers to share them and to learn how to use them. Countries vary greatly in the way these tasks are carried out. Holland, for example, was well known for its extensive "School Support Structure" in the 1980s. The Dutch Support Structure was allocated a stable proportion

(2 percent) of the national budget for education to support the implementation of government-initiated reforms. A key variable across countries is the extent to which the locus of control over the support system resides with governments, employing authorities, or professional teacher bodies.

The key components of a professional development system are:

(a) the *governance* or decisionmaking component. This component is concerned with control questions such as: Who determines what goals and purposes the professional development system will serve, the allocation of resources, and the legitimation of some in-service education activities over others (e.g., for credit; for promotion)?

(b) the *knowledge* component. This concerns the goals of the PD system: How are the goals and purposes the professional development system determined? What is the basis for determining what should teachers get better at? Is the main goal of the system to help teachers learn how to implement government or employer determined policies? Or, does the system depend on the development and review of profession-defined standards? Does the system support or undermine the growth of research-based knowledge in the profession about practice?

(c) the *incentives* component. This concerns the mechanisms by which teachers are given recognition for evidence of their professional development. What value is placed on advances in teachers' knowledge and skill relative to administration? How are these advances related to career stages and organisational structures in schools? Does the pay system reflect the critical importance of high quality teaching to the success of school systems?

(d) the *provider* component. This concerns who provides PD activities and courses. Who designs and runs them? Who decides how teachers will learn? What is the basis for their credibility and their legitimacy? Who accredits the providers? How are they funded? Who pays?

In the past, teachers rarely exercised control or leadership over these components. Choy, Henke, Alt, Medrich, and Bobbitt (1993) report that only one U.S. teacher in three felt they had any influence over the content of in-service training. However, there are signs that a basic shift is taking place in control of the in-service education system; the locus of authority seems to be shifting from bureaucratic control to some, as yet unclear, model of professional leadership and control. For example, Little and McLaughlin (1991), following their research with teachers who are active members of professional networks such as the Urban Maths Collaboratives, talk about a shift from a "training" paradigm to a "professionalism" paradigm in the development of teachers (p. 34). While the traditional in-service education system has been an instrument primarily for the implementation of central policy, the emerging system is more an instrument for encouraging teachers to deepen their skills in the specifics of their teaching or subject over the long term of their careers.

This shift in the way goals for PD are defined raises some interesting questions about funding and whether a new "economy" of PD is emerging also. In the policy-driven system it is reasonable to expect employers to cover the costs of in-service training, as in other industries. In a standards-based model there may need to be a different equation. Teachers preparing for NBPTS certification, for example, might be expected to cover part of the costs if they gain personally through promotion or enhanced opportunities for career advancement and mobility. Long-standing policies for granting salary increments for course credits may need to be reconsidered with the advent of a standards-driven system.

This shift also has implications for the traditional role of universities. The system for gaining formal awards for advanced professional qualifications has been controlled in the main by universities, not the profession, unlike occupations such as accountancy and medicine. Although universities have a valuable role to play in professional development, a standards-guided model raises questions about whether universities should retain a monopoly over the provision of further qualifications for teachers, and why a professional body for teachers should not establish its own advanced certification system. University courses for practising teachers may not necessarily meet the profession's need for an advanced certification system based on the demonstrable attainment of high standards of practice, a certification which is credible to employers as a basis for career path and salary decisions.

## A STANDARDS-GUIDED PROFESSIONAL DEVELOPMENT SYSTEM

At a conceptual level, the relationship between teaching standards and the professional development of teachers is straightforward. Standards for accomplished teaching, such as those of the NCTM and the NBPTS, provide long term goals for professional development. They make explicit the educational values that teachers continually seek to embody in their practice, particularly in the relationships they build between themselves and their students, and the subject matter in question. They clarify what the profession expects its members to get better at. The NCTM's *Professional Standards for the Teaching of Mathematics* (NCTM, 1991) for example, is an excellent model of challenging profession-defined teaching standards, one that would take most math teachers many years of reflection, training and feedback from colleagues to attain.

The key components in the standards-guided model are:

1. Profession-defined *teaching standards* that provide direction and milestones for professional development over the long term of a career in teaching;

2. An *infrastructure for professional learning* whose primary purpose is to enable teachers to gain the knowledge and skill embodied in the teaching standards;

3. Staged career structures and pay systems that provide *incentives and recognition* for attaining these teaching standards;

4. A credible system of *professional certification* based on valid assessments of whether teachers have attained the levels of performance defined by the standards.

In the standards-guided model, teachers' professional bodies develop standards for career advancement *as practising teachers*. They also develop and operate a system for assessing teacher performance for professional certification. Teacher associations, in collaboration with employers and universities, provide appropriate development opportunities for teachers to reach the standards and, eventually, to prepare for certification by professional bodies. Attainment of these standards, as validated by performance assessments developed by the professional body and conducted by trained peers, is regarded by employing authorities as a prerequisite for promotion through a series of three to four career stages over the period of a teaching career.

At a political level, however, resistance to the standards-based model is to be expected. Apart from the public, three groups have a vested interest in in-service education; employing authorities, universities and the teaching profession. For a long time, teachers have come a poor third in this triangular struggle over the allocation of resources and the determination of goals for in-service education. Early attempts to place responsibility in the hands of the profession, such as teachers' centres and school-based in-service education, failed to gain widespread support from governments. An attempt to build an in-service education system around professional standards would represent a fundamental shift in the balance of authority and control over teachers' work and its evaluation. It would also change the traditional methods for allocating and distributing resources for PD. For these reasons, initial resistance to the idea of a standards-guided model is likely until employers and universities and other providers realise they have much to gain from a system that provides incentives for most teachers to engage in processes for attaining high teaching standards.

Technically, there is a long way to go before a standards-driven approach could be implemented on a national scale. The most advanced example is the National Board for Professional Teaching Standards (NBPTS) in the US. Few professional bodies have been as rigorous as the Board in its quest for credible standards and assessments, yet the Board would be the first to recognise that more needs to be done. Since it was established in 1987, the NBPTS has invested over $60m in research. In 1994 it announced the first cohort of Board Certified teachers. In this chapter it is only possible to provide a glimpse of the technical expertise, as well as political acumen, that is needed to set standards, to develop valid and reliable performance assessments, and to conduct a national professional certification system. (For a fuller account and discussion see, for example, Haertel, 1991; Jaeger & Bond, 1995; Moss, 1994; Ingvarson, forthcoming).

## RATIONALE FOR THE STANDARDS-GUIDED MODEL

A few years ago I was asked to come up with a strategy for enhancing the professional development of science teachers in Australia. My first step was to talk with a lot of science teachers across the country about what was wrong with the present arrangements. It seemed important to define what the problem was before developing the strategy. These interviews pointed to some major weaknesses which meant that the traditional patterns of professional development provision were unlikely to touch or engage the majority of teachers.

Three will be mentioned here:

(a) *Unclear, short term goals.* There was insufficient clarity or consensus about what science teachers should get better at *over the long term*. As a result, planning and provision of in-service activities lacked coherence or a developmental sequence. Most courses were one-off activities. When looked at in total, provision could be described, at best, as diverse, but aimless was probably a more accurate term.

(b) *Weak incentives.* There were few extrinsic incentives for professional development. Career structures and pay systems were only loosely aligned with evidence of professional development and the attainment of high levels of knowledge and skill in the teaching of science. Most teachers said they just "did their own thing". There were no outside reference points or standards with which they could compare their own teaching.

(c) *Weak professional control.* Teachers, relative to most professional groups, had little control over policies and practices related to their own professional development. Even teacher/subject associations devoted most of their course effort to helping their members cope with changes in government policy, not to helping them progress to higher teaching standards. There was a need to strengthen the capacity of teacher associations to exercise professional leadership in relation to the quality of teaching.

These interviews pointed to the powerlessness that teachers feel as an occupation in relation to their own professional development. The standards-guided model is designed to address these weaknesses. In this model, teaching standards provide clear, stable, profession-defined expectations for professional development over the long term, in contrast with the short term, one-off character of traditional modes of in-service education driven by rapid shifts in government or employer policy. Teachers come to feel that the development of standards is their business.

These weaknesses are consistent with those identified by others in the field. As Fullan (1995) argues, one reason PD has had a poor track record is because it lacks a theoretical base and a coherent focus or purpose. In-service education is mainly "just courses", and, as a result, "it fails to have a sustained cumulative effect, or to engage teachers where they work. At best it serves to support the implementation of specific innovations, but it lacks any integration with the day to day life of teachers" (p.253). For Hargreaves (1995), most PD ignores or undermines the place of moral purpose and commitment – the desire to realise values in practice, which is a necessary condition for growth. Teaching standards, such as the NCTM's Professional Standards for Teaching Mathematics and those developed by the NBPTS, directly tackle questions of moral purpose in teaching and learning and clarify what the profession believes teachers need to know and be able to do to make those purposes a reality.

Elmore (1996) draws attention to "the problem of scale" in educational change – that few reforms this century have ever managed to engage more than about 20–30% of teachers in "ambitious" practices. He argues that an over-reliance on intrinsic incentives in teaching is one of the main reasons. The rate of adoption is roughly equal to the proportion of teachers who are motivated highly enough by intrinsic rewards, and the chance to affiliate with pockets of 'true believers' engaged in a common endeavour. A related reason is that the types of extrinsic incentives that have been used in the past, such as merit pay bonuses and career ladder schemes, lack the capacity to shape practice, or if they do, they do it in counter-productive ways.

The standards-guided model aims to strengthen extrinsic incentives and tangible forms of recognition for professional development, such as career advancement, leadership opportunities and status. Elmore argues that part of the solution to the problem of scale is to create alternative forms of "harder-edged" incentives based around performance standards related to salary or career progression, such as those embodied in the NBPTS standards. This means the basis for assessing teacher performance must change from simple conceptions of student outcomes and observational checklists to more complex evidence of teaching performance such as the portfolio exercises required from candidates who apply for NBPTS certification.

In a talk to the 1995 Annual Meeting of the American Educational Research Association on incentives and systemic reform, Clare Pelton, Vice-President of the NBPTS, gave a brief history of her experiences with in-service education over a period of more than thirty years as a teacher. Her aim was to distinguish what worked from what did not.

For Pelton (1995) the defining feature of effective PD experiences was that teachers controlled the agenda. Most courses left barely a trace on thought or practice because they were "someone else's agenda". Teachers were subject to the whims of district administrators and university researchers. Decision making about in-service education aims and funding was also usually someone else's turf – that of the district office or the university. In contrast, effective PD experiences were based on real tasks – issues and evidence that grew out of classroom work. Often it was a focus on subject matter learning that seemed to turn teachers on. They were not "courses", or someone's project, but on-going activities sustained by the mutual desire to match aspirations to reality and the opportunity for discussions with teachers from other schools who were trying to do the same.

What really worked, in Pelton's experience, were those marginal, but on-going, projects based around networks of teachers wherein teachers played the major role in setting the agenda, such as the Bay Area Writing Group that started in the early 1970s. Others have written in similar vein about teacher networks (Little & McLaughlin, 1991; Lieberman & McLaughlin, 1992). Pelton reported that teachers preparing for National Board certification, often as members of local networks, claimed the process was the most valuable PD experience they had ever had.

The standards-guided model aims to place greater responsibility for the professional development agenda in the hands of teachers, individually and collectively. As a result of that responsibility, and tangible incentives, the model predicts teachers will be more likely to become involved in on-going networks of the kind Pelton describes.

## STANDARDS AND TEACHING: THE EMERGING PICTURE

*Two purposes for standards*

For the purposes of this chapter it is important to distinguish two purposes for the development of standards. One is to ensure student welfare and provide public safeguards, based on the undeniable requirement that teachers be publicly account-able. The state, in collaboration with the profession, has the major responsibility for defining these basic standards or duties. The second emphasises the complementary need to ensure that teachers keep up with developments in research and knowledge in their area of teaching and review their practices in the light of this knowledge. The major responsibility for developing these standards for high quality practice should rest with the profession.

Lee Shulman provides the useful analogy of restaurant evaluation to illustrate the difference between these two necessary types of standards for teaching. Restaurants must meet two types of standards, each serving important, but differ-ent, purposes. A restaurant must meet a set of health and safety standards if it is to remain open to the public. It is important to note that the standards in this case are *necessary* standards, not desirable standards, as in Scriven's concept of "duties" (1994). A failure to meet even one of the health or safety standards means that the restaurant may be closed. This failure can not be compensated for by meeting other standards satisfactorily. It is also important to note that the standards are generic. They apply to every restaurant.

There is another type of evaluation of restaurants that serves a different purpose. This is the *Guide Michelin* model. It is carried out by a different type of evaluator, with very different qualifications and experience from those of the health inspec-tor. Their evaluations aim to tell you how good the restaurant is, for that type of restaurant. This evaluation requires an expert critic; a connoisseur of that type of cuisine. Its aim is to lift the quality of restaurants; and the standards provide a guide to the kinds of improvement that might be made, without presuming that there is only one way to improve. Lifting standards in this case does not imply standardisation.

Both evaluations serve valuable functions. They clarify what is valued. They aim to have important consequences. Their validity rests on the extent to which the evaluation has beneficial effects on future performance. While Department of Health standards aim to provide common public safeguards, the restaurant critic aims to lift both quality and diversity.

There are obvious parallels to this analogy in teaching. Michael Scriven (1994), for example, provides one of the most rigorous approaches to defining the neces-sary, generic standards for the appraisal of teachers in the public interest. His duties-based model of teacher evaluation is derived from an analysis of the contractual duties that all teachers are employed to carry out. It complements the US NBPTS (1989) standards, which are based on descriptions of highly accomplished practice in particular areas of the curriculum. These criteria aim to articulate what teachers need to know and be able to do in order to promote high quality student learning in particular subject areas. This work indicates that teachers can reach a workable consensus on advanced standards specific to the teaching of particular subjects in particular contexts.

Superficial lists of teacher competencies based on task analyses abound in the teacher evaluation literature. Professional knowledge, however, is another thing, especially as it relates to the implementation of educational values and what counts as quality student learning in particular curriculum areas. Competency lists can provide useful descriptions of what teachers are expected to do, but problems arise when we need to know what counts as doing it well; that is, when we start to use them as standards for professional development, or as a basis for recognising quality learning and teaching. Even greater problems occur if one expects them to provide research-based guidance on what teachers should be expected to get better at.

### Minimum, competitive and developmental standards

Another relevant distinction between types of standards comes from Bacharach, Conley, and Shedd (1990). They distinguish three types of pay systems based on different types of standards: minimum, competitive and developmental. Minimum standards specify the base level of knowledge and skill required of teachers to enter and retain a position in the profession. Competitive standards relate to job-based career ladders. They help to regulate the allocation of limited promotional positions and monetary rewards. Neither minimum nor competitive standards provide incentives or direction for professional growth.

Developmental, or skills-based, standards are based on progress along dimensions of increasing knowledge and skill about practice. They define targets for professional growth, but do not impose quotas on promotion. They assume a gradual transition from novice to expert based on research and reflective practice. Pay systems for professions tend to be based more on the developmental standards model because they provide incentives and recognition for professional growth, growth which is in the interests of both the employer and the public.

### "Professional Standards for the Teaching of Mathematics"

There are now several examples of advanced or quality teaching standards produced by professional bodies. The NCTM's *Professional Standards for the Teaching of Mathematics* (NCTM, 1991) is one of the best known examples of the leadership that teachers' associations can provide in standards-based reform. It is also an example of the fruits that follow from viewing standards development as a long-term process of consensus building across major stakeholders. There are numerous examples of professional development networks that now take the NCTM standards as their frame of reference (e.g. Schifter & Fosnot, 1993; Barnett & Ramirez, 1996).

Romberg (1988) provides a case study of the role that the NCTM standards have played in the reform of school mathematics in the US over the previous ten years. He argues that the NCTM's emphasis on standards represents a major shift from earlier strategies for promoting curriculum and teaching reform. According to Romberg, the big differences are that:

1.    Leadership for the reform activities has been assumed by professional organisations.
2.    Consensus has been reached among these organisations about the direction and the form the needed changes must take.

The National Council of Teachers of Mathematics provided three reasons for their involvement in standards development: to ensure quality, to indicate goals, and to promote change. The NCTM also believed that it was part of its professional responsibility and an appropriate thing for a professional body to be doing. The interesting question for the NCTM was why they and similar associations had not been doing it for many years. For the NCTM, ensuring quality required the professional community to take the intellectual reins for mathematics education away from textbook and test publishers, legislators, and administrators whose control had yielded a low-level, basic skills curriculum.

As goals, the standards indicated what was valued in terms of student and teacher development. As the Preface of the NCTM standards document (1991) states:

> This document spells out what teachers need to know to teach towards new goals for mathematics education and how teaching should be evaluated for the purpose of improvement. We challenge all who have responsibility for any part of the support and development of mathematics teachers and teaching to use these standards as a basis for discussion and for making needed change so that we can reach our goal of a quality mathematics education for every child.

The way in which 'we' is used in this quote encapsulates the underlying theme in this chapter – it illustrates the kind of self-esteem that comes to an occupation with growing confidence in its expertise and with the exercise of important responsibilities.

A significant feature of the NCTM *Professional Standards* was the way they demonstrated how teaching standards could be embedded in the teaching of a particular subject. In fact, research through the 1980s demonstrated that standards for teacher evaluation *should* be specific to the teaching of particular subjects because the subject being taught, and a teacher's knowledge of that subject, had profound effects on teaching methods and their effectiveness. Despite these findings, subject effects were not reflected in the dominant types of teacher evaluation favoured by school administrators. NCTM's standards are an attempt to capture what teachers of *mathematics* should aspire to. They were not derived from a task-analysis of competencies based on what teachers currently do. They are an attempt to respond to the question, 'What do teachers need to know, besides generic teaching skills, to teach mathematics well?', a deeper question that points to the need for professional, as well as managerial, models of teacher evaluation and accountability (Darling-Hammond, 1986).

One of the main reasons the NCTM became involved in standards was to change in the way teachers defined themselves as a profession, and what their professional responsibilities as an organisation should encompass. The NCTM case is an excellent example of the kind of responsible leadership that a subject association can offer, and the beneficial effects that can follow from the increased credibility and influence of the organisation in national policy concerning teacher licensure, PD, advanced certification, curriculum, testing and teacher evaluation. Becoming involved in standards has done the NCTM no harm at all. According to Romberg and Webb (1992), NCTM experienced a rapid growth in membership (from a low of 55,000 in 1983 to 100,000 ten years later) that they attribute, in part, to its active involvement in mathematics education reform.

## STANDARDS AND PROFESSIONAL DEVELOPMENT

Professional standards can be seen as an attempt to conceptualise the main dimensions along which teachers can be expected to improve in their practice. There have been many attempts to describe stages of teacher development in the past, often using theoretical perspectives from disciplines such as psychology and adult learning (e.g., ego-self development, self-actualisation). (Sprinthall, Reiman, & Thies-Sprinthall (1996) provide a comprehensive review of models for teacher professional development.) Though helpful in other contexts, these stage theories of development are not particularly useful when the task is one of describing what teachers need to know and be able to do produce quality teaching and learning for the purpose of performance assessment .

Two complementary approaches to conceptualising dimensions for development are being used as a basis for developing standards for accomplished or high quality teaching. The most common approach emphasises the domain- or subject-specific nature of expertise (NBPTS, 1989); the other emphasises the generic nature of high level, or meta-competencies (Dreyfus & Dreyfus, 1986; Elliott, 1993; Sternberg & Horvath, 1995). It is not possible to do justice to this literature here, other than to sketch out some of its main features and contributors.

Approaches to standards development, such as those used by the NBPTS , the Interstate New Teacher Assessment and Support Consortium (Darling-Hammond, Wise & Klein, 1995), and the NCTM (1991, begin by identifying what counts as quality learning in particular curriculum domains, following recent research on teacher knowledge and the domain-specific nature of expertise (Leinhardt, Putman, Stein, & Baxter, 1991). Their next step is to identify what teachers need to know and be able to do to promote quality learning. A common dimension in this literature, for example, is the development of the capacity to engage students in discourse consistent with teaching for understanding and the educational values inherent in the subject area (Lampert, 1990; Ball, 1993). This area of research indicates that teaching for understanding is heavily dependent on sound understanding of the subject matter being taught (Cohen & Ball, 1990) as well as research knowledge about how students learn that subject matter (Fennema, Carpenter, Franke & Carey, 1993).

This research is providing greater confidence that we can articulate a knowledge base for teaching and standards for what counts as quality teaching. It also indicates that when teachers' subject-matter knowledge and pedagogical content knowledge are more explicit, better connected, and more integrated, they are more likely to teach the subject dynamically, to represent it in more varied ways, and to encourage and respond more fully to student comments and questions. A principal focus for professional development then is the knowledge that teachers hold about the subjects they teach and the beliefs they hold about how students learn them (Borko & Putnam, 1995).

From a different, but not contradictory, tradition of teacher research, development is a standards-driven search for greater "situational understanding" (Dreyfus & Dreyfus, 1986). Situational understanding is enhanced when professionals reflect on practice and evaluate factors that help or hinder their ability to realise their educational values in practice. The direction of growth is guided by educational values. Standards are statements of educational values (Elliott, 1993), moral purpose (Fullan, 1995), or procedural principles (Peters, 1966) indicative of educational quality in the settings a teacher provides for student learning that serve reflection. They provide a lens through which teachers perceive what is significant in a practical situation and decide on appropriate action. Elliott's earlier work with others on action research leaves no doubt that this type of action research can lead to rich insights and new knowledge about teaching for other teachers to consider. The PEEL (Project for Enhancing Effective Learning) Project in Australia, is similarly convincing (Baird & Northfield, 1993). This teacher-controlled action research was driven by standards grounded in conceptions of active learning derived from theories of meta-cognition and constructivism. Case studies written by PEEL teachers illustrate not only enhanced levels of situational understanding, but sophisticated contributions that teachers can make to professional knowledge. Case studies from these examples of action research written by teachers could make convincing entries in portfolios submitted to professional bodies for advanced certification (Wolf, 1994).

Like the domain-specific work, Elliott's (1993) image of the PD process is consistent with the standards model. He emphasises that, "The quality of a teacher's performance is constituted by its consistency with *educational values* that constitute the ends of education" (p. 56). Teachers' understandings of educational values are shaped by their biographies. This understanding also grows with experience and increased skills in reflection within professional communities. The aim of PD here is to promote growth toward what turn out to be ever receding value-concepts or standards. According to Elliott, "There are always new meanings and understandings to be grasped, and therefore fresh implications for action to be discovered. Values, including educational values, are never perfectly realised in any particular form of action, . . . " (p. 62).

Changes in the way teachers' work is defined also affect how we conceptualise what should teachers get better at and, therefore, the way we conceptualise standards. For example, emerging conceptions of teacher leadership and schools as professional communities broaden the definition of teachers' work and therefore the bases for conceptualising teacher development. Teachers in professional communities must be more than just classroom teachers. Their work will incorporate contributions to leadership and management as well as teaching.

Fullan (1994), for example, argues that a necessary condition for reform to work is a "substantial broadening of teacher leadership until it embodies the majority of teachers in a given school, a given district, a given state, a given profession (p. 1)." Mohrman, Mohrman, and Odden (1996) argue that schools have much to learn from the research on "high involvement" organisations about how to decentralise management effectively and build the self-management capabilities of teachers. Kelley (1995) explores the implications of emerging models of school organisation for the kinds of knowledge and skills that teacher career structures and pay systems should reward. She argues that in high involvement models, "The older model of teaching in which the career educator eventually moves out of teaching into administration is replaced one in which "master" teachers take on additional leadership responsibilities, but remain connected to the classroom throughout their careers" (p. 22).

These writers point to the need to change the way teachers' work is defined in relation to school management. In professional communities, teachers assume more school-wide leadership functions. These changes have major implications for the way we should conceptualise teacher development and what teachers should get better at. As well as needing teachers with increasing depth and breadth of expertise in teaching and classroom practice, professional communities need teachers who develop a variety of leadership and team management skills in matters related to school policy, curriculum and teaching. Consequently, pay structures have to provide better incentives for teachers to develop educational leadership, as well as depth and breadth, skills.

## STANDARDS AND TEACHERS' CAREERS

The standards-guided model aims to strengthen the links between professional development and career advancement. Career structures and pay systems have powerful long term effects on conditions that enhance the quality of teaching overall. These include: the ability of teaching to attract and retain its share of talented graduates; motivation to improve professional practice; the organisational culture of the school; and teachers' perceptions of whether their work is recognised and valued. The effects of typical pay systems for teachers on these conditions are more often negative than positive. There is increasing recognition that re-invention of teacher pay systems is a pre-condition for the "re-culturing" of schools as professional communities (Mohrman, Mohrman, & Odden, 1996).

Attempts to reinvent pay systems during the 1970s and 80s, such as merit pay systems and career ladder schemes, proved to be either unacceptable to teachers, because of detrimental effects on staff relationships (Smylie & Smart, 1990), or irrelevant to the enhancement of teaching (Smylie, 1994). The concept of career development, or "skills-based" pay, is a promising alternative (Lawler, 1990). Bacharach's idea of developmental standards was introduced earlier. In this conception, the main basis for the career structure shifts from years of experience, extra jobs, or credits for courses, to evidence of growth in those areas of professional knowledge and skill that are critical to a school's effectiveness. This is the heart of the standards-based model.

Unlike competitive job ladder schemes, skills-based pay systems provide *all* teachers with incentives to enhance their professional development. They overcome the negative effects of merit pay schemes by making the criteria for extrinsic professional recognition consistent with the intrinsic rewards that teachers seek and that come with professional development efforts. The vital links in this chain are teaching standards and performance assessments that teachers consider to be valid, realistic and challenging, such as those the NBPTS is attempting to develop.

Career development is a more appropriate concept than career ladders for organisations that employ professionals. With professional careers, changes in pay and status are based on advances in the person's knowledge and skill and consequently their value to the organisation. But the principal nature of the work that is done does not change substantially with career advancement. The role may enlarge, teachers may offer more leadership, but senior staff are still expected to practice and model good practice in a community of practitioners. Similarly, it is expected that all teachers will contribute to the school managerially, as well as educationally, if they wish for career advancement. Leadership and positional authority are thereby decoupled.

Emphasis on standards and career redesign is also warranted by recent research that suggests we may have overestimated the importance of focusing on the school as the unit of change and improvement. An equally important focus for reform policy may be the teacher, or the profession. This is the essential aim of the standards-based model. The research program of Rowe, Holmes-Smith, & Hill (1993), for example, shows that teacher effects far outweigh school effects on student achievement:

> It is essentially through the quality of teaching that effective schools 'make a difference'; in fact, on the basis of our findings to date it could be argued that effective schools are only 'effective' to the extent that they have 'effective' teachers. (p. 15)

This research shows that class/teacher effects, mediated by teacher professional development, have more powerful effects on student achievement outcomes than school effects. The clear implication is that educational reform should focus as much on teachers and the profession, on using career paths to attract. prepare and retain the best teachers possible, as it does on school restructuring and changing models for school management.

As yet, there are few examples of career development models in operation. Ingvarson and Chadbourne (1997) outline some of the difficulties encountered when a pay for knowledge and skills model (the "Advanced Skills Teacher") was introduced in Australia. Traditional assumptions about what it means to have a career in teaching proved difficult to change, especially in the absence of valid standards for advanced practice. There was a need for more evidence that teachers have much to get better at beyond the first 7–8 years of teaching.

*Matching teacher career cycles to professional development*

The above developments in career structures can be related to Huberman's (1995) work on career cycles or stages, which focuses on the subjective experience of teaching over the long term. One of the problems many have pointed to in teachers' work is its lack of career stages, such as those in traditional professions that provide cycles of effort and a sense of achievement and professional recognition when the standards for each career stage are attained. In those professions, unlike teaching, people tend to be promoted within, not out of, the profession. They still keep practising after promotion.

Huberman found about 4–5 stages in most teaching careers; from an entry/ survival stage, through stabilisation and experimentation, to serenity and disengagement. It would be an interesting exercise to try to match Huberman's subjective stages with the kinds of career structures that seem necessary for the "re-culturing" of schools as professional communities.

The highest levels of career satisfaction for the teachers in Huberman's study seemed to rest finally with those who 'stuck to the knitting' and concentrated on classroom experimentation and enhancing their teaching skills. Huberman points out that his findings are consistent with those of Ashton and Webb (1986) on the quality of work life: "Work is likely to be satisfying when we value what we do, when it challenges and extends us, when we do it well, and when we have ample evidence confirming our success" (p.162). Standards would make a contribution to the quality of work life by providing frameworks for self evaluation, challenging projects for personal development and a valuable sense of achievement and professional recognition.

While new forms of licensure standards (Darling-Hammond, Wise, & Klein, 1995) might correspond to negotiating the survival phase successfully (years 1–3), National Board Certification would seem to come somewhere in Huberman's experimentation phase (between 7–18 years). The call for pay systems based on knowledge and skill, as outlined above, seems compatible therefore with Huberman's findings.

THE NBPTS: AN EXAMPLE OF AN EMBRYONIC STANDARDS-
GUIDED PD SYSTEM

The National Board for Professional Teaching Standards is the most ambitious
attempt by any country to establish a national professional body for the advanced
certification of teachers. It has the potential to revolutionise the professional
development system for teachers in the U.S. The Board's mission (NBPTS, 1989),
"is to establish high and rigorous standards for what accomplished teachers should
know and be able to do, and to develop and operate a national, voluntary system
to assess and certify teachers who meet these standards" (p. 1). It aims to build a
national certification system for *all* teachers, one that is recognised by local education authorities for career advancement, and by state licensing authorities for license
renewal purposes. President Clinton recently (Feb. 1997) pledged to support the
NBPTS in its goal of certifying 100,000 teachers over the next decade.

The NBPTS approach embodies the main features of the standards-guided
model outlined at the beginning of this paper. Standards development is conducted
by committees of teachers and other educators appointed by the NBPTS to advise
its Board of Directors. So far (1996) seventeen standards committees have
developed standards in twenty-one certification fields (eventually there will be 34
fields in all). The Board seeks a professional consensus about current best practice
and thought. A key consideration in standards development is managing the
politics of the operation – who gets to sit at the table? The Board pays attention
to sorting out the intellectual landscape of the field and building in the variability
that exists in terms of philosophies, values, and positions. This task goes well
beyond task analyses of basic competencies, or the identification of generic teaching skills. Each NBPTS Committee has the job of articulating a vision of highly
accomplished learning and teaching in its field of practice. According to David
Mandel from the NBPTS:

> The first thing is that you have to have a vision of what you are trying to
> accomplish with kids, one that you can agree on. And then you have to ask,
> 'What are the critical aspects of practice that allow someone to get these
> results with a wide range of kids?' That's the beginning of the standards
> conversation. (Interview with author, April 1995)

From the outset, each standards committee interacts regularly with the relevant
subject associations, inviting input, advice, and commentary. Extensive periods of
wide consultation also accompany the release of draft standards in an effort to
ensure the validity of the standards.

The development of performance assessments based on the standards has been
conducted by Assessment Development Laboratories (ADLs). ADLs have usually been based in regional laboratories, testing organisations, research institutes,
or universities. Their assignment has been to design and test performance assessment packages for the initial certification fields. Teacher associations play a
significant role in both standards and assessment development. The NBPTS works

from the view that quality in teaching does not imply uniformity of style. Like performance in the arts, quality teaching may be recognisable, but not predictable or standardised.

The *English Language Arts* ADL, an early example, created a performance assessment system with three types of exercises: 1) School Site Portfolio; 2) Content Knowledge Examination; and 3) Assessment Centre Exercises. These exercises are designed to provide windows into what teachers and their students actually do. They are ways for teachers to represent their knowledge and skill. The School Site Portfolio, for example, includes three exercises that teachers complete in their schools over several months. These require them to provide evidence of their teaching, by means of videos and examples of student work, with reflective commentaries for presentation to the Board's assessors. Candidates are strongly encouraged to involve colleagues in the process of preparing their portfolios.

The Content Knowledge exercises consist of three essay prompts, which are completed in an assessment centre. One and a half hours is allowed for each prompt. The purpose is to assess candidate's knowledge of literature, their knowledge of the reading and writing processes, and their knowledge of language development. The Assessment Centre exercises are simulations of situations akin to those that accomplished teachers might face, such as analysing a colleague's lesson, or selecting textbooks.

Performance assessment methods undergo rigorous tests to ensure they meet the highest pyschometric standards, Valuable descriptions of the R & D work of the NBPTS on standards and assessment development can be found in Jaeger & Bond (1995); Mandel (forthcoming) and Pearlman (forthcoming). Six certification fields are now (1996) fully operational.

*Professional development and the NBPTS:*

National Board certification has the potential to provide more powerful incentives for professional development than we have had in the past. The Board's system of external professional assessment aims to provide a valuable, expert and independent indication of professional development that schools can use in making high-stakes decisions about career advancement. In time, as National Board certification becomes recognised more widely by local employers for salary and career purposes, it may provide an alternative to further university study as an indicator of professional development and, therefore, value to the employer. For this reason, Board certification could pose a threat to the virtual monopoly universities have had over courses for credit and further qualifications for teachers.

In practice, new forms of collaboration between professional associations and universities appear to be emerging. Some universities are beginning to provide a meeting place for support groups of teachers preparing portfolios for Board certification. Partnerships are developing between professional associations and universities in the provision of relevant professional development. As mentioned above, teaching standards can provide very useful reference points for group debate, self-evaluation and peer review and support.

National Board certification is based on an assessment of teacher performance against Board standards. It is a professional body certification, not a university qualification. The Board does not provide or require courses to be taken. How a teacher prepares for Board assessment is left to the teacher, although the Board, of course, provides detailed guidelines for its assessment exercises and encourages teachers to collaborate as they prepare. Ideally, preparation for Board certification would a very appropriate focus for the work of professional networks and communities within and across schools.

It is not difficult to see how a standards-guided model could spawn a wide variety of professional development activity designed to support candidates. A limitation I see in the current NBPTS certification process is that it requires teachers to complete most portfolio tasks over the relatively short period of one year. The process of promoting professional development, which is one of the main purposes of the Board, might be better achieved if teachers were expected to prepare entries for their portfolios over a period of four to five years of part-time work with colleagues in various networks within and across schools. Younger teachers may then see the advanced standards of the Board as goals they work towards over several years.

There may be alternative ways in which teachers might prepare for the equivalent of a Board assessment. Masters degrees could be geared more closely to preparing teachers for assessment by a professional body – a "Professional Masters" degree might serve this purpose. The preparation period could be planned over several years. It is conceivable that a Professional Masters level course for teachers could be structured around the main dimensions of NBPTS standards such as subject matter knowledge, pedagogical content knowledge, knowledge of students and learning processes, knowledge of classroom teaching and management, as well as other dimensions based on expanded school roles, such as curriculum and professional development leadership and the building of professional community in schools. Assignments for such courses might be based around the equivalent of portfolio entries described above for the English ADL.

*Greater integration with existing professional networks and associations*

There is another level at which a standards-guided model, such as the NBPTS, could have profound effects on teachers' engagement in and commitment to professional development. The standards model strengthens the roles and responsibilities that teachers' professional associations can play in regard to several important professional functions. One of the major potential benefits of the NBPTS, for example, is the opportunity it offers for many teachers to become involved in its operation – at local, as well as state and national levels – and not just as members of the Board or as candidates. The operation of a standards model itself requires the kind of teacher interaction and involvement in networks typical of best kinds of professional development.

The summative nature of professional body certification can have highly beneficial consequences on formative evaluation of practice and peer support at the school level. Case discussions about standards and their meaning create vehicles for generating helpful feedback about practice. Standards provide something to be collegial about. At the school level, the criterion-referenced nature of NBPTS assessment minimises competition between teachers, unlike merit pay and career ladder schemes. A pay system based on skill-development, with no quotas, will encourage teachers to help each other work toward professional certification. Some independent schools in Australia, for example, are building a requirement into their *Advanced Skills Teacher* pay schemes that applicants make informal presentations at staff seminars from time to time based on reflective case studies, videos of their teaching and other kinds of classroom-based evidence.

At wider levels, the operations of a body like the Board require the involvement of large numbers of teachers in the conduct of assessment centres and in the actual assessments of evidence for certification. Grassroots understanding and support for what such a body is trying to do will be essential. A professional body will need to work with, and build on, the kind of state and local networks that teacher/subject associations can provide. Subject associations, for example, could provide a cadre of specially trained assessors from among its experienced members. The experience of carrying out such "real" tasks, as perceived by teachers, would almost certainly provide a rich and rewarding source of professional learning. Tasks associated with the implementation of teaching standards and a professional certification system would seem to have the potential to precipitate informal, though powerful, processes of sharing, learning and accountability at all levels.

## HOW CAN STANDARDS FOSTER PROFESSIONAL COMMUNITY?

This final section will indicate some of the ways in which a standards-driven approach is consistent with and builds on some of the best of current thought and practice in the PD field. In summary, the argument is that professional standards are an essential foundation for the development of the kinds of professional communities that so many commentators now associate with the best opportunities for professional development. Professional communities and networks seem to be important "mediating structures" for significant change at the level of teaching practice (McLaughlin, 1995).

Louis, Kruse, & Marks, (1996) provide a valuable synthesis of the critical elements of professional communities. According to their research, professional communities are strong when the teachers in a school routinely engage in activities characterised by: reflective dialogue; de-privatisation of practice; collective focus on student learning; collaboration; and shared norms and values. Standards can provide a valuable framework for such activities.

Professional communities are sometimes more effective when their membership runs across schools and districts or even states. Huberman (1995) describes a progression of PD models that move from the individual teacher coping with problems, to cross-school, self-managed groups of teachers with common interests, such as the subjects or the grade level they teach. Huberman calls these cross-school networks the "open collective cycle" model. Huberman emphasises that these groups need challenging ideas from research from outside the group if they are to survive. These ideas widen the deliberations of these groups as they share experience and experiment. Teaching standards can provide valuable ideas and reference point for these networks. Networks could be based on groups of schools, subject associations, or nearby tertiary institutions.

On close inspection, most conceptions of professional community rely, either explicitly or implicitly, on some conception of professional standards to underpin their activities. Fullan (1995), for example, believes that teachers need four core capacities to learn on a continuous basis and contribute to a professional community: personal vision building; inquiry; mastery; and collaboration. Where might standards fit into this conception?

Standards help teachers to articulate a vision and to address Fullan's question, "what difference am I trying to make personally" (p. 253). Standards also help to clarify the purpose of inquiry. While change comes from within, inquiry needs to be guided and validated by external reference points. The emerging forms of non-competitive performance assessment in the standards model, such as portfolio entries, provide encouragement, settings and recognition for the kind of collaborative reflection and learning among teachers that Fullan advocates.

*Standards as a focus for case writing and discussion*

Some the most effective professional development activities in which I have participated over recent years have used "case methods" (Shulman, 1992; Merseth, 1996). Cases are candid stories that teachers have written about particular events that have arisen in their own teaching. They are usually brief, first-hand, accounts (1–3 pages) of their experiences in teaching particular topics or ideas, often including rough and ready evidence of what students have said, done or written in class. Teachers come together in case methods groups to read one another's cases, or cases that other teachers have written.

Case writing and discussion groups epitomise the idea of professional community. Cases are written to stimulate collaborative reflection through discussion. They are a means for teachers to share insights and reflections, to identify dilemmas and problems, and to find support and challenge in a professional environment. Cases provide teachers with windows into each others' pedagogical reasoning and practice. Most importantly, they come to see their own experiences and assumptions through the eyes of respected and sympathetic others, a critical prerequisite for change in beliefs, or "seeing anew" as Jenny Nias (1987) puts it.

Case methods groups require a focus. Barnett has been using the NCTM standards as a backdrop for her valuable research on case methods with elementary teachers for several years (Barnett & Ramirez, 1996). Citing Hargreaves and Dawe (1990), she says "we have evidence to support the claim that one of the most important purposes for case discussions may be to support 'critical and collaborative teacher cultures which develop curriculum and pedagogical reform from within the profession' " (p. 2). Barnett found that, through case discussions, teachers began to take responsibility for their own professional development agenda. They became empowered and, "Once this happen(ed) to them, they seem(ed) eager to empower their own students in a similar way" (p. 2).

Deborah Schifter, in her work on mathematics cases (Schifter & Fosnot, 1993) also used the NCTM standards as a reference point. Shifter explains:

> We saw them as a Rorshach, something that can be interpreted in different ways. So you need the detailed descriptions of classrooms in order to start the dialogue about what the NCTM standards mean in terms of day to day practice – and you need the cases, narratives, videos in order to start thinking about what the standards mean. (Interview with author, May 1995)

Ingvarson & Marett (1997) used the Victorian Curriculum and Standards Framework as a the focus for their case methods groups. These groups consisted of teachers from different schools who meet weekly for four months to write and discuss "cases" arising from events in their own teaching of subject matter – in this instance, science. We found that case methods were more successful initially with cross-school groups. Our teachers said that in their own school departments "faculty discussion never lasts more than five minutes. . . because you just want to be out of there."

In theory, funding for these sessions was to support the implementation of the state's Curriculum and Standards Framework. In practice, the writing and discussion made the meaning of implementation problematic because the teachers probed deeply into what it meant to teach toward particular outcomes or standards in the framework. Implementation turned out to be far too pallid a term for what they were doing. Through their writing and discussion the teachers were in fact contributing to professional knowledge about the relation between standards and practice. Although the teachers were often critical of the standards, and in fact they wrote to the developers about their limitations, the standards themselves provided a valuable framework for detailed writing, reflection and discussion about practice.

Some commentators regard a focus on standards as a threat to teacher autonomy. Experience suggests this attitude may reflect a somewhat patronising attitude to teachers, as well as a misunderstanding of the rationale for professional autonomy. As with Barnett and the science teachers above, McLaughlin (1995) found that,

> Somewhat ironically and contrary to the fears of those who worried that reforms based in different and more rigorous standards for instruction would usurp teachers' professional autonomy, standards-based reforms potentially

can shift authority back to the profession. Indications are that standards-based reforms represented as broad goal statements and not precise directives for practice actually have enhanced teacher professionalism. (p. 19)

Profession-defined teaching standards would seem to have the same potential to shift authority for the professional development system to teachers and their associations at national and state levels and to "confer new authority on teachers at the local level for specifying the practices and activities appropriate for particular communities, schools and classrooms" (McLaughlin, 1995, p. 19).

CONCLUDING COMMENTS

Many have argued for some time that our systems and structures for professional development need fundamental reform. What has become clearer recently is the intimate relationship between the reform of professional development and the development of teaching as a profession. A fundamental contradiction lies at the heart of professional development systems. While policy rhetoric espouses teacher empowerment and strengthening professional community, in reality teachers still exercise little control over the professional development system in comparison with employing authorities and universities; its goals and the allocation of resources, its provision, and its links to career advancement and other forms of professional recognition. My suspicion is that there is a relationship between the low level of teacher control and the frequency of less effective PD methods.

Teaching standards have great potential for improving the quality of PD planning and provision. Professional development planning driven by standards – whether they be standards for initial registration, appraisal, or promotion, looks to the long term. It focuses on teachers as persons, where they are and what they might become, not just the present policy change. Standards provide stable long term goals for professional and career development based on the profession's assessment of what teachers should get better at. Standards provide a basis on which teachers can set the agenda for their own professional development.

A basic assumption behind this chapter is that the capacity to set standards is a necessary credential if teachers' organisations are to claim the right to exercise greater authority over their own professional development and to take the major responsibility for its provision. The development of teacher-defined standards is central to the evolution of teaching as an accountable profession and schools as professional communities.

The development of a standards-based model will require a long term perspective. It is a direction in which to move gradually, through seeding programs that will steadily establish the structures and conditions that support a more self-regulating profession. The rationale for the standards-based model is that professional development needs to be seen as part of a wider set of mutually reinforcing policies designed to enhance the quality of teaching, which include accountability standards for governments, teachers and schools respectively (Darling-Hammond,

1992), increased opportunities for collaborative work within and across schools, redefined career structures and incentives, and work redesign and redefinitions of teachers' work. These components have profound effects on the capacity of the in-service education system to 'engage' most teachers in long term professional development planning.

The standards-based model requires policies that support knowledge growth in the profession, rather than changes in employer policy, as the principal basis for determining professional development goals and provision. Teacher associations, such as the National Council for the Teaching of Mathematics (NCTM) in the USA, have demonstrated a capacity to generate challenging standards and assessments based on research and best practices. There are indications, for example from the work of the NBPTS, that this capacity can now be mobilised more effectively in the service of a standards-driven in-service education system than has been managed in the past.

A central message from the research on change is that it is worth investing in people and their development. Change policies that focus on teacher quality and the quality of teaching lead to the accumulation of experience and 'instructional capacity' (Corcoran & Goertz, 1995). They pay off in the long run, not only in terms of student achievement, but in terms of the bottom line. And higher salaries and better career paths in teaching are more likely to attract and retain teaching candidates with higher academic ability. It is important for the quality of education in our schools that we learn how to value quality in teachers' work. Standards demonstrate that the profession is capable of being explicit about what counts as quality; that practice is not just a matter of "doing your own thing." They enhance accountability within the profession by clarifying reasonable targets for professional development. Standards based on professional knowledge may protect teachers from arbitrary, inconsistent and invalid evaluations of their performance.

The strong surge in interest in standards among teacher organisations generally is a sign of frustration with dominant assumptions underlying recent government policy designed to enhance the quality of education. Teacher organisations have begun to realise that they must demonstrate their capacity to be explicit about what counts as quality teaching if they are to be taken seriously in national policy debate and to counter policies designed to de-professionalise teaching. The development of policies for locally managed schools, which devolve almost all 'quality assurance' functions to school management teams, tend to leave teachers and their national organisations out of the equation. These policies overestimate the effectiveness of managerial models of control over teachers' work. They underestimate the potency of professional networks to influence what teachers actually think and do, and they fail to understand or exploit the potential of professional forms of control and accountability. They are not based on sophisticated analyses of quality learning and the expertise in teaching required to promote it; that is, professional teaching standards.

*Note:* I am indebted to Rod Chadbourne and the late Matt Miles for their helpful comments on earlier drafts of this chapter.

# REFERENCES

Ashton, P., & Webb, R. (1986). *Making a difference: Teachers' sense of efficacy and student achievement.* New York: Longman.

Bacharach, S. B., Conley, S. C., & Shedd, J. B. (1990). Evaluating teachers for career awards and merit pay. In J. Millman & L. Darling-Hammond (Eds.), *The new handbook of teacher evaluation* (pp. 133–146). Beverley Hills, CA: Sage.

Baird, J., & Northfield, J. (1993). *Learning from the PEEL experience.* Melbourne: Monash University Printery.

Ball, D. (1993). With an eye on the mathematical horizon: Dilemmas of teaching elementary school mathematics. *Elementary School Journal, 93,* 373–398.

Barnett, C., & Ramirez, A. (1996). Fostering critical analysis and reflection through mathematics case discussions. In J. A. Colbert, P. Desberg, & K. Trimble (Eds.), *The case for education: Contemporary approaches for using case methods* (pp. 1–13). Boston: Allyn and Bacon.

Borko, H., & Putnam, R. (1995). Expanding a teachers' knowledge base: a cognitive psychological perspective on professional development. In T. Guskey & M. Huberman (Eds.), *Professional development in education: New paradigms and practices* (pp. 35–65). New York: Teachers College Press.

Choy, S. P., Henke, R. R., Alt, M. N., Medrich, E. A., & Bobbitt, S. A. (1993). *Schools and staffing in the United States: A statistical profile, 1990–91.* Washington, DC: NCES, US Department of Education.

Cohen, D., & Ball, D. (1990). Relations between policy and practice. *Educational Evaluation and Policy Analysis, 12,* 331–338.

Conley, S., & Odden, A. (1995). Linking teacher compensation to teacher career development. *Educational Evaluation and Policy Analysis, 17*(2), 219–237.

Corcoran, T., & Goertz, M. (1995). Instructional capacity and high performance schools. *Educational Researcher, 24*(9), 27–31.

Darling-Hammond, L. (1986). A proposal for evaluation in the teaching profession. *The Elementary School Journal, 86*(4), 531–551.

Darling-Hammond, L. (1992). Creating standards of practice and delivery for learner-centred schools. *Stanford Law and Policy Review,* Winter 1992–93

Darling-Hammond, L., Wise, A., & Klein, P. (1995). *A license to teach.* Boulder, CO: Westview Press.

Dreyfus, H. L., & Dreyfus, S. E. (1986). *Mind over machine: The power of human intuition and expertise in the era of the computer.* Oxford: Basil Blackwell.

Elliott, J. (Ed.). (1993). *Reconstructing teacher education: Teacher development.* London: Falmer Press.

Elmore, R. (1996). Getting to scale. In S. Fuhrman & J. O'Day (Eds.), *Incentives and systemic reform.* San Francisco: Jossey-Bass.

Fennema, E., Carpenter, T., Franke, M. L., & Carey, D. (1993). Learning to use children's mathematical thinking: A case study. In C Maher & R. Davis (Eds.), *Relating schools to reality.* Allyn and Bacon

Fullan, M. (1994). Broadening the concept of teacher leadership. In D. Walling (Ed.), *Teachers as leaders* (pp. 241–254). Bloomington, Ind.: Phi Delta Kappan.

Fullan, M. (1995). The limits and potential of professional development. In T. Guskey & M. Huberman (Eds.), *Professional development in education: New paradigms and practices* (pp. 253–267). New York: Teachers College Press.

Haertel, E. H. (1991). New forms of teacher assessment. In Gerald Grant (Ed.), *Review of research in education* (Vol. 17). Washington, DC: American Educational Research Association.

Hargreaves, A., & Dawe, R. (1990). Paths of professional development: Contrived collegiality, collaborative culture and the case of peer coaching. *Teaching and Teacher Education, 6*(3), 227–241.

Hargreaves, A. (1995). Development and desire: A post-modern perspective. In T. Guskey & M. Huberman (Eds.), *Professional development in education: New paradigms and practices* (pp. 9–34). New York: Teachers College Press.

Huberman, M. (1995). Professional careers and professional development: some intersections. In T. Guskey & M. Huberman (Eds.), *Professional development in education: New paradigms and practices* (pp. 193–224). New York: Teachers College Press.

Ingvarson, L. C. & Chadbourne, R. (1997). Reforming teacher pay systems: Some Australian experiences. *Journal of Personnel Evaluation in Education.*

Ingvarson, L. C. & Marett, M. (1997). Building professional community and supporting teachers as learners: The potential of case methods. In L. Logan & J. Sachs (Eds.), *Meeting the challenge of primary schooling for the 1990s.* London: Routledge.

Ingvarson, L. C. (Ed.). (Forthcoming). *Teacher evaluation for professional certification: The first ten years of the National Board fro Professional Teaching Standards*. Greenwich, Connecticut: JAI Press Inc.

Jaeger, R., & Bond, L. (1995). *Psychometric evaluation of performance assessments: new solutions to some traditional problems*. Paper presented at the Annual Meeting of the American Educational Research Association, April 18–22, San Francisco.

Kelley, C. (1995). *Teacher compensation and organisation*. Consortium for Policy Research in Education, University of Wisconsin-Madison.

Lampert, M. (1990). When the problem is not the question and the solution is not the answer: Mathematical knowing and teaching. *American Educational Research Journal*, 27(1), 29–64.

Lawler, E. E. (1990). *Strategic pay: Aligning organisational strategies and pay systems*. San Francisco: Jossey-Bass.

Leinhardt, G., Putnam, R., Stein. M. K., & Baxter, J. (1991). Where subject knowledge matters. In J. Brophy (Ed.), *Advances in research on teaching, volume 2, teachers' knowledge of subject matter as it relates to their teaching practice*. Greenwich, CT: JAI Press.

Lieberman, A., & McLaughlin, M. W. (1992). Networks for educational change: Powerful and problematic. *Phi Delta Kappan*, 73, 673–677.

Little, J. W., & McLaughlin, M. W. (1991). *Urban Mathematics Collaboratives: As the teachers tell it*. Centre for Research on the Context of Secondary School Teaching, School of Education, Stanford University.

Little, J. W. (1993). Teachers' professional development in a climate of educational reform. *Educational Evaluation and Policy Analysis*, 15(2), 129–151.

Louis, K. S., Kruse, S. D. & Marks, H. M. (1996). Schoolwide professional community. In F. M. Newman & Associates, *Authentic achievement: restructuring schools for intellectual quality* (pp. 179–203). San Francisco: Jossey-Bass.

McLaughlin, M. W. (1995). *Teachers' professional lives in the United States*. Paper presented at the Annual Meeting of the American Educational Research Association, San Francisco, April 18–22, 1995.

Mandel, D. (Forthcoming). Developing professional standards: lessons from the National Board for Professional Teaching Standards. In L. C. Ingvarson (Ed.), *Evaluating teachers for professional certification: The first ten years of the National Board for Professional Teaching Standards*. Greenwich, Conn.: JAI Press Inc.

Merseth, K. (1996). Cases and case methods in teacher education. In, J. Sikula (Ed.), *Handbook of research on teacher education. Second edition* (pp. 722–744). New York: Macmillan.

Mohrman, A. M., Mohrman, S. A., & Odden, A. (1996). Aligning teacher compensation with systematic school reform: Skill-based pay and group-based performance rewards. *Educational Evaluation and Policy Analysis*, 18(1), 51–71.

Moss, P. (1994). Can there be validity without reliability? *Educational Researcher*, 23(2), 5–12.

National Board for Professional Teaching Standards. (1989). *Toward high and rigorous standards for the teaching profession*. Detroit: NBPTS.

National Council of Teachers of Mathematics. (1991). *Professional standards for the teaching of mathematics*. Reston, Virginia: NCTM.

Nias, J. (1987). *Seeing anew: Teachers theories of action*. Geelong, Victoria: Deakin University Press.

Pearlman, M. (Forthcoming). An architecture for NBPTS performance assessments. In L. C. Ingvarson (Ed.), *Evaluating teachers for professional certification: the first ten years of the National Board for Professional Teaching Standards*. Greenwich, Conn.: JAI Press Inc.

Pelton, C. (1995). *Incentives and systemic reform*. Paper presented at the Annual Meeting of the American Educational Research Association, April 18–22, San Francisco, 1995.

Peters, R . S. (1966). *Ethics and education*. London: Allyn and Unwin.

Romberg, T. A. (1988). NCTM's curriculum and evaluation standards: What they are and why they are needed. *Arithmetic Teacher*, 37(9).

Romberg, T. A., & Webb, N. L. (1993). *The role of the National Council of Teachers of Mathematics in the current reform movement in school mathematics in the United States of America*. (OECD) documents: Science and Mathematics Education in the United States: Eight innovations (Proceedings of a conference).

Rowe, K., Holmes-Smith, P., & Hill, P. (1993). *The link between school effectiveness research, policy and school improvement*. Paper presented at the annual conference of the Australian Association for Research in Education, Fremantle, Western Australia. 22–25 November, 1993.

Schifter, D., & Fosnot, C. T. (1993). *Reconstructing mathematics education: Stories of teachers meeting the challenge of reform.* New York: Teachers College Press.

Scriven, M. (1994). Using the duties-based approach to teacher appraisal. In L. C. Ingvarson & R. Chadbourne (Eds.), *Valuing teachers' work.* Camberwell, Vic.: Australian Council for Educational Research.

Shulman, J. H. (Ed.). (1992). *Case methods in teacher education.* New York: Teachers College Press.

Smylie, M., & Smart, (1990). Teacher support for career enhancement initiatives: program characteristics and effects on work. *Educational Evaluation and Policy Analysis,* **12**, 139–155.

Smylie, M. (1994). Redesigning teachers' work: Connections to the classroom. In L. Darling-Hammond (Ed.), *Review of research in education,* (Vol. 20, pp. 129–179). Washington: American Educational Research Association.

Sprinthall, N. A., Reiman, A. J., & Thies-Sprinthall, L. (1996). In J. Sikula (Ed.), *Handbook of research on teacher education. Second edition* (pp. 666–703). New York: Macmillan

Sternberg, J., & Horvath, J. A. (1995). A prototype view of expert teaching, *Educational Researcher,* **24**(6), 9–17.

Wolf, K. (1994). Teaching portfolios. In L. C. Ingvarson & R. Chadbourne (Eds.), *Valuing teachers' work: New directions in teacher appraisal.* Hawthorn, Vic.: Australian Council for Educational Research.

# International Handbook of Educational Change - Table of Contents

## FUNDAMENTAL CHANGE
*Michael Fullan, Editor*